AF816027

Changing Face of

Processed Food Industry

in India

Changing Face of

Processed Food Industry

in India

Rajat Kanti Baisya

Deptt. of Management Studies
Indian Institute of Technology
Delhi

Ane Books Pvt. Ltd.

New Delhi ◆ Chennai

Changing Face of Processed Food Industry in India

© **Author**

This Edition : 2019
Pages : xvi + 318 = 334 (Hb)
Size : Royal (6.25" X 9.50")
Price : Rs.1495/-

Published by

Ane Books Pvt. Ltd.

Head Office 4821, Parwana Bhawan, 1st Floor, 24 Ansari Road,
Darya Ganj, New Delhi - 110 002, India
Tel.: +91(011) 23276843-44, Fax: +91(011) 23276863
e-mail: anebooks@vsnl.com, Website: www.anebooks.com

Chennai Avantika Niwas, 1st Floor, 19 Doraiswamy Road,
T. Nagar, Chennai - 600 017, India
Tel.: +91(044) 28141554, 28141209
e-mail: anebooks_tn@airtelbroadband.in

ISBN (10) : 81-8052-166-4
ISBN (13) : 978-81-8052-166-9

No part of this book may be reproduced in any form including photocopying, microfilms, photoprints, storage in any retrieval system, transmission in any permanent or temporary form, without the prior written consent of the publisher.

Printed at Milan Enterprise, Delhi

Dedication

To my wife Susmita and children Deepshikha and Rishabh for their constant support and encourgement and for the inconvenience that they have gone through. More particularly to my elder daughter Deepanwita, a brilliant student who did not survive to see the publication of this book. Cruel hands of destiny had snatched her from us. This book is dedicated to her memory.

Rajat Kanti Baisya

Preface

For decades Indian Economy was largely dependent on Agriculture. Even today majority of our population are dependent on agriculture. However, agricultural growth rate has been declining and our economy is now dependent more on the performance of service sector which contributes to about 55 per cent of our GDP. Contribution of agricultural sector to our GDP is constantly declining whereas manufacturing sector has been still showing the promise and is growing. In spite of the low growth rate, India has achieved the distinction of becoming the largest or the lead producer of many agricultural commodities including say milk production. Also, in spite of low farm productivity and poor infrastructure and limited access to farm implements and loan, our farmers have delivered. The price of agricultural commodities at the farm level is still lower than that prevailing in many other countries in the world. But when it comes to processing our processed food products are not cost competitive in the global market. In the domestic market also the consumption is not growing and marketers are not seeing any significant growth and one reason is that our processed products are much costlier in comparison to the fresh produce. Poor infrastructural support, high wastage of fresh produce because of lack of storage and preservation facilities and complex and inefficient distribution infrastructure and high and multiple tax structure make the processed products all the more costlier. As a result, our processed food industry did not perform in spite of the fact that we have all the basic ingredients including the availability of raw material and government's policy support emphasizing on the growth of agriculture and processed food products. We have an independent Ministry of Food Processing Industry for almost two decades now to give impetus and support for the growth of this sector. But nothing significant seems to have happened so far.

Processed food industry in India has been receiving all kinds of support and attention of government since last two decades when a separate Ministry of Food Processing Industry was formed with an independent minister being in charge of that. Although this industry has been identified as sunrise sector with huge potential with emphasis on our agriculture based economy, the food processing sector did not perform. Since the inception of liberalization and open market driven policy from beginning of 1991 the industry suddenly got a new challenge from the players from abroad looking at the market size of India.

Local players were not doing well in one hand and had to face the big global players all of a sudden forced them to view their businesses from different perspectives exploiting other opportunities and alternative models as available to them. Many of our domestic industry thus got acquired by multinationals. And that journey for the local players for survival is still continuing. As a result, the face of our food industry is constantly changing.

The series of articles under the theme "Changing Face of Processed Food Industry in India" was started about a decade ago and regularly being featured in the magazine "Processed Food Industry" (PFI), a leading monthly journal focusing on the happening on this sector. Some of the articles were also published in other leading journals on processed food industry including "Indian Food Packer" (IFP), "Indian Food Industry" (IFI), Modern Food Processing(MFP), and Asia & Middle East Food Trade (AMEF) etc. I have compiled, updated and even modified select articles from the same series appeared in different times in PFI, IFP and IFI and in other journals. My friends and colleagues in industry have been asking me to put the entire series so far published in the form of a book for reference by the numerous professionals involved in this industry directly or indirectly. Moreover, my teacher Late Prof. A. N. Bose former vice chancellor of Jadavpur University and a pioneer in Food Technology education and research in India has constantly encouraged me to compile all these articles in the form of a book. This is an attempt in that direction.

These articles were placed under various section in a chapter corresponding to the sub sectors of the industry category in order to provide a perspective regarding what is happening to that sector due to change in policy as well as with the entry and competition from multinationals.

With opening up of the economy, the market has become so dynamic that there are rapid changes in the business environment. To succeed in this highly competitive market one has to be highly pro-active with total knowledge of trade structure and competition in the food industry. This book is an attempt to capture that environment.

This book made an attempt to capture the development of the processed food industry in various sectors, categories and sub-categories and also traced the reasons of performance. If India has to occupy the lead position in the global economy our agricultural sectors as well as our processed food industry including primary processed food industry have to achieve global standard and earn a place in the global trade. At present our global trade is only about 1.5 percent. It can go up to 3-4 percent if we can improve our supply chain performance. There is a distinct hope now because leading corporations like Reliance, Bharti Group, ITC etc. have now ventured into food business. Their combined effort with large resources and technology back up will make the difference. With retail revolution, market is also expected to grow. This book will provide the status of the various categories of food industry and also should give some insight on the critical issues responsible for the performance. I hope that professionals, researchers, academicians and businesses will find this book useful.

Rajat Kanti Baisya
New Delhi

Acknowledgement

This book covers the history of development of Indian Processed Food Industry under various product categories for last two and half decade or so. I was covering these developments in the various sectors of the industry in the magazines and journals including Processed Food Industry (PFI), Indian Food Packer (IFP) and Indian Food Industry (IFI) for over a decade now. Some of these articles were presented in various national and international seminars and published in other journals as well. I therefore, gratefully acknowledge the permission received from the publisher of PFI, IFP and IFI to reproduce some of my own contributions to be incorporated in this book. I acknowledge the support of the editor of PFI Mr V.R.Dhingra and his staff in this regard. Also would like to acknowledge the support of Dr.V.H.Potty editor and Mr G.C.P Rangarao former editor of IFI as well as Mr K.L.Radhakrishnan , chief editor of IFP. Mr. Saleem Akbar of PFI has rendered help in taking some of the photographs included in this book which I gratefully acknowledge.

I also would like to thank The Ministry of Food Processing Industry (MOFPI), Govt. of India for permitting me to incorporate some of the data including strategies and action plan as drawn by the ministry. I thank the management of Rabo Bank who have been working very closely with the ministry to create a vision and strategy document for the MOFPI for allowing me to include some of the data from their document.

I would also like to put on record the support of my institute (Indian Institute of Technology, Delhi) and the faculty and staff of the Department of Management Studies at IIT Delhi while working on the project.

My teacher Late Dr. A.N.Bose, former vice chancellor of Jadavpur University, Kolkata had encouraged me to write this book after he saw and read some of my articles in various journals. I gratefully acknowledge this although he did not survive long to see the release of this book which was my desire. I also would like to thank my teacher Prof Tarun K.Ghose, former head of

Biotechnology & Biochemical Engineering Department of Indian Institute of Technology, Delhi for his support. I had the good fortune to be the student of these two stalwarts in the fields of Food Technology and Biochemical Engineering respectively.I also thank Prof Sunit Mukherji, former Professor of Food Technology at Jadavpur University, Kolkata for the encouragement that I have received.

I also would like acknowledge the help rendered by my students. Although list is long but I would like to specifically acknowledge the help of Parikshit Charan and Ganesh Das –both are my doctoral students and Sumit Mathur and Shibashish Bhattacharya – both postgraduate MBA students. I would like to acknowledge the significant effort from my publisher Ane Books India to bring out the book as per schedule.

Finally, I would like to acknowledge the unstinted support and encouragement received by me from my wife Susmita, daughter Deepashikha and son Rishabh. Lastly, I acknowledge the blessings that I abundantly received from my parents Late Dr Rabindra Kumar Baisya and Mrs Vidyut Prava Baisya.

Rajat Kanti Baisya

Contents

Table 1.1 : Contribution of various sectors in national economy

Item	1980-81	1990-91	2004-05
GDP (in INR bn)	1224	4778	34875
GDP gwth rate (%)	3.5	5.6	6.9
Agriculture %	39.7	28.3	20.6
Processed Food %	4.82	6.45	6.3
Service %	36.6	43.69	51.4
Manufacturing %	23.7	25.38	28.1

It can be seen that processed food industry contribution to overall GDP has gone down over the years along with agriculture. Manufacturing sector and more significantly service sector's growth are much higher than agriculture sector. We are therefore, not achiveing a balanced growth.

Performance of food industry over the last four years is shown in Table 1.2. It can be seen that both in terms of total sales and domestic sales the year 2004-05 performance is lower than those of the earlier years although export sales has marginally gone up.

Table 1.2 : Industry Performance

Performance criteria	2001-02	2002-03	2003-04	2004-05
Total Sales (INR billion)	763.39	837.05	914.94	885.81
Domestic Sales (INR billion)	720.17	789.77	860.27	828.34
Total Exports (INR billion)	43.82	47.28	54.67	57.47

Source : Total sales from CMIE data base, Total Exports from MOFPI annual report, 2005-06

India's share of global trade is now 1.4 percent.

The production, export sales(both in value and volume terms) and domestic sales of select processed food items for last five years have been given in the following Table 1.3. Most of the dominant categories are stagnating in terms of sales performance. Only exceptions are marine products, confectionery items, alcoholic beverages including spirits, wine and beer.

Table 1.3 : Performance of select categories of processed food

Milk Powder and Condensed Milk

	2000-01	2001-02	2002-03	2003-04	2004-05
Production (Tonnes)	146866	128588	155067	147372	146952
Export Quantity (MT)	8535	20210	13714	6282	33351
Export Value (INR Billion)	6.68	1.539	9.29	5.47	2.651
Sales Value (INR Billion)	9.50	9.25	9.75	9.50	9.50

Malted Milk Foods

	2000-01	2001-02	2002-03	2003-04	2004-05
Production (MT)	116930	109030	108719	109146	110000
Export Quantity (MT)	1840	4819	2970	2185	2337
Export Value (INR Million)	199	406	297	214	214
Sales Value (INR Billion)	12	13	13	13.5	14

Butter, Ghee and Other Fat From Milk

	2000-01	2001-02	2002-03	2003-04	2004-05
Export Quantity (MT)	1815	1760	1939	1846	3411
Export Value (INR Million)	237	233	255	262	413
Sales Value (INR Billion)	5.867	5.594	4.886	4.097	3.273

Icecreams

	2000-01	2001-02	2002-03	2003-04	2004-05
Export Quantity (MT)	14	28	77	107	299
Export Value (INR Million)	1	3	8	8	25
Sales Value (INR Billion)	4.5	4.1	4.1	4.25	4.5

Poultry

	2000-01	2001-02	2002-03	2003-04	2004-05
Export Value (INR Billion)	1.048	1.483	1.821	2.536	2.570
Sales Value (INR Billion)	6.6	6.5	6.5	6.6	6.8

Biscuits

	2000-01	2001-02	2002-03	2003-04	2004-05
Production (MT)	883474	920132	944544	968926	1071384
Export Quantity (MT)	4091	6626	16575	13201	19900
Export Value (INR Million)	197	326	616	562	854
Sales Value (INR Billion)	37	38	39	40	41

Break-Fast Cereals

	2000-01	2001-02	2002-03	2003-04	2004-05
Production (MT)	5840	5252	3312	3990	4630
Export Quantity (MT)	961	571	770	716	1201
Export Value (INR Million)	65	37	42	44	60
Sales Value (INR Billion)	.626	.537	.526	.572	.278

Fruit Juices / Pulp / Concentrates

	2000-01	2001-02	2002-03	2003-04	2004-05
Export Quantity (MT)	5628	4205	9055	6544	9477
Export Value (INR Million)	205	168	278	250	351
Sales Value (INR Billion)	2.552	1.761	2.210	2.149	2.079

Sauces / Ketchups / Jams

	2000-01	2001-02	2002-03	2003-04	2004-05
Export Quantity (MT)	7995	9526	10177	15898	14254
Export Value (INR Million)	357	413	460	602	532
Sales Value (INR Billion)	1.67	1.861	2.102	2.46	2.10

Confectionery

	2000-01	2001-02	2002-03	2003-04	2004-05
Export Quantity (MT)	3137	4163	6053	8976	9808
Export Value (INR Million)	268	353	439	629	697
Sales Value (INR Billion)	15	16	17.2	18.5	19

Marine Products

	2000-01	2001-02	2002-03	2003-04	2004-05
Production (MT)	5655350	5955930	6199680	6399390	NA
Export Quantity (MT)	502599	468033	527873	409494	379864
Export Value (INR Billion)	63.673	58.983	69.281	61.056	56.952
Sales Value (INR Billion)	264.56	289.38	316.93	316.72	320.00

Tea

	2000-01	2001-02	2002-03	2003-04	2004-05
Production ('000 MT)	827.4	842.1	837.6	850.5	830.8
Export Quantity (MT)	202.4	180.1	184.4	177.8	178.3
Export Value (INR Billion)	19.764	17.192	16.629	16.373	17.952
Sales Value (INR Billion)	70.9	66	65	63.5	64

Coffee

	2000-01	2001-02	2002-03	2003-04	2004-05
Production ('000 MT)	312.6	304.3	284.5	257.0	296.0
Export Value (INR Billion)	18.56	17.72	18.56	18.93	16.13
Sales Value (INR Billion)	50	50	51	52	52.5

Wines, Spirits & Liquors

	2000-01	2001-02	2002-03	2003-04	2004-05
Export Quantity (Kls)	10720	10426	13185	13274	16934
Export Value (INR Million)	634	599	777	732	832
Sales Value (INR Billion)	62.647	58.154	62.436	68.584	69.122

Beer

	2000-01	2001-02	2002-03	2003-04	2004-05
Export Quantity ('000 Litres)	8094.0	7319.1	7003.7	9420.2	11411.8
Export Value (INR Million)	239	207	205	263	297
Sales Value (INR Billion)	14.692	17.070	16.033	16.382	18.784

Source : CMIE data base

India is a front ranking producers of perishable commodities. But processing is insignificant and still in the nascent stage of development. In spite of the fact that India is a leading producer of many basic food items in the world and our cost of production is one of the lowest but the processed products are not competitive in the global market. The following Table 1.4 and 1.5 will illustrate this.

Table 1.4 : Production and processing of perishable agricultural products in India

China : $195 bn; USA : $150 bn; India produces	**India - $105 bn. India has**
• 50% of world's mango, • 23% of Banana, • 36 % of cashew nut, • 11% of onion, • 28% of cauliflower, • 28% of Green Peas. • 10% of Fruits and Vegetables • 16% of Milk	• 53% of world's buffalo and • 17% of goat And a 8000 km of coastline

Food processing still at a nascent stage

Level of processing (Fruits & Vegetables)	**Level of Processing** (Perishable products)			
		Organized	**Unorganized**	**Total**
USA - 80 %	Fruits / Vegetables	1.3%	0.8%	2.2%
France - 70 %	Milk /milk products	13%	22%	35%
Malaysia - 80 %	Buffalo Meat	21%	-	21%
Thailand - 30 %	Poultry	6%	-	6%
India - 1.3 %	Marine Products	8%	15%	23%

India share in global production (2001-03)

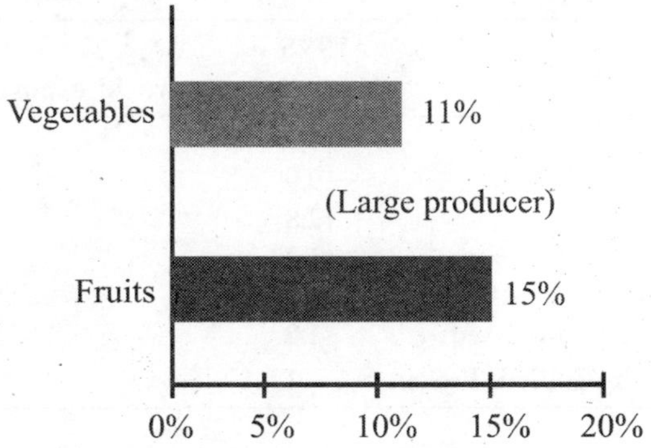

Indian Prices as a % of World Prices (2001-03)

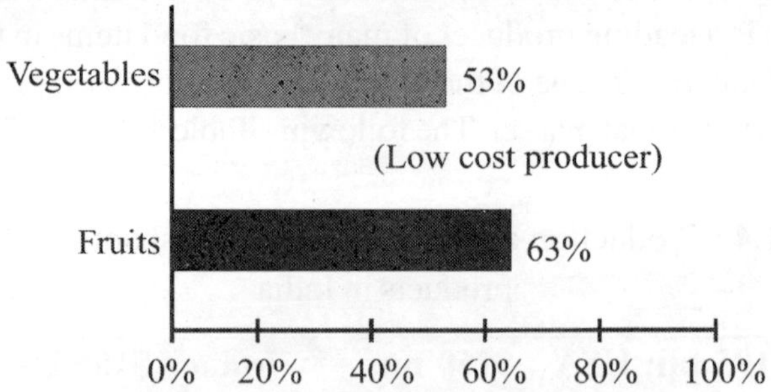

India share in global exports

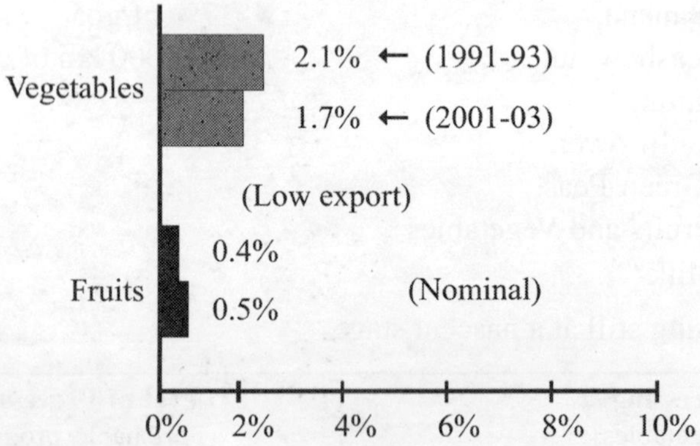

Source : UN COMTRADE Statistics, World Bank Staff Estimates

Indian share of food and agricultural products in global trade is only about 1.4 per cent. It can be observed that excepting rice which has gone up from 17.7 percent in 1998 to 29.7 per cent in 2002 other products did not show any significant growth. In fact, tea and spices have shown degrowth. Dried fruits and beef have grown slightly over these period.

Table 1.5 : Share of select food categories in global trade

Item	**1998**	**2002**
	(% share in world exports)	
Rice	17.7	29.7
Tea	19.9	13.4
Spices	12.8	10
Beef	1.2	1.9
Fruit / Nut- Fresh / Dried	1.7	1.8
Fruit / Preserved / Procssed	1.2	1.4
Vegetable Fresh /Chilled, Frozen	1	1.1

Source : UN ITC

The performance of agricultural products during last decade for other Asian countries including China is shown in Table 1.6. In the post liberalization era import of processed food has gone more than double whereas for other countries growth was not that high. Again share of agricultural products in export has remained same at around 18 per cent in case of India whereas for others it has gone up significantly. This means India's import is increasing but export is remaining static.

Table 1.6 : Share of Processed foods in Agricultural Products

	Exports		Imports	
Country	**1990-91**	**2001-02**	**1990-91**	**2001-02**
China	28	42	20	19
Malaysia	36	64	35	38
Thailand	29	40	21	33
Indonesia	21	38	19	24
India	18	19	20	41

Source : World Trade Report 2004

Table 1.7: FDI in Processed Food Sector

Year	1999-00	2000-01	2001-02	2002-03	2003-04	2004-05
FDI Inflow Received in FPI Sector (INR in Billion)	4.4406	1.9813	10.3612	1.7653	5.1085	1.7408

Source : Ministry of food Processing Industries, GOI

Till date total FDI inflow is said to be INR 52.74 billion. What this money has done to the industry? Not much as can be understood from the fact that Coca Cola company itself has written off INR 20.00 billion to adjust their cumulative losses. Also SaraLee and Nutricia closed down their Indian operation in processed food.

About 30 per cent of total fruits and vegetables grown in the country is said to be wasted due to lack of processing facilities and also due to inadequate infrastructure for marketing of perishables. The primary grading and collection centers, cold chain, quality certification system, transportation for perishables etc. are almost non-existent. Warehousing and cold storage facilities are inadequate. There is complete lack of infrastructure in rural markets. Wholesale markets are in government control and they lack modern facilities and private direct markets not permitted. Paradoxically, marketers find it difficult to sell whatever little is processed. Domestic market for processed food is not fully developed and infrastructure is lacking for marketing fresh perishables.

The current status of the industry can thus be summarized as below:

- Processeing industry is not growing.
- Domestic industry stagnating, export growth insignificant
- MNCs struggling for survival, local companies disappearing/ surrendering-last one is Parrys confectionery
- Imported foods coming through trading route. Even MNCs prefer this route (No investment, easy to exit).
- Our basic farm level price is low in global standard but when it comes to processing it is costlier.
- Low level of technology, lack of automation and low productivity makes it costlier.
- Low level of scale of operation makes it costlier.
- Infrastructure inadequacy makes it costlier
- No big domestic player (excepting in alcoholic beverages) in the game

We are not competitive and we are not able to add value. Not much of value captured in the industry as can be seen from the following figures. Value addition thus one of the lowest.

Table 1.8 : Value addition in processed food industry

Country	Value added in food industry
India	7%
China	23%
Philippines	45%
UK	188%

Source : MOFPI.

What we Need

Hub and Spoke format should be adopted for the terminal market where state of the art services for electronic auction, grading, washing and packing lines, processing and exports, banking, transport including reefer vans etc., advisory on input, price and quality are to be made readily available. Government has created many food parks around the country which are not fully utilized so far. We should create these infrastructure facilities around those food parks. This will take care of supply side of the industry.

On the other hand marketers should look at global market opportunity to create demand for the processed items which require improved technology, economy of scale, international quality and packaging systems, resources to match the huge task of marketing 'made in India' processed food in international market. The task ahead is therefore enormous.

Indian Family Owned Food Industry

With our open market policy many felt that small family owned businesses would disappear or would decline gradually and finally would meet the inevitable in closure. But that did not happen. Small and medium businesses have survived and played a vital role in economy in all industrially developed countries. In India they not only survived, but continued to play a very useful role in our economy. In United States more than ninety percent of the businesses are owned by families. Although small businesses are thriving, yet some of the family owned enterprises have become so big that they have taken a multinational dimension. For example, Wriggly and Johnson Wax - both are family owned companies and have become global players. Hence, being small as such is no constraint for survival and growth. On the contrary, small players have better ability to be flexible to adjust with the changing market conditions and therefore are dynamic to remain in business.

Incidentally in food industry in India, we have many such small family owned enterprises. Questions being asked as to what is happening to them. Unfortunately in India, we don't have that class of family owned entities which are large and organised, barring, of course, a few of them. Food Industry was always seen as low technology industry by the prospective entrepreneurs. A fellow who is running either a sweetmeat shop or Halwai shop or even a cake and pastry shop suddenly decides to put up a few equipments in his backyard and applies for registration under Industries Act to elevate his status. K.C. Das's Rosagulla (a popular Bengali sweet) in sixties decided to produce Rosagulla in cans to sell only at its own retail outlets in Central Kolkata and later on in one more outlet in Bangalore. K.C. Das's shop later became K.C. Das and Sons Pvt.Ltd. Licia macaroni is a fifty year old family owned brand which still exists in Kolkata, but still same, living on small local volume of business. Similarly, we have in Delhi - quite a few small canneries running in Lawrence road producing local brands and also Midlands Foods at Mathura. In my definition, they are not industrialists, they don't have vision, they are basically either a short term opportunists or took to setting up an enterprise as a means of earning a living. They therefore could not do anything. The products that they had introduced could not become successful brands and business.

Those who had visions have done well, created a good brands and grew well. The former category did not chalk out for them any role and they thus will disappear (if not already closed down) and will not remain a part of the future history of the Indian food industry.

But in the latter category, they will remain a strong force. In this, we have Dabur, Parle, Dharampal Satyapal Group of Industries (manufacturer of Catch brand of Salt and Pepper), Pioma Industries, Nutrine, Gits, Kissans amongst others. They will remain. Some of them might have changed hands - for example, Kissans got acquired by HLL or Parle Beverages by Coke, but that is a different matter because even in that case the brand and the business still exists and will continue to exist.

Family owned businesses who have not created any significant brand or a distribution infrastructure, will never be the target of MNCs' for acquisition. They, therefore, have nothing to lose or gain with the entry of large global corporations. They would have been disappearing otherwise also. Unfortunately, we have many of these types. If you don't believe, contact our All India Food Processors Association. Majority of their members exists only in name and I have been observing this trend for last twenty-five years discussing the same issues like OTS (open top sanitary) cans and PFA rules and tax structures on processed foods. They have not changed. Those who have been successful should not also worry. They will continue to grow and prosper provided they change, upgrade and do aggressive marketing, innovative and introduce more value-added products. But they will always be the target of large global players seeking entry into the Indian market.

Still there are other categories of family businesses. They fall in the category of either traditional sectors or special category of foods such as meat, fish and poultry and also spices etc. In these sectors Indian family owned businesses can even fight large corporations and they have demonstrated better results. For example, Allanas in meat and fish processing, Venkateshwara Hatcheries in poultry, MDH in spices and Haldiram in Indian snacks (bujjias). They will continue to flourish as long as they keep on imbibing the technological changes and also follow a focussed marketing approach.

Besides, all these local companies have demonstrated that they can stay ahead of the race. Of course, in meat, fish and poultry we still did not see any big international players but in bujjias Pepsi is making serious effort and Haldiram is still well ahead of Pepsi.

Family businesses with strong brands and core competencies in their respective category of foods have therefore nothing to fear provided they keep on upgrading themselves and remain competitive in a dynamic market environment. Global giants, of course, will always knock at their doors with attractive offers which they will have to carefully ward off because selling it off will mean permanently being out of business. Creating a new one from scratch even if they have money will not be as easy as they might think it is.

The family owned businesses who have already aligned themselves with MNCs' as their reliable contract manufacturer (co-packer) will also remain in the business provided they can sing and dance to the tune of their principals. But a good strategy for them would be distributing the total capacity amongst a number of principals as it has been done by Lotus Chocolate Company Ltd. (LCCL), a Hyderabad based chocolate manufacturer. They have their own brand in South Indian market but they also make for big brothers like Nestle and Cadburys. Of course, recently they are in the news that Hershey of US has made a bid to acquire them in order to have a manufacturing base in Indian subcontinent. But that is a different matter and such type of acquisitions will not be many.

The problem is really with the third type of family owned businesses. They do not have any strategic alliances and they don't have any core competencies. They are, therefore, not the natural owner of their businesses. They thus will have to die. And they would have been dying otherwise also, if not dead already irrespective of liberalisation.

Some Traditional Indian Food Brands Survived the Test of Time

In this world only certainty is change. Everything, therefore, changes with time. So does the products and brands. As we know that the products move through its life cycle from inception to growth and then to maturity and decline and finally disappears. Marketers do everything possible to extend the product life cycle during the growth and maturity phase and to arrest the decline. But still a stage comes when product loses its significance and had to be withdrawn. Sometimes new product is introduced to take the position of the declining product to engineer the death of an apparently non-relevant product. If, however, brand is constantly rejuvenated to remain contemporary and relevant then product goes through transformation and brand remains and continues to be enjoying customers support and patronage. Those brands gradually grow to become power brands and those brands are always vibrant and modern and through ages they become part of the culture. In international market we have many such food brands. For example, Coca-Cola which survived over a century and still very much relevant. In domestic market we don't have many such instances. We have seen many such brands of food and food products which were launched and nurtured for a long time and then disappeared. We also have instances of a few food brands which are still going strong. But the fact of the matter is that we also have some food products which survived the test of time. Although their numbers are not many.

Like Coca-Cola which was originally introduced through chemist shop, many of us may not be knowing that hundred years old summer drink "Rooh Afza" was originally introduced as drug way back in 1907. It had a distinctive taste, unique formula and unusual colour and very high brix (that gives higher dilution ratio) that clearly set it apart from other syrup and sherbat. Hakim Adbul Majeed, the founder of Hamdard did not possibly dream that his Rooh Afza would turn into a market leader in sherbats for nearly a century. Traditionally, syrup market is divided into three categories - herbal syrup such as khus, fruit syrups and synthetic flavoured syrup such as rose, strawberry, keora etc. Rooh Afza is actually all three types combined into one. It is made of twenty one ingredients including carrots, watermelon, orange, lemon, pineapple and rose water. And also consisted of special herbs with medicinal properties and extracts of fruits, vegetables and traditional flowers. That in short is the concoction formulated to give consumers enlightenment (Afza) to the soul (Rooh). The product does not contain, as manufacturer claims, any artificial ingredients or preservatives and the formulation still remains the same. Rooh Afza claims to be effective for fatigue, anaemia, giddiness, restlessness and irritability. The 700 ml glass bottle can be spotted in every household in summer. The packaging is still traditional but the manufacturing over the years, have been mechanised to cater to the increasing demand. Branded sherbat or syrup segment is about INR 2000 million in size and Rooh Afza is about 50% of the market. To get chunk of this market Dabur launched its Sherbat-i-Azam.

Fig. 1.1 Some traditional Indian Food brands that survived long and still growing.

Haldiram also launched a similar product. In Kissans, we worked a great deal to market an equivalent of Rooh Afza and we did formulate one and marketed it but the product did not get the volume, as expected. Rooh Afza still reigning supreme. This product is being patronized by older generation and youngsters still drink only because their parents insist. I therefore, have doubt whether the product will have same appeal, in years to come, as it has so far. Hamdard need to rejuvenate the brand to remain contemporary to stay ahead. And it seems that the company is making some conscious efforts in that direction. It has been reported that the enterprising grandsons of Hakeem Majeed- Hameed Ahmed and Asad Mueed are planning high pitched advertisement for Rooh Afza in order to keep sustained level of interest of the consumer in the brand. They also seem to be extending uses of the product in custard and jellies etc. This according to me is a good idea because brand has to be seen as relevant and contemporary if it has to have an extended life cycle. Besides, Roof Afza is the flag ship brand of Hamdard group and therefore its profitable continuance can only ensure Hamard's survival in the long run.

The other Indian brand of food product which survived the test of time is Lizzat Papad. Of course, lizzat also make and market spices now but their over fifty years old papad is still a leader in the segment. And most importantly the beneficiaries from this venture of Maharashtra Mahila Sanghathan are many and they are all needy families. Lizzat papad has significant export market now. But the product is still made in a traditional way. The dough is distributed to women of slum areas to return next day. In the early morning dry papads are collected by the mobile van from specific locations for final packaging and distribution. Lizzat survived because of low cost operation and relatively higher value delivery. Whether cost equation will remain same in years to come is a question. Most probably will not. But in this event the brand will be threatened for its existence. The traditional papad business now will have to be run on modern scientific line and discipline. The improvement in productivity, quality of product, packaging and process mechanisation would be the key imperative. And concerned authorities need to do something.

Fig. 1.2 Time Tested Indian Brand.

There are not many Indian food brands survived long. Hajmola - a candy from Dabur's stable is also a very old product, all most over fifty years old. This product, however, has undergone metamorphosis. The original Hajmola was a digestive powder promoted as ayurvedic medicine. Then came tablet which is still there selling in the market. The brand got a real boost when candy was introduced. Hajmola is now a favourite of the kids and children and thus can hope to have an extended life. The ball game can change only when some other brand of similar nature will outsmart Dabur and they should always be prepared for that as Hajmola is a significant brand for them contributing about INR 750 million in sale.

I would like to take up the case of yet another Indian brand coming from a small business house in Pune and that is Gits Food Products Pvt. Ltd. This company manufactures instant food mixes for over forty years now and is a market leader. While working for Corn Products India Ltd (now known as International Best Foods) we were competing with them in Idli, Dosa and Gulab Jamun mixes. I saw them thriving in those days with very limited advertisement budget. They even survived the onslaught of Hindustan Lever. HLL introduced the total range of instant food mixes with lot of promotional fund as usual for Levers only to withdraw later on. HLL had many stalwarts in food and nutrition working for them but that did not make any difference in the market place. Dr Varadrajan was HLL's Research Director during that time who later on moved to CSIR as their Director General and subsequently to IPCL. Nutrition was at the heart of Dr. Varadrajan so much so that while at IPCL he initiated a project on production of yeast (single cell protein) from petroleum hydrocarbon. A lot of work was done at RRL - Jorhat and even pilot plant study was also done for single cell protein to tackle the problem of protein- calorie malnutrition. While producing protein from all possible sources could be an interest to the food scientists but that cannot be a priority research programme for IPCL. I can only imagine that even after being at the helm of IPCL Dr Varadrajan could not forget his past association and interest. All these now a history. While on the subject of instant food mixes, Gits has shown that with consistent focus and single minded effort one can really succeed. For CPC and HLL, instant mixes was one of their many business lines but for Gits this was the only business and hence their survival hinges on that.

A couple of days ago while carrying out some survey in Mumbai retail market I was happy to see the visibility of Gits brand in most of the food stores. Today Gits is about INR 700 million brand and still going strong.

These brands although survived the test of time but the market dynamics are changing so fast that there is no guarantee that they will survive in future. It all depends upon what is being done in relation to these brands' own competitive sets, to keep them going. In United States, brands disappear in a period of even six months. That stage has not yet come in India. But that stage is not very far either and Indian businesses need to learn that lesson - sooner the better.

2

New Competition From Multinationals in Processed Food

Dominance of Multinationals in Food and Dairy Industry

The Face of Indian food and dairy industry has started changing ever since Late Rajiv Gandhi formed an independent ministry of food processing industry and gave it a priority status by putting it under Appendix 'A' category. And first contribution of this ministry was to grant entry to Pepsi Cola which Parle resisted tooth and nail without success. Pepsi formed a joint venture with Voltas and Punjab Agro giving significant export commitment which in later years they found very difficult to deliver. In their anxiety to get faster entry into the Indian market Pepsi had accepted all kinds of conditions and the project cost which was originally envisaged at INR 300 million was completed reportedly by spending INR 800 million. Voltas and Punjab Agro could not put up with the pressure of bringing in additional matching equity required to complete the project and finally walked out of this collaboration. Only time will tell us when Pepsi will recover the accumulated losses but apparently they are not bothered considering it as an investment for the future.

Seeing Pepsi's move and decision to enter Indian market with minority holding, Coke openly declared that they made a great mistake by taking a decision to quit during Janata rule in 1977 when the then industry minister George Fernandez only asked them to dilute the foreign equity to sixty percent. Coke, therefore, immediately submitted a proposal for clearance in joint venture with Late Biscuit King Rajan Pilai's Britco Foods Pvt. Ltd. who played a pivotal role for the re-entry of Coke in India. Ramesh Chauhan of Parle again tried to resist the move but when saw no hope, finally decided to join hands with Coke and Parle brands were acquired by Coke at a reported price of INR 1600 million.

Rajiv Gandhi's government was selectively granting the entry to food multinational by asking them to provide significant export commitment but Narashima Rao's government opened up the Indian market to global players and declared its policy of liberalization with no strings attached. All big food MNCs immediately, therefore, jumped into the fray. Close on the heels of Pepsi and Coke the British confectionery giant Cadbury Schweppes entered into the Indian carbonated beverages market with their Crush and Canada Dry range of products bottled through Pure Drinks bottling plants. When Coke acquired Parle brands for which Pepsi was also racing, the latter then acquired Dukes from Pandoles family, the number one in ready-to-serve fruit beverages in bottle (Mangola brand) and soda water in western India. Only a few years ago Parle was an all India player controlling sixty percent of the country's carbonated beverages market and only other two regional big players were Pure Drinks in north and Dukes in west. Today the entire soft beverages market is dominated by the global players namely Pepsi, Coke and Cadbury Schewppes. Cadbury Schewpes, of course, later on withdrawn from the cabonated beverages market leaving the fight between two global giants Pepsi and Coke. Interestingly enough, even after the onslaught of the global brands like Coke and Pepsi, Thums-Up is still a very strong brand and was the largest selling number one cola brand in the country for quite sometime after its acquisition. But the brand no longer belongs to Parle, it has become now Coke's property. If Ramesh Chauhan could visualize this scenario earlier, he possibly would not have sold his business to Coke. Multinationals do not believe in fragmented brands. Instead, they would like to put their entire resources behind their global brands. The popular Indian consumer products brands will be gradually replaced by the global brands. Coke tried to under play Thums-Up in the market place but did not succeed. Even today Thums-Up sells more than Coke. Coca-Cola India will end the year 2006 with sales of 215 million cases. Thums-Up accounts for nearly 30 percent of the sales with 50 million cases, Sprite follows with 40 million cases and Coca-Cola 32 million cases. It is interesting to note that Thums-Up sells more than Coke which is considered most valuable global brand in 2006 ranking by interbrand.

Hot beverages, particularly tea and coffee industry was traditionally dominated by multinationals and the lead players are Lipton, Brook Bond and Nestle. Policy of liberalization now thus helped MNCs to monopolise soft beverages market as well which was hitherto dominated by Indian business houses. Health beverages, both white and brown variety, signified by Horlicks and Bournvita brands respectively are already the monopoly of two British multinationals namely SmithKline Beechem and Cadburys in that order and their only Indian competitor Jagatjit industries with brands like Viva in white segment and Maltova in brown segment have now been acquired by Smith Kline Beechem. The total Indian beverage market is now the domain of the global players.

Dairy industry, particularly, the handling, processing and marketing of fluid milk was till recently reserved for co-operative sector and was not open to private sector. In 1991 this sector was thrown open to private sector and during that time many new private dairy projects came into being and the prominent among them are J.K. Foods, Heritage Foods and Amrit Foods and there are a few licensees who are in the process of setting up the projects and still there are a few who will never install any plant. They are, in fact, waiting for the prospective buyers to sell their license and most likely takers will be multinationals. Because of pressure from Dr. Kurien and his NDDB lobby this sector has again been closed to private companies and the only route that would be open to the MNCs is acquisition. Till recently, only multinationals in dairy field were Glaxo, Nestle, Smith Kline Beechem, Cadburys and Hindustan Lever and leading Indian players were Dalmias, Foremost, Jagatjit, Dempo and Raptakos and there was a balance in the market place. While MNCs were dominating the baby food and weaning food segment, their Indian counterparts were dominating the milk and other milk products such as ghee, butter, SMP etc. But the scenario is fast changing. For example, taking the advantage of Narashima Rao's govt policy of liberalization, Unilever group soon took the initiatives. As a fallout of an international acquisition Hindustan Lever got merged with Lipton and Brook Bond and became the number one in hot beverage market. Before that, Hindustan Lever's food activity was limited to owning a dairy plant in Etah in UP.HLL failed in seventies with their launch of convenience foods in the form of dehydrated foods (Hima peas) and instant food mixes which is well known to everyone. Subsequently, Brook Bond acquired Kissans and Dipy's from UB group which in turn got acquired by HLL to become number one once again in processed fruit and vegetable products industry.

At present, manufacture of ice creams is reserved for small scale sector. Only marketing of ice-creams is permitted by large companies. Confectionery giant Cadburys diversified and introduced "Dollops" range of ice-creams through franchising route. They could not make it a profitable venture in three years time and by then their mainline business came under pressure which forced Cadburys to sell Dollops brand to Hindustan Lever. After acquiring Dollops, Lever has struck a strategic alliance with the biggest ice cream company namely, Kwality which is owned by different members of the Ghai family independently in four regions of the country. Those factions resisted this move, later on persuaded to fall in line.

Kwality's arch rival Milk Foods (a Jagatjit group company) manufacturing and marketing flavoured yoghurt and 100% ice cream also joined hands with Levers. These alliances have excellent strategic fit with Levers overall plan, by then the company secured permission to manufacture and sell its Walls range of frozen desserts and have set up a state of the art plant at Taloja by spending INR 16 million to produce ice cream mixes. HLL has thus become the most dominant player in the ice cream market over the last couple of years. An industry which is reserved for small scale sector is now being dominated by multinational through a different route. The controversy relating to whether ice-cream is a frozen dessert for which HLL was given a license was in fact again re-examined by Ministry of Food Processing Industry and Law ministries and finally issue was put to rest.The dairy industry was dominated once by small and co-operative sectors but HLL has become the most dominant and also biggest player through a different route namely, through the acquisition and strategic alliances. In another development, American multinational HEINZ has acquired the food division of Glaxo, the manufacturer of leading brands like Complan, Farex, Glucon-D etc, to set up their 100% owned entity in India. Others will shortly enter in dairy field include Kraft General Foods. If this trend continues the co-operative movement in dairy and operation flood will soon face a grave crisis.

Because of the dominance of the multinationals in beverages and dairy industry, the market size is increasing and quality and variety are improving which is a result of intense competitive activity. Ultimately, consumer is the king and he has a wider choice now.

Global Competition in Processed Food

Decades ago Indian processed food industries were crying about high taxation, lack of infrastructural support, non-availability of quality raw material at competitive price, non-availability of latest packaging machineries and packing material etc. as the major reasons for poor or sluggish growth of this sector. But the industry was still growing then albeit not at the expected level. Competition was also there amongst domestic processors with their MNC counterparts. Because, large MNC food companies like Nestle, SmithKlein Beechem, Britannia, Glaxo, Hindustan Lever etc. are there for ages. But domestic industries were not worried about their presence. There were healthy competition. In some areas domestic industries were doing even better than some of their nearest competitors in multinationals. What went wrong then? Why domestic industries are now not able to fight multinational giants? This is because the rules of the game have changed. Post liberalisation, we have now entered into an era of survival of the fittest.

Only couple of years ago we had only Amul Cheese. Britannia first successfully introduced cheese from cow milk followed by the introduction of French cheese "Le-Bon" from Dabur-Le'-Bon joint venture. Philips Morris - owner of Kraft Foods - is sitting with a formal licence to set up 100% owned company in India. They carried out lot of research for introduction of Kraft cheese in India. Their project now has been put in cold storage and they are still waiting and watching the market for processed food industry.

Upto mid eighties Kissan was the number one brand in Tomato Ketchup and around that time the competition came from Maggie - a Nestle's brand. With Maggie launching several varieties of Tomato Ketchup there was a growth in the market. With Kissan and Maggie fighting neck to neck other smaller but established brands like Dipy's from Herbertsons, Volfruit from Voltas, Noga of Nagpur Orange Growers Association were also co-existing. The biggest global player in Tomato Ketchup Heinz came much later after a long wait and watch. Some of the unknown local brands of tomato ketchup are still existing only on price competition.

The price competition has also kept some of the other categories of food products still alive. For example, the age old Corn Flakes from Mohan Meakin under the brand name Champion still sells almost the same quantity (reportedly 500 MT per annum) against the much better quality Kellogg brand which sells around 3000 MT per year with all its variants.

Till today we have only Parle and Britannia as two major brands in biscuits. Kellogg has entered the category but withdrawn later on. Cadbury and SmithKlein Beecham have nominal presence with specialilty biscuits. Sara Lee introduced specility biscuits and cookies but withdrawn after three years incurring consistent losses.

In the snack foods category we have two successful Indian players namely Uncle Chips brand of Amrit Foods and Pepi of SM Dye Chem. Others are local, such as Fun Flip, Crax etc. Soon entered Pepsi with their Ruffles brand and then extended to Indian snacks by introducing bujjias which Bikanerwala makes for them to market.

In confectionery we have over half a dozen global players struggling here for brand share and fighting against Indian players like National, Norton, Parle, Parrys etc. Amongst MNCs in this field leading are Perfetti, Wriggley, Agrilimen, Park Davis (with their Chicklet brand)

Competition is also seen in organised fast food retail chains. Couple of years ago we had only Narula running such an organised fast food chain. Today we have everybody namely. McDonald, Kentuchky's Fried Chicken, Dominos, Pizza Huts of Pepsi and many more.

In some of these categories domestic brands are still a leader - for example, Uncle Chips, Frooty, Rasna etc. But how long they will be able to retain their leadership is a big question mark? Having failed to establish the potato chip brand Pepsi finally acquired the number one in the category the Uncle Chips from Amrit Foods. When potato price goes up local players find it difficult to run with the brand - for example Billy's Ltd.- an Indian company in technical assistance with Florigo of Netherlands had successfully introduced potato chips in Eastern India and was reportedly doing well. As potato price started shooting up the company could not afford to sell its brand at a competitive price and therefore closed down. With highly fluctuating input price, domestic industries will be all the more vulnerable like the one as we have seen in the case of Billy's.

Imported Foods in Indian Market

Not too long ago, for buying imported foods we had to go to select markets - such as Modern Bazar, Vasant Vihar in Delhi or Fort in Mumbai. In other places one has to literally search for such choice food items. In those days importing foods were not permitted. And we were told that these foreign made chocolates and soup mixes and cheese find their way to Modern Bazar through diplomatic routes in the sense that persons in diplomatic services bring with them these foodstuff and sell them to local stores. But the fact of the matter is that these food items are brought to India through what is called "Suitcase trade" in the concerned trade circle. It will not take time for readers to understand what the "suitcase trade" is? It simply means to carry suitcase full of foodstuff by people frequently travelling overseas and selling and or delivering those to local traders and this happens in an organised manner. Those who can afford, have to pay a fancy price for those foreign foods. Although price was exhorbitant but the quality used to be distinctly better. Children love their Swiss chocolates, French Cheese and Italian pastas.

General Foods (now known as Kraft Foods International) - subsidiary of Phillips Morris has a synthetic orange beverage by brand-name "Tang" found to their dismay that so much of Tang is selling in India and Nepal now that they started thinking what would be the loss of sales to their South East Asian subsidiaries from where it finds its way to Indian market, once they start manufacturing it locally.

In the last couple of years these imported foods are available almost in all leading shops in most of the shopping centres in the city. To my surprise while taking a stroll in Greater Kailash shopping centre, I found couple of those shops have stacked Champaign, sparkling wine and imported mineral water outside the shop alongside soft drinks and on getting curious when I peeped inside I found everything is available. You name it - it is there. I bought some MARS chocolate and came out.

Fig. 2.1 Imported food brands that flooded Indian market.

The way things are moving, some of these foreign companies in course of time will do only trading in foods. There are local agents who now represent many foreign companies and regularly import foods in turn to supply to local retailers and stores. In big stores like Nanz, Bigbazar and large food stores like Foodland there are regular requirement being catered to by their local agents. In earlier years we used to see these phenomena in countries like say in Middle East. This trade in imported foods will be on the increase as the custom duty goes down. It will also fuel the growth of partial processing in India to take the advantage of price equation. For example, importing the product in bulk and carrying out re-packing operation here will be more economical than importing the finished product itself.

As we know that India has now signed the WTO (World Trade Organization) agreement. As per the terms of reference to this agreement, India has to put most of the items under Open General License (OGL) for import which means that these items can be freely traded. Over two hundred odd food items now put under OGL and in that list shrimp, strawberry, raspberry and other fruits, have already featured.

Another 414 items are removed from the “restricted” list allowing these to be imported against Special Import Licence (SIL) that can be procured in the market by importers at a small premium. Fruits like oranges and pomegranates, soft drink concentrates etc. are falling in SIL category whereas a range of marine food products, vegetables, assorted fruits and juices, spices, edible oils, jams, jellies etc. are brought under OGL.

The outcome of the same is that in India we now get "KIWI" - an Australian fruit from select outlets if we want to. Shrimp is also now imported into India. In a recent wealthy marwari marriage reception that I had attended, I found in the fruit counter all the fruits look different than what I am familiar about. For example, Guava and Apples were almost double the normal size that we get here. Plus there were unknown fruits. And I was told that all these fruits were imported from Bangkok. I was so tempted that I tried all varieties and filled my stomach with all these tasty exotic fruits only. And later on started thinking that what will happen to our fruits if these fruits are available at a competitive price in India. Can our farmers and fruit merchants become globally competitive in terms of price and quality. We should see the writing on the wall and work in that direction. The Agricultural Products Export Development Authority (APEDA) should quickly assess the scenario and rise to the occasion to take appropriate action. All of us have seen the ongoing battle European banana growers were fighting in the forum of WTO against Americans refusal to permit entry of European Banana in that country.

If international fruit brands like "chikita" and "Del Monte" start selling here, who is going to buy local fruits from our mandis and roadside vendors selling fruits on the top of hand-pulled trolleys?

Food Traders Launching Global Brands Through Free Imports

Exim Policy 2001-02 was designed to remove 670 items from the QR list. And this included all food items. We are thus going to witness a truly global market in India. All kinds of processed or even fresh food and food products will now be seen in Indian stores. The indications are already there. Bigwigs in fast moving consumer goods (FMCG) like HLL, Cadbury, Marico, Pepsi, Coke, Nestle, Smith Kline Beecham , Mother Dairy met under the umbrella of Confederation of Indian Industries (CII) in the month of November 2000 to discuss the consequences of removal of QRs affecting their sales performance. Imported products have eaten into the market share of desi and videshi FMCG companies alike. At the CII meet, the general consensus among members was that imports have cornered almost six per cent share of the domestic market during the same year.

A related concern expressed by the members was that there are no quality check on food items imported in the country. In fact, it has been reported that some of these imported food items do not adhere to the Indian food laws and package commodities regulation order. Our regulatory mechanism seems to have no infrastructure to check the inflow of the imported food stuff quality after the flood gate of import is being lifted.

Processed food manufacturers abroad have been gearing up to encash on this new found opportunity and appointing agents in India to start trading activities. Many such distributors regularly displaying their products in the Ahara trade fair.

To protect farmers from the onslaught of imported fresh fruits and vegetables, government however, will be imposing peak rate of duty. Some of the processed fruit and dairy products will also be covered under this peak rate of duty structure. The products to be covered will include copra, coconut oil, potatoes, yoghurt, cheese, fruits, vegetables, packed fruit juices, poultry products like chicken legs, sugar, rice, etc. The tariff rates could be as high as 150 to 300 per cent. This move can best be described as to build confidence in the minds of farmers that they are not left in the lurch - although protectionism is not going to be favoured by the Government in the long run. However, even after paying import duty at the rate of 150%, the fresh fruits can still compete with the local produce in certain selected category of fruits as it would be in certain other categories as well. Among the agricultural products which are expected to make a beeline for India include Australian mangoes which would be available in winters, apples, potatoes and rose flowers. India has already experienced Australian Apples and Kiwis before the QR phase out. Australian apples with their blood red skins have been available in South India at about the same rates as the Kulu variety and there was a shift in consumer preference for the more attractive imported variety.

Even the alcoholic beverage industry will have to face the threat. Earlier they faced successfully the challenges of the scotch whiskey manufacturers in India. Now they will also have to face the competition from the directly imported scotch in Indian market. With the prevailing duty structure the popular brands of scotch whiskey can be easily marketed in the price range of INR 300 to INR 500 a bottle. Who will then drink the local liquors or even India made scotch whisky? Those players who can derive advantage from the global scale production operation now will do trading activities in India without really making any investment on manufacturing. Realising the potential threat, local liquor manufacturers are taking up the issue with the government to raise the import duty structure for the scotch whisky but the reality is that they will have to face this new challenge. United Breweries (UB) Group, the largest in the country with global vision is trying to create barrier for the global players. Their recent acquisition of controlling interests in Associated Breweries (manufacturer of London Pilsner brand in Maharashtra) and Sandpiper brand in north and also the strategic tie-up with the Mohan-Meakins brands of liquors for marketing under UB groups Millennium Alcobev will give them significant advantage and a dominant position in liquor trade and distribution. In another move UB is going to acquire 26 per cent equity in their fifteen contract bottlers thereby having indirect control over them. This is what we call golden share strategy which is normally leveraged when need arises. This move, if successful will put UB in a very dominant position in the liquor trade. McDowell - an UB Group company through its trading arm were selling foreign liquors in Indian market. Earlier this trade was limited to certain market segments like hotels, diplomats and embassies. Now this trade has the opportunity to develop once the QRs is withdrawn. And seeing the opportunity they are planning to start pub-cum-departmental stores in all metro cities to start with. First such pub will be opened shortly in South Mumbai this year. McDowell International Brands, the new trading subsidiary of McDowell & Co. will be selling foreign spirits, wines, beers, cigars, perfumes etc. through these stores.

There will be fifty such life style stores (two per state) proposed to be set up in the country with an investment of INR 1000 million and these stores will also sell food albeit imported food items. UB Group thus will be marketing non-UB products of global players.I find that consumers have started now buying McVitie's biscuits made in U.K., sold in Delhi stores imported by Universal Corporation Ltd., Chennai in place of Britannia and Parle brands as we used to buy earlier. And the retail price of 400 gms of digestive biscuits is INR 98 and in some stores it is even cheaper. Earlier, whenever people go abroad used to bring good cheese, drinks and biscuits back home.They need not have to do this anymore. This trading activity opens up easier avenues to Indian market as the manufacturing investment need not have to be done. We have seen what has happened to Sara-Lee's food venture - Sara Lee Bakery India Ltd. (SLBI). Sara Lee acquired Nutrine brand of biscuits and launched their own brand and in two years time, they found after losing INR 73.6 million at the before tax profit level on a sales of around INR 599.8 million that India is too tough a market and then they decided to hand over the business to their contract manufacturer, Vasana Agrex & Herbs Ltd. of the Vasana Group to call it a day. This only proves the point that MNCs are not finding the going too easy in the Indian market. But those who are getting into the Indian market through trading route by appointing local distributors have nothing to lose. We are therefore going to see many such traded food brands in India. And I am wondering how our local industries are going to fight this competition on cost, quality and marketing front? The sooner they realise the competitive threat from yet more global brands through trading channels the better for them. The post liberalisation mantra is "if you cannot shape up, shake out".

Foreign Fruits & Vegetables Flooding the Indian Market

As per the commitment given to the WTO we are gradually withdrawing the control and barrier for free import of most of the fresh fruits and vegetables into the country. Foreign fruits and vegetables are cleaned, graded, neatly packaged and well branded. They are gradually flooding the Indian market. The inflow of these items are not limited to exotic asparagus and melon but also includes very commonly grown apples, grapes and cauliflower. Initially we have seen that the market for foreign fruits and vegetables were limited to those which are either not grown here such as kiwi and some variety of melons or those which were made available as non-seasonal product. But it is no longer so. Markets for foreign fruits and vegetables have truly opened up as will be evident from the doubling of their imports from the earlier year. Doubling of imports just cannot happen only from the imports of exotic fruits and vegetables as the demand cannot jump so drastically within one year and it is everybody's knowledge that commonly grown fruits like apples and grapes are being sold all over which are imported from countries like Australia. As per the statistics published by the Government, imports of fruits and vegetables nearly doubled to INR 171 billion in 2002-03 from INR 928 million during 2001-02. The data also reveal that imports of peas, for example, has gone up by almost four times during the last four years. This should be seen against our failure to establish branded frozen peas in the market. Even a company like Hindustan Lever had to withdraw their product. Industry was not able to establish the volume for canned green peas in brine. But you can see now many imported brands of canned peas in the organized food retail stores. One has to see the growth of these organized retail stores in big cities. These retail stores not only provide the right ambience for shopping but also offer the competitive price because they command enormous muscle for getting better negotiated price most often by sourcing directly from the manufacturers by short circuiting the normal trade channel. Our Indian products are not able to penetrate into these stores as they are still not able to pack and brand the fruits and vegetables as required for this segment.

Our farmers are suffering from the problems of quality, price, packaging, presentation and also from their inability to access the organized retailing channels. Deshi fruits and vegetables still sell in mandis and local markets and road sides whereas foreign fruits and vegetables are sold through organized retail distribution in shops and supermarkets. We give statistics and say that thirty percent of our total harvest of fruits and vegetables go waste due to the lack of processing facilities and inadequate storage and distribution infrastructure. I was all along arguing about the fact that processing facilities and storage infrastructure will automatically fall in place if the market for the same is developed because market forces will dictate those investment. Exactly the same is happening. Otherwise, how foreign fruits and vegetables could do a business in excess of INR 170 billion in India in 2002-03 albeit at the cost of Indian farmers. Foreign fruits and vegetables are now also selling through wholesale market like Azadpur Mandi in Delhi.

In India, we are still one of the largest producer of fresh fruits and vegetables but there is no significant value addition in the trade of fresh fruits and vegetables. Keeping in mind that large part of our trade on this flows from the local whole sale market through the involvement of multiple agencies and local traders who ultimately bring those to sell on the road side or local markets, there is a need to develop parallel structure of procurement directly from the farmers and processing those in large scale plant. National Dairy Development Board (NDDB) had only set up one such plant in Delhi and their products are only selling through Mother Dairy outlets. Private ventures in the similar line or even initiatives from state co-operative agricultural corporation would be required to enable our farmers to find a competitive platform to enter those food retail and organized super markets where most of those foreign fruits and vegetables sell.

Punjab Agro appears to be taking such initiatives to bring marketers, processors and growers under one umbrella to form a synergistic chain in order to be competitive.

The government of Punjab is also taking many new initiatives in terms of cutting tax on eco friendly crops further to attract corporations to procure these fresh produce for processing preferentially from this state. As per the announcement made, tax rate will come down to about 2 per cent from the prevailing 9 per cent. The state otherwise charge in taxes for procurement of crops including rice from local mandis. The new tax rate , as stated will be levied at specially designated mandis. We have set up many agri export zones in the country for the designated agricultural and horticultural produce of that region. But not all of them are functioning well. The reason being that the entire linkages connecting those to the end buyers are not developed. Besides, marketing channels could not be effectively exploited. Some initiatives in that direction as taken by APEDA although commendable but not enough for the magnitude of task that we have in hand. We need to involve the large MNCs who are globally active in the trade of fresh fruits and vegetables such as Del Monte to invest in India to market our produce not only in India but elsewhere in the world. If Del Monte can sell Malaysian pineapples and Kenyan mango all over the Europe and America why not ours. In noth eastern states during season , pineapple and jackfruit grown in the region are really rotting on the road side.In fact, ripe jackfruit is just not available in Delhi. Here it is sold as vegetable. Our pineapple and mango scores significantly above in terms of quality and taste over those sold in Europe and US markets. We only need to access the trade cutting across the barrier and put our act together to make best presentation of our products. And I don't see any reason why it is not possible for us to achieve.

MNCs' Entering Traditional Foods Sectors

Mckinsey did a study on the opportunity in India for food and agri business at the behest of Confederation of Indian Industries (CII). And as expected they projected a huge potential in food sectors and said that the real potential lies in traditional, local food and grocery items - but not so much in westernised processed food. Some of our big multinationals seem to have swallowed the Mckinsey advise-pill and got into this sunrise sectors.

Historically, traditional food items were the domain of small local players. Grocery items earlier were sold loose and unbranded. Then some progressive traders started the cleaning, grading and primary packaging. And the next stage of development was branding of primary foods such as Atta (wheat flour), Rice etc. but those were mainly regional brands. Popular among these were "Rose" and "Shakti Bhog" brands in northern India.

In traditional food items such as spice and pickles there are host of local brands with regional strong-holds such as 'Cookme' spice powder in East, 'Bedekar' pickles in West, 'MDH-masala' in North etc., to name a few. And the food ingredients - nobody thought of. Only food ingredient that was there was tomato puree and paste in cans which in the recent times Godrej introduced in tetrapack. Dabur introduced a range of curry paste as kichen aid food ingredients in the market.

Edible oil in tin pack and later on in polyester jar and tetrapack were the first major step in branding grocery items. "Postman" - peanut oil from Ahmed Mills was one of the oldest popular brands. Today we get variety of edible oils and NDDB and Marico are the leading players in this sector. Amongst MNCs we have "Mazola" corn oil from CPC and "Sundrop" from ITC Agro - a sunflower oil which subsequently has been acquired by CONAGRA - the fastest growing food company in America. With CPC and CONAGRA being involved in edible oil market this sector is going to be soon dominated by MNCs.

The next major attempt to market a branded grocery item was done about a decade ago by Tatas by introducing the first refined iodised salt in poly bag by brand name "Tata Salt" and that was a success. The next big brand in this

Fig. 2.2 Multinationals have entered into the traditional food segments.

category is "Captain Cook" from DCW Chemicals who had plans in branded grocery items and thus the company introduced other items including wheat flour under the same brand name. But that was shortlived. During 1997 DCW Chemicals suffered a major setback and the company decided to divest this food business. The acquirer is Corn Products Co. (India) Ltd.- a wholly owned subsidiary of CPC-International a nine billion US dollar American multinational in food and grocery business. The company has recently changed its name to Best Foods Ltd. CPC was a sleepy company operating in India for over fifty years and their performance was lacklustre. With their limited range of Rex and Brown and Polson brands of convenience foods, the parent company, although doing well globally did not have any commitment in India. In late seventies and early eighties when I was heading their project department many investment proposals were sent and notably among those were dextrose manufacturing project as CPC has a flavoured glucose brand in the portfolio and Knorr soup project. But project work used to be carried out by us endlessly but nothing got implemented. In post liberalisation era, this apparently sleepy company seems to have become active. The third brand of salt is "Kissan Annapurna" which is making a sustained effort to get market share. This brand which is now in Hindustan Lever's fold through Brook Bond acquistion who in turn acquired Kissan in early nineties have reportedly spent INR 180 million in advertising and got 14% market share in a INR 20 billion branded salt category in a span of one year. Tata Salt still holds 26 percent market share and Captain Cook's share is about 20 percent and balance forty percent is still with the smaller players. With the acquisition of "Captain Cook" by Best Foods International which in turn got acquired by Hindustan Lever , in branded salt market MNCs are the dominant players controlling sixty percent of the market.

The value addition in branded salt and pepper was really done successfully by a Delhi based local company Hi-Tech Foods belonging to Dharampal Satyapal of premium "Baba Zarda" (chewing tobacco) fame. Hi-Tech Food's `Catch' brand of salt and pepper in dispenser pack is a success story with upper middle class household and restaurant segments as the main customers.

The first MNC to get into the branded spice business was Brook Bond who introduced the select premium priced spice range by name "Sona" in late eighties. The products were priced and packaged for higher income group. They struggled for couple of years to establish “Sona” brand but failed and was forced to withdraw in later years. Apparently, we don’t see any major MNC in branded spice but world leader in exotic spices “McCormick” seems to have plan to enter Indian market. They formed a joint venture with A.V. Thomas group of south for sourcing Indian spices for the global market.

The first MNC to introduce Indian pickles was Nestle with their Maggie brand. The products are still in the market. And as mentioned earlier, the first MNC to introduce traditional snacks (bujjias) is Pepsi under the umbrella of “Leher Namkins”. It can be concluded that in traditional Indian foods MNCs cannot add much value through the involvement of their principals abroad. On the contrary, they will have to learn from the locals to derive advantage of their brand and resource muscle.

Hindustan Lever has entered branded grocery items though Kissan route in a big way. The company does significant export of branded rice particularly in Middle East market and therefore expected to introduce the branded rice shortly in domestic market as well. Otherwise, in India so far branded packaged rice is limited to Basmati rice and there are many brands in this category and leading among them is “Kohinoor” — but all are from small manufacturers. The grocery business is basically low margins and high volume business and thus it required multiple supply source to be strategically located to reduce the cost of freight and excellent distribution infrastructure and logistics management capability. Big houses like HLL, therefore are expected to do much better in this sector.

In the food ingredients business MNCs have not yet traded. The only big player in this area is Dabur with their range of pastes such as onion, garlic, ginger and also mix of these for particular application. Current sales of these items which are sold under the umbrella brand “Hommade” is said to be INR 50 million and going by that standard it can be considered as a reasonable success. Very recently, “Cookme” curry paste has been launched in Kolkata. The market indicators point towards growth in the branded food ingredients business in coming years. Pepsi is expected to get into this category and with their backward linkages with farmers whom they support with the high yielding variety of seeds for better crop yield, it stands to have an edge over others in this sector. One could have expected that Nestle would also jump into the fray in this sunrise food business - but their new Italian Managing Director Mr. Carlo Donati seems to have other priorities and they want to focus on major key brands.

Price and quality are expected to be the major determinant in the success of grocery items and basic foods. Consumers in India would not be willing to pay much as the price of convenience. Big global brands of MNCs' in that context are therefore not much of significance.

MNCs Competing with Local Brands

It is said that whereas basic questions remain same but answers change with time because dynamics of market place is always changing. Many Indian businesses have made big from a small and simple idea just because they moved in first in the market. One of these is Pioma Industries - makers of Rasna brand of soft drink mixes. The success story of Mr. Khambatta, owner of Pioma stems from the fact that he has created a business of INR 1.5 billion in value terms of soft drink concentrate (SDC) from nothing when the market was dominated by squashes, cordials, ready-to-serve (RTS) fruit beverages and carbonated soft drinks.

In earlier days, squash and cordials were the main beverages for in-house consumption. Things drastically changed with the entry of multinationals. As fruit drinks in cartons and colas in 1.5 ltrs. PET bottles attacked "Rasna" for in-house consumption segment, its soft drink concentrate volumes began to shrink. For the past three years, concentrate sales have been shrinking at the rate of 7 per cent per year as against a growth of ten percent per year in earlier years. It is not that carbonated beverages in PET bottles and RTS beverages in cartons are the new ideas. In seventies these were tried by all leading players in the field including Parles, Campa Cola (Pure Drinks of Delhi), Kissans and others. But things did not work presumably because the market was not ready at that time and also because such a high pitch marketing activities as it is happening now was not affordable by Indian industries. As a result "Rasna" was keeping its growth in the home consumption segment unabated.

Rasna was first launched in mid seventies. Initially the product was distributed by Voltas and after two years when Mr. Khambatta decided to withdraw from Voltas the sale was only INR 15 million then. Mr. Khambatta knocked the doors of Rallis and Corn Products (now known as International Bestfoods and a Uni-Lever group company) to give the all India distribution right but that did not materialise. In Corn Products I was then Project Manager and was working on the development of a me-too formulation to be launched under the brand name "TRINKA" and therefore taking up distribution of "Rasna" would have been a counter strategy for us.

Pioma Industries then decided to set up their own distribution infrastructure and Mr. Khambatta did not look back since then. In the following years Rasna faced competition from Trinka of Corn Products, "Dipy-Sip" from Herbertsons. "Ju-C" from Voltas, "Harsas" from Kissans and Rooh Afza from Hamdard. All these companies were much bigger in size and therefore also in terms of resources. But none could compete with "Rasna" and gradually withdrawn one by one from the market exeepting Rooh Afza which is an established brand. We used to admire Mr. Khambatta's ability to manage logistics because with his volume increasing he still used to manage the status of a small scale industry by not resorting to the use of electricity and thereby gaining in terms of taxes particularly the excise duty which others had to pay. Pioma Industries was in fact having not only a first mover advantage but also a cost advantage over others and thus Mr. Khambatta was playing the same game what "Nirma" did to Hindustan Lever in case of detergent. But the rules of the game seems to have changed now.

Pioma signed collaboration agreement with Del-Monte and Del-Monte brand of squashes have already been launched. But Pioma's prime brand 'Rasna' in in-home segment is now under attack. To counter that move the company has tried to stem the tide by creating a hitherto unknown aerated fruit juice category with its recent launch of Oranjolt. An aerated orange drink with three percent orange juice content, Oranjolt was marketed in Ahmedabad. Positioned as the "fruit with the fizz", Oranjolt comes in 1.5 litres PET bottles. Orange segment is 17 percent of the total INR 35 billion aerated soft drinks market. But Oranjolt will have to compete with Pepsi's Mirinda with 45 per cent market share and Coca-Cola's Fanta and Crush having 40 per cent and 15 per cent market share respectively. It is interesting to note here that Crush was a Cadbury Schweppes brand which has now been acquired by Coke.

Rasna was hoping for success with Oranjolt having 3 per cent natural juice as a major differentiator against Fanta and Mirinda but it did not work. The orange segment alone is INR 4 billion and growing reportedly at a rate of 50 per cent per annum is an encouraging scenario. In earlier years, before the entry of Pepsi and Coke the whole category of soft beverages were growing at a rate of about 12 to 15 per cent. Thanks to the escalated level of marketing and both Coke and Pepsi fighting to get the dominance in soft drink markets as they do elsewhere in the world, the whole market is growing almost three times higher a rate than the category's traditional growth rate.

Rasna earlier tried successfully the do-it-yourself route by not adding sugar in the SDC which consumer has to add. This one-minus concept had a duel advantage. Firstly, it reduces the cost of the beverage which is an attraction to the middle class consumer and secondly housewife gets satisfaction that she has some contribution to make in the beverage she serves to her family members and guests. New flavours were launched every year to keep the excitement around the brand and their ad-campaign with this little girl with big eyes saying "I love you Rasna" was a success. Pioma Industry in subsequent years also launched powder variety in 500 gms Jars in Orange and Mango flavour similar to Kraft Food's "Tang" - which has around 7 per cent contribution in INR 1.5 billion sales of Pioma.

The new launch from Rasna will face stiff competition in in-house segment from Cola giants as well as from "Real" from Dabur and "Onjus" from Enkay Texofood. Cola giants will not take it lying down. Mr. Khambatta has to face new realities now. He, of course, churned out yet another first mover advantage with 3 per cent real juice in aerated orange drink. But this time it could be a new story and new lesson for him. And as I said in the beginning, in marketing there is no sure answer for all time to come.

MNCs Facing Difficulty in Establishing New Foreign Brands

In Europe and America brand share of products change very fast changing the fortunes of the company. But in India brand loyalty is so high that even if the marketing effort is temporarily withdrawn the brand is still preferred by the loyal customers. Coca-Cola after acquiring Parle brands were trying to convert "Thums-Up" share to coke and for that purpose they were making many deliberate efforts. The reality is that "Thums-Up" is still a brand to reckon with. Coke left India in 1977 after working in Indian soil for about two decades. When coke decided to close their operation as Coca-Cola Export Corporation they did not make any money in India till then because they were engaged in concentrate selling and the money was in the distribution and franchising. This time when they entered the Indian market for the second time, they not only decided to acquire Parle brands to get quick access to Parle's extensive distribution network but also to acquire all franchise bottling plants. This has necessitated a large sum of investment but in longer run this investment will pay for it. Multinationals, particularly those who are late entrants just cannot match the business knowledge and distribution complexities that Indian food businesses have so painstakingly developed slowly but surely over the years. On the top of these, brand loyalty in India is so high that MNCs find it easier to acquire Indian brand and business for growth rather than fight it out only on the strength of superior product knowledge, technology and resources that are available with them. MNCs therefore are grabbing businesses one after another from Indian family owned business houses. The latest in the list is "Uncle Chips" from Amrit Banaspati Group which has been acquired by Pepsi. This is possibly for the reason that Pepsi has now realised that their desparate attempt with "Ruffles", "Lays" and with all their variants are no match to Uncle Chips distribution and the brand loyalty it enjoys. It is generally said that everybody has a price. And hence Amrit Banaspati has also finally sold the brand and the business to Pepsi, of course, at a price, which is higher than the profit that it would have been making from the brand. And for multinationals like Pepsi, this price would be a drop in the ocean. So it is a win-win situation for the both.

A study on the Indian family owned businesses have revealed that only three percent of family owned businesses have survived third generation which means ninety seven percent of the family owned businesses have disappeared or declined in the second generation itself. It, therefore, makes good sense for the second generation of family owned businesses to sell off when the residual value of the business is still there instead of waiting further to erode the value and altogether disappear from the business arena. In that sense Indian food businesses may be taking strategically right decision in disposing of the brand and business and that too at an attractive price to the MNC competitors.

But the issue is what they will do next with the money received as the compensation. Here again the study shows that family owned businesses have done much better as an entrepreneur rather than as an inheritor of the businesses. And it is time that the sales proceeds of the Indian food businesses should be used as a start up activity of yet another food business. And Mr Ramesh Chauhan has proved that he can be successful in yet another brand like "Bisleri" mineral water which has established itself as the number-one bottled mineral water brand controlling about sixty percent of the market share. And what we are seeing - MNCs like Nestle and Danone are talking to Mr Ramesh Chauhan to acquire the brand again. Although Rameshbhai is keeping a public posture that his talks with Nestle has fallen through and he is not selling his Bisleri brand but here again there will be a walk-out price from Nestle which Rameshbhai possibly cannot refuse. Are we therefore again going to witness another bottled water brand being acquired?

MNCs like Pepsi, Coke and Nestle having launched mineral water brands, but to fight Bisleri is not going to be easy, particularly for the reason that Bisleri now has become synonymous with bottled mineral water and MNCs cannot tolerate that for long. If Rameshbhai is not going to take sanyas in Himalayas, my advice to him is that he should not sell his Bisleri brand to MNC at any price. But whether he will listen to my advice is another matter.

Because businessmen's mind works in terms of return on investment and cashflow. But Rameshbhai should not expect that he can create yet another brand of food products. The other day I was making strategy presentation to the owners of the one of the leading and well known natural spring water brand and when I was explaining that the huge investment in the fixed asset that they have made is unwarranted and it would be extremely difficult to justify the investment in terms of return that they can expect.

Quick came the reply from the Chairman of the company saying that if they did not invest in the state-of-the-art imported plant no multinational will ever buy their plant. This means that the entrepreneurs are waiting for the MNCs to pay the price so that they can get out recovering their cost with a hefty profit. Such is the mentality of the Indian family owned businesses. They don't have any permanent value proposition for the shareholders. There are many family owned businesses in abroad which have become global players now. But in India, we don't see that global vision amongst family owned food businesses. And now that nothing remained excepting Parle products (manufacturers of Parle Biscuits) is worth mentioning in food businesses which is still being controlled by Mr Vijay Chauhan and Mr Sarat Chauhan. A friend of mine who is in the business of selling herbal and fruit beverages and squashes came to me to help him strategising his business to become around INR 200-250 million in size and then he expects that some MNC will pay him double this amount so that he can peacefully retire. In America, we have ninety percent of the businesses which are family owned and many grown in size to become even global corporation.

But in India we find that most of the family owned food businesses are either already sold or are waiting for the big offer which they cannot refuse. I am expecting the next big acquisition in food business would be in spices and in that direction MDH and Everest - both of them jointly controls over forty percent of the total INR 12 billion spice market. Hindustan Lever has just got into the spice business after the failure of "Sona" brand of Brook Bond. And world giant in Spice "McCormick" in collaboration with A.T. Thomas is already here with big ambitious plan.

Although food processing technology has not undergone any remarkable change in the recent past but the communication technology and global competition have been really changing the face of the industry and that too very fast. Department of Food Processing Industry seems to be busy identifying new opportunities and also ascertaining the issues facing the industry. Ministry is projecting a huge potential for food processing industry and to make it happen Govt is providing all kinds of support to the industry.

Multinational Food Companies to Upgrade the Industry

Eating habits in India are still traditional and as a result the processed food industry did not grow as expected. It takes long time to change the consumer food habits and it requires a lot of development efforts and resources to popularise the processed convenience foods. The survey indicates that the Indian housewives would always like to add some value to the food she serves to her family to get a satisfaction that she herself made the dish to the liking and also for the nutritional requirements of her family members. This attitude of Indian housewives seems to be there even with the working women. Marketers therefore could not realise the price of convenience that they were expecting that the consumer will pay. The result is inevitable. There were many product failures and one out of twenty products that were launched in the recent past could only see the light of the day. And the rest fell by the wayside. The industry which was till recently dominated by the local entrepreneurs and business houses have suffered serious setbacks and there are only handful of local industries which survived and grown in this sectors whose names are worth mentioning. Parle, Nutrine and few industries in dairy sectors are falling in that category and they are now the take-over targets for the multinationals. Nestle signed an MOU with Nutrine with an intention to take over but the deal fell through. Majority of the process food industry categories are in the small to medium scale sectors whose existence are threatened because of multiplicity of problems including low capacity utilisation, high cost of production, non-availability of quality raw materials, seasonal nature of the industry, multiple taxes, poor infrastructural support and most importantly small market, low growth rate and high cost of market development.

Fig. 2.3 Kellog upgraded the quality of breakfast cereal.

It requires a lot of resources and skills and capacity to sustain the financial pressures. Local industries tried this for many years but with very limited success. It is in this area multinationals' marketing skills, technology, and resources and financial muscle that can come readily to develop this sector for the benefit of not only the food industry but also for the benefit of the farm sector. We may or may not like it but that is what is going to happen. And that will be for the good of all concerned – consumers, farmers and also for the development of our economy. Local industries' role will then could be largely to provide support services and also to manufacture as subcontractors for the multinationals. Local brands which are small will thus disappear and the market will get flooded with the global brands.

We are expecting these new MNC entrants to develop export market for the value added processed foods and agro commodities and in many instances export obligation has been a condition for granting license. Reality is that international trade is highly competitive and one can compete if the cost of production is really low here. Export trade cannot be sustained on incentives and drawbacks if structurally it is unviable. For the cost of production to be competitive domestic industry should develop and become mature in the first place which is not happening so far. Otherwise, value addition can never take place within the country. That is the reason why value added export in this sector has not grown even after the entry of MNCS. In the name of export, large houses are actually buying the export performance of small business units by paying a premium to meet their own export commitment. This hardly helps the country.

Statistics always float around that because of lack of adequate storage and processing facilities country loses about thirty percent of its total harvest of fruits and vegetables but fact remains that if all these raw fruits and vegetables were converted into processed fruits and vegetables losses would have been even much higher because of lack of ready market or demand for those products in domestic and international market. Prime task therefore is to create market demand for the processed foods. All other issues would then fall in place as market forces would have levelled other constraints. We have over three thousand fruit and vegetable processing industries operating as cottage, small, medium and large scale industries using low level of technology with little or no ability to market their output resulting into unviable operations. Many of those units are now virtually closed down or existing only in name.

The financial institutions which had funded such units could not recover the interest payments, not to speak of recovering the principal amount. Majority of these units therefore are beyond recovery even if fresh dose of fund is injected into them. We have thus one option and that is to invite MNCs who knows the business and can bring in their global synergies with commensurate resources to establish the food industry in India and this is what exactly going to happen in next couple of years. Whether we like it or not existing industries which are doing reasonably well and have developed good distribution infrastructures will have to be ready to be acquired by new MNCs which have arrived here to stay. Those industries which are either sick or unviable should get ready to produce for MNCs on contractual basis. Those who will not be ready for either of these two new role should be ready to die a natural death.

Competition Led to Superior Quality

Food processing industry in India has undergone a total metamorphosis over the last one decade, in terms of types, variety, quality and presentation which is a result of liberalisation leading to foreign direct investment in frontiers of processed food sectors. Multinational and transnational corporations made significant contribution. This was possible due to the significant technological upgradation in this sector. It is not that the latest state-of-the-art technologies in this sector were not known to us. On the contrary, we had the fullest capability and technical know-how. In seventies and eighties we used to talk about in seminars and conferences the new types of packaging, products and processes but industries never felt the necessity to upgrade or invest in new technology. Nor did they have the resources to support such programme. Reason was the apprehension all around that there would be no market for such products. And we continued to produce products that are of traditional in nature using age-old technologies. Besides, there were licensing restrictions, reservation of many categories under small-scale sectors etc., resulting into poor or negligible upgradation of the industry. Things have changed since then.

With the technological upgradation we now see an all round improvement in processed food product's quality. The competition has forced the processors to improve and to upgrade the quality. Earlier we had limited categories, for example, jam, jellies, marmalades, squashes, cordials, ketchup and sauces in fruit and vegetable sector, ice cream, spray dried milk powder, condensed milk, butter and ghee in dairy sector, bread, biscuits and cakes in bakery sector, hard boiled confectioneries, one brand and type of chewing gum and limited variety of chocolate in confectionery sector. Today we have not only better quality of these but also a lot of variants and product types and choices. There is also a significant improvement in packaging quality. In seventies we had only glass and cans as packaging materials. In eighties we had seen laminates and other plastic materials coming in. Today we have the host of packaging types being used to market processed food products. Earlier we used to get fruit juices and ready-to-serve (RTS) beverages only in glass bottles. Today we have tetra pack and also asceptic carton pack. Similarly, tomato paste earlier used to be sold in metal cans and the market for this was also very small. Today tomato paste is sold by Godrej Foods in asceptic consumer pack.

In packaging of cheese and other dairy products considerable improvement in the product and packaging quality are evidenced. Cheese, as a product was not known to the Indian consumer in seventies and eighties. Only cheese that we had was cottage cheese. Processed cheese was not there, not to speak of varieties of cheese as they are found and consumed in other countries. Amul introduced processed cheese much later. I remember, during early eighties we had to develop a particular party near Delhi to supply mozzrella cheese required for pizza topping to be sold through Mcdowells Fast Food chain which subsequently closed down. Today although we don't have all varieties of cheese but we have seen a beginning. Britannia and La-bon cheese are definitely gaining ground. And we expect that when Kraft will enter this market there will be a revolution in processed cheese sector in India. Kraft International has done considerable research on the possibility of producing world class Kraft cheese for Indian market and they came to the conclusion that the milk quality in India is not good enough to produce cheese of Kraft grade. Besides, Kraft cheese is produced from cow milk where as in India bulk of our milk is from buffalow. They even thought of importing the compressed casein block to Nepal under refrigerated condition and set up processing plant there for Indian market in order to take the custom duty advantage because quality is what they can not sacrifice. But that also was not found to be viable. I told Mr. Puno who is in charge of South East Asian region including Indian sub-continent that starting early is the key. I advised him to start the operation first and cow milk can be made available or can be organised. But they had still the apprehensions. Britannia subsequently introduced cheese and their sole claim was "Cheese from cow milk" and has done very well. And it is everybody's knowledge that Britannia is not manufacturing it themselves but it is being manufactured in a local plant near Pune under a subcontract manufacturing arrangement. Britannia is only marketing it. Although process technology support might come from their respective French collaborators namely BSN and LA-BON, but this only proves my contention that technology is known to us but we did not put it to application to tap new and emerging market. Competition is forcing the marketers to look for better products and new products, which is a direct outcome of the liberalisation policy.

Even the traditional item like Indian snacks (bhujjia) and Bengali sweets manufacturers are also thinking to upgrade their manufacturing technology and product quality. Mr. Agarwal, Managing Director of Bikanerwala who supplies bhujjia to Pepsi Foods recently invited me to visit his plant at Lawrence Road in Delhi and said Pepsi's global chief also visited his plant and was highly impressed to see their process. When asked what exactly the improvement they have made in their age-old labour oriented process, Mr. Agarwal commented that the packaging of Bujjia is now fully mechanised. Similarly sweets are also a serious trade worth INR 165 billion and in West Bengal alone the market is estimated to be INR 10 billion. The Sweetmeat Traders Association in West Bengal recently held a seminar in Calcutta to devise ways and means of making the sweet making process more hygienic and to ensure optimum use of technology - said Mr. Robin Pal, General Secretary of the Association. The implications of liberalisation has also reached these so-called traditional foods and the traders now are eyeing for the global market.

Under liberalisation regime consumer is the king. They are getting better value for money and they have now a wide choice to select from.

Why MNC go Through Acquisition Route for Growth Strategy

Different corporations adopt different growth strategies. Some choose to grow organically exploiting the potential of their main business operations, others look for growth opportunities in diversification or in acquisition of existing and or competitive business units. Acquisition option is often more attractive to many companies because it seems the faster way to grow.

Acquisition also offers many other advantages. It provides faster entry into a new and alien market and thus gives an immediate knowledge base for the acquirer which is required to run a business profitably. It also eliminates a potential competition in the market and thus helps acquirer to sell their own products through the same selling and distribution channel. For fast moving consumer goods (FMCG) like processed foods, it takes years to build an efficient distribution channel in a highly complex and large market like India. Whatever might be the reason, the acquisition has to ultimately enhance shareholder value. These conditions can be summarised in three essential tests (Michael Porter, Competitive Advantage, The Free Press, 1985):

- The attractiveness test: The industry chosen for acquisition must be structurally attractive.

- The cost of entry test: The cost of entry must not capitalise all the future profits.
- The better off test: Either the new unit must gain competitive advantage from its link with the corporation or vice versa.

The first major acquisition in processed food industry was seen when Brook Bond acquired Kissans and Dippys from UB Group. And subsequently Brook Bond got acquired by Hindustan Lever (HLL). After acquisition, HLL quietly dropped Dippy's brand and manufacturing units. Under UB fold there were nine manufacturing companies including one in Nepal and another one in Ooty (dedicated only to Mushroom production and export, which UB retained). But HLL closed down all these satellite units and concentrated on one brand "Kissan" and focussed factory concept and gradually introduced many new product including branded grocery products under umbrella brand of "Kissan-Annapurna", which has become INR 2500 milllon business in a short span, built in-roads virtually from the scratch. They thus, followed the third rule of acquisition as mentioned above.

Coke acquired Parle Brands by paying reportedly INR 1500 million but the integration with their own business was not managed properly. Also to get entry into the Parle distribution infrastructure in a hurry they possibly paid much higher price for the acquisition and thus cost of entry was very high and therefore likely to fail to pass the second test of acquisition as enumerated above. Coke is facing financial crunch not only in India but also in global scenario which is evident from their unceremonious exit of their CEO and their decision to reduce 6000 emp'oyees globally. Of course, Coke is a giant and financial situation only in India cannot trigger those decision globally. In later years Coke has to write off the big losses in Indian operations.

Pepsi decided to enter agro sector by joining hands with Punjab Agro with their grand plan to integrate backward linkages with farmers which ended up in a fiasco and thus failed to pass the attractiveness test. Although now, they seemed to have recovered a lot of their lost ground by focussing on their core brand and business and acquiring smaller businesses like Dukes who have their presence in only western India market with dominance in Soda and Mango - an RTS beverage under the brand name "Mangola".

In later years we have seen Heinz acquiring food business from Glaxo. Heinz reportedly not doing well and are over dependent on Nycil sales which is not their strategic business. Both "Nycil" and "Complan" sales are dropping and thus Heinz delayed introduction of their Tomato Ketchup for which they are famous globally. Of late, Heinz introduced tomato ketchup but it is not doing well.

We can, therefore, clearly see that the acquisitions which were made earlier by leading MNCs did not give them very attractive returns. They only gained on two counts, namely getting access to the distribution infrastructure and in eliminating one competition from the market.

HLL also acquired many other brands and went for strategic alliances. They also divested their dairy plant at Etah in UP to Nutricia although HLL is in dairy business in a big way. This is their planned strategy as the products which are produced from Etah factory including Anik Ghee and Skimmed Milk powder were not doing well.

The recent acquisition of the only public sector food company-Modern Food industry (MFI) is being seen as a positive move for HLL. The INR 1.05 billion outlay for acquiring equity and another INR 200 million as capital infusion for reviving MFI will increase HLL's exposure to branded processed food items.

The money that was paid by HLL was for acquiring 74% of MFI and the business that will add to HLL's balance sheet is approximately INR 2.0 billion should allow HLL to move up in value chain from flour to bread and other processed foods. For acquiring that HLL has accepted the condition that all 2000 employees of MFI will be kept at their current terms of employment and to make sure that HLL does it Government has retained 26% of equity in the venture. Through MFI, HLL will get immediate presence in 110 Class 1 towns and daily distribution reach into 0.1 million outlets. Besides the unit in Delhi, HLL will get access to other 14 units of MFI and 24 franchisees in various parts of the country. Apparently, HLL is making another attempt to gain competitive advantage. And in the process, the only PSU in food which has all India presence has now gone in the fold of this giant MNC. Considering the fact that MFI has an asset worth over INR 20 billion mostly in real estate the price that HLL has paid for acquiring 74% equity is very attractive.

The latest acquisition in the processed food industry is of health food drinks brands like "Viva" and "Maltova" from Jagatjit Industries Limited (JIL) by Smith Kline Beecham Consumer Health Care (SBCH) the Indian associate of SKB - UK. The deal is said to have been clinched for a price of INR 862.5 million. Viva and Maltova enjoy about 8% market share of the health food drink market which is estimated around 90000 tonnes per annum. With this acquisition SBCH will dominate health drink market with 70% market share. As a result, post acquisition SBCH share rose to INR 4.76 billion from the previous closing at INR 4.43 billion.

SmithKline globally is getting out of food but their Indian arm is so strong that it is not only continuing but also has gone for an acquisition. This is because at the current level of market capitalisation no one will find SBCH an attractive proposition for acquisition as it will fail in cost of entry test. SBCH has thus to continue making healthy profits and reward their share holders. SBCH has also made significant investment of INR 800 million to upgrade and mordernise their manufacturing facility. Alfa Laval has been entrusted to do this job. If the post acquisition integration process are managed properly SBCH stands to gain from it as there is a strategic fitment in the operations of both the companies. They have done their home work also well as for sometime JIL's facilities was used by SBCH for contract manufacturing of their own brand "Horlicks".

Both these recent acquisitions are note worthy in the sense that they are not only big but also trying to draw synergy from the operations.But with these two acquisitions possibly nothing in the Indian business houses in the processed food sector left to be acquired.Only one name which is still going strong is Parle Products Ltd. (PPL). But how long Mr. Vijay Chauhan can keep his fight on against giant MNC's to retain control on his popular brands like Parle-G and Krack - Jack? United Biscuits has started their operations in Bombay, Britannia acquired regional biscuit brand "Kwality".

Acquisition of Domestic Food Business by MNCs

Liberalisation has brought in through the entry of large multinational and transnational corporations, foreign investment in this sector. This resulted in competition, technological upgradation and market expansion. In the face of the competition, domestic industries are gradually losing market share and thus selling their businesses to the new entrant MNCs well before the value of the brand and businesses drops further due to ongoing onslaught of multinational brands. This is happening because MNCs' have much greater resources to put behind their brand and business and also have long term vision and sustainability. Domestic industries are no comparison. The first attack came in soft beverages industry with Coke acquiring Parle brands and Pepsi acquiring Dukes and with the entry of Cadbury Schweepes in this sector entire soft drink industry is now in control of MNCs'. Earlier only hot beverages (both white and brown segments) were controlled by MNCs' such as Nestle, Brooke Bond and Smithkline & Beechem. But soft beverage sector was dominated by domestic industries. With Coke and Pepsi acquiring Indian businesses, total non-alcoholic beverage industry is now under control of MNCs.

Britannia is already under control of Danone group of France. Only large bakery and confectionery left to be acquired in private sector is Parle Products.

And with the entries of confectionery giants like Perfetti, Wriggly and Agrilimen (a Spanish confectioner in joint venture with Dabur but later on acquired Dabur's equity to have 100% control) confectionery and bakery sector, will also become the domain of MNCs.

With Nestle's strong presence in Tomato Ketchup and Pickles and Hindustan Lever acquiring Kissan and Dipy brands from UB group through Brooke Bond route fruit and vegetable sector is also dominated by multinationals.

Heinz, the world's largest Tomato Ketchup manufacturer had acquired food business of Glaxo. Due to strategic restructuring of portfolio Glaxo decided to divest their dairy business with established brands like Complan, Glucon-D and Farex. Hindustan Lever, on the other hand, through a strategic alliance route, took control of Kwality Ice-cream as well as 100% Ice-cream brand of Jagatjit. Hindustan Lever with their own presence in dairy sectors, and with the introduction of Baskin Robbins and Walls has emerged as a dominant player in dairy, segment, in general and Ice-cream segment, in particular. Hindustan Lever (HLL) also acquired Dollop Ice-cream brand from Cadbury's.

HLL, however, recently announced their intention to sell-off their dairy unit in UP. Ice-cream industry which is reserved for small scale sector has now been in the control of multinationals through a different route. The argument that ice-cream is actually a frozen dessert - a nomenclature that has been accepted by both food and law ministry of Govt. of India - paved the way for Hindustan Lever for this strategic acquisition. The earlier successful domestic businesses such as Dalmia Dairy, Foremost Industry and Jagatjit Industry in dairy sector are all in deep trouble - and MNCs have taken a control of this sector as well.

National Dairy Development Board (NDDB) with its strong brand Amul and with its deep root extended upto farmers level as a means of backward integration will of course, remains a significant force to reckon with. But nobody will deny that in branded dairy products Amul has to put up a constant fight against multinational brands. Vadilal is also a significant player in ice-cream but their presence is limited in Western India and for how long they will remain has to be seen. Kraft Foods a unit of Phillips Morris is holding a licence to set up 100% owned entity and they are expected to come and set up their operation anytime.

In the convenience foods - 'Corn Products', a US multinational is fast making progress. This is an old company which did not make any significant contribution in the Indian food business largely because of lack of interest from their principals. CPC - International is now fast making progress with their well known Rex and Brown & Polson and Knorr soup brands. Recently they announced the acquisition of DCW Chemicals - makers of Captain Cook brands, which ran into rough weather because of the objection taken by some miller in Haryana to whom allegedly DCW has contractual obligations. Shortly, we will also have products in joint venture with Pioma Industries, the manufacturer of Rasna soft drink mixes and Campbell a world leader in canned foods. Godrej, on the other hand, has joined hands with Pilsburry a leading player in the convenience foods business to boost their business activities. Pilsburry has already introduced instant Cake mix. In subsequent years, of course, this alliance fell through and both Godrej Foods and Pilsbury have charted their own independent course of business. In this category others including Gits brand are relatively smaller and regional players.

Apparently, first change that we have witnessed is of acquisitions of domestic brands in frontiers of food business by MNCs and alongwith, although at a much lower scale, a few joint ventures. Even the public sector undertaking, Modern Foods although making profit was put up for sale which Hindustan Lever acquired, in due course of time.The first lesson that we have learnt as the fall out of liberalisation is acquisition of successful domestic food business by MNCs.

Recent Acquisitions in Indian Food Industry

BUNGE is an unknown entity in food processing industry. It is a south American group but have very large presence in North America. And is a family owned company. Through a number of acquisitions Bunge has emerged as a leading oil seed processing company in the world market. They are the largest producer and marketers of fertilisers in South America and world's leading player in edible oil. Nobody has heard about this company before as they are mainly in commodity trade and that too focussed on the edible oil trade. Sometime ago a friend of mine Monoj Sarma came to India and met me. At that time I did not know that he is working for Bunge Foods in USA as Project Leader. He was making lot of enquiries with me about the HLL's brand Dalda which is generic to the category of the hydrogenated vegetable oil. It was in the news for some time that HLL wants to exit from this business identified as nonstrategic to their core businesses. When Monoj was enquiring and collecting details about Dalda little did I know that Dalda is going to be acquired by Bunge. The edible oil trade is very difficult. It requires very specific skill to manage. The margin of contribution in this business is also low and that too largely depends on the procurement skill and the volume of business. Small or even medium size players who are not having deep root in in this trade are unlikely to succeed. In CPC (Now known as Best Foods International and an Unilever group company) we had introduced Mazola corn oil and withdrawn the product later. Although Unilever now owns Best Foods but Mazola brand which is quite popular edible oil in US and also in part of Europe is still in the CPCs fold. ITC, although now has been re-entering the category but have failed earlier. They were in Sunflower oil having Sundrop as their brand name. Britannia had set up large soyabean processing complex in Vidisha in Madhya Pradesh and introduced Vital brand of soya oil in the market but after incurring losses sold the business to S.M.Dyechem. The leading player in the category now is Marico. The other lead players are Cargil again is an US based commodity player. Even the well known brand like Postman from Ahmed Mills is fast disappearing. In fact this family owned business has distintegrated.

All businesses cannot therefore, sustain this category. Although Dalda is an old business that HLL had, but inspite of the fact that it is generic to the category there was very little contribution that the business division was making for the company which has prompted the company to look for the buyer. After acquiring the brand Dalda, Bunge Ltd, its new owner is now extending into the soya oil to improve the profitability of the business. Bunge also acquired Gee Pee Ceval Proteins and Investment Ltd – a company promoted by Mr Mahendra Mansingka. These two companies will be, in course of time integrated under Bunge Group. A company not known for their existance have appeared in the scene from nowhere and acquired a company and one important brand and are getting ready to launch new product in edible oil. We will shortly have Bunge soya oil in the market.

The next big acquisition in the processed food sector that took place in the recent times is that of Parry's confectionery of the south based Murugappa Group. This over 100 years old business got sold for INR 640 million. South Korean group and a confectionery giant Lotte Confectionery Company acquired the entire 60.39 % stake of Murugappa Group to have the total control in this business. Lotte Confectionery is a USD 1 billion company and have significant presence in chewing gums, candy and bakery segments. The Murugappa group chairman Mr M. V. Subbiah said while briefing the press that with the MNC competition increasing in this segment the group felt that they cannot bring in matching investment required for product development and promotion to survive and therefore this deal is in the best interest of the company (Parry Confectionery Ltd) and its shareholders. Lotte group was looking for the opportunities to get entry into the Indian market and this was a great opportunity for them. According to the deal, Lotte group will use

Parry logo for a fee for five years. It has been said that Lotte will pay an annual royalty fees of INR 0.5 million for using the logo of Parry which cut across many categories. Parrys confectionery's leading brands are Coffee Bite and Lacto King.

Parrys confectionery was losing money all these years. Only in the year 2003-04 through a financial restructuring they have been able to report a marginal profit. The half yearly financial report published at the end of september 30, 2003 shows that they made net profit of INR 0.4 million only on a turnover of INR 464.1 million. They reported a turnover of INR 938.2 million in the finacial year 2002-03 did not show any growth in subsequent years. It may be mentioned here that earlier I predicted that both Parry and Nutrine will soon change hands and possibility would be some MNCs coming and acquiring these two companies. At that time I did not realise that it will happen so fast. Parry was using the only synergy that the group had with this confectionery business is its integration with their sugar business.

They had this advantage but to remain in business in globally competitive category one needs to be innovative which has not happened. In the confectionery category many new players have lined up and we have seen many new brands. I can only see the possibility of Parle continuing with this busness as they have the ability to fight MNC competition which they have displayed earlier.

Indian food business, particulary the large Indian food business have to quickly upgrade themselves in the value chain and also deliver lot of innovation in the category that they represent to remain in the business failing which they should sell their enterprise to prospective buyers when the residual value is still high. Murugappa group just done that. We all are being watched by global players who are evaluating many options for entry into the large market like India. We need to think global and act local to survive and grow.

Proliferation and Extension of Food Brands

Food items are primarily processed to extend its shelf life and to preserve its nutritional value. The secondary purpose of processing of food is to deliver convenience, taste and appeal to the target consumers. Depending upon what consumer segments we are targeting the processing methods, type of food and its taste and packaging and total presentation varies widely. In a country like India where local taste preferences differ from region to region it poses a much bigger problem to produce food products which can have a much larger acceptance and hence a bigger market potential. But there are some food categories and types for which there is a universal acceptance and hitherto Indian processed food industry only were processing those generic category of foods for all India market. Even new entrants in the processed food industry were only adding brands in the traditional sectors. We have witnessed this phenomenon before liberalisation in different categories. And as a result, mortality rate of processed food brands were quite high. For example, when Amul came into the market with their Amul Butter - Polsons butter disappeared from the scene. And the successful brand went on extending it to other categories. Having tasted success, Amul brand has been extended across a range of items including cheese, cheese spread, shrikhand, chocolate and ice-cream.

Creativity in food industry was, to say the least, very low. There were of course small local companies who attempted to create products for catering to the local taste preferences but the market was so small that the products did not survive the test of time. For example, Kissan launched "Bisebelle Bhath" a South Indian delicacy in Southern market in mid eighties only to withdraw a year later. We at Kissans did considerable work and developed instant rice but market research indicated that the market for instant rice would be insignificant and thus we had to drop the idea. The same instant rice was used to formulate "Bisebelle bhath". Phillips Morris who got clearance for setting up 100% owned entities in India had announced their plans to introduce the instant rice under their global and popular brand "Minute Rice". But later they changed their mind altogether and did not enter the Indian market till date.

And still there are others who tried to create universal appeal and introduced mass market product and have demonstrated big success stories. The example is Rasna from Pioma Industries who created a success story and now even challenging Tang of General Foods in other markets. Yet others have failed in such attempt. In mid eighties steel merchant of Mumbai Mr. Ravi Kiran Agarwal in a joint venture with Kwality Frozen Foods had set up Tasty Bite Eatables Ltd. - a company to get into frozen foods and North Indian and South Indian vegetarian and non-vegetarian ready-to-serve foods. The concept was - 'warm and serve'.

A modern plant was set up near Pune. The products including Mutton curry etc. in retortable pouch were introduced but it did not click. A couple of years later they faced serious financial problems and subsequently the company was sold to Hindustan Lever - who tried hard to establish "Green Valley" frozen foods. It was also later on withdrawn. Tasty Bites finally got acquired by a NRI group from US for sourcing ready to serve ethnic foods from India for US market. Welga Foods in Badaun near Bareilly similarly had to close down their frozen foods plant. Tarai Foods who were also a contract manufacturer for Hindustan Lever is still struggling to exist. The only long term player in frozen foods particularly frozen vegetables is "Mafco" - a co-operative in Maharashtra. Food products that were in the high price range and were well ahead of their time did not succeed in India. And thus casualties in certain category were very high.

Before nineties the food industry in India was struggling to establish only the traditional food brands and there was very little or no effort to introduce new foods. In post liberalisation era we have host of new MNCs with superior marketing skill and bigger resource to their command have extended their brands to a wide variety of local foods and their variants including the areas which were protected niches of small local players. For example, Indian traditional snacks were only local brands even a couple of years ago. But there we have now even global brands. Kissan under UB-group used to sell and market only fruit and vegetable products. Today Kissan brand has been extended to even branded grocery items which were earlier the domain of small local players. Pepsi's primary business is in soft drinks but in India they have gone into branding of traditional snack foods. Similarly Nestle - a swiss Food major - has introduced pickles in Indian market. In the traditional food items local companies should be able to add better value and hence can score higher in the market place.

In seventies, 'Bisleri' was the only mineral water which had national presence and the sale was to the tune of approximately one hundred thousand cases valued at about INR 6 million. Today mineral water market is said to be of INR 8 billion and over hundred brands of mineral water are there. Mr. Ramesh Chauhan of Parles thinks that mineral water market in next five years time will become INR 200 billion and based on that he has drawn up ambitious plan for his Bisleri mineral water. The competition in mineral water is so high that Mr. Ramesh Chauhan's own brother Mr. Prakash Chauhan who owns "Frooty" brand also introduced a mineral water under the brand name "Bailey". Of late, we have multinationals entering the mineral water scene. "Evan" is recently launched which is a well known international brand.

Earlier we did not have any fruit juice in the market. Only canned juice and ready-to-serve beverages in bottles were available. Today we have number of brands in carton and tetrapack. Such as 'Onjus' of Enkay Texofood, 'Real juice' of Dabur, 'Jump-In' and "Xs" of Godrej, 'Tropicana' from Pepsi etc. all packed in convenient asceptic cartons.

The proliferation of brands are also seen in branded grocery products. A few years ago we had 'Tata-salt' as the only refined iodised salt selling in the market and subsequently we had 'Captain Cook' from DCW, 'Kissan Annapurna' from Kissan Products and Catch (with dispenser) from Hi-Tech Foods and more brands to come in. In some areas such as meat and poultry products branding, packaging, processing and distribution on a national scale has yet to be witnessed. But in many of the processed food categories, as we can see that the existing brand is either extended to a wide variety of foods such as Britannia to Cheese and Long Life Milk in tetrapack etc. or there are proliferation of brands.

In this process, ultimate beneficiary is the consumer as they can expect to get the best value for their money. Competitive pressure will make that possible.

In Key Categories it is Now the Fight Amongst only Multinationals

The market seems to have never seen so much of excitement and exposure of processed food before. It is all due to high pitch marketing activity initiated by multinational giants. And as expected in this battle for market share of our domestic companies are gradually slipping behind. The fight thus is now amongst only multinationals - at least in key food categories. Earlier we have observed that Bisleri mineral water is having its head above the rest but now in that category also we find Aquafina of Pepsi and Kinley of Coke are fast emerging as winners. If the visibility in the market and the market report are any indication Bisleri cannot hold the dominant position for long. By switching the age old and faithful Bisleri bottler Goenkas in Eastern region to Coke has given a severe jolt to the Bisleri. Marketing is a war like situation and there is nothing unfair in this as long as beating the competition is concerned. And the better financial resource definitely is helping the MNCs to gradually inch upon the competition and finally eliminating them. In their attempt to capture the market everyday we are seeing the new product being introduced. In a category like water we are now going to see introduction of flavoured water from both Coke and Pepsi. Consumers are in to see many variants to their delight.

In soft drinks, it is everybody's knowledge that local players are almost non-existent. It is the fight between Coke and Pepsi. The same is the story in case of health beverage and that too both in brown and white health beverage segment. The fight there is between Cadbury and Smith Kline Bechem. In white segment Complan is also having a reasonable market share but that too is in the fold of Heinz who acquired food brands from Glaxo a couple of years ago.

a. Hot beverages

b. Cold beverages

c. Health beverages

Fig. 2.4 In beverages segment the fight now only amongst multinationals. **(a)** Hot beverages, **(b)** Cold beverages, **(c)** Health beverages.

In fruit and vegetable products category the major segment is tomato ketchup and there we have again two formidable players - Hindustan Lever and Nestle. Heinz is a world leader in this category but they could not make any significant breakthrough with their tomato ketchup in India so far. But the fight in this category again is limited to two multinationals.

In branded grocery items we had host of domestic brands including many local brands which are quite popular. The names that are coming to my mind are Shaktibhog, Rose etc. Although these brands are still there but they are nowhere near the MNC brands like Kissan Annapurna or Pilsbury. A scenario is gradually emerging in processed food business that the fight for market share is getting restricted between multinational brands. And in the process domestic brands are getting marginalised. Cargil is really a giant in grocery items and it is expected that it will soon become a big player here in India as well. This market will be gradually extended further into the convenience staple food category. Hindustan Lever has completed its extensive research on the chapati (roti) in packed form to be introduced shortly into the Indian market and the volume expectation is enormous. They are said to be covering the railway stations for distribution of chapati with the assumption that passengers returning home would like to buy chapati so that they need not have to prepare it after reaching home tired of long journey.

Both Nestle and Cadbury are gearing up to fight the chocolate war. The traditional leader in chocolate segment was Cadbury. But with a series of successful launch of new products in chocolate category Nestle has established itself as a dominant player. Nestle was first to launch white chocolate in 1991 followed by the launch of Kit Kat in 1995 and Munch in 1999. With the launch of Munch which is basically a chocolate-wafer priced at INR 5, it has been reported that they could double the INR 5 segment. During August 2001 Nestle also launched another new segment with Milkybar which has a soft white fudge center enveloped in a white chocolate covering. On the top of all that new products, Nestle recently launched Chocostick in Tamil Nadu. Within four months of its launch this product has cornered about 11 percent share of the chocolate market in Chennai and as per the available report over six million units of Nestle Chocostick are being consumed every month in just Tamil Nadu itself. This can be largely attributed to the low price point of INR 2 which opens up lot of distribution opportunities in upcountry territory in rural areas. Apparently, Nestle has taken away the new initiatives in chocolate market from the stronghold of Cadbury's. Although Cadbury has reacted by launching a product in the same segment in Andhra Pradesh. While both are currently test marketing the product but both are upbeat about its potential. Although Nestle is so far a clear winner which can be seen from the fact that Nestle's growth stands at 14 percent in the chocolate industry which is above the industry growth rate of 9.2 percent. And against that background Cadbury's growth rate has been reported as 6.7 percent. The next chocolate war of the titans, Nestle and Cadbury, is going to be fought again in down south with this new innovative product in chocolate segment which can be described as liquid chocolate mass. It is in fact a semi solid chocolate mass in a see-through plastic pack in a stick format.

There are two lessons that we learn. And these are - domestic companies are out from the race in these categories and there are a lot of innovations that are taking place in all key segments which has helped the marketers to expand the market. And I wonder why this could not happen earlier. Why we have to wait for MNCs to come in to show us the way. There could be various reasons but technological capability is not definitely the one.

Opportunities for MNCs in Indian Processed Food Sector

INDIA is an agricultural economy and we are already a leading producer of sugar, milk, tea etc. Food production & processing account for 26% of our GDP and over 60% of our employment. But if India wants to become world's largest food factory as we are contemplating we have still miles to go. Our productivity is still low and level of utilization of farm machineries are much at lower levels in comparison to many other Asian countries. Although this sector is one of the first areas to receive high level of development support but value addition is still one of the lowest. The value addition in the food sector is only 7% to food production as compared to 23% in China and 45% in Philippines and 188% in UK.

Indian food industry is also characterized by its dominance by small and unorganized sector which accounts for 75% of the total industry. In spite of all these limitations, food is a profitable sector in all emerging markets including India. Food sector gets the place only after the communication. The involvement of MNCs in the post liberalization era has helped the industry to improve upon the value chain to a certain extent where MNCs have their own interest linked with that sector. For example, Pepsi has helped farmers to increase tomato output by 266%. Similarly, Cargill's effort achieved sunflower growth by about 100% and Tarai potatoes have grown by over 50 %. This increased output in turn helped in increase in farmers' income for Tarai potatoes by 125%, and for tomato grower by 230 %. Similarly, sunflower growers' income went up by 100%. The food consumption has over the decades changed from the subsistence level in to basic and finally to premium foods. The processed food sectors can only cater to premium segment of the market, which is said to have grown by about 150%, but this segment in terms of number of households is still very small. Some estimate puts that figure as 5 million household. The size of the market as it exists is not attractive enough to make room for many players to thrive. Our food industry is also suffering from the problem of too many intermediaries adding to the cost, besides low yield. Success has to come from only large scale integrated approach. The price of the product is a major issue in the game which has prompted Coke and Pepsi to launch an option at INR 5 price point which has triggered the growth. It has been estimated that the value loss in the food chain is almost INR 5000 billion. The name of the game is therefore, efficiency.

MNCs have both resources and technological advantage over their domestic counter-parts. They also have the staying power over a longer period. This has been demonstrated by the large global and transnational corporations like Kellogg and Pepsi. Indian food industry now has poised for growth and there are several factors that show that the industry will gradually evolve to global standard. But exploitation of that opportunities are not possible by all players. Only large global players who have long term vision can make it. Others including MNCs with short term vision or those who have set up operation with certain expectation which is not realistic may not be able to sustain operation in Indian conditions for a long time. For example, we have seen the failure of large companies like Heinz although they have not yet given up the operation but their efforts to sustain the level of operation that is required are still at low key. Heinz, a world leader in tomato ketchup could have taken more aggressive and innovative steps to establish their products line. But that is not happening. In seventies and eighties tomato ketchup market was only of INR 200 million approximately and leading player was Kissan followed by Dipy's both under the UB group fold then. But Maggie tomato ketchup launched by Nestle really expanded the market. Today tomato ketchup is almost INR 2000 million market, a ten fold growth in the last decade. Heinz could have given the incremental boost in the same market which did not happen. Another example of MNC failure is Dutch multinational Nutricia's decision recently to exit Indian market. Nutricia India, a subsidiary of Royal Numico entered Indian market through acquisition of Hindustan Lever's dairy business along with the brand Anik and production plant at Etah in UP. HLL could not make a successful brand out of Anik Ghee and baby food etc. and finally could sell the brand and business to Nutricia. But Nutricia also could not sustain the business. This dairy business and the plant they finally sold to the INR 370 billion Ruchi group who are the largest in the edible oil sector. And Nutricia decided to quit Indian operation. The point that is being made is that only MNCs with long vision can make it and the opportunity is there for them.

MNCs dominance in the Indian food market can be seen in categories where large prospect of growth is visible. For local players either select categories or regional opportunities are there for exploitation. For example, for Ruchi, Anik ghee could be an opportunity but not Anik baby food where both HLL and Nutricia failed. In future, we will witness fight between MNCs in large categories and they will exploit and trigger growth.

Yet Another Major Food Joint Venture Breaking up

We have been experiencing the failure of many joint ventures in the post liberalisation era in all categories of industries - processed foods included. Readers will remember that initially Pepsi venture was also a tripartite joint venture between Punjab Agro (a cooperative sector), Voltas (a Tata group company) and Pepsi. But both Punjab Agro and Voltas could not put up with the magnitude of losses Pepsi venture was incurring and the way the project was being implemented with a significant overrun requiring additional infusion of funds. These are operational issues but if a joint venture between an Indian company and a multinational has to succeed there has to be a cultural fit in the work environment and business ethics and values. The parties involved in the joint venture must know working in a cross cultural environment. If the association is not synergistic and the business performance expectation is not based on reality and there is no transparency in work practices and functions, sooner or later all joint ventures will end up in breaking up.

We have many other examples of the joint ventures breaking up. Dabur exited from the Excelsior Foods after Nestle acquired the control of the company through the overseas acquisition. Excelsior was initially a joint venture between Dabur and Osem group of Israel. Osem was in fact a specialist in cookies and speciality biscuits manufacturing. Osem group was subsequently got acquired by Nestle overseas which has changed the equation in the Indian joint venture. Till that time Dabur was a part of the management control of Excelsior Foods. When Nestle came into the scene Dabur had to take the back seat leaving the business affairs to be managed by local Nestle and their representatives. The performance of this company even after significant investment was poor to say the least and Dabur got into a situation of holding only a portfolio without any return. What followed next was inevitable. The relationship between Nestle and Dabur got sour which ended up with separation after prolonged negotiation for deciding an exit price for Dabur. Dabur subsequently also exited from other joint venture - with the Spanish company Agrilimen and what I gather is that they are in the process of getting out from other joint venture as well, the one with the French company LeBon. Although Dabur gave the reason as they would like to concentrate on their core business areas to exploit their core competencies but the fact of the matter is that the goings were not good. Otherwise, Dabur is in any case in food business, although not finding it very profitable. Parles could not continue association with Coke for the full term as per the original understanding. Coke has many allegations against Parle related to breach of contract. Truth is that the association failed.

The question is why these joint ventures are breaking up? Any association or any joint venture to last has to be based on win-win situation. In post liberalisation era Indian food companies - both existing and upcoming - thought that they needed the involvement and support of established multinationals to derive advantage from their strengths to fight the increasing global competition.

Thus we saw a set of joint ventures coming up in the subsequent years. On the other side, the multinationals which were keen to enter the Indian market found that they did not know the local market and trade practices well and distribution systems as prevalent in India also quite complex. As an entry strategy some of those decided to join hands with locals or acquire the local companies to get immediate access to the market. By acquiring they also eliminate a competition. Those who have joined hands with local industries gave rise to another set of joint ventures. And we have couple of them in foods. But the trouble is that we find that these joint ventures are not lasting long.

The latest that I read is that the Godrej Group and the US-based food major Pilsbury are finally parting ways after a four years of not-so-happy alliance. Pilsbury Co., part of the $21 billion global food and drinks giant is buying out the 43.5 percent equity stake of Godrej Group in their joint venture Godrej Pilsbury Ltd. This stake acquisition will help Pilsbury to increase its stake in the venture from the existing 56.5 percent to 100 percent thus converting it to a wholly owned subsidiary. Pilsbury initially introduced Cake mixes and then went on to introduce Chakki Fresh Atta and Green Giant Canned Corn. This joint venture was supposed to market Godrej Food's Fruit juices Jumpin, edible oil Cooklite and Godrej Sunflower oil and Shakti. This marketing arrangement was called off later following some hiccup in the alliance. According to Godrej, their brands were not getting any value addition from the association and in fact some of their brands lost penetration so much so that Jumpin market share which was 35% at the start of the alliance dropped to 23% by the time marketing rights were called off. Godrej Pilsbury has a sales turnover of INR 600 million with its Chakki Fresh Atta having 25% market share in southern region. Godrej Pilsbury is marketing joint venture where Pilsbury holds stake through Selvic Netherlands BV.

Possibly, Pilsbury found Godrej distribution infrastructure as a good reason for joining hands to create a marketing success. It can be mentioned here that for the similar reason Proctor & Gamble also joined hands with Godrej for the detergent and personal care business which broke up in later years. This gives rise to the suspicion that possibly MNCs join hands with the local company to understand the trade and to take an entry into the complex but large market in India and when they acquire sufficient knowledge, they create situation for taking the complete control of the business and the stake. Under the circumstances, Indian companies possibly will do better by concentrating on their business with total focus and trying all along to acquire the global best business practices. After all, it is well known that one of the major disadvantages of globalisation is the decline and death of domestic industries. And our players should learn how to thrive the global competition for their own good.

Alternative to that is to have only minority partner in the joint ventures. But where they are going to find such partners. Vijay Mallya is scouting around for 49% strategic partner in their beer business and of late, as we all know Bisleri also on the look out for a strategic partner to give away 48% equity in the proposed set up. The situation as can be seen is that the Indian food companies are neither able to hold the joint ventures and at the same time finding it difficult to go it alone. The crucial issue is the resources, which Indian companies cannot match the deep pocket of MNCs. And that is the reason why they must learn global games to extend the frontier outside India.

3

Dairy and Dairy Products

Indian Dairy Industry

For sheer numbers, India's dairying has no match in the world. The figures are simply mind boggling. For example, some 70 million farmers, maintaining a milch herd of a little under 100 million – 57 million cows and 29 million buffaloes fed largely on crop residues having the milk yield estimated at 71 million tonnes in 1996. Starting as a trickle of one to two liters per family in some 500,000 remote villages, a unique collection system transforms this feeble flow into a veritable flood of 100 million liters for urban Indian consumers everyday.

Indian white revolution is thus a unique phenomenon by itself. Operation flood has linked 9 million farmers in about 200 districts into 70,000 milk societies. These milk societies supply milk to 170 milk unions for processing and marketing. The key success of Operation Flood is that it offers these small and marginal farmers having very little financial liquidity, an assured market for their milk output. The dairy sector today provides some 70 million families the triple benefit of nutritive food, supplementary income and productive employment. Traditionally, cows have been primarily reared to produce bullocks, while buffaloes are largely bred for milk production.

The Indian dairy sector is characterized by the following key features:

Number one commodity: Milk is India's number one commodity in terms of its contribution to the national economy. However, investment in dairying made under the five – year plans is not commensurate with its output. Consequently, its potential has not been adequately tapped.

World's number one producer: The growth in milk production is really phenomenal, having trebled to 67 million tons between 1970 and 1995. During this period, the production of food grains and oilseeds doubled to 191 million tons and 22 million tons respectively (source: Economic Survey 1995-96, Dairy India 1992, Indian Poultry Industry Yearbook 1994).

Value of Dairy Output: The value of output from dairying, based on consumer prices, is estimated at INR 1050 billion in 1997 and INR 1500 billion in the year 2000.

Buffalo Advantage: India's milking machine, the buffalo, constitutes less than 40 per cent of the total bovine population, but accounts for more than half (52%) of the total milk production in the country. Cows account for the 45% and goats produce only 3% of the total milk. All our milk processing plants are therefore, largely dependent on the buffalo milk.

Internationalisation of Operation Flood: The white revolution has evoked interest among planners around the world. Other developing countries including Sri Lanka and the neighboring countries are making concerted effort to emulate it. In fact, a joint venture proposal was also mooted between Sri Lankan government and NDDB in 1996.

Dairy sector therefore, offers considerable scope for setting up new venture. Dairy based products thus are expected to attract foreign maiden or joint ventures in India. Main reasons for the world focus in India in this sector will include low cost economy characterized by low rate of inflation, inexpensive labor, presence of world's third largest pool of technical manpower, world's largest democracy, an independent judiciary, businesses free from government interference, developing infrastructure, big and growing untapped market and most importantly the process of liberalization has already been initiated here. We have thus seen a few players in dairy products have already arrived and a few are in the offing. We will cover those separately under each category of dairy product groups.

The processed food industry has always been regarded as sunrise industry since the formation of Food Processing Ministry in 1984 and nothing significant has happened so far. And hence, doubts were expressed in all quarters that whether the sun will ever rise in this sector. Dairy sector has always been doing good but for its cyclical ups and downs. Indian dairying thus has the potential of emerging as a sunrise industry. India represents one of the world's largest and fastest growing markets for milk and milk products due to the increasing disposable incomes among the 200 million middle class.

With an annual growth rate of over 5 per cent, the country's milk production in 1997 had exceeded 200 million liters per day or 74.3 million tons per year. By 1998, it became the world's number one milk producer with the estimated output as 78 million tons (Ref. Aneja R.P. and Puri B.P.S., India's Dairy

Riddles Unravelled, Dairy India, 1997, 3-27). The Indian dairy industry has been profiled in Table 3.1.

Table 3.1 : Profile of Indian Dairy Industry in 1997

Human Population	953 million (70 million dairy farmers)
Milk production	74.3 million Tons (203.5 million liter/day)
Average annual growth rate (1995-2000)	5.6%
Per capita milk availability	214 gms per day or 78 kgs per year
Milch animals	57 million cows, 37 million buffaloes
Milk yield per breedable bovine in-milk	1,250 kgs
Cattle feed production (organized sector)	1.5 million tons.
Turnover of veterinary pharmaceuticals	INR 5,500 millions
Dairy plants throughput	20 million liters per day
Throughput as percentage of total milk output	10
Value of output of milk group (1994-95)	INR 500 billion (based on producers price)
Value of output of Dairy Industry	INR 1050 billion (based on retail price)

Source : Dairy India 1997

Agriculture plays an important role in the Indian economic growth and in that live-stock sector has special significance. It is increasingly being realized that dairying could play a more constructive role in promoting rural welfare and reducing rural poverty. For example, milk production alone involves more than 70 million producers, each one raising one or two cows or buffaloes. Cow dung is an important input as an organic fertilizer for crop production and is widely used as fuel in rural areas. Cattle also serve as an insurance cover for the poor households, being sold during times of distress. About 40% of the total income of the rural household in the small and marginal category come from dairying. Efforts to increase milk production by farmers are strongly influenced by increase in demand as transmitted through the prevailing marketing channel.

Availability is Still Lower than World Average

Although India is the largest producer of milk now but still per capita availability of milk in India is much lower than the world average. As against the world's average per capita milk availability of 285 gms per day, in India per capita availability has increased from 107 gms in 1970 to 200 gms in the year 2000 availability (Table 3.2).

It may be noted here that world average per capita is just half of the per capita consumption of US.

Table 3.2 : Per capita milk availability in India and world average.

Year	Per capita Availability (in gms per day)
1970	107
1980	128
1990	178
1994	183
2000	200
World average	285

Source : Mckinsey Report

Urban India Consumes Most

The bulk of the milk is consumed in the urban. Urban market consumes more than fifty per cent of the total fluid milk produced in the country. The reason for the rise in consumption of the milk is that its demand is highly income elastic. The dairy expenditure of the richest household is ten times that of the poorest. This is in contrast with most other countries where rich substitute milk with other sources of protein including meat and poultry. The following Table 3.3 will illustrate the milk supply in urban and rural India as per the 1995 estimate.

The supply scenario has improved further in subsequent years as can be seen from the following Table 4. It can be noted that by year 2000 supply to urban areas has increased significantly from 56% in 1995 to 60% of the total milk production in 2000 whereas in rural areas there is a decline presumably because there is an incremental demand in urban market for the increase in urban population during that period triggered by the migration of the villagers to urban areas in search of employment. Also rural farmers need to sell the extra quantity after retaining the minimum that they need. It can be noted however that cooperative sectors was concentrating on the business of pasteurised fluid milk whereas private sector was more on milk products. Whereas the demand of the fluid milk and also the availability of the fluid milk increased but the corresponding demand for the milk products did not go up in the same proportion. As a result, the projected utilisation norms were not materialised. The product was available and as Indians love milk and milk products, the issue of acceptability was not there. The only reason the milk products did not grow as expected was their affordability. Of course, this needs a detailed analyses category wise.

Table 3.3 : Supply of Milk to Urban and Rural areas

Group	Population (million)	Milk supply in million liter (gms per day)	Per capita availability per day
Urban Areas			
Class I cities**	174 (19%)*	75 (41.4%)	431
Other towns	80 (8.8%)	26.5 (14.6%)	331
Total	254 (27.8%)	101.5 (56%)	400 (average)
Rural Areas			
Milksheds	292 (32%)	40.5 (22.2%)	140
Outside milksheds	367 (40.2%)	39.5 (21.8%)	110
Total	659 (72.2%)	80 (44%)	123 (average)
All India	913 (100%)	181.5 (100%)	199

* Indicates percentage to the all-India population

** Class I cities: population of over one hundred thousand.

Note : 1. Population data is as per 1991 census projected to 1995.

2. The availability of milk production in rural areas has been calculated on the assumption that the producer retains 36% of the milk produced and non-producers in rural areas consume another 9%. The balance 56% moves into urban areas, with class I cities accounting for 74% of this supply.

Table 3.4 : Breakup of Urban Milk Supply 1995 and 2000

Sectors	Availability in 1995 in million liter per day	Availability in 2000 in million liter per day
Total Milk Production	180 (100 %)	230 (100 %)
Volume retained in rural areas	80 (44%)	90 (40 %)
Surplus for urban areas	100 (56%)	140 (60%)
Share of organised sectors	18 (18%)	30 (22%)
Share of traditional sectors	82 (82%)	110 (78%)
Break up of organised sector share:	18	30
Cooperative/Government	11 (60%)	15 (50%)
Private sector	7 (40%)	15 (50%)
Utilisation of fluid milk and milk products:		
Cooperative/Government	90: 10	80: 20(projected)
Private sector	20: 80	30: 70 (projected)

Milk Utilization Pattern

Liquid milk is still an important component of the Indian diet. And therefore about 46% of the total milk consumed in India is consumed as fluid milk.

Indian dairy products which include ghee, milk sweets, khoa and paneer account for about 47% of the rest and western dairy products which include cheese, ice cream, condensed milk and milk powder (both skim milk and whole milk powder) constitute the remaining 7 percent. Although the percentage of dairy products in Indian diet has increased significantly and has seen a rapid rise but the share of western dairy products has not changed to that extent. In last 35 years, share in consumption of western dairy products has increased from 4 percent to seven percent of the total. This reflects the situation that for lower income group, preference for Indian products is much higher than that for western style products. The utilization of fluid milk for various types of product groups is as shown in Table 3.5.

Table 3.5 : Utilization of Milk for various product types (Milk Products Consumption profile.)

Types of use	Percentage of total
Liquid milk	46
Ghee	28
Curd	7
Khoa	6
Butter	6
Others (western type products)	7

Although this sector has shown remarkable growth in the production and distribution of milk, no significant new investment was forthcoming. The success of the coop-erative sector is directly influenced by the strong farmer based cooperative movement. For example, in Gujarat, the cooperatives are successful in collecting over 80 percent of the total milk production in the state. Earlier there were couple of private industrial groups including multinationals managing dairy business and all of them were focused on dairy products and that too western types. These include Dalmia Dairy Industries, Foremost Dairy Industries, Hindustan Lever Ltd, Glaxo India Ltd in the north, Dempo Dairy in the west etc.

All of them are not doing well. Hindustan Lever has sold the business to Nutricia who in turn has put the same business up for sale again and finally exited from the business. Glaxo sold it to Heinz who are finding it difficult to run. Only Nestle is doing well and still growing but SmithKline Beechem (SKB) the producer of Horlicks is declining. Of late SKB is taking several marketing initiatives to regain the market. In seventies and eighties, we used to consider this sector attractive for the simple reason that all players were doing well. We will cover the various subsegments separately. The purpose for which these names are being mentioned here is that this sector needs big investment which is not forthcoming particularly for the reasons that in the post liberalisation era Indian players are not doing well and some of them like Foremost Dairy has, in fact, closed down. The only major success story of recent times is the launch of cheese and sterilised milk from Britannia positioned as Cow milk cheese which has now been transferred to new joint venture with the Cooperative Dairy of New Zealand.

But they have also not made an investment in the manufacturing facility and thus only a marketing success so far. Britannia's joint venture partner BSN Group of France is big in dairy business in Europe. Their yoghurt brand 'Danone' is well known globally. But in spite of expectation nothing significant happened in terms of BSNs foray into dairy sector as yet. However, the small players in this sector selling pasteurised fluid milk in polybags or Indian type products are doing well operating within their own limited geographical areas that they cater to and also the niche segment that they have decided to serve. In this respect Mahan Foods Ltd in north has done well. But there are many small and medium size players who have created success story in dairy business like Nanak Dairy in north and Keventer in East.

The Problems of Dairy Sector

The success of the Anand model should not give rise to an impression that all cooperatives are doing well. In fact, most of them have been facing numerous problems and therefore are not able to demonstrate the success story. The cooperative movement thus have limited success in Maharastra and north India. In south and East, it is almost a failure. There were times when there were proliferations of many cooperatives which were not managed well leading to poor profitability of those cooperatives which in turn led to their inability to pay farmers adequately and thus there was no investment to mobilise the available supply. This resulted in the inevitable poaching of farmers by agents and small players who have little incentive for any extension work to stimulate demand. Large dairies suffered for not having adequate supply and the whole sector got coiled into a vicious circle.

Those who made the investment did not succeed and thus there was no fresh investment in this sector. The failure of the coperatives could also be traced for the increased politicisation of coperatives which led political parties to treat them as potential vote banks and source of employment which led to numerous problems including over-staffing, low capacity utilisation, weak marketing orientation and poor financial controls coupled with the appointment of managers by the government who are neither farmers nor professional managers with appropriate industry skills. As a result, the managers do not truly represent the interest of the farmers or the industry to maximise the returns. The second major problems is government dictating the input-output pricing. For example, government fix a minimum producer price in Maharastra and Punjab, fixes selling price to government dairies in Maharastra and determines the selling price based on the on the spot intervention in Andhra Pradesh and Karnataka which has resulted into inefficiencies in processing and marketing of the dairy products.

As mentioned in the Mckinsey Report, with the only exception of the cooperatives in Gujarat, the cooperatives movement in the rest of the country has very poor financial performance resulting in annual losses of over INR 5 billion. This has happened in spite of the fact that the cost of production of milk in India is lowest in the world (almost 70% of the cost prevailing in US), the prices of the dairy products are amongst the highest in the world. The price of butter and whole milk powder are 130 per cent of the international price. This will explain the magnitude of inefficiencies.

The realities of the post- GATT world are reflected in the Report of the Working Group on Animal husbandry and Dairying for the formulation of the ninth five year plan (1997- 98 to 2001-2002). Effective animal health disease management is critical not only from the point of view of livestock enterprises in reducing the economic losses from diseases but also to improve the milk quality and milk output. The proposed outlay on Animal health in the ninth plan was INR 5.52 billion (28.1%) out of the total of INR 19.65 billion for the livestock sector. For the dairy development, the plan outlay in the ninth plan is INR 4.85 billion representing about 24.6% of the total allocated for this sector. As per plan, steps will be taken to bring down the population of the non-descript cows and buffaloes, while upgrading and conserving proven breeds of cattle and buffalo. As mentioned in the document, special attention would be paid to the Jaffrabadi and Gir breeds using embryo transfer technology and good farm management practices. The Jaffrabadi buffaloes are high yielding breed averaging 2,000 liters per lactation cycle with fat con-tent of 9.5 per cent.

To extend the benefits of the operation flood to the other areas, integrated dairy development project would be further strengthened to cover even hilly and back-ward districts by duplicating the Anand model. A serious review needs to be undertaken to understand why this objective has not been fully realized.

In 1991 as part of the economic reforms, the dairy sector was delicensed much against the strong objection from NDDB and its mentor Dr Kurien. Basic philosophy underlying delicensing was encouraging competition in procurement and marketing of milk and thus enhancing the value for both producers and consumers. It was also expected to spur increased flow of capital and new technologies. Concurrently, government of India promulgated the Milk and Milk Products Order (MMPO) in June 1992. All plants having a handling capacity 10,000 to 75,000 liters per day or producing milk products containing between 500 to 3,750 tonnes of milk soilds per year are required to be registered with the respective state authorities, while those processing over 75,000 liters per day of fluid milk or more than 3,750 tonnes per year of milk solids require registration with the central government as well. Till 1996, a total of 734 applications were received for registration and 319 were granted registration under MMPO. Many of those approved plants have not come up. A few came up and became sick for their inability to find market for the products and for capacity utilisation. Those which have continued to market fluid milk and that too in northern regions have survived. In the mean time, market also has seen sterilised milk in tetra pack although the volume is still low.

This sector offers tremendous potential if the prices for the milk products are lowered to bring them within the affordable range. This is possible as supply is increasing and raw milk price is still low. What it needs is to organise the intermediate storage by installing chilling centers in strategic locations and managing the logistics. And most importantly, setting up large integrated facilities to derive the advantage on economy of scale coupled with good management practices. Only Amul is showing that the dairy business can be very successful. But it needs to be a mix of cooperatives and private large investment as it is in United States and in many other countries. But where is the new investment of this magnitude. The current Chairman of NDDB Ms Amrita Patel initiated the move, much to the dislikes of Dr Kurien, by allowing Mother Dairy Foods Ltd (MDFL) to form marketing joint venture with any interested parties including MNCs where MDFL will hold 51% control in equity. This move is likely to provide the key impetus to marketing of dairy products that this sector so badly requires.

Indian Dairy Industry: Total Change in Complexion

Dairy industry in India is divided along the line of fluid milk and milk based food products. Broadly, we can classify Indian dairy industry into two categories, namely, those who deal in fluid milk and those who deal in milk based products. Of course, still there is a third category and they are into both fluid milk and milk products. Interestingly enough, all these sub categories have different characteristics in terms of their ownership, size of the business and profitability. For example, in fluid milk we find the dominant players are either in cooperative sector or have private Indian ownership. The state cooperative dairies have presence all over but the successful ones are in north and west. In east, milk production is very low and thus the state dairy cooperative units are dependent largely on the reconstituted skim milk powder for the fluid milk supply in the cities. In south, only successful cooperative dairies are in Andhra Pradesh and also in Bangalore.

While cooperative dairies are present all over, the private dairies for fluid milk supply have only regional presence such as Paras and Nanak in north and Kevender in east. Although large cooperative dairies like Amul in Gujarat or Vijaya in Andhra Pradesh are also significant players in both milk and milk products. Yet the business of milk based products, in reality, are in the control of multinationals. In the pre-liberalised era we had couple of Indian business houses quite successful in the dairy business, particularly in the milk product business but almost all of them have disappeared now. In this list includes the names of Dalmia Dairy Industries and Foremost Dairy Industries Ltd. One cannot find Swapan brand of Dalmia Dairy any longer in the market.

Dalmia Dairy was a very profitable unit for the group. There was a time when Foremost Dairy launched Gold Cafe in competition with Nescafe and has given Nescafe a run for their money but that was short lived. Like many other Indian brands we were not able to put up a long drawn battle against the multinational brands and the decline was much faster once the market was opened up for dairy sector as well. Indian dairy businesses only have been busy making short term profit. Long term brand building for sustained development was not their cup of tea. The result we have seen in the later years, Dalmia, Foremost, Dempo etc closed down one by one. They only met their inevitable, as expected. The other leading Indian player in dairy was Jagatjit Industries with their Ovaltine and Viva brands but this got acquired by Smith Kline & Becheem. And Raptakos Brett is limping with Threptin brand of protein biscuits sold only through medical outlets. The dairy business of Raptakos is almost finished now.

We have thus all milk product business now in the control of the multinationals. The latest entrants in dairy include Britannia with their cheese and milkman fluid milk in aspectic pack, Dabon, a joint venture between Dabur and LeBon of France with their range of cheese. The only formidable player in this segment is Amul which is still a force to reckon with. In fact, the strategic strength of Amul is so strong that it can give easy fight to all these multinationals. But the reality is that we have only one Amul. We will not be able to create a second success story like Amul again.

Nestle occupies a very special and unique position in Indian dairy industry. It has always been seen as innovator and trend setter. Nestle's performance therefore, was consistent all along. Others who were in dairy business include Glaxo, Hindustan Lever, Cadbury and Smith Kline Becheem (SKB). While Cadbury and SKB are still the leaders in the milk based brown and white beverage segments respectively both Glaxo and Hindustan Lever have withdrawn from the dairy sectors totally. Glaxo, in the name of concentrating on their core business in pharmaceuticals decided to withdraw and finally sold the business to Heinz although they had a successful brand like Complan. But Hindustan Lever, in spite of the fact that they were one of the early entrants in dairy, their Anik brand was, in fact, a non starter and therefore HLL finally decided to sell their business to Nutricia, a late entrant in the Indian dairy market.

Nutricia bought HLL's plant in UP only for the manufacturing facility and they have modernised the plant making fresh investment.But Nutricia also did not succeed and finally decided to exit from India. Anik as a brand is of little or no consequence to Nutricia. HLL is deeply into the ice cream business and with Kissan, Lipton, Brook Bond in to their fold they still have decided to sell their Etah dairy manufacturing plant. HLL also bought Dollop ice cream business from Cadbury and subsequently withdrawn the brand and currently focussing only on Walls and Baskin Robbin business. HLL, as everybody knows, also had tied up with Kwality Ice Cream and Milkfoods for their 100% Ice cream brand in an attempt to have total monopoly in ice cream business in India. Although it is stated to be a strategic alliance where is the 100% ice cream brand now? Instead, Mother Dairy has a successful brand of ice cream in Delhi and the adjoining market. HLL is thus emerging as a leading player in ice cream second to Amul. In terms of milk products each sub segment is now dominated by a leading multinational corporation and they are white beverage (Horlicks) by SKB, brown beverage (Bournvita) by Cadbury, ice cream by HLL, infant and weaning food by Nestle, Cheese by Britannia etc. SKB is making significant investment of INR 850 million in modernising and automating their plant.

In good old days when food business was thought to be difficult we found success stories in dairy sectors in the sense that most of the dairy ventures were seen to be successful. Today the ball game has changed and all the Indian business houses either have already sold out or closed down. There are no buyers in the market to buy their physical assets to bail them out from their debts. In just ten years time the total complexion of the Indian dairy Industry has changed. Only the co-operative dairies are still keeping their flag flying high largely because of their strong distribution infrastructure and their fluid milk business which has helped them to be in touch with the ultimate consumers and most importantly for their superior value delivery. In the earlier days we had a good business on flavoured milk which is gradually growing in volume. In seventies when Energy was launched by Maharastra State Co-operative Dairy in Mumbai there were hoarding all over the city and the message was "In Calcutta we have only Banerjee and Chatterjee but in Bombay we have Energy". And the product was an instant success. Couple of years ago A&M in their annual function organised in Hyatt Regency hotel in Delhi honoured Dr V. Kurien for his contribution in the field of marketing and while accepting the honour Dr Kurien cited that hoarding on Energy saying that was his only marketing activity in his career. Aarey Milk Co-operative in the outskirts of Mumbai is now in deep trouble and incurring losses and is now up for sale.

The pasteurised fluid milk was initially supplied in returnable glass bottles with aluminum foil lid to be collected from the nearest milk booth and there was a system of milk card introduced for each family and depending on the size of the family a fixed quantity of milk was made available. Although all three types of milk namely, double toned, toned and full fat milk was supplied. The quantity restrictions were withdrawn later on as operation flood becoming successful.

The only milk product that was available was Amul butter. We did not know what actually the cheese was. Of course, cottage cheese was available always from sweetmeat shop till such time late Morarji Desai's government stopped production of cottage cheese to help increase supply of milk for the infant and children. In those days there was lot of unrest and agitation by sweetmeat shop owners which is a big industry in West Bengal even now. Later on, glass bottles were withdrawn and polyethylene pouches were introduced which is still in vogue. But, in addition, we also have dispenser installed in all milk booths. The fluid milk business has come a long way and it is increasingly seen to be graduating to a brand. We also have now ultra high temperature (UHT) milk in aspetic and in carton pack.

Cheese business is something which has taken some root in the Indian market only recently and we have many players now. Leading among them are Britannia, LeBon and Amul. We have varieties although limited and we also get sliced cheese for sandwiches and that is a major development. Also packaging is improved significantly and are comparable to international products. We expect that kraft cheese is shortly going to be introduced and once that happens market is going to be bigger resulting out from the intense activities of all the players.

If we now try to take a view of the dairy industry in India we have multinationals on one side and cooperative dairy on the other side. Multinationals are all India players but cooperative dairies are regional players excepting Amul and to some extent Mother Dairy. And private milk suppliers and also local milk products manufacturers such as Vadilal ice cream in west etc. are all marginal players. And it is likely that these privately owned domestic industries are increasingly going to be marginalised. Behind Britannia is Danone who has strong interest in dairy products. Britannia has formed a separate organization in joint venture with a co-operative dairy in NewZealand for their dairy business.

Amul has a big task in hand to keep their dominance over other MNCs in dairy industry. All the big players particularly the multinationals have excellent network of chilling plant and collection centres for milk from the remotest villages. And the days are not very far when we will see that local industry is reduced to play the role of Doodhwala to multinational players.

Sweetmeat Industry Talking about Going Global Fearing MNCs

If Pepsi and Britannia can start selling and competing with local traders in Bhujia they can also enter into this protected domain of Indian sweetmeat makers - fears the office bearers of Paschimbangal Mistannya Bebosayee Samiti (Sweetmeat Traders Association of West Bengal). The total market of milk based sweetmeat in the country has been estimated to be around INR 165 billion and West Bengal market alone is of the size INR 100 billion; big enough market to draw the attention of multinational food companies. This is largely a cottage scale or home scale industry employing over 3.0 million people in West Bengal alone. Because of the traditional nature of the industry the trade has been passed on from father to son. There were some established family names, which got famous for a category of sweetmeat. For example, Rasogolla of K.C. Das, Sandesh of Bhim Nag, Dahi of Ganguram etc. But some of them are now losing their strong hold either because of fragmentation in the family or because of the fact that they could not keep the quality standards over the years. The major problem that this industry (if at all we can call it so) facing today are:

- Low level of productivity

- Lack of standardisation and hence variation in quality.
- Low shelf life of the product and high incidence of rejects and unsold stocks.
- Lack of infrastructural support. Only equipment that they use is a refrigerator - to keep the stock. Small or tiny traders even don't have that. Refrigerated stocks don't taste as good as fresh which consumers prefer.
- No control on the raw material and other inputs. No process control resulting in batch to batch variable cost of production.
- No standard packaging
- No scientific management principle.
- No organised marketing.

Local shop has its own loyal clientele to thrive. If becomes popular opens another shop in another locality or in the neighbourhood. Cumulative effect of this is that this unorganised industry is now caught in the grip of fear psychosis. They started now knocking at the door of the professional bodies like Association of Food Scientist and Technologist (AFST) or All India Food Processors Association (AIFPA) etc. to seek their help to organise and upgrade themselves on the modern scientific and management lines. Whenever they see the report in the press that Rasogolla is being patented by Americans they rush to these professional bodies to know more about it and its implications. They therefore are very much scared about what is in store for them? Are they going to lose their business, which has been started and painstakingly developed by their forefathers, to new food MNCs?

That this question constantly haunts them is apparent from the statement of their General Secretary who recently said that "we need to mechanise and adhere to Global Standards of Quality so that not only we organise ourselves to control the domestic market but we also should eye for selling our products in the Global Market". And to do that they need the support of the professional bodies like AFST. Paschim Banga Mistannya Bebasayee Samiti (PMBS) has organised a National Seminar in Association with the AFST - Eastern Regional Chapter to work out a national agenda and action plan to sort out some of these pressing issues. AFST has taken initiatives to resolve some of the quality, packaging and machanisation related issues facing this industry with an objective to upgrade this industry and also to improve the prospect of market penetration and geographical expansion. It is true that if the shelf life of some of these traditional sweetmeat is extended, the relatively bigger traders can eye for overseas market at least for the ethnic population. But at the same time it is also true that if some of the typical issues this industry is facing are resolved, it will attract the attention of the large business houses including MNCs simply because merely the size of the industry is mind boggling. Another factor PMBS should clearly keep in mind that by seeking more mechanisation, the employment potential will also significantly reduce. Besides, once large industry enters the sector there will be other issues like value addition and convenience which only organised sectors can deliver. The greatest value for a fast moving consumer goods (FMCG) is the strength of the brand which these small time traders will never be able to build. They, therefore, run the risk of someone entering the trade and creating a brand to capture significant size of this market. To that extent their fear is valid.

Earlier this industry could create some established brands but these could not be sustained mainly because of fragmentation of the family owning those brands. Once the family got divided each one of them were trying to encash on the goodwill of the parent brand but in that process the consumers lost faith in the product. Once famous "Bhim Nager Sandesh" (Sweetmeat from Bhim Nag) started operating in the later years as "Bhim Nag and Sons", "Bhim Nag and Grandsons", "Bhim Nag and Brothers" by the different factions of the same Bhim Nag family and all were trying to co-exist on the goodwill of the parent brand unsuccessfully. Same thing happened with Ganguram who was famous for his Dahi (Curd). It also got fragmented into "Ganguram and Sons" etc.

Fig. 3.1 Can traditional sweetment be standardized for global opportunity.

What is required for this industry to thrive is training and development of their workforce in terms of food safety, good manufacturing practices, testing, quality control and standardisation in one hand and marketing and modern scientific and management principles on the other hand. They can possibly form cooperatives and work on franchising principle and create a few brands for each category of product and establish themselves as manufacturers and marketers of value added quality sweetmeat delivered through most cost effective and convenient manner.

Some private sector initiatives can also be taken to organise this industry. If Haldiram can do it for bhujias and namkeens and can go global and can put up a fight successfully against multinationals why not the same game be played for sweetmeats. The major issue would be shelf life and quality standards. But the efficient management of the logistics and distribution will partly solve this problem to make an attempt to create Haldiram model.

And our professional bodies should help them deliver the same. Otherwise, I am afraid soon, we will see, for example, McDonald's and Pillsbury's sweetmeat proliferating in the domestic market and PMBS dream of becoming a global player on their traditional business will remain only a pipe dream?

Milk has Graduated from the Status of Commodity to Brand

India produces about 90 million tons of milk every year and out of that 31 million tons are processed to produce dairy products including skim milk powder (SMP), baby foods & weaning foods, butter, ghee and cheese etc. The balance 60 million tons can thus be assumed as consumed as fluid milk. The estimated installed capacity of handling fluid milk in the country is approximately 33 million tons and that too particularly concentrated in the co-operative sectors. These co-operatives are also known to use SMP to produce reconstituted milk to be sold as fluid milk. Cooperative dairies in the early sixties first introduced pasteurized fluid milk in glass bottle with aluminum foil cap. In subsequent years polybags substituted the glass bottles which are costly due its weight, breakage and high handling cost. Also there is an incidence of additional cost and inconvenience in recycling of glass bottles. The pasteurised milk in polybags and fluid milk dispensed through the vending machine were sold from milk booth owned by the manufacturers (largely co-operative dairies and state owned dairies) and are located strategically in all localities for better distribution and reach. This arrangement continue even now and is quite effective in terms of availability, delivery on time and quality for an essential, perishable and mass consumption product like fluid milk.

India also has the distinction of becoming the largest milk producing country in the world but per capita consumption of milk is still low. The white revolution that was initiated by Dr. Kurien can be considered as successful but his co-operative movements did not work in all states. In the north eastern states the co-operatives are either non-existent or their performance is very poor. In large cities like Calcutta and Mumbai, milk supply is largely from the state co-operative dairies but due to the fact that local milk production and supply is inadequate from their own chilling centres and collection units to run the central dairy plant to required capacity, these units therefore are largely dependent on the import of milk from Gujarat. Additionally, SMP is reconstituted to produce fluid milk to be pasteurized to meet the growing demand of the local market. Consumers may not be knowing that most often than not what they really consume is actually reconstituted milk and not the fresh milk.

But becoming a surplus in terms of milk production from a state of affairs that existed in early fifties when not only that we used to import milk but there was acute shortage of milk, is no mean achievement of our co-operative movement. During my childhood, I myself have witnessed long queue of public to get a litre of milk per family reconstituted from SMP donated by Christian missionary organizations and I don't have any hesitation to say that I myself also stood in those queues with my brother in my hometown at Silchar in Assam where milk is still a very scarced commodity. In north eastern states there is no co-operative dairy. One exists in Guwahati, but that is for the name sake. Thus people are largely dependent on the local doodhwala (milkman) to supply daily milk and that too adulterated with water. My father who was a doctor by profession used to tell the "Goala" (doodhwala as called locally) - "don't add too much of water and ensure that you mix good potable water". The situation is no better today. Similar situation was prevailing even in Bengal. There were times in sixties and seventies when West Bengal Government banned production of milk based sweets to counter the situation arising out of acute shortage of milk. Today when the production is adequate barring seasonal shortages say in summer months, the issue is basically the distribution. The private players who created hurdles for the co-operative movement to succeed have been still flourishing in milk businesses. In northern states it is in fact the private players including large MNCs such as Nestle and Smith Kline Beechem have been able to set up successful dairy project to produce milk based food and food products. The Indian players who were also once dominating the market in dairy industry include companies like Foremost Dairies, Dalmia Dairies etc. They have already become sick and now on the verge of closing down.These are major management failures in the private dairy sector. Incidentally, these private companies and MNCs' are in dairy products and not in the distribution and selling of fluid milk.

Private companies who have ventured in fluid milk distribution are still thriving and there are many local players in each state. "Nanak" and "Paras" are two favourite names in fluid milk business in north in addition to "Amrit" marketed by Amrit Vanaspati. Similarly, we have "Keventer" in east. Of late, we are witnessing completely different scenario in fluid milk marketing. There are proliferation of branded and / or private labeled pouch milk selling in the market. In Ahmedabad (the home state of National Dairy Development Board, NDDB) alone there are twenty brands and in Mumbai there are about a dozen brands of fluid milk. Pouch milk is like the friendly neighborhood doodhwala, has loyal following because it is felt to be fresh and is produced and consumed on a daily cycle. The ultra high temperature (UHT) milk, on the other hand, obviously works on a different longer term cycle. Theoretically, the UHT milk in glass bottles should have very long shelf life if the sealing integrity of the pack is proper. Britannia has already launched their UHT milk "Milkman". Some of the co-operative dairies are also venturing into UHT milk. Andhra Pradesh Dairy Development Co-operative Federation (APDDCF) the manufacturer of Vijaya brand of milk and milk product saw an opportunity in this. It has UHT milk at fat level of 5, 4.5 and 3 per cent. It has recently launched a low fat UHT milk with 1.5 per cent fat priced at INR 19 per liter and APDDCF, in the first six months of the launch sold about 0.1 million litre of Vijaya low fat milk - which is quite an impressive performance. Vijaya is also launching a new UHT category milk with a shelf life of six months. And for that they are setting up a new INR 250 million plant in Hyderabad. The product will be sold in plastic bottles.

Amul is planning three variants of its Taaza UHT milk to be placed in the market at various price points. It is expected that Nestle will also introduce shortly UHT milk in the market. Unlike pasteurized milk in pouches which has to be sold immediately because of its low shelf life and thus the market is local, UHT milk has an advantage of long shelf life and hence can be marketed on the global basis. All players are therefore going for all India market for their UHT milk just like any other FMCG products. UHT milk is distributed under normal storage conditions and stocked in all outlets like any other long life food products as against refrigerated transport and storage required for the pasteurized milk which is a major advantage which offsets the large part of cost of UHT milk.

Fig. 3.2 Milk has now become value added branded item.

Earlier we had branded milk powders and condensed milk to meet the longer term requirement of fluid milk for tea, coffee, sweetmeats and also, if required, for direct fluid milk consumptions. Consumers were reconstituting the powder milk or condensed milk for that purpose. In northeast or even, in West Bengal market, imported particularly from Australia and New Zealand milk powder in tin containers are available in most of the outlets which consumers prefer. Large part of that stock comes to India through either Bangladesh or Nepal and are competitive with domestic brands. Now we have UHT milk to meet the requirement of fluid milk for longer term use.The milk trade has thus graduated from Doodhwala supplying milk directly to individual homes, to pasteurized milk in bottles and then polythene pouches through co-operative dairies and then the variants in pouches by both co-operative and private dairies and finally UHT milk in carton and aseptic packs and in plastic bottles. This is a long treacherous journey for milk from being a plain commodity to a preferred brand.

What will happen to these so called doodhwala? With e-commerce coming of age, these doodhwala can don the mantle of delivery guys and some enterprising entrepreneur may even dream of organizing them under a banner and start a milk supply service business. A milk supply service industry to support the big players might eventually develop.

Why Milk Food Beveages Category is Stagnating

Milk food beverages (also known as milk food drinks) as a category is very important for some businesses. This includes both white (such as Horlicks, Complan, Viva) and brown (such as Boost, Bournvita, Milo) beverages. All these are well known brands, some are coming from very large MNCs, such as Milo of Nestle is a leading global brand. But still they are under performing leading to the stagnation or decline of the category. In 1999 this category was 82000 MT in volume terms and INR 11 billion in value terms. The category now has dropped to 70000 MT valued at INR 12 billion. Although in value terms there is a marginal growth but that is due to sporadic price increases taken by the players. In real term therefore, there is a decline. In this health drink business category we have witnessed many acquisitions and takeovers during the last decade. For example, Jagatjit Industries brand Viva in white segment and Maltova in brown segment were acquired by Smith Kline Beechem Consumer Care (SKB) who owns the Horlicks brand. Complan which was earlier with Glaxo was acquired by Heinz along with all other food brands as an entry strategy for Indian market. In fact, Complan was a unique category created by Glaxo successfully. They ran their advertisement campaign – "Complete planned Food with 23 vital nutrients that body needs" very successfully for decades. Nestle's Milo was, of course, a late entrant in the category but they are a major force to reckon with their global presence. But in India despite their best efforts Milo has only two per cent share in the category. At the end of all these acquisitions and mergers, the players that remained in the business include Cadbury with their major brand Bournvita, Nestle with Milo, Heinz with Complan and most importantly SKB with Horlicks, Boost, Maltova and Viva.

The most dominant player in this category is thus SKB whose only business is Horlicks. SKB was demonstrating significant performance with single product for all these years. So profitable is the company that their principals in UK who have long exited from the food business were not able to take decision to sell their Indian business so far. The dividend being paid by the company and their market capitalisation are indicators of the fact that the company has delivered shareholders expectation year on year. Bournvita was a dominant player in brown segment although Boost was able to take significant market share in course of time. When the fight now is limited to only four major players and all are global leaders in food business with their success stories in their key brands and when all were doing well with no constraints on the resources what really happened that the performance of these brands have really started declining leading to the decline of the category as a whole.

To understand this phenomena we need to analyse the category in little more detail. Firstly, it must be noted that white segment represented by Horlicks, Viva of SKB and Complan of Heinz constitute about 65 per cent of the market. The brown segment represented by Bournvita, Boost, Maltova and Milo constitute the rest of 35 per cent. This white and brown segments are again highly polarised in the sense that over 60 percent of sales of white beverages comes from south and east, south accounting for over 45 per cent. Whereas, major part of the brown beverage sales comes from north and west. Apart from these polarisation in terms of territorial influence on white and brown segment's performance, these two segments are often at loggerheads. While brown beverages are positioned in lines of energy and fun, white beverages are positioned on health and nourshiment platform. As children like chocolate or cocoa taste, brown beverages tried to exploit the taste aspect of the beverage. As for the positioning, the distinction and dividing line for both white and brown beverages are very narrow or almost overlapping and therefore, brown segment often erode the white segments market. Another factor that has influenced the sales of this category is the level of noise in the media these players were able to make. The sales performance of these products were therefore, directly fluctuating with the level of advertisement spend. And players have reduced the advertisement significantly which has impacted their own brand performance in particular and the whole category in general.

When this category is advertisement sensitive, why it was that players were not making attempt to keep the brands alive in the consumers mind by relaunching the brand and also by making enough promotional activities, innovations around the brand to make it contemporary and relevant. I think that players have taken it easy and have decided to milk the brand. But for

SKB it is the only business that they have and thus they have nothing else to do excepting to keep the brand growing. The only plausible reason that SKB can have is that the brand is not relevant in their international portfolio and therefore, there is no interest from their headquarters. Horlicks have thus declined in sales to the extent of 17 per cent this year over the last year's performance. Everyone in SKB now have woken up to this fact and is trying to stage a come back. Recently they have redesigned their packaging and also the label. They also have launched three new variants – vanilla, honey and chocolate apart from the regular malt variety. Over the years Horlicks had taken the position of a beverage for all age group where as the youngsters at the age group of 8 to 14 years were the earlier target segment and that is the largest segment. When the beverage is seen to be taken and liked by older people including patients, young children switched to brown segment. Complan is also restaging a come back with new set of advertisement campaign. For quite sometime, Complan advertisement was not seen at all, particularly after Heinz took over this brand. Heinz, as a company incidentally is not doing well in India.

Besides, the lack of adequate marketing support behind these brands there are some fundamental issues which have altered the ground reality. When milk was in short supply this malted milk foods was and other milk beverages have found relevance. And as such the brands grew in volume during earlier years. With the success of operation flood the relevance of these health foods reduced to a certain extent and growth rates went down. This coupled with indifference on the part of the marketers in the recent times that fueled the accelerated decline. Time has now come when players have realised that they need to reposition the products, create innovations around those propositions, target the relevant segments and remain contemporary to the changed market situtation and new consumer expectation. They will thus have to act a fresh with renewed vigour and only time will tell us whether they will succeed in revitalising the category.

New Generation Ice Cream Parlours to be Designed Like Coffee Parlours

The concept of coffee house where both tea, coffee and snacks are served is age old in India. Some of those coffee houses have historical association which were frequented by many big and well known personalities. In some of those, big ideas were born and still remembered with nostalgia - for example the Indian coffee house at College Street in Kolkata. The concept of parlours are relatively new. Till the other day the concept of parlours was limited to only ice cream but although they exist even today there was no big success story to talk about. Ice cream parlours are therefore not a big industry in its own category. But it looks like that they are staging a come back. Presumably they are getting encouraged with the success of Coffee Cafes and notably amongst those are of Barista coffee parlour. Barista was promoted by Turner Morrison Group. But seeing its success Tata Tea has taken an equity in Barista venture. Recently, a north Indian group came to me for help in giving a shape to their concept of a Tea Parlour to be designed on Barista line.

While we were discussing that coffee has many possibilities of value addition and there could be many variety such as Cappuccino, Irish coffee, cold coffee etc. was there any possibilities of creating such exciting options in tea. It may be pointed out here that over ninety percent coffee market exists in south, east and north together only represent five percent of the total coffee market in India. In spite of that Barista coffee and south based Coffee Cafe parlours are success story in Delhi. It is the reverse in case of tea consumption in the sense that major market is in east and north. We had coffee houses in north and east but never Tea houses. I have now realised that several options of tea could be possible, such as Iced tea, Lemon tea, flavour rich Darjeeling tea, strong tea, masala tea etc. Hopefully you can see the tea parlours also in town. In Bangalore this has already started.

Hindustan Lever (HLL) has attempted to dominate the ice cream trade through a series of acquisition and strategic alliance route. HLL has never succeeded in introducing a successful food brand from inception. All of their ventures failed. Food business in India therefore has been built through a series of acquisitions. But even after that, food business portfolio for HLL is a drag on HLL's book whereas it is the major source of income and the largest portfolio for UniLever. HLL had acquired all brands of ice cream in India including Kuwality but they withdrawn all these brands which they acquired. Instead, they launched Walls and Baskin Robins. It can be recollected that Cadburys was running their own and also franchised ice cream parlours under Dollops and Yankee Doodle. But they disappeared once HLL in post acquisition period decided to withdraw form this brand. Some of these ice cream parlours chain were either shut down or taken over in course of time. There were reasons why these ice cream parlours did not succeed and therefore when food retailing is booming and coffee parlours are creating success stories and fast food chains are making fast buck our ice cream parlours still maintained an icy silence all these years. Apparently they are now making noise and their plans are being lined up. Few of them will be new and few are staging a come back.

They have learnt from their old experience that merely having a "high priced hole-in-the-wall kind of ice cream parlours" will not work in India any more. There has to be a value perception and variety and ambience to attract the customers. The new set of ice cream parlours are therefore going to be designed to serve coffee, snacks and of course, a variety of ice creams in a contemporary ambience. Home grown Nirulas is launching its ice cream chain shortly. Swiss-born Movenpick is talking about appointing franchisees and also for tieing up with the supermarket chains and departmental stores for rapid expansion. Movenpick which entered India a few years ago with similar cafes offering ice cream and coffee was quick to expand its menu to include snack items. Typical ice cream parlours designed in line with what we have abroad will not work here particularly for the reason that in India we have a very low per capita consumption of ice cream and it has a high seasonality. Also Indian consumers do not believe in picking and moving with his ice cream cone. He prefers to sit and share the experience with his family and friends. Per capita consumption of ice cream in India is only 250 ml as against 1.2 liters in China and 22 liters in USA. Besides, real estate cost in India also make the whole proposition unviable.

While some smaller known brands had displayed limited success, such as chains like Arun in south and Vadilal in west but there was no big step forward taken by leading players in the game. HLL has opened ice cream parlours in Bangalore and Kolkata but these are still a low key limited operations. No one has so far been able to develop a business model which is financially viable on a national scale. Hatsun Agro, a company that manufactures and sells Arun ice cream through approximately 1000 franchised outlets in four southern states is a limited success story in this ice cream parlour business but they are a twenty years old player in the game. The new format for ice cream parlours designed in line with coffee parlour style, ambience and offering are going to be set up by some leading corporations. It is expected that Nestle is also going to enter the ice cream trade soon with their international brand. There will be therefore many chains and as usual some will be national and still some others that will continue as regional players. Consumers will have to watch and experience the new ice cream cafes which are going to be appearing shortly in their new avatar.

Amul Emerging as a Giant in Dairy Industry

Amul is getting into a host of products and subproducts categories in foods to emerge soon as a giant in food processing. Amul has placed the sales target for the year 2006 at INR 1000 billion which is a very ambitious target. A very tall order indeed. But plans are being drawn up to achieve that. Amul, although in cooperative sector, its marketing success is quite well known and must be the envy of the many large MNC food giants. Amul has succeeded in almost all the products that it had launched over the years barring possibly the two products namely, dahi (yoghurt) and chocolate. In yoghurt segment no one has succeeded so far because of the nature of the product which every Indian household produces at home. In chocolate both Cadbury and Nestle are well entrenched players. Of late, however, Amul had tied up with Campco to launch an eclair to compete with Cadburys. Eclairs is manufactured by the Campco and marketed by Gujarat Co-operative Milk Marketing Federation (GCMMF). With about fifty percent market share in the cheese segment and an enviable twenty seven percent share of the national ice cream market Amul has already thrown down the gaunlet in several well entrenched turfs. Now the butter girl and cheese boy are prowling around for more kills.

Amul's success can be traced from its excellent brand image and a still better distribution network. Amul has a well networked cold chain distribution which I am sure, others would dream to have it. Amul now is leveraging this cold chain for new range of frozen foods beginning with Pizza and targeting the microwave household in urban areas. Their new launch of twenty-rupees Amul Pizza has captured public imagination like no other food launch in recent times. Another key factors for the success of Amul is the fact that Amul always delivered better value for money for the customers. Prices for Amul products are always lower than the competitors with as good or sometimes even better quality. Amul therefore, was close to its customers heart which helped the brand to create one success after another. Pricing the Pizza at INR 20 will again give them a shot in the arm. At this price point MNCs and even imported foods will find it difficult to take on. But with so many brands in the market it will not be easy for Amul to create a success story. But this new launch of Pizza from Amul did not succed.

Fig. 3.3 Amul is the market leader in all dairy segments.

Although Pizza is the hot item on the Amul's plate for new launch, several other products are also on the cards. Amul has been working with the coffee growers' cooperatives in south India to create the ideal Amul blend but so far not been able to come up with a product that passes the test. "We will launch coffee sooner than later. Give us a little more time" - said Amul Chairman, Amul will shortly introduce biscuits as well. This means that Amul will now extend its portfolio from confectionery items to bakery items as well.

This magical figure of INR 1000 billion is not going to happen just like that. To reach this figure GCMMF has estimated that it will have to double the number of sales offices from the present 46 to 100, the stockists from 3000 to 7500 and retailers from 0.4 to 1.0 million. To implement this it will require the increased managerial manpower which is one of the challenges today. This manpower is going to be provided by the Institute of Rural Management, Anand (IRMA). Founded by the National Dairy Development Board (NDDB) in 1981 IRMA has evolved into a world class business school focussing on rural management.

To extend the market coverage Amul is now tieing up with other cooperatives in various states including Maharashtra to process and market Amul brands of milk and milk products. Amul ice cream is now manufactured and marketed from seven different locations in the country. Amul is a low cost operation that compares with the best in the world. They have no debt. The working capital requirement is only INR 220 million on a sales of INR 23 billion which speaks good about their inventory and trade debt management. Amul pays much lower trade margin than its competitors but they still have the loyal customer base. Amul's retail commission on ice cream is around 17.5 percent which is ten percent lower than what competition pays. Today Amul is using information technology to its advantage to raise its efficiency level and bring down its costs further. Headquartered at Anand, Gujarat, it is networked with all its marketing locations. Tata Consultancy Services has implemented Enterprise Application Systems for Amul to provide the connectivity. Its 3000 distributors have e- mail connections and 1000 more are on online environment. Amul's B2B operation claims an encouraging response with the dealers in Mumbai, Kolkata and Ahmedabad placing orders through the internet.

Amul now stretching from the dairy farmers from rural hinterlands to the microwave pizzas in urban homes is all set to take many food MNCs directly head- on in coming years. And going by the action plans and other criteria which are essential for creating success story it is likely that Amul will soon realise its dream. Although MNC giants will not remain only a silent spectator during this phase but they should know that Amul has a definite advantage over them.

Value Addition in Dairy Industry

Dairy Industry in India: The dairy industry in India is considered to be a category which has been growing and profitable. This category is better organized amongst other categories of processed food industry in India. When the world production of fluid milk stands at around 613 million tonnes and is growing at a rate of only 1.1 percent India's milk production stood at 91 million tonnes growing at around 4 per cent per annum. This means that 15% of the world's milk is produced in India and that too growing at a rate four times of global growth rate giving India the status of the largest milk producing nation in the world. There are two differences , namely, about 58 percent of this milk is from buffalo and despite being the highest milk producing nation in the world the per capita milk consumption in India is still lower (229 gm per day) than the world average (285 gm per day). Our milk production , processing and marketing channel as it exists is unique in nature. About 70 million rural households are involved in cattle rearing and milk production, out of which only 11 million farmers are linked with the 0.1 million dairy cooperative societies generating about 18 million tonnes of the fluid milk daily. This milk from dairy cooperatives form the major source of fluid milk supply to cities and towns across the country.

Fig. 3.4 Many new products launched in dairy sector.

Out of 91 million tonnes of fluid milk produced in the country rural consumption is about 39 million tonnes (45 percent of the total) and another 17 million tonnes (20% of the total) also consumed as fluid milk supplied to urban areas from the nearby villages. Thus 65 % of the total milk produced in the country is consumed as unprocessed fluid milk. The balance 35% is processed into the value added products of which unorganized sector utilizes about 24% or 22 million tonnes of milk .As unorganized sector utilizes lower level of technology and also low quality control measures, value addition in those are not much. And in the organized sector the remaining 11% or only 10 million tonnes of fluid milk really goes for processing , out of which about 6 million tonnes is utilized as packaged fluid milk like UHT milk and only 4 million tonnes is processed by the organized sector for real value added dairy products. About 50 per cent of the total milk production is consumed by the urban population either as fluid milk or as value added processed milk products.

The operation flood programme initiated in 1970 and the cooperative movement helped us to reach this stage. The cooperative sector over the years have created many successful brands including Amul which is a leading dairy brand with all India presence. Others, which are also well known but has a very strong regional presence are Aarey in Maharastra , Verka in Punjab , Nandini in Karnataka, Vijaya in Andhra Pradesh , Saras in Rajasthan, Mother Dairy in Delhi and Kolkata. Out of all these, Mother Dairy has now graduated to a level that they can claim an all India presence now in addition to AMUL which has an advantage of scale and cost. AMUL has emerged as the largest food industry in India which was possible because of its inherent character of low cost and easy and assured access to the raw material.

It should be noted that large part of the production of milk has to go for direct consumption as fluid milk and we still have milk shortage areas to feed. Primary task is therefore ,to ensure safe and hygienically packed fluid milk that retains the quality and standard to reach the uncovered rural and milk deficient areas. In this process, we can add some value through standardization , packaging , distribution and supply chain management and also through the brand building exercise. The major value addition possibilities has to be seen in the context of surplus milk available for processing by the organized sector and also helping the unorganized sector to go up in the value chain. The task is therefore, multifaceted.

Market for Value added Dairy Products: Flavored milk is increasingly becoming popular in the certain market. As consumers are getting more health conscious there is a growing tendency to buy health foods in place of other forms of beverages. Flavored milk thus constitute a good substitute for carbonated soft beverages and significant value addition is possible either through packaging or through the innovative formulation. For example, flavored milk can be both synthetically flavored as well as can be mixed with real fruit juice and pulp.

Although the base is still small, the flavored milk market is said to be increasing by around 27 per cent in value terms. There are host of brands mostly regional are being sold in this segment. Additionally, Nestle's Fruit & Milk and Amrit Foods Gagan are quite popular in the northern region. In the recent times, we are witnessing lot of activities in the dairy segment and there are products in this segment which are actually diet milk, fortified milk. Both Amrit Foods and Nestle have launched low fat milk with less than 0.5 % fat recommended for people with high cholesterol and blood pressure. There are number of brands in the UHT milk segment in tetra pack and the volume in this segment is said to be about 70 million liters and growing at a rate of about 20% per annum in volume terms.

Both plain and flavoured yoghurt (Dahi) including misti dahi are now selling in volume and we have Amul, Mother Dairy and a host of local brands in the game. Fruit yoghurt and stirred yoghurt are yet to gain a meaningful volume. Earlier attempts in this direction have failed and the current market is largely for the set yoghurt. But there are number of curd based products now in the market such as lassi , butter milk, chhas etc. which were earlier the domain of the unorganized sectors served through local shops and made to order but now being introduced by both cooperatives dairies and private players. Other traditional products such as paneer , khoa and khoa based sweets are actually the stronghold of small and unorganized players. Amul has introduced paneer in the market , otherwise all are the local and traditional players. There is lot of opportunity for this segment to go up in the value chain to help the dairy segment to deliver higher value.

We did not have good quality cheese earlier. Only Amul was selling processed cheese and cheese consumption was nothing much to mention about. Of late, this segment has grown and has become INR 4.5 billion in size and processed cheese is still the leading contributing about 60 % of the total category and growing at a rate of 15% annually. Additionally , we have cheese spread and mozzarella which goes mostly in pizza topping. Britannia has influenced the growth in the cheese market introducing cheese from cow milk. Dabon International's brand Le Bon also has captured significant market in this category. Earlier we had only Amul cheese cubes wrapped in foil and packed in containers but now we have cubes , slices , spreads etc. fuelling the growth of this segment so much so that "Laughing cow" , a foreign brand also sells in leading urban outlets.

The market for dairy whiteners , creamers and condensed milk has been reported to be to be about 200 MT valued at INR 3 billion. The products are available both in pouches , tins and as well as in tetra packs. In this segment also we have regional players such as Vijaya , Parag and Swapan and all India players such as Amul , Nestle.

The ice cream market is estimated to be about INR 15 billion of which organized sector contributes about INR 9 billion (equivalent to 40 million liters). Amul is the leading player controlling about 28% of the total market, Hindusthan Lever has 8% and Vadilal and Mother Dairy has about 7% share each. The share of the unorganized sector is gradually shrinking.

The other dairy products include butter, ghee and milk powder. Of which, milk powder which is a INR 255 billion category is entirely with the organized sector. But in butter and ghee unorganized sector is the larger player. Butter is a INR 65 billion category of which organized sector represents only about INR 5 billion and ghee is INR 245 billion of which organized sector is only INR 35 billion and the balance is with the unorganized sector. Small local brands have been able to create a niche and competing on price equation.

Value Addition in Dairy Products: In last one decade the processing scenario has changed. There are more players in the segment both Indian and overseas than before. Some of the private players and their brands also disappeared during this time as they could not play the new rules of the game. Local new players are not able to play the high pitch marketing game and therefore gradually reduced to become the subcontract manufacturers for the large players. Both Dabon International and Britannia are therefore, marketing the brands of cheese sourcing from Indian local players. In the cooperative sector Amul has overshadowed other state cooperatives. They have their success stories but not been able to grow beyond the regional level.

The large part of the processed dairy products are still with the unorganized local and small players including halwais and dudhias who operate in small pockets using traditional methods of processing where large players cannot easily reach. The task in hand is thus how we can integrate those unorganized players to upgrade them in the value chain? Can we help them to produce using better technology maintaining quality standard so that large organized players can market those at higher value through a franchised chain of outlets spread all over which can be owned by the same unorganized players so that they get higher value and at the same time play a larger role in the national interest? This is both technology as well logistic management task and we need to create a model for the success.

Future Challenge: Although, a pessimist will argue that in post liberalization, agricultural growth rate has reduced, it was 3-4% before 1990s but in the first three years of the 10th plan period (2002-2007) agricultural sector growth plummeted to near about 1% but the economy has the resilience to absorb that pressure and we still delivered the growth rate supported by the service sector. We need now another successful green revolution focusing on horticulture, floriculture and dairy sectors. By year 2020 our domestic demand for milk and milk products likely to reach a level of about 170 million tonnes and we can achieve this target provided we continue to maintain the current level of growth. In the global trade we have the products like butter & milk fat, cheese, condensed milk, whey casein etc. When paneer industry is organized and the volume picks up whey protein isolate, milk lactose will be produced and exported. Our products are based on buffalo milk whereas in global trade cow milk products are traded. Our surplus can be marketed globally in the processed form provided we can develop the market for those. For this purpose we need to forge global level collaboration. But the way market is developing for health related products including milk we will not have any difficulty in finding market for the increased milk output as projected in the domestic market itself. Currently, India's share of global trade is less than 1 per cent despite being the largest producer. We still have low milk yield per animal coupled with our inability to create brands in the global market which makes our task in the global trade more difficult. But I can foresee that Indian players have to play a role in future in the global market by forging alliance with global players.

The domestic consumption for milk products will grow heavily. For example, it is projected that cheese market in India will grow from the current level of INR 4.5 billion to about INR 11 billion by the year 2015. Dairy whiteners market is projected to go up from 200 MT currently to 300 MT during next five years. Value added fermented milk products are already in the market. We will see the introduction of many nutraceutical beverages based on milk and fermented milk in the coming years.

The significant value addition to the products is possible only through aggressive marketing and brand building exercise which require both resources and skill. Global market will be competitive and our players have to create and capture value at all level of interfaces starting from the procurement. Cooperation and competition and integrated supply chain management will be the key if Indian dairy sector has to play its legitimate role to deliver higher value and take its products and merchandise all over the world.

4

Sugar and Sugar Confectionery

Sugar Confectionery Industry has Seen Many New Products From the New Entrants

In an apparently commodity market the two new players Perfetti and Joyco who entered the Indian market only ten years ago created a success story. They seem to have succeeded in building quite a few brands where others have failed. But they have built this business hard way and experienced many failures. Perfetti and Joyco virtually unheard-of-companies which had a very tough time at the initial stage now together control more than fifty percent of the industry. The size of this industry is said to be about INR 120 billion and the sales of Perfetti has been estimated to be INR 3.3 billion and that of Joyco INR 2 billion.

This is quite an achievement particularly because none of the players in this category with the exception of Nutrine has ever crossed INR 1 billion mark in spite of the fact that all of them are here in this market for over decades. These two new players have really brought in many innovations in the category and made the industry more vibrant to attract new players where others did not see any viable proposition in this low value, low margin and fragmented industry. Till 1990 this market was therefore, largely underdeveloped. On one side there was a dominance of the unorganized sector in the sugar and hard boiled candy category and on the other side the gum based confectionery variant was almost non-existent or unheard of. We used to have only traditional chewing gum from National Products (NP) whose sales was about INR 200 million and there was no other brand in this category. Today you don't see this NP's Chewing gum any more. It should be noted here that in this category these two small unknown players have succeeded where giants have failed. HLL and ITC both had entered in this category in the recent past. HLL has entered the category with its brand Max and used its beverage channel to distribute it.

Later on HLL began creating a separate distribution channel for sugar confectionery. Cadbury who has acquired Adams globally is said to be re-entering, after its first foray with the launch of Googly in 1997 which did not really work for them. Cadbury is in the process of re-launching Halls and Clorets which the company has recently acquired with the global merger of Warner Lambert. ITC, which is a new comer to the category launched its hard boiled candy in the semi-urban and rural segment. Parry Confectionery which is over 100 years old company seems to be looking safer zones of niche opportunities for growth and to avoid any direct confrontation with new comers particularly the MNCs. Finally , this also got acquired.

How did the duo made it in a difficult category? The answer lies in the total focus and constant innovation. Both Joyco and Perfetti have the advantage to have a heritage in confectionery, something that most of the previous players lacked. Indians do not always adhere to the well established norms of the developed market where there is gradual up-gradation of the category to maturity –graduating to bubble gum to chewing gum to functional confectionery. But both Perfetti and Joyco tried to upgrade the category exactly in that line with many variants which helped to keep consumers locked into exciting new experience and they succeeded. They initially focused on kids and now turning to adults as well. Because of the sustained effort on the part of these two successful players market has really changed beyond recognition. In 1994 we had only 50 SKUs (stock keeping unit) in this category and today it has grown to almost 500, a ten fold growth. Earlier, excluding chocolate there were about seven to eight brands in the category and the total advertisement expenditure was INR 70- 80 million.

As against this there are all most 70 brands (excluding chocolate) in the category now with total advertisement spent of INR 600 – 700 million. The qualitative shift that these two players have brought in is significant and praiseworthy which makes them leaders in the industry category. They seem to have created a template of success in the category for others to follow. One will recollect the great campaign of the Candico (a Bakeman group company) who even formed an expert panel drawn from children to try, test and approve the products before they were launched. They also introduced couple of products with big advertisement budget support but they were short lived. Where is Candico now? It requires inner strength to sustain in a highly competitive field. Candico failed because it lacked that. Both Perfetti and Joyco have global experience in confectionery and others have lot to learn from them. From a clear distribution driven approach as it used to be earlier, the focus was on consumer off- take involving the ultimate consumers now. Extensive sampling at schools and promotions at the point of purchase were experienced in the recent times to drive growth in the category which were earlier unheard of. That is why a single brand Alpenliebe from Perfetti sells INR 1.6 billion which is equivalent to something like 3.2 billion pillow packs at 50 paise each followed by Big Babol which is INR 800 million. Similarly, Joyco boasts of the INR 1 billion Boomer bubble gum and Solano INR 500 million brands today. Although these two brands can be considered as cash cows but there are many other brands in their portfolio which have star status to be grown as tomorrow's cash cows.

The route followed by Perfetti and Joyco is not similar. While Perfetti is a fully owned subsidiary of their USD 1.5 billion parent company, Joyco is essentially a 51:49 joint venture of the Euro 300 million Spanish company with Dabur. Perfetti has an expatriate heading the business whereas Joyco has a local in its helm of affairs. Perfetti was seen to be more aggressive with more visibility in the market place supported by the high pitch advertisement whereas Joyco was more on the promotion and ground level activities. No wonder that within couple of years Perfetti has been able to create seven successful brands in its portfolio in India – Big Babol, Centerfresh, Brooklyn, Alpenliebe, Chlormint, Mentos and Golia C. Centerfresh is the leader in its segment with 35% market share. Earlier Wrigley was the leader in that segment.

In that environment most of the Indian old players are playing safe game trying to consolidate their position instead of launching new products as is being seen with the new comers. Nutrine, Parrys and Campco – the three south based companies are seeing the expansion possibility by exploiting weak territories. But one lessons that they have learnt that low unit price products are the big success. Nutrine thus is focusing their 50 paise and INR 1 brands like Maha Lacto, Koka Naka and Honey Fab. Nutrine is also focusing on their fruit bar segment.

Fig. 4.1 In sugar confectionery MNCs have introduced new products and accelerated the category growth.

In a fiercely competitive category like this new innovation is the only answer. Market is waiting for the re-launch of the brands from the giants like HLL and Cadbury. No one can ignore their enormous distribution strength. There is no doubt that both Perfetti and Joyco have demonstrated significant success by following two different models. But for both, innovation is at the core and common factor for success.

Confectionery Industry is Seeing Major Activities for Growth

We have discussed earlier about the major innovations that this industry has registered after the entry of new MNCs, particularly triggered by the high profile activities of organizations like Perfetti, Wriggly, Jayco etc. And therefore, confectionery industry in India in post liberalization era really showed significant performance in terms of growth, penetration and new products formulations and packaging. There was thus lot of excitement one witnesses in this category. The new things are happening till now in this category.

The competition has forced the industry to be innovative and cost competitive and the environment is such that the industry has to harness knowledge, eliminate redundancy in business processes, use innovative methods and techniques to go up in value chain to capture the incremental value and deliver those better than the competitors to ensure success. Not all are able to display that kind of skill sets required for survival and therefore, we can see even those who were best performers a couple of years ago are no longer able to perform that well. For example, Hindustan Lever (HLL) has been reporting lower level of performance for quite sometime now.The food portfolio of HLL has shrunk in the reecnt times and the company also has phased out various food brands. During last one year food business did not perform as per expectation. Incidentally, HLL also got into the confectionery category.

The confectionery industry is desperately trying to get incremental volume by introducing products at lower price points. FMCG category in personal care range including the products like shampoo etc. has tried this very successfully with fifty paise and one rupee sachets. Smaller companies have utilized this concept even more effectively. Alpenleibe, by introducing fifty paise a toffee really enlarged the market drastically and were able to create a remarkable success story. Seeing the success story of Alpenliebe, all FMCG food companies including Perfetti, Proctor & Gamble, Cadbury, ITC have now decided to introduce products at 50 Paise price point to accelerate the growth through higher penetration.The businesses have to look into that kind of possibility. We are seeing that confectionery industry has been actively considering the ways and means to reduce the price. As per AC Nielsen estimate this category contributes almost 5.1% in volume in terms to the domestic confectionery market at 6,617 MT. However, in value terms this translates into a sizeable 11.5 % of the market. In fact, the market is divided by two price points, namely INRe 1 and 50 paise and it is the latter category where the growth is maximum. The shopkeepers these days even give two lozenges worth INR 1 to the customer instead of change which most of the time they don't have. Recently, I was standing in front of a small retail shop in a posh south Delhi colony where a child came to buy detergent sachet of 100 gms and a match box and the retailer, instead of giving back small change, gave her two Alpenliebe and the little girl did not object. I could see that this small child is from a very poor family and therefore I got curious to know from where she comes. I stopped her to ask that and she replied that she is the daughter of a construction worker in a closeby site. I then asked her whether she will enjoy eating that, she replied one she will eat and the other she will give to her brother. We say that brands are built at touch points. This is how large brands percolate down all sections of the society.

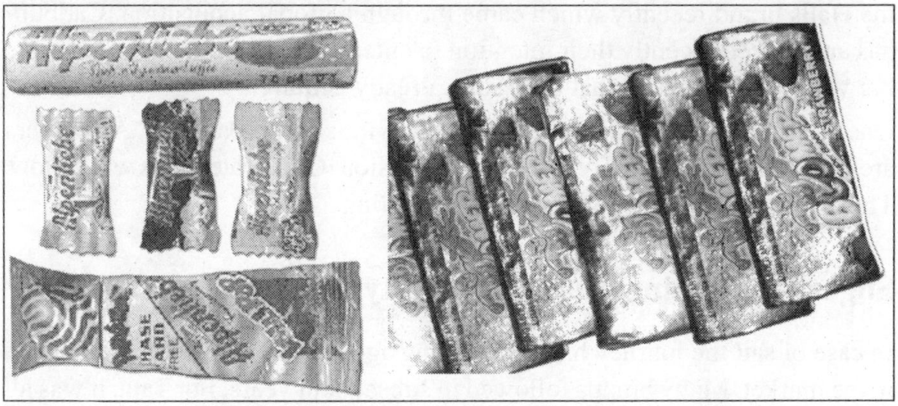

Fig. 4.2 Low unit price of confectionery helped significant growth of the category.

In the fifty paise segment Chloromint of Perfetti and Halls of Wander Ltd dominate. On the other hand P&G dominates the INR 1 category controlling 72% of the segment by Vicks. But Vicks sells predominantly through the chemist segment whereas 50 paise category sells mainly (approximately 30 % of the total) through the smaller outlets. By launching a fifty paise option Vicks can increase sales significantly. ITC is working on its novel product offering under the Minto- fresh brand for the adult segment. ITC is now considering the low price options to increase the sales. I personally think such options should be given to the other food categories as well to really tap the mass market.

There is other things happening in this confectionery category. We know that when organic growth is not possible acquisition offers prospect of the growth. In confectionery industry also we are seeing many acquisitions being happened of late. Delhi based confectionery company Candico announced the other day US$ 100 billion acquisition in Tanzania, Africa. The company also plans to set up 6000 MT manufacturing plant in Johnnesburg in South Africa with an investment of US$ 5 million. Candico made high profile entry in this category not long ago in India but failed. They are now focusing in third world countries. They also plan to enter Nepal, Bangladesh, Srilanka by setting up manufacturing operations. Although they are no longer a big player but they have about thirteen brands including Loco Poco, Gol Maal etc and they also claim to have 8% market share in this INR 150 billion confectionery market predominantly dominated by the MNCs. The point here worth noting that an Indian company is now looking at the global opportunity which other food companies should look at. Cadbury, after coming into the controversy over the insect found in their products in the market lost significant sales. They now are looking at the sugar confectionery as the major avenue of growth and not remaining confined only to chocolates. Cadbury has again acquired the Halls brand recently which came through a global acquisition. Cadbury has announced recently their intention to enter the confectionery market in a big way with the brand that they have already acquired.

One can therefore see that there is lot of activities in this category. All players are exploring the possibility of market expansion. Other categories will follow. The lesson of confectionery is worth emulating.

Sugar Graduating from Commodity to Value Added Brands

In case of salt the journey had started long ago when Tata Salt was launched in the market. Many brands followed in subsequent years. For Tata, it was all together for different reasons as salt was a byproduct for Tata Chemicals and they were required to refine it and market it rather than spending money to tackle this corrosive chemical otherwise as an effluent needing costly treatment for disposal. The latest in the branded salt business would be the entry of Nirma having set up a 10000 MT per annum capacity salt refining and processing plant. Incidentally, Tata's plant is also located in Gujarat. Tata's salt brand being a first entrant is a great success story which has helped them to create a very well entrenched and effective distribution set up for mass market and they are now contemplating a big entry into many other branded grocery products exploiting inherent strength of the distribution net work that salt business has created. But of late, we have been observing that Sugar is being branded and promoted with attractive pack forms and variants.

There were times when sugar was supplied through public distribution system. When it became free to sell in open market it used to be traded like any other commodity through grocers. It was subsequently used to be also sold as packed in poly bags in various sizes but it was unbranded at that time. Some sugar manufacturing companies then started putting their own label as private label and sugar distribution reach was enlarged and it started selling in food and provision stores. The things have remarkably changed now. It can be pointed out here that the sugar industry normally goes through a cyclical performance of having a good and a bad year. It is also energy intensive and therefore those who have been able to implement energy saving and conservation practices and also those who have captive power plant using bagasse as boiler fuel have been able to get an edge over others in terms of incremental contribution.

Modi Sugar Mills have been said to be highly energy efficient. Most of the sugar industries are concentrated in Uttar Pradesh and Maharastra states and they will be invariably also having the distillery which generates enormous amount of liquid waste with very high BOD (Biological Oxygen Demard) level requiring expensive and very elaborate biological treatment plant which most of these plants cannot afford unless they have the down stream alcohol based chemical plants or producing IMFL for either marketing their own brands or producing for other established players in this field. Because of this complexity and price control, some of these sugar mills got sick. They were therefore trying to get favourable deals from the government through collective effort. Sugar lobby thus is quite strong, at least in Maharastra. Some of the players like DCM even tried to produce invert sugar and fructose syrup by setting up a plant based on the technology from BARC (Bhabha Atomic Research Centre) but the fructose syrup and invert sugar market is very limited and that too restricted to some select pharmaceutical industries. Also it is workable only when sugar price is very high. In India therefore, fructose sugar including high fructose corn syrup did not succeed. Sugar industry players, particularly those who have read the future direction of the business well, are now trying to play a different game. Marketing value added sugar in various variants at much higher price than what usual crystal sugar will sell is therefore seen to be the new name of the game. The leading amongst those players are Dhampure, DCM (Daurala) Sugars Mills and Balarampur Chini Mills. Modi Sugar Mills are now trying to put their act together in the same direction.

These days sugar cubes are also quite popular. Most of the offices and institutions and even some of the affluent households use sugar cubes for tea and coffee. Offices find sugar cubes and tea bags quite convenient when most of them have dispensing machine and have introduced self servicing system. One can therefore find sugar cubes in various pack sizes in most of the food retail outlets in metro cities. During late seventies when I used to work for Herbertsons Ltd - manufacturers of Dipy's brand of processed food products belonging to the United Breweries group, imported a sugar cube making machine.This cubing machine was standardized to market sugar cubes under Dipys brand. The parameters particularly the temperature, pressure and moisture content for cube formation were optimized so that it does not break during transit and storage under normal trade conditions. Various packaging, storage and transportation studies were carried out and finally product was perfected.

Fig. 4.3 Sugar has graduated to brand.

The market research work was also going on through a research agency to understand the market and also to project volume of business for this. The project was dropped after finding that business would be too small and it will not be worth launching from a big business house like Herbertsons. The plant was later on sold to DCM Sugar Mills who were not able to utilize its capacity even after two decades. Of course, it was making immense sense for the DCM to buy this plant as they are the basic sugar manufacturer. But only now they might be seeing some utility of the plant when the plant is almost written off and fully depreciated.

Sugar industry now can be seen to be taking many new initiatives. Not only you have both white and brown sugar in the market giving options for the health conscious people but also you have other variants. You have in the market now sulphur free sugar. Sulphur is used to remove or bleach the brown colour that comes from the molasses, the mother liquor during crystalisation of sugar and earlier more whiter the sugar was it was considered to be better and therefore marketers did not bring this issue in front for a commodity like sugar. But today environment friendly, pollution, natural and other health related connotation etc are the buzz words and sugar was seen in those light in order to create a product differentiation. In this context Dhampure in fact is one step ahead of others.

They have also introduced branded jaggery. Circularly cut individual cake is vacuum packed using cellophane wrapper to preserve the quality. These individual blocks have been put inside a mono carton and then one kilogram of the product again in outer pack made out of printed brown paper which makes it natural looking. Both packaging and branding are so designed to give an impression of premium pack and is attractive to draw attention of the consumers on the retail shelf. The Gold-n-Brown brand of jaggery getting an entry into home. You will not believe the price. It is being marketed at INR 28 per kg. We say marketing is everything. Creating a demand for a product is the job of the brand managers. And in the context of today's dynamic business environment only excelling in the current environment is not enough – one must envision the future. These products are being created for the future food market in mind. And we need many of those.

5

Food Service, Retailing and Fast Food Restaurants

Food Retailing has Now become Industry

Food retailing has come of age - from a period when food items were sold in small road side grocery shops & mandis and bazzars to a stage when food products are retailed through supermarket stores where consumers can inspect, select and pick up the products they like in a comfortable ambient and still pay a fair price for the product and the merchandise and sometimes even pay less than the price they would have paid at the nearest food stores. Shopping foods is no longer a strenuous and uncomfortable affair. Instead, it is a pleasurable experience. From simple trading activity, food retailing is now graduating to a status of an industry.

The first visible sign of the change in food retailing was seen in mid-eighties. Around that time a few new food stores were set up in all metro cities in India. Calcutta was the only exception where it started a little later. We had at that time couple of leading food stores started operating such as "Morning Stores" and "Modern Stores" in Delhi, "Nilgiri" in Bangalore, "Food Land" in Mumbai "Spencers Food Stores" in Chennai.

Food business analysts are of the opinion that food retailing will be changing and supermarket will soon be established in various smaller towns and thus food retailing industry has been predicted to be an in thing. To a large extent we can see that it is happening.

Spencers were the first to tie up with a Singapore based large retail chain - "Dairyland" and had set up the food stores in Chennai. This was a technology tie up. The most crucial issue related to retail business is system and inventory management. A great deal of knowledge and experience are required in these areas in order to achieve ideal or optimum stock rotation and pricing for perishable and nonperishable foods and also for processed and fresh foods. Failing which one can lose money in the retailing business.

In Mumbai, Garware group during late eighties had set up large food store which is now reported to have been closed down. But Food Land is still operating.

Prior to that, in cities like Mumbai and Delhi we had co-operative stores like "Apna Bazzar" in Mumbai and "Kendriya Bhandar" in Delhi. Both were very successful and are operating many outlets in all strategic localities in the city. When Escorts group was thinking in late eighties to diversify into non auto sectors which is their main business we deliberated a great deal and decided to get into agri business or food business. Escorts' the then Chairman Mr. H.P. Nanda had also rationalised that decision by saying that "we sell tractors and harvestors for agricultural sectors and our decision to diversify into agro sectors therefore is but a natural extension". And I was hired to give their dream a shape. Having worked in food business earlier for long years I knew that both failure rate in food business and the gestation period are higher than those of other consumer product businesses where risks are relatively lower. We, therefore, were looking for a relatively lower risk food project and finally zeroed in on food retailing after drawing up an ambitious plan. At that time MRTP provisions were restricting large group's entry in many industry sectors. But the then prime minister Late Mr. Rajiv Gandhi first created a ministry of food processing and gave it a priority status by putting it under Appendix I category. Nanz Group of West Germany, a two and half billion dollar food retail store chain was roped in in joint venture with Goetze (an Escort group company) and all clearances were obtained which paved the way for setting up first foreign food retail store in India. Later on "Marsh" food chain of USA also joined this by taking 30% equity in the joint venture.

In course of time there were twenty food stores under "Nanz" operating in northern India alone - some directly owned and some are franchised. Recently, I enquired about the financial performance of Nanz stores. I was told that they are still not making profit although very close to the break even point. The first "Nanz" store that we had started at South Extension was in 1990. Today after a decade later of the stores existance the company Nanz was in the red and Escorts group finally divested this business. Some stores are making money but some are still losing. Spencer's food store in Chennai which belongs to the RPG Group said to be making profit. But still all such food retailing ventures did not work. Mr. K.V. Rao of Dolphin International also ventured into food retailing in Delhi and subsequently in Bangalore. The name of the store was changed to Green Food Store located in Green Park which was closed down after running it for three years.

In India, particularly in metro cities the real estate cost is very high and to make a store of good size financially viable daily sales has to be minimum of INR 10 million which many stores could not generate. And as a result, like any other food industry the failure rate is very high here as well.

Oberio hotel group runs a few stores of processed and frozen meat and meat products including sausages, chicken drumstick, hotdogs etc. One such shop is located in Vasant Vihar in New Delhi. The product quality is comparable to what one gets in Europe or American stores.

The process of development and growth of food retail stores might still be slow. But as we can witness today, the future is going in that direction.

Once developed, these food stores will become really a dominating trade partners for the food industry, who will be forced to give special discount and liberal trade terms for them to get the shelf space in those successful food stores. Once established, the store label brands will become also a threat to the industry as manufacturers have to compete with the store label brands which are normally sold at a lower price. In Great Britain we have such big food stores namely "Sainsbury" and Tesco". Soon we are going to see either these stores in India or atleast their equivalent.

Food Retailing will help in the Growth of Indian Food Industry

The retail sector has now been thrown open to the foreign direct investment (FDI) with a cap of 49 percent holding. Immediately after this was announced all major global retailers have started looking at the investment opportunity here. World's largest retailer and the number one corporation in the fortune 500 list Wal Mart has announced that they are looking for a reliable and resourceful partner. Wal Mart CEO was here to survey the opportunity and to make the announcement. The other big players such as Carrefour, Tesco, Sainsburry are also in the queue to enter the market.

In the Food retailing so far we have Food Land in Mumbai, Spencer's food store – Food World in south in collaboration with Dairy Land of Singapore (of course they are now dissociating) and BigBazar of Pantaloon which have come into being in last couple of years. All these have ambitious plans. Nanz Food store came too early in the scene and their format in the form of very large retail outlets did not work. But they have definitely a very valid reason to come back again. Food retailing, once the global big players are here will make lot of difference to many small scale manufacturers provided they can produce volumes and deliver the quality and maintain the supply line schedule. The quality food manufacturers which are finding it difficult to market their merchandise in a highly competitive market will soon find a different kind of opportunity.

These new retailers are looking for even global sourcing from India for their other locations elsewhere in the world. Currently Wal Mart buys around US dollar one billion worth of merchandise from India which can go up manifold if the supply source is reliable. These new generation food retailers will be launching their own store label brands which will have the guarantee of premium quality at competitive prices. There is therefore the expectation of big customer shift for those store label brands against national advertised brands. This kind of shift is quite visible in stores abroad. One can find in Tesco and Sainsburry's carbonated beverages in cola, orange and lemon-lime flavours selling alongside the Coke and Pepsi priced a few pence cheaper. You name any food product there are store label brands and these are equally accepted in the market by the consumers. These products are produced in the well known food manufacturing plants in those countries.

One difference of course is still there. In European countries or even in other developed countries food distribution is controlled by the handful of organized retail chains and therefore they are very powerful as all manufacturers-marketers need their support to retail their products which is still not the case in India. Our market is big, too much diversified and extended in terms of geographical boundaries and in terms of complexity. Products sell here through millions of stores, groceries, provision stores and roadside shops. As such the manufacturers are not solely dependent on the large organized retailers. But sooner the scenario is going to change. Besides, the large retail chain will have big volume requirement and therefore will have the muscle power to negotiate better terms. Manufacturers cannot do without their support.

It was also seen that these big retailers are highly competent in terms of their ability to ensure customers loyalty by providing individualized service and also by introducing the innovative products. As they are closer to the customers they know them better and thus have opportunity to have much better interface with the customers. They are able to maintain the customer database on their buying and spending habits to work out special programme to build customer loyalty. In course of time they might pose a threat to the smaller retail stores.

There are couple of issues which these global retail chains need to address. These are : the management control of the local stores, high real estate cost in the metro cities, availability of the trained man power to run, control and manage the stores. The existing players who have made significant investments already and have great expectation are finding that getting trained manpower is a big problem. There is huge projection for the retail trained people. This industry has still not got the support of the government in terms of recognition as an industry. Only recently policy makers, trade associations like CII, FICCI etc are talking about it and holding series of conferences and seminars but ground level reality has not changed much. Of late, we are seeing that management institutes have started offering specialization on retail management. There are some institutes offering short term courses and diplomas on retail management thinking that there are opportunities emerging in this new found industry category.

The food industry in India is going to gain from this new policy as many manufacturers are going to find the avenues to market their products – of course, as the store label brands. This will have its chain reaction to provide the necessary support to other linkages of total supply chain management. What we need to improve is the productivity and reduce the cost through the economy of scale.

Fig. 5.1 Food Retailing is going to give a great momentum to processed food industry.

The other opportunity that I can see is that with this up-gradation of retail experiences we will have many more items such as fresh produce, processed meat and meat products, frozen foods and more importantly the grocery items and commodities will mature to a more convenient, packaged form of presentation which will provide the assurance to the customer about their reliability, hygiene and quality. The local road side small vendors will soon find themselves that they are not providing any benefits to the customer – not in terms of price, quality and convenience. I am therefore, expecting that entire middle income group will soon shift to buying from these organized retail stores.

There are people who are worried in the sense that small traders in large cities will find going difficult when large organized retailers will also open small format local stores through franchising route. But they can then switch over to specialized stores. In the over all terms one can see a definite sign of improvement in the entire processed food sector. And we should welcome that.

Food Service Industry has Come to Stay

Every industry has a canteen to serve food to their workforce. Traditionally, those are normally contracted out and employers sign a renewable contract with the food service provider based on a fixed menu to be served to their workers and staff controlled through a committee consisting of representatives of employer, employee and the vendor is partly or fully subsidised depending upon the industry and its management. This practice is prevalent in most of our industries employing large workforce in factories. Often the issue related to quality of food, quantity and quality of service as well as the general hygiene etc. become a subject of dispute between employees and the management. And sometimes that snowballs into a big tension and takes a much wider dimension. Running a canteen effectively has thus always been seen as a headache of the Personnel Managers.

Usually this canteen service is provided by small timers with or without any organised skills to manage quality and logistics required for the purpose. Time has now come that such food service vendors have to reorganise themselves in modern scientific, technological and management lines as required to run an industry. Food service thus will soon be seen as an organised industry and those who are not falling in line will have to fold up sooner or later. In large projects or the projects which are in remote locations or for the projects where lot of expatriate work force will be engaged, the demand on quality food service will be all the more stringent which only organised industry can manage. Organisations which are in the business of hotels and restaurants will be increasingly seen getting into this trade.

The three most important parameters of managing food service industry are logistics, quality and variety. Those wanting to get into food service industry can only add value for the customers by developing superior skills to manage these basic key attributes better than their competitors to demonstrate an edge to remain in business profitably. And in that score those who will be doing better can expect to extend such operations in hospitality business beyond the geographic boundaries of India and go overseas. A few have already demonstrated that ability in India.

Raju Shete has built up a specialist food service operation with sophisticated logistics management. His Radhakrishna Hospitality Services (RKHS) is not the run of the mill, common or garden variety catering company. Whether the location is at high sea, on oil rigs or remote sites far away from civilisation Raju Shete is there with his food chain. Dabhol power project is commissioned on schedule - Bechtel Engineers worked there round the clock to make it happen but the food service was controlled and managed by RKHS. Freshly baked bread and fresh fish from sea are served for Indian palates. If one looks at the kitchen and cafeteria of Dabhol Power Project one gets a feeling that the quality is no less than any five star hotel foods. Raju Shete could give a five star touch in the wilderness. RKHS could get this contract in competition with Taj, Oberoi and other international competitors and that was possible according to Shete for his better understanding of the logistics involved in remote site catering.

RKHS has a tie-up with Eurest International, part of the global food service giant, the INR 2760 billion Compass Group - where Eurest has 50 percent share in the business. It has also tied up with Ticket restaurant, the food chain promoters which is a part of the French Accor Group. It has operations spread over 150 sites and eight states, 2500 employees and serves seven million meals every year. During 1997-98 its income stood at INR 390 million.

RKHS operation is also spread across Burma, Bangladesh, Singapore, Thailand, Malaysia, China, Oman, UAE and South Africa. It has even catered to US forces in Bosnia. Its client list include bluechip companies like ABB, Compaq, Daewoo, Siemens, Hyundai, Whirlpool. RKHS is planning now inflight catering.

Fig. 5.2 Food service industry has now come of age.

In managing the food service chain it is less about cooking and lot about managing complex logistics control. In a typical food supply chain supplies are transported starting from raw material to processing plant and then processed food to stockists to wholesellers to sub-distributors and finally to the end users. As a result, transportation accounts for 40 percent of the total cost. The first step to developing effective food service chain is therefore to invest in infrastructure. RKHS has invested INR 150 million on a 40000 sq.ft. hubs at Thane with a 2400 cuft. deep freezer, 1200 cuft. chiller and 6700 cuft. refrigerated cold room under the banner of Foodland (Mumbai's pioneering food store) and subsequently one more hubs was set up in Delhi. These hub centres supplies stock to most of the remote outlets of RKHS. For distribution, a fleet of refrigerated buses with chillers are used. All distributors are networked and logistics are controlled through an ERP system and employees are empowered to take decision regarding placing and executing orders. At Dabhol power company site which is 350 Kms from Mumbai the employees at construction site can cool off at a small bar after a hard days work. According to Bechtel - "Food service at the Dabhol site is similar to a Bechtel site anywhere in the world - it is world class". And this was possible by managing the key performance criteria and also by training and empowering the employees. In line with international standards RKHS has set up in 1995 "International Catering Institute" at Powai where employees are trained in multilocational catering. It also offers advisory service for setting up catering facilities in a holistic manner covering all issues related to project management upto the minutest detail of even garbage disposal.

With more multinational corporations setting up their operations in India demand for first class catering services at project sites, factories and offices will be on the increase. We can expect a boom in this Industry when infrastructural development projects as planned will be underway. Most of our caterers are now small and family owned with no expertise in delivering quality food at optimal cost as it involves technology and management skill. Being small is not a constraint but they will have to gear up to manage logistics issue with clockwork precision failing which they will get marginalised.

The future of the food service industry in India will have to learn from what Raju Shete has created. Nothing short of global standard will do. And the opportunity in this sector would be enormous.

Fast Food Restaurants in India

Earlier we had successful restaurants doing brisk business in all major and even in smaller cities. Those restaurants were frequented by customers and were thriving only on price-quality equation. Those who have done very well have opened a few more branches in the same city or town. And those who have done still better have ventured in other cities.

We have therefore the types of "Moti Mahal" in Delhi and "Ambar" and "Kwality" in Calcutta. And of course, their fortune fluctuated by the local competition again fighting on price-quality and also may be on decor, ambience and service. In these category of restaurants customers could get all variety of foods but popular amongst those were Indian and Chinese.

The next phase of development was restaurants specialising in Cuisines. In that list we have now specialised Thai and Italian food in addition to Indian Mughlai, South-Indian and then Chinese and Continental. Product specific specialisation in restaurant business worked well in Indian market. But it did not go beyond that. Of course, it had a consequential effect in other traditional restaurant business. In Mumbai, for years Iranian restaurant did good business with their cake and pastries. These Iranian restaurants also used to serve full meal. In seventies when I was working for Parles I used to visit frequently for meal and snacks at an Iranian restaurant just outside Andheri (West) railway station. That popular restaurant does not exist now. A large department store has taken its place. Upto mid eighties in almost all localities in Mumbai particularly close to the suburban railway stations one would confront couple of Iranian restaurants as one emerges out of the exit gate of the railway platforms. Now those are dying businesses. The only asset that is left to the owners is the possession of high priced real estate property in prime locations of Mumbai city. The usual crowd that used to visit Iranian restaurants earlier now has shifted to fast food restaurants proliferated in and around all major cities.

Parallely in some of the major cities like Mumbai and Calcutta home delivery restaurants and fast food service joints also came up. These restaurants distinguish themselves on faster delivery from other sit-in types and also mostly owned by small time entrepreneurs - enterprising ladies included.

The only successful fast food chain owned by an Indian that is worth mentioning and still going strong is Nirulas' of Delhi. They are operating units in Nepal as well. Nirula's have couple of outlets in Delhi and were able to imbibe the logistic management skill and systems orientation. They therefore survived the onslaught of MNC chains, which have opened shops after the liberalisation of Indian economy. In mid eighties this opportunity in fast food business was recognised by couple of big business houses. In United Breweries Group (the original owner of Kissans and Dippy brands) at that time we were working on a blue print of fast food chains of restaurants. The outcome of our tireless work was setting up UB-Groups' first restaurant in Connaught Place N-Block under the name Pizza King. Within a short period of time two more restaurants were opened - one in South Extension Part I and the other one in M-Block Market of Greater Kailash I and subsequently two restaurants also in Bombay-Worli area.

Fig. 5.3 Rapid growth of fast food restaurants chain.

When the first restaurant in CP in New Delhi was opened the initial response was very good. At any given point of time we have seen people were standing in queue outside the restaurant for the space to be available inside. When South Extension restaurant was opened the queue outside the CP restaurant disappeared but both the restaurants were still running in full capacity. But when Greater Kailash I restaurant was opened CP and South Ex restaurants were not delivering the expected sales. We thus learnt our first lesson that our original plan of operating one such unit in each locality would not be feasible. Bombay experience was also not good. But had set up the back up services for much bigger scale of operation. We had our Central Kitchen, which was like a mini Industry located at Okhla Industrial Area in Delhi and Sakinaka in Andheri (East) of Bombay. While restaurants were running well, the overhead costs were killing. We had started doing various researches and studies to find out ways and means to make it viable. UB was a very large and respectable group and thus would not be happy only to own a few restaurants and therefore we faced the inevitable. After three years of operation the restaurants were closed down. Thinking in retrospect I now believe that if we had cut all costs to run only three restaurants which we had set up to make them viable financially, today UB - group could have reaped rich dividends.

In those days there were frequent articles used to appear in leading English

Dailies describing the ill effects of consumption of this so called junk foods being sold through these fast food restaurants. Notably amongst those writers I recollect the name of Mrs. Thankamma Philips-Principal of Catering and Applied Nutrition Institute of Mumbai.

The leader among the big names in fast food chain, which are now operating in India is "McDonald". Look at the magnitude of the operation they run - their global scale is quite impressive. The company has 18700 McDonald's outlet serving 33 million people everyday and adds 3000 outlets every year. Of course a few closes down also but that is a part of the game. Managing quality, systems, decor and uniformity throughout the world is no easy task. But the same is achieved. McDonald's restaurant is same all over the world. The basic principle of growth lies in successful franchising. Franchisee in each country or city manages everything. The principal only provides system, controls, strategy and quality - of course for a fee. And most importantly the marketing.

US based Domino's Pizza India Ltd., has laid out a plan for setting up 100 outlets in India . Domino's India - master franchisee of Domino's Pizza Inc. has so far invested INR 250 million in setting up around 28 outlets in India. Each additional outlets requires investment of INR 7.5 million. Indian operation entirely owned by Delhi-based Bhartiyas is expected to break even by the year end-the company spokesman said. Currently the company has outlets in Delhi, Mumbai, Chennai, Pune and Bangalore. A couple of more units in each of these cities are under construction. Part of the emphasis on service is centred around "deliveries on time". Pizza Hut - Pepsi's restaurant wing also started operation in India but their progress in my reckoning is a bit slow. Pizza Hut- a division of Tricon Restaurants International is currently having 11 outlets in India and would be having 25 outlets all over the country.

Kentucky's fried chicken did not do that well as reported-presumably because what Kentucky sells is what we can call "Chicken Pakora". In India Chicken Tandoori is favourite but not chicken pakora. I understand that Kentuckys have realised the same and are now selling many new items through the same unit. Their progress is therefore is little slower but I am sure they will also flourish as they have in many other countries.

When our Indian or Deshi varieties like South Indian will go global? For example, why cannot we see so many Dasaprakash restaurants specialising in South Indian dishes all over. Some are seem to be making efforts. For example, Bhukara and Dum Pukht - the restaurant brands belonging to the ITC welcome group Hotels, will open more eating shops overseas notably in England, the US, West Africa and South East Asia.

In doing so, they hope to exploit further the brand equity they enjoy amongst regular overseas visitors. Mrs. Hilary Clinton two-years ago made it a point to visit Bukhara. Delhi based restaurant Chor Bizarre, for instance, now runs a successful London Branch. Bukhara specialising in Lucknow "Nawabi" cuisine is already present in Singapore and Kathmandu but hopes in five years to be serving in many more places. Plans have been firmed up for Dubai and Saudi Arabia as per the source from ITC hotels - Maurya Sheraton, Delhi. Bukhara serves food which owes its origin to the North West Frontier Province, a historically rich region with strong cultural links with India. Food is mostly cooked in tandoori style and stress is laid on the rugged atmosphere one might witness in this region.

Dum Pukht's Lucknow food is cooked in sealed pots for long periods and dishes sport succulent sounding names like "Kakori Kabab" and "Murgh Purdah". At Dubai, Bukhara will be a part of a five star hotel - The Kempinski and in Saudi Arabia; Dum Pukht is planned as a stand-alone restaurant with a renowned local restaurant chain.

Latest in the restaurant chain is with the opening up of its first unit in Mumbai recently which will be patronised by film stars who will receive money for patronising and frequently dining there - to attract customers.

Efforts are to be directed to open chain of restaurants abroad specialising in Indian cuisines. South Indian food has a distinct possibility. But before venturing out one needs to create the image of managing large global business here. Indian cuisine ranks second after the Chinese in popularity and demand. Why cannot we extend our operations successfully like other global chain then? Possibly a beginning is being made and success story will soon follow.

Retail Revolution is Finally Arrived Impacting our Food Industry

Wal-Mart, the world's number one company in the fortune 500 list has finally firmed up a plan to enter India through a 50 : 50 joint venture with Bharti Telecom. Bharti Group had been discussing their retail business with the Tesco for quite sometime and it was reported earlier that they were going together. Only recently Bharti has withdrawn from that discussion and the very next day announced the formation of JV with Wal-Mart. This only indicates that the discussion continued by Bharti parallely with both Tesco and Wal-Mart and finally the decision was taken in favour of Wal-Mart who were very actively scouting around for the joint venture partner in India and the choice was for the large all India group with significant presence. Reliance could have been the other choice for Wal-Mart along with some of the big groups like Raheja Construction including the existing players in retail domain like Shopper Stop, Pantaloon etc. Even the domestic group like Godrej was also named as prospective partners for Wal-Mart. Finally the issues are resolved and Bharti-Wal-Mart joint venture is formed. Mr. Sunil Mittal of Bharti gave the press statement that it is not necessarily the joint venture of equal equity participation but a joint venture of two equals. The real term retail revolution therefore, is about to begin in India and that will impact the prospects of our processed food industry.

The success of processed food business requires intensive distribution. Our retail universe is very complex. There are about 12 million retail outlets in India. More than 80 per cent of these retail outlets are run by small family businesses which use only household labour. We are therefore, a "nation of shopkeepers" and the retail industry is highly fragmented and unorganized. Organised retailing is still in a very nascent stage. With Wal-Mart's entry and Reliance Group's foray into the retail business things are going to be different from now on. We can therefore say that retail revolution in India is about to begin. The left parties in the UPA government has started making noises and expressing concerns over the repercussions of entry of such big giant in the world of retailing. Commerce Minister Mr Kamal Nath is also reportedly saying that the Government is going to examine the impact on the neighborhood retailers because of big players entry into the field including the foreign players.

Indian retail distribution is so complex that it becomes an enormous task for the marketers to build a good and efficient distribution system. And as efficient distribution is at the core of creating any success story in business and more so in fast moving consumer goods (FMCG) business like processed food, many MNCs have gone ahead for acquisition of domestic business form this consideration itself. For example, the major attraction of Coke acquiring Parles brand is to get access to their distribution. Similarly P&G and Pillsbury have tied up with Godrej Soap only for the consideration of easy access to the retail universe to ensure the availability of the products. Hindustan Lever is the most efficient in distribution of FMCG goods. HLL has direct access to over 1 million outlets which they serve directly. Most of the other FMCG companies in food and personal care products category service anything between 2 to 5 lacs outlets directly through their channel distribution systems. Smaller companies even cater to even lesser number of the outlets directly. The companies have to thus depend on largely secondary distribution triggered through the wholesale route. The wholesaler play a very important role in the entire distribution system to ensure that goods and merchandise reaches other outlets which company cannot cover through direct route coverage. Our distribution cost is thus more and between C&F agent, distributors, superstockists, wholesaler together constitute about 25 to 35 % of the product cost given away as commission including freight and insurance cost at primary level. The Wal-Mart entry and Reliance investment in the efficient supply chain management will significantly reduce the length of this chain and will be more cost effective. Reliance and Wal-Mart will also bring in quality merchandise at lower cost because of their scale of operation. The product will thus be available in these organized retail outlets at costs which will not be more than the price at which neighborhood retailers are selling. It could be even less costly because of efficiency of the system and in addition there will be daily low prices at these stores. I know of many new investors willing to play a role in the entire supply chain linkage for Wal-Mart and Reliance. This is a new found investment opportunity by setting up cold chain and logistics provider businesses. Apparently therefore, one can think that our traditional retailers are going to face a threat.

Organised Retailing in India

Existing Players	
RPG Retail	Foodworid, Spencer's, Health and Glow
Piramal's	Piramyd Megastores, Crossroads
Pantaloon	Pantaloon, Food Bazar, (Future Group) Big Bazar, Central
K. Raheja Group	Shopper's Stop, Crossword, Home stop hypercity
Tata (Trent)	Westside, Star India Bazar
Tata (infiniti)	Croma
Landmark Group	Lifestyle, Max
Reliance	Reliance Fresh
Others	Subhiksha, Trinethra, Nilgiri's, Vivek's, Vasnath's
Players Set to Enter	
Bharti-Wal-Mart	
Tesco	
Carrefour	

However, we should not think that these small retailers eventually will have to perish and will be thrown jobless or will lose their livelihood. It is not going to be so if they are enterprising and agree and most importantly act to play a different role in the new value chain. Essentially there are two different kinds of roles that these traders will have to play. One, to become a franchised outlet in those localities where they are operating now. But this will be possible for those who own a real estate which meets the criteria of the big organized retail players or have the ability to invest to create new facilities. The other possibility for them is to become sourcing agents and quality inspectors for large players after taking the necessary training. There will be opportunity for those who can invest large fund to create storage and warehouse and packing stations for the Wal-Mart and Reliance. Of course, these possibilities are not going to cover all small retailers who earn their daily livelihood from whatever they sell from their shops. But they will still remain. India is a vast country and Wal-Mart and Reliance will not be able cover all such small pockets of market. The new role has to be played by at least those reasonable size retailers in metros, cities and towns. Because these local retailers will not have any value proposition for the consumers, they will not be able to provide ambience to make shopping pleasurable nor they can offer lower price than what Wal-Mart and Reliance will offer. Besides, the variety of merchandise in orgainsed retailing will be more where each customers will be treated with grace to make him or her feel important. Why then customers will go to these small outlets?

There is going to be a need of huge trained work force to work in these retail outlets. Some institutions are already come up for providing those training to simple graduates and non-graduates to be ready for working in organized retail outlets where customer care is an important part of their business. Business Schools have started offering programme on retail management. The impact of the retail revolution is going to be very positive in our economy.

In processed food industry small and new players will be able to find ways to place their products in these stores by producing store label brands for them. This will also help them to sell their products abroad through say Wal-Mart itself. Processed food industry should therefore welcome this new development. Everything is going good for them. Food processors should quickly line up to capture this new opportunity.

Reliance Chairman Mr. Mukesh Ambani has said that our country is too big and thus there is a room for them also to play their part. This is true. There is no reason for other organized players in retail to get panicky about Wal-Mart entry because they have other global and successful players to tie up with. And lastly Wal-Mart is not the last word. Even they also failed. After losing money for consecutively for eight years in Germany to the local players and incurring huge loss Wal-Mart had withdrawn couple of months ago from German market. Who knows Reliance and other established local players can put up a good fight against Wal-Mart and outsmart Wal-Mart as well in terms of performance. Only advantage that Wal-Mart have is that they are the biggest and they know the game better than anyone else.

Food & Grocery Retail Market in India

Food and grocery segment constitutes about 62 per cent of the total INR 12000 billion (USD 270 billion) Indian retail market. There are about 12 million retailers in India and 80 per cent of those are actually mom and pop shops run by family members. The modern organized retailing is about 3 per cent of the total. In South, however, the modern retailing is said be 10% of the total. As per IMAGES F&R Research estimates organized food and grocery retail market was a mere 0.5 per cent of the total in 2004. This organized segment has now grown to just about 0.8 per cent in 2006 valued at INR 500 billion at 2004-05 prices.The organized food and grocery retail sector grew at the rate of 35.6 percent in 2005 and at 42.5 per cent in 2006 over the previous year.

Until recently , this segment was dominated by players with regional presence as most of them had established themselves in local markets only such as Subhiksha in Chennai, Trinethra in Andhra Pradesh and Margin Free Markets in Kerala. Food World tried to expand to West India (Pune) but failed. This was primarily attributed to inefficient supply chain management and lack of investment in establishing effective SCM network in different regions. But players like Food Bazaar has established a pan-India presence and Subhiksha has moved towards north India and currently testing the NCR market.

It can be noted that grocery retailing accounts for nearly half of the packaged fast moving consumer goods(FMCG) sales. AC Nielsen study indicates that there will be significant switch in spending from traditional grocery stores to modern stores in the region. (*Source:* India Retail Report 2007. An images F&R Research.)

Key Drivers to F&G Retail Growth

- Changing consumer preferences due to increased disposable income.Consumers are demanding wider range and unique merchandise with consistent quality –'all under one roof'
- Gradual increasing cosmopolitization of Indian population due to western influence and internationalization of palates and lifestyle created the need of wider array of products and services
- New types of packaged and convenience foods such as processed meat and meat products requiring refrigerated storage and transportation and retail shelf space

As of now the emphasis in food and grocery retailing is on dry groceries.The wet groceries like fruits , vegetables and meat products accounting for only 3-5 per cent of the over all offering of the organized players. However, consumer spending indicate that about 40% of total consumer spending is on wet groceries.The major challenge would thus be putting appropriate supply chain management infrastructure for wet products and those who will be able to do it faster will have a major differentiation advantage to leverage.The signs of eliminating involvement of middlemen and backward integration in SCM among Indian retailers are increasingly visible.

Major players in the fray are Big Bazaar (belonging to Pantaloon), Giant (rechristened as Spencer's), Star India Bazaar (of Tata Group), Landmark (in association with South African Retail giant Shoprite), Reliance Industries, Rainbow Retail (of Raheja Group), Godrej, Adani, Trinethra (now under AV Birla Group), Dairy Farm, Jubilant Group among others.

Factors that will Determine the Success of F&G Stores

- Ability of the companies to achieve economies of scale and supply chain integration leading to cost reduction , improved stock turnover and better credit terms from vendor
- Building scaleable model that is replicable across regions and extending models to smaller cities and towns
- Passing on benefits of lower costs to consumers offering better value proposition than what neighbourhood stores offer
- Home delivery to match the customer convenience offered by the unorganized segment
- Better shopping environment benchmarked to international standard
- Focus on private label particularly for staple foods
- Extend into other categories for private label brands

Challenges to be Overcome

- Efficiency related issues in supply chain management areas for significant cost reduction
- Food and grocery is still a localized affair. People are unwilling to travel far off distances for grocery shopping when options are available nearby. Finding solution to this issue is thus a big challenge

An analysis of grocery retailers performance has shown that in year 2006 there was a growth of 73 percent in number of cities covered as against only 18 percent in 2005. Although no of outlets doubled in 2005 and there was 65 percent growth in 2006.

Spinach from Mumbai currently has 60 stores in three western cities. They plan to make it big with 1500 stores in 100 cities by year 2010. Spar, an international FMCG retailer also made its foray into the Mumbai market in November 2004. The retailer who has signed a license agreement for the Mumbai region with Radhakrishna Foodland Pvt.Ltd presently has one store in Mumbai with total retail space of 27000 sqft. Bangalore based Jubilant

Group's Monday to Sunday has two stores in the city across a total retail area of 12500 sft.The Kolkata based C3 supermarket chain has six stores now and Tai chain has four stores with a single city presence. Hyderabad's Heritage Foods have also launched their Fresh supermarket store in the city in December 2006.Owned by Chandrbabu Naidu , former chief minister of Andhra Pradesh, Fresh F&G chain plans to make it to 80 outlets by 2008.

Leading F&G Retail Stores

1. Subhiksha:

Chennai based retail chain is the largest discount stores in India with over 315 stores.Started in 1997 it is the first company to start tie ups with the manufacturers for cost saving. In 2006 it had 315 stores with 60 stores in Bangalore & Mysore and one store in NCR. The turnover of the company is INR 3.34 billion.They have launched aggressive television campaign to reach masses.They plan to invest additional INR 1000 million to add 180 more stores in eight cities of which 100 stores will be in Mumbai city itself. As per plan they would like to have 600 stores by the year end 2007.

2. Fabmall:

Bangalore based Fabmall operated 12 stores and achieved INR 500 million in sales in 2003-04. It has been acquired by Trinethra of Hyderabad with 80 outlets in eight cities in Andhra Pradesh covering retail space of more than 1300000 sqft . Post acquisition, Trinethra had added five more stores under Fabmall and now operating both the formats.Trinethra super retail with 172 stores subsequently got acquired by AV Birla Group which acquired 90 percent stake.Balance 10% is still with India Value Fund managed by GW capital , a private equity fund. By year 2006-07 Trinethra has 198 stores in more than four cities with total area of 525566 sqft and sales INR 2.78 billion.

3. Foodworld:

Dairy Farm International entered Indian market and took over Food world from Spencer as a route to dilute the shareholding in RPG group.It had a four city presence and 100 stores in 2005-06 as compared to the previous years 79 oulets.Dairy Farm now plans to set up bigger stores as well as large format stores. As per plan they would like to set up 500 outlets by year 2010.

4. Spencer's Retail:

A RPG group company entered into F&G retail in 2001.In the year 2006-07 they had 68 stores in 17 cities with retail space of 582490 sqft.They have both small (2000sqft) as well as large(8000-15000 sqft) format outlets selling both fresh products and durable item under one roof. Small format outlets sell fresh food, groceries, chilled and frozen foods.

5. Food Bazar:

Food Bazaar, the Pantaloon group's F&G chain, has in all 45 outlets across more than 20 cities and is located within the group's value retail format Big Bazaar.Food Bazaar's value proposition –selling below MRP which helped in high stock turn over. It has launched private label brands of tea, salt, sugar, spice and processed foods.The turnover for the year 2003-04 was INR 1.5 billion which is expected to go up to INR 32.5 billion by year 2010.The company plans to have 110 outlets in 2007 and 250 outlets in 2010. They have over 10000 SKUs.

6. Trumart:

Launched by Piramal group and managed by Mumbai based Crossroads. First outlet was opened in Pune in upscale Bhandarkar Road of 6000 sqft size.They have 12 oulets in five cities in 2005-06 although started initially in Pune and Mumbai. Now they have 42 outlets (2006-07) in 14 cities with plan to have 150 outlets in the year 2010.They project 82 outlets in 2007.The theme of their stores is AUOR(All under one roof).

7. Nilgiri's

It has pioneered the organized retail operation in the country –started as early as 1905 in Bangalore.In 2004-05 it has about 140000 sqft retail space which has now gone up to 200000 sqft.They have mainly franchisee and a few company owned format outlets. They have pioneered franchisee model in India in F&G retail.

8. Arambag Foodmart:

Belonging to the Arambag Hatcheries and is a household name in Kolkata. Spread over Kolkata and other cities in West Bengal company operates 24 stores with an average area of 600-1000 sqft of retail space. Deals in groceries, confectioneries, toiletries, frozen foods and of course its products Arambag Chicken (dressed chicken). The unique features of these stores is below MRP price, good quality and convenient location.There has been gradual increase in sales from INR 181 million in 2004-05 to INR 212 million in 2005-06 to the current to INR 260 million now.

9. Namdhari's Fresh:

Namdgari's Fresh (NF) a sister concern of Namdhari Seeds Pvt.Ltd , a leading Seed company was started four years back with a vision to be the leader in Quality Fresh Produce following Integrated Pest Management Practices with eco friendly bio- agents. Currently they have 13 outlets in Bangalore and 3 more in NewDelhi.

10. Reliance Fresh:

Reliance entered the F&G sector recently with its Reliance Fresh outlets foraying through the Hyderabad stores. First set of roll out included 11 stores all located in the same city. First day turnover was INR 2.2 million. Targeting at least 35 outlets in major cities. Expansion is planned and is in progress to cover immediately Delhi, Mumbai and nearby areas in the first phase. They are planning 70 cities and 784 urban towns and 6000 odd rural mandi towns to cover 100 million sqft of retail space backed by about 68 strong distribution network by year 2011. The company expects to get sales approximately of INR 1000 billion.

Restaurant and Catering Services Market in India

Indian catering services sector is estimated to be worth INR 570 billion which includes restaurant business. Out of which about INR 40 billion or 6.9 percent is accounted for organized sector. The vast unorganized segment mainly comprising of street side stalls and kiosks, on- premise service constituting the majority of consumer food service units and is characterized by intense fragmentation and a virtual absence of standardization of operations. The retail segment was INR 350 billion in 2004, which grew by about 18 percent to INR 414 billion in 2005 and in 2006 the segment recorded a growth of nearly19 percent over previous year and stood at INR 492 billion at 2003-04 prices. Food and Beverage retail constitutes about 4.7 percent of the USD 270 billion Indian Retail Market. (*Source:* India Retail Report 2007. An images F&R Research.)

Home grown as well as international restaurant chain present in both high street location as well in malls represent orgainsed F& B sector. Most of the leading multinational food service chain like Pizza Hut, McDonald, Dominos, Kentucky Fried Chicken (KFC) followed the franchising model. Whereas local chain like Nerulas setting mostly company owned units.There was a 70 percent increase in the total number of outlets in the year 2006 which is significantly higher than 29 percent of the previous year. This is indicative of the fact that Indian consumers are seeking variations and are willing to experiment with new cuisines.KSA Technopak studies show that as against in USA where seven basic types of meal which covers all types of dinner menu, in India 15 different types of meals cover only 60 percent of dinner menu. The home delivery segment is also fast growing during last couple of years.

Vegetarian section of the society needs vegetarian menu which perhaps forced KFC to introduce the vegetarian menu. At the same time Indians have accepted Chinese, Italian, Mexican and Thai menu and these restaurants are also proliferating now. The catering service industry in India is in the growth phase and offers opportunities across a variety of cuisines in various formats like Fast food restaurants, multi cuisines food courts, Living space and Home delivery.

Major Players

1. Cafe Coffee Day:

The Bangalore based Amalmagated Bean Coffee Trading Co. Ltd. is the parent company. The company today has 500 outlets spread across 80 cities as compared to 300 outlets equivalent to 500000 sqft of retail space in 64 cities in 2005-06. Each outlets attract about 400-800 customers everyday.

2. Barista:

Barista Coffee company started the coffee revolution in Indian market way back in 2000 first in northern India and then extended to other regions. Today Barista have 225 outlets in over 35 cities whereas in 2005-06 they had 129 outlets in 25 cities. It also has franchise stores for setting Espresso Bars and Coffee Kiosks in smaller towns. Average outlet size is 1000 sqft and by year 2007 they plan to have 300 outlets and projecting 1000 outlets by 2010.

3. Baskin Robbins:

World's largest chain of ice cream specialty shops with presence in 40 countries and more than 5600 outlets. Currently they have about 200 outlets in 30 cities in India offering many options of ice cream flavours an increase from 120 outlets in 2004-05 to 160 outlets in 2005-06 in 25 cities.

4. McDonald's :

McDonald opened its first outlet in October 1996. Indian operation is a joint venture between (50:50) McDonald's corporation of USA and two Indian businessmen. Hardcastle Restaurants Pvt.Ltd owns and operates its western India operation and Connaught Plaza Restaurant Pvt.Ltd operates the northern operations. There are 100 outlets in 22 cities with total retail space of 275000 sqft. McDonald also developed specific vegetarian menu to suit Indian food habits. McDonald do not offer any beef or pork items in India. It plans to have 200 outlets in 45 cities by year 2010 that will make total retail space of 700000 sqft.

5. Dominos:

Dominos Pizza India Ltd was incorporated in March 1995 as the master franchisee of Dominos International Inc, USA for India, Srilanka and Nepal. The first outlet was opened in 1996 in NewDelhi. Now they have 140 outlets in 32 cities and 154000 sqft of retail space and is a leader in its segment. It plans to add 45-50 more outlets by 2007-08.

6. Pizza Corner:

First started operation in India in 1996 by Global Franchise Architects India Pvt.Ltd (GFAIPL). Currently it has a chain of 92 outlets in 24 cities with total retail space of 79543 sqft. The emphasis of the operation in northern and western regions, GFAIPL is a Geneva based company plans to invest USD 1.1 million this year towards expansion plan to add 30 more outlets of Pizza corner and 10 outlets of Coffee world.

7. Pizza Hut:

Pizza Hut the flagship brand of the Yum Brands Inc launched 'Great Indian Treat' its first Indian menu offered in International format. Pizza Hut also entered India in 1996 and presently has 163 outlets in 25 cities. Expansion plan is through mainly franchising route.

8. Pulse Foods:

Belongs to Podder Heritage group serving Indian food through its chain. Currently has 60 outlets across India. This chain follows quick service format. This chain now has opened its international outlet in London.

9. Jumbo King Vada Pav:

Jumbo King opened its first outlet in 2001 in Mumbai. Presently has 50 outlets covering 3 cities in western India covering retail space of 11000 sqft.In 2004-05 it had only 9 outlets in one city. They now plans to have 500 outlets in 39 cities by year 2010 covering 200000 sqft.

10. Comesum:

It focuses on railway catering . The concept came up when Indian Railways catering and Tourism Corporation signed up the company for opening restaurants at various railway station across India. The chain has three retail models : Comesum Food Plaza, Comesum Restaurants and Comesum Takeaway. Currently it has 10 outlets across 7 cities. Two more outlets are coming up in Gaziabad and Gurgaon in north.

In the regional sector there are number of new players emerging. For Example, Arambag Hatcheries has recently opened Arambag Adda Bites, 700 sqft coffee shop in Kolkata.Three more outlets are being added in the same city.

Kamat is another chain operating in Western and Southern India. Sukh Sagar and New Shanti Sagar dominate the market in southern cities in India.

In north India we have Sagar Ratna of Delhi which is also a major player in the catering retailing area.

6

Alcoholic Beverages

Category Review of Alcoholic Beverages–Indian Made Foreign Liquor

IMFL industry in India, roughly estimated to be 85 million cases valued at INR 280 billion, is growing at the rate of 9-10% per annum in volume terms. The liquor industry in India is highly government regulated in terms of constraints on manufacturing, storage as well as distribution. The industry faces threat of prohibition, high excise duties, exorbitant import duty, restrictions on advertisement, restrictions on inter-state movement. Besides, there are barriers of control over distribution and near-monopoly status of retailers and distributors. Among the various categories of the food industry, alcoholic beverages have attracted the maximum foreign direct investment (FDI). This is because the liquor industry elsewhere in the world is witnessing a declining trend whereas in India it is still growing in spite of the earlier recessionary trends in the economy and the anti-growth liquor industry policy of the government.

Alcoholic beverages industry, in general, covers Indian made foreign liquors (IMFL), country liquor and beer. IMFL include wine which is still a small category but is growing at a very high rate and therefore merits separate attention. The industry is so large that each category needs to be covered separately. There is no valid reason why in India we describe potable alcohol made by distilleries as IMFL. The only plausible explanation could be that we have an established country liquor industry and trade running in parallel and whisky, brandy and other white spirits clubbed under IMFL will be easily distinguishable in trade and commerce.

The liquor market comprises of premium and regular segment having 20% and 80% of the market respectively. Besides, there is a large unorganized segment consisting of local country liquor manufacturers. In the post-liberalization era, many global players made entry to the Indian market with their international brands and consequently domestic players also being seen revamping their existing brands to meet the competitive threat from the international players.

Indians are largely whisky consumers as that provides a relatively cheaper source of intoxication and, therefore, whisky accounts for more than 60% of the entire market. The trend, of course, is changing. The market size under IMFL categories is shown in Figure 6.1.

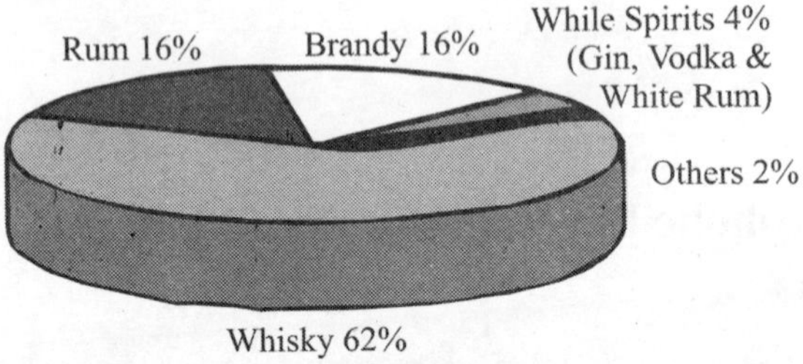

Fig. 6.1 : Market size under IMFL Category.

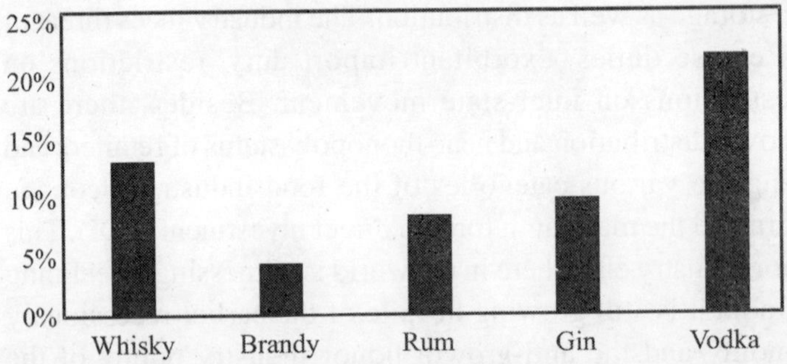

Fig. 6.2 : Growth rate of IMFL categories

Although the entire category is growing at the rate of about 10% in volume terms the growth of individual segments are different. Here again whisky is the largest growing segment. The Figure 6.2 will show the growth rate of various product categories under IMFL. One can see that vodka is the fastest growing category now.

Whisky

The whisky market, which is estimated at 43 million cases, is further classified into categories like medium, regular, prestige, premium, super deluxe whiskies, and Scotch whisky. The regular segment is the largest, constituting nearly half the volume of the total whisky market. The sub-category-wise market size distribution and the key brands under each such category as given in Table 6.1.

The Scotch segment consists of two categories - Bottled in India (BI) and Bottled in place of Origin (BO). Bottled imports of Scotch are still not permitted, but bulk im- ports are allowed, at import duties of approximately 240%. The official figure of the number of BO Scotch sold is 85,000 cases per annum. While estimates for the BO Scotch sold through legal channels stood at 110,000, smuggled imports have been estimated between 300,000 and 500,000 cases per annum. In spite of high expectation of the trade, Scotch whisky manufacturers could not display expected level of performance and the primary reason is high price and those who could afford that price also have direct access to the duty-free or other genuine scotch stock.

Leading Players in the Liquor Market

The market leader is United Breweries (UB) Group which has many distilleries under its fold but now they have rationalized the operations and are driving the liquor business through two group companies McDowell & Co. Ltd and Herbertsons Ltd. Kishore Chabria's group BDL Distilleries (owner of Officers Choice brand) has acquired significant stake in Herbertsons – a dispute being fought by the two groups in the court of law although it is still under the control of UB group. UB achieved a sales of over 30.08 million cases in 2002-03 which is 14.5% growth over the previous year (26.5 million cases). The other important domestic players in order of ranking in market leadership are Shaw Wallace, Mohan Meakin and Jagatjit Industries (both located in the North) and Khoday distillery. UB and Shaw Wallace are fighting it out in the market place and are therefore setting the market trend. Other players including Jagatjit and Mohan Meakin and Radico Khaitan don't have that much of visibility although they have some significant high performing brands. Khoday's premium whisky Peter Scot is quite popular in this segment. The company-wise performance is summarized in Table 6.2.

Quite a few of the international majors such as Seagrams, IDV (now UDV - United Distillers & Vintners) and Bacardi have set up shop in India. They initially launched themselves in the premium category of the liquor industry, but then have also started penetrating into the middle segment. For example, UDV has launched Gilbey's Green Label whisky in the regular segment, where the brand's volumes have crossed 2 million cases per annum. Experiencing the success and realizing the fact that price is a major issue for the growth, all the major global liquor players are launching their brands in the lower market segments. However, they face major hurdles in distribution and are unable to access large and lucrative markets like that of Tamil Nadu.

IMFL Production

The production figures between 1996-97 and 1999-2000 are as given in Table 6.3. One can see significant rise in production in alternate years.

The production of IMFL and country liquor in India for the period 1996 to 2002 is given in Table 6.4.

One can see that now country liquor production is almost same as that of IMFL.

Table 6.1 : Whisky sub-categories and key brands

Sub-categories	Key brands
Medium	Hayward's Whisky
Regular (18 million cases)	Director's Special (3.5 million cases), Gilbey's Green/White (12%), Bagpiper, Diplomat (7%), 8 PM (2.5 million cases)
Prestige (10 million cases)	McDowell No.1 (4 million cases), Royal Stag Whisky, Bagpiper Gold Whisky
Premium	Peter Scot, Royal Challenge (75%)
Deluxe	Antiquity, Single Malt, DSP Black Brand (25%)
Scotch (0.9 million cases)	Black Dog, 100 Pipers, Long John

Table 6.2 : Company-wise performance

Company	Market Size (mn cases)	Lead Brands
Herbertsons	8	Bagpiper Whisky
McDowell & Co.	17.9	No.1 McDowell Whisky, No.1 McDowell Brandy, Diplomat, Old Cask Rum, Kerala Malted Whisky, No.1 Mcdowell Celebration Rum
Shaw Wallace	10	Directors Special, Royal Challenge, Antiquity, Rare Premium Whisky, Old Tavern Whisky, Mutiny Rum, White Mischief Vodka
UDV	3	Green Label, SmirnOff
Bacardi	0.1	Bacardi Rum
Seagram	0.8	Royal Stag
Radico Khaitan	4.5	8 PM, Contessa Rum, Black Cat
Jagatjit Industries Ltd.	6	Aristocrat, Bonnie Scot, Aristocrat Supreme
Khoday Distilleries Ltd	2	Peter Scot

Table 6.3 : Company-wise Trends in Production of IMFL between 1996-2000

	Units	1996-97	1997-98	1998-99	1999-00
Mcdowell & Co.	'000 litres	42531.4	52401.4	66071.4	78331.0
Balaji Distilleries	'000 cases	3325.6	3290.0	3751.3	3533.5
Shaw Wallace & Co.	'000 litres	12830.0	11864.0	8446.0	12115.0
Jagatjit Industries	'000 litres	26090.0	28548.0	28295.0	28295.0
Mohan Breweries	'000 Cases	2323.0	2989.8	3018.1	3498.8
& Distilleries	'000 litres		8385.4	6178.9	10887.3
Pearl Distillery	'000 bulk litres		5678.0	10276.3	13646.4
	'000 Cases		555.3	2440.1	3612.6
Shiva Distilleries	'000 litres		35580.1	41508.1	41508.1
Herbertsons	'000 litres				
Lakh proof kls		7944.4	9057.6	9825.2	10389.5
Maharashtra Distilleries	Lakh proof kls	4857.0	8595.0	7406.0	6931.0
South India Corpn.	'000 cases			13.0	1366.6
(Agencies)	'000 litres			3127.4	3392.7
Mohan Meakin	Lakh proof kls	14288.0	15112.2	10832.0	14655.3
Chandigarh Distilleries					
& Bottlers	'000 litres				26797.0
Khoday India	'000 litres	7373.8	6698.2	8054.7	8162.1
Seagram Manufacturing	'000 cases			855.1	855.1
G M Breweries	'000 litres	14377.1	14377.1	13297.6	14810.0
B D A	Lakh proof kls	4775.9	5211.2	5070.5	5070.5
I F B Agro Inds	'000 litres	896.0	748.0	1038.0	1211.0
Lakh proof kls		18795.0	21797.0	23983.0	21718.0
U D V India	'000 litres		4836.0	4836.0	6914.0
Mysore Sugar Co.	'000 litres	65977.5	60387.6	66048.6	66048.6
Baramati Grape Inds	'000 litres		10902.5	11275.2	13393.3
Total for the sample 98 Cos.	'000 bulk litres		30284.0	32347.4	40896.6
	'000 cases	7758.5	9162.9	12607.4	14233.0
	'000 litres	460554.1	556058.6	591359.8	633120.1
	'000 nos	129.8			
	Lakh proof kls	130932.5	140629.2	86258.7	92115.9
	Mln. Gallons	0.1	0.2	0.8	1.7
	Tonnes	182	474	121	388
Total production					

Source: Industry: Market Size & Shares, Centre for Monitoring Indian Economy – August 2001

White Spirits

The white spirit market consisting of vodka, white rum and gin is estimated to be about 2.5 million cases. This category, although small in relation to overall liquor market, is growing at a healthy rate of 25-30% and there is an increasing trend of white spirits being adopted by the consumers over brown spirits particularly whisky. The white spirits growth is primarily led by vodka which is growing at a rate of 25% per annum. Out of 5,00,000 cases of vodka sales premium vodka accounts for 1,50,000 cases per annum. The leading players in this category are UB's Romanov, Shaw Wallace's White Mischief, UDV's

Smirnoff. Bacardi is leading in the white rum category. Brand-wise, performance of white spirits are as given in Table 6.4.

Table 6.4 : Industrial Production of IMFL and Country Liquor in India

	April	May	June	July	Aug	Sept	Oct	Nov	Dec	Jan	Feb	Mar	Total
Indian Made Foreign Liquor (IMFL) (kls)													
1996–1997	2205	2382	2275	2247	2138	2354	2357	2522	2908	2736	2211	2468	28803
1997–1998	2149	3001	2873	3457	3647	3086	3096	2901	2880	3958	4646	4402	40096
1998–1999	4127	4205	4411	4818	4445	3934	4082	4522	4191	4294	4191	4402	51622
1999–2000	2905	3669	3531	3571	3120	3325	3287	3656	4435	4111	3878	3789	43227
2000–2001	3427	3767	3470	3976	4057	5032	4565	4879	5006	4720	4541	3954	51394
2001–2002	4805	4579	4378	4655	6513	6266	5914	6123	6723	5355	6261	6376	67948
Country Liquor (kls)													
1996–1997	1989	1902	1857	2110	1997	1965	2131	1530	1920	2106	1962	2470	23939
1997–1998	2426	1486	1891	2347	2325	2187	2246	3035	3737	3159	3631	2999	31469
1998-1999	2974	3078	3009	3328	3024	3672	3013	2881	3069	3162	3100	5193	39503
1999–2000	4716	4404	4858	5189	4796	5123	4971	5044	5524	5087	3752	4544	58008
2000–2001	4121	4424	5623	5638	5247	5767	5674	5523	5733	5613	4881	5050	63294
2001–2002	6784	6947	8253	7862	7669	6791	8172	9400	9646	6945	7876	9016	71930

Source : Monthly Abstract of Statistics – December 2001 – CSO

Table 6.5 : Brand-wise performance of white spirits

Brand	Cases
UDV India's Smirnoff Vodka	1,10,000
Bacardi	1,20,000
Kilachand's Alcazar	40,000
Shaw Wallace's White Mischief	85,000
Romanov Vodka	1,40,000

Fig. 6.3 : In alcoholic beverages domestic players still having bigger market.

Liquor Trade

Excepting a very few brands which can claim national distribution, the liquor market is highly fragmented dominated by the regional players. The distribution of liquor also follows multitude of systems and it is controlled in many states, except in Maharastra, West Bengal and Assam, where com- panies can sell their products freely in the open market. In certain territories, it is a government controlled market, for example Delhi. The other forms of control are auctions and Army supplies through canteen stores department (CSD). Under the auction system, government fixes a floor price for the shops and the bidders have to quote prices. The license would go to the highest bidder and the bid price would have to be paid in equated monthly installments. This system operates in Punjab, Rajasthan, Bihar, Orissa, Uttar Pradesh and Madhya Pradesh. States following the open market system provide flexibility to marketers. But in states where controls are exercised, dis- tributors have lot of influence on the kind of margins that will be available to the manufacturers and marketers. In the government controlled system, the distribution is managed through state agencies such as TASMAC in Tamil Nadu, BEVCO in Kerala, the Andhra Pradesh Beverage Corporation in AP, the DSIDC in Delhi and so on. Since these agencies are the sole wholesalers they also have significant power in deciding which brand to buy which restricts free availability and marketability of a company's products. There are restrictions in selling through restaurants and hotels too. The Table 6.6 below describes the distribution channel available in specific states in the liquor trade.

Table 6.6 : State-wise distribution channel for liquor trade

Open Market	Maharashtra, West Bengal, J & K, Goa, Assam, Meghalaya, Tripura, Arunachal Pradesh
Auction Market	UP, Rajasthan, MP, Bihar, Punjab, Chandi- garh, Haryana
Government-controlled	Tamil Nadu, Delhi, Kerala, Andhra Pradesh controlled
Prohibition States	Gujarat, Manipur, Mizoram, Nagaland

South India is the largest consumer in the Indian liquor market, with Andhra Pradesh showing the highest consumption, at 15 million cases, and a growth rate of 100%. In Kerala too, the consumption of liquor is high. Consumption in South India has been growing at a very high rate, compared to North India, which grew at 2% last year.

The State-wise consumption of liquor is: Andhra Pradesh (15 mn cases), Bengal (1.7 mn), Assam (1.5 mn), Bihar (2 mn), Mumbai (2 mn), Maharashtra (2 mn), Delhi (2 mn), Haryana (2 mn), Punjab (2 mn) and Rajasthan (3 mn).

There are an estimated 25000-27000 licensed retail sales outlets in the country for alcoholic beverages. As these retailers have virtually a monopoly of the liquor trade in their respective states and they have a ma- jor role to play in popularizing any particular brand.Thus the trade relationship is the key in this trade. This is particularly important where the advertisement is restricted or even prohibited. Indian companies spend about INR 1 billion on promotion of liquors and leading brands amongst those are Bagpiper, Royal Challenge and Chivas Regal. But the government is further tightening the regulatory measures to curtail growth in an already over-regulated industry category.

The government has now imposed 10% sales tax on liquor sales across the country to be paid by the distributors when buying from manufacturers/ marketers. This is being done to capture the real volume of busi- ness which is believed to be understated. IMFL industry shows, as per official statement, only 0.2 % of turnover as profit which is raising this suspicion.

Indian Broadcasting Foundation (IBF), TV channels apex body has put a stop on surrogate liquor advertisements on TV. They also said that members of the Confed- eration of Indian Alcoholic Beverages Companies (CIABC) must get the advertisement copy approved by the IBF subcommittee in advance.

The export market for Indian liquor is very small. The primary reason is that molasses based hard liquors are less in demand. All international players including Scotch whisky manufacturers are in fact from grain alcohol. Besides, the quality of IMFL does not meet the requirement of the international market. Indian players are waiting for the opportunity when the market for molasses based alcohol will find acceptability. Figure 6.4 below provides figures for export, alcoholic beverages during the last five years. In 1996-97, the value of the export was around INR 1.8 billion only and thereafter it was declining further. Shaw Wallace accounts for the largest share in the liquor export market (around 50%).

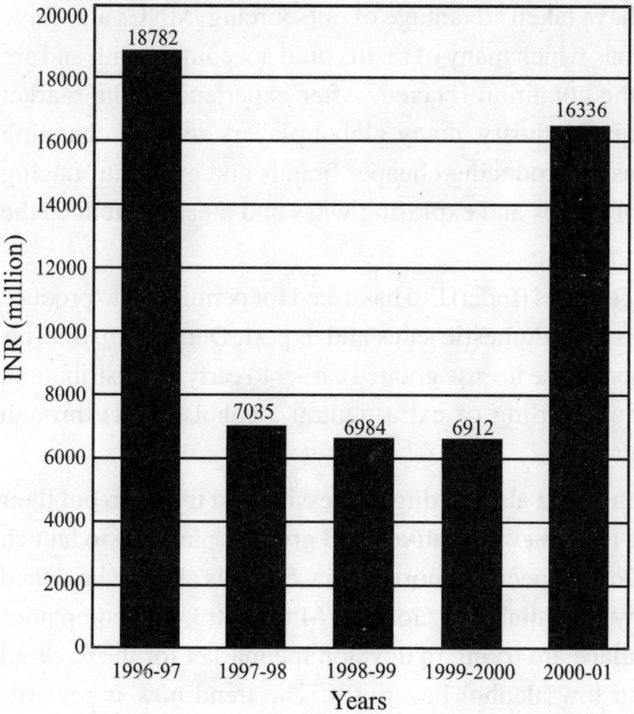

Fig. 6.4 : Export of Alcoholic beverages (1996-97 to 2000-01)

Source: Export Statistics for agro & Food Products-APEDA-India 2000-2001

Recent Trend

The mere size of the market has attracted many global players to set up operation in India. The scotch whisky consumption has declined substantially globally due to growing apathy to hard liquor. The scotch MNCs are therefore anxious to locate new markets for their surplus whiskies and India offers them an opportunity. The import duty on alcoholic beverages is still high and the liquor lobby is trying to influence the government to keep that entry barrier but as per WTO commitments duties have to be phased out to 150%. But MNCs performance so far is not impressive particularly for the reason that they face hurdles relating to the regulatory framework and distribution infrastructure. Scotch whiskies are in the premium segment and therefore have limited market opportunities for them. Foreign Investment Promotion

Board (FIPB) subjects MNCs to a capacity ceiling of 10,000 Kiloliters. Of course, some of them have taken advantage of outsourcing. MNCs also have to meet export obligations which many of them could not comply with and are now lobbying to get the condition relaxed. After experiencing the market dynamics of Indian liquor industry, many global players are now changing their strategies in terms of producing cheaper brands and even introducing molasses based alcohol blends and exploring ways and means to reduce the cost of operation.

Allied Domecq Spirits & Wines (India) Ltd has asked for permission to produce rum from molasses spirit for domestic sales and export. Demera Distilleries Ltd is seeking amendment to the license granted earlier to carry out distribution, marketing, blending and bottling of extra neutral alcohol (ENA) through contract manufacturing route.

Leading Indian companies are also getting aggressive and trying to put their act together and taking many new initiatives. UB group is planning to launch low alcohol Shotz & Derby Special in north India. Shotz is already launched in Rajasthan and Derby is available in Goa and Maharastra. The companies like UB and Shaw Wallace are trying to develop the market for the cocktail and ready-to-drink and low alcohol beverages. The trend now is towards white spirit and low alcohol beverages and therefore this category will witness many new variants of the beverages.

MNCs Fail to make Dent in Domestic Alcoholic Beverage Industry

Alcoholic beverage industry has gone through uncertainties with the change of government in power each time. The excise component in liquor which is a state subject varies widely from state to state and as a result the product has to move from the state where it is being manufactured to the state where it has to be sold under bonded store. Each state is therefore a different market for the liquor trade and it not only has to pay for the interstate tax and state tax but it also has to conform to many regulatory mechanisms for the movement and for selling and marketing of goods. On the top of all these the trade has to face continuous threat of prohibition. There are even instances of a state which was 'wet' earlier, became 'dry' when different political party came to power and again became wet when the party in power got defeated in the next election. This was exactly what has happened in Haryana. And because of that the industry has to suffer huge losses in terms of closing down the manufacturing operations, trade infrastructure etc. There was loss of direct and indirect employment. This industry therefore could not utilise the normal potential for growth opportunities. They were constantly trying to adjust to the controls of the regulatory mechanisms. Most surprising factor of the whole episode was that there was inconsistency in terms of the policy framework of the central government and that of the local state government. This restrictive and also conflicting policies of the government has given rise to the proliferation of unlicensed and spurious liquor production for which not only government has lost tax revenues but many innocent people died because of the consumption of spurious brew.

During eighties no new licences were issued. Besides, the allocation of potable alcohol as well as the molasses allocation and its price were controlled by the government and as a result liquor trade could not flourish. During seventies many new licences for breweries were issued and then new licences were again stopped. The companies which were issued licences for setting up of breweries did not set up the plant themselves. Most of them took the licence to sell to others to make money. We have thus seen that new breweries were also set up by the four domestic players only namely, UB, Shaw Wallace, Khoday and Mohan Meakins although the licences were issued to many others.

Mohan Meakins is the country's oldest brewery. Most of the country's brew masters have learnt the trade at Mohan Meakins which have supplied majority of the brew masters working in other breweries in the later years. Coincidently, the majority of the brew masters are Punjabis who seem to have monopolised this trade.

There were restrictions in the liquor marketing in terms of advertisement and sales promotion etc. The focus of the marketers were thus only on product, packaging and pricing. We have therefore seen many new product launches at various price points. The organic growth that has happened to this industry was mainly due to trade level activities and thus the growth was much slower than it would have been possible.

As there were very limited scope for innovative marketing in liquors; the attractive packaging was a very important marketing mix for the liquor industry. Product Managers working for the liquor brands were thus changing the pack design and label very frequently to keep the interest in the trade alive. Social gatherings, frequent parties and organising musical evenings were the usual occasion for promotion and public relations activities.This trend seems to be still continuing. The INR 280 billion liquor industry is increasingly moving towards a fashion oriented platform. The hundreds of varieties of sculpted bottles, shapes, sizes, labels and corks have become as important to the over all selling of liquor as perfume bottles are to the fragrance industry. As liquor companies cannot advertise above the line and need government permission for any price corrections, packaging seems to be the only rescue in the brand's marketing mix.

UB group, even in seventies and early eighties introduced PET bottles for packing some of their premium liquor brands. In the recent years the significance of packaging innovation has assumed much larger significance. Most of the leading liquor companies including McDowell, Herbertsons, Shaw Wallace have commissioned European design firm such as Design Bridge at London or Paul Simmons Associates - a British design firm to develop the new generation packaging for them to compete with the international scotch brands and spending crores of rupees on the packaging development. With the estimates of adulteration varying from anywhere between five percent and twentyfive percent, liquor companies want to ensure that they sell is what they produce. For example, Guala caps are being used by a lot of liquor companies despite it being twice as costly as roll-on-pilfer-proof (ROPP) caps. Guala closure is the only element in liquor bottling that cannot be counterfeited. Brands like Seagram, Royal Challenge, Antiquity, Vintage, McDowell Premium, Aristocrat Supreme and Colonel's Special, have already switched from ROPP caps in favour of Guala.

In post liberalisation era many new licences were issued to scotch whiskey manufacturers and we have seen United Distillers, Seagram starting the marketing operations in India. In the later years, Bacardi, Foster Beer were also given licence and they introduced their product in the Indian market. Only South African Breweries licence application is still pending before FIPB because Supreme Court has yet to decide who will finally issue the licence - state or the central government? In fact, SA Breweries has told the government that it would set up shop in China instead of India if its application for a tie up with Narang Industries does not come through.

The original licences that were granted to these foreign players stipulated that they will bring in latest generation grain alcohol technology and distill and bottle the product locally to be marketed in India alongwith an export obligation to be adhered to. In reality, however, what has happened is that most of them have started only third party bottling operation in India by importing the basic flavour concentrate and initiated a trading activity here. The government has now asked them to fulfil the commitment or quit and as a result Black and White, Black Dog and Vat 69 may soon vanish from the Indian liquor market. The export obligation also has not been met fully by these companies. The scotch whiskey manufacturers have now realised that the market is not big enough for them as they had earlier estimated. Besides, those who drink scotch might be still preferring to get the original stuff available in duty free shop and from other sources. Most of the scotch whiskey manufacturers are not doing well and after having realised that the market here is price sensitive and those who can afford have their own source of imported scotch, some of them introduced mid priced range in the domestic market such as Seagram's 100 Pipers etc. Those who could not adjust to the local conditions have decided to close shop and still there are some who are operating at sub-optimal level.

The beer industry on the other hand has not witnessed any significant technological upgradation. Canned beer, light beer, strong and extra strong beer etc. we had experimented earlier, the only thing that is happening is that their volume has increased and like canned soft drink canned beer is also now popular. But the largest volume is still from bottled beer in amber coloured and white bottles, green to much lesser extent.

UB Group now aspires to become global leader in alcoholic beverages and all their strategies are now directed towards achieving this objective.

Besides UB, there are three other major liquor companies in India and these are Shaw Wallace, Khoday, Jagatjit and Mohan Meakins and there are lesser known players like Narang, Kedia etc. Jagatjit is suffering from management crisis. In fact it does not have any meaningful organisation. And very often their name appears as a company up for sale. Jagatjit's food business is already sold and very soon liquor business is also likely to be acquired by some one. Now Mohan Meakin is also up for sale. After seeing that foreign players could not deliver the much publicised performance, the top performing local players like UB and Shaw Wallace have been now concentrating their resources only in liquor and beer business. With the acquisition of liquor business of Shaw Wallace UB group now positioned themselves as leader in the category.There is a distinct possibility that UB will emerge as a strong global player. Herbertson's Bagpiper whiskey is already the third largest liquor brand in the world.

The fact of the matter is that large global players have not been able to create any major impact in terms of market expansion, new product and new market creation, any technological upgradation or innovation. And in absence of those the old domestic players are not only doing as well but also flexing their muscles to become global player. And in that direction UB group is taking the lead role.

Beer Industry is Going to Witness Many New Brands

With the intense marketing activities of the domestic players and multinationals in brewing industry with powerful brands the beer market has witnessed significant growth in the recent years. Many local brands also have changed hands. For example, Associated Breweries in Maharashtra producing London Pilsner brand got acquired by the United Breweries (UB) group. UB group also has acquired the popular north Indian brand Sand Piper who had introduced beer in green bottle and positioned the product in premium segment in Indian market for the first time. This acquisition will help UB group to have the dominance in north Indian market. United Breweries has also introduced new beer brands through its subsidiary Millennium Alcobev and the brand has become quite popular in the western Indian market if one has to go by the visibility of the product and the brand. The Millennium Alcobev also has the marketing tie up with the age old brewery - Mohan Meakins for marketing their brands. These strategic tie ups and acquisitions has definitely strengthened the position of UB group in the beer industry.

Besides UB, the other leading domestic player is Shaw Wallace with their brand Haywards. Although Shaw Wallace is also a formidable player but UB has definitely preempted them in some key initiatives. Both UB and Shaw Wallace are going for major expansion plans. Shaw Wallace has announced their plan to expand the capacity of their Uran plant in Maharashtra and also expressed an intension to set up few more green field projects. UB on the other hand wants to set up a large brewery in Andhra Pradesh and also to double the capacity from two lakh hectolitres per annum to four lack hectolitres per annum in its Kalyani, West Bengal plant. The group has also submitted a rehabilitation package for Castle Breweries Ltd (formerly known as Jupiter Breweries Industries Ltd). The age old player in the game Mohan Meakins Breweries Ltd although still has a significant presence in the domestic beer market are gradually losing in terms of their stronghold which they enjoyed as an oldest brewer in the country. They are not seen to be taking any major proactive steps to keep their position in the market secured. It is therefore a matter of time when they will either be acquired by some other players or will lose the market share fast. The possibility of its acquisition by some big MNC brands cannot be ruled out. There are host of regional players who are selling their brand in the local market such as Arlem in Goa.

Bombay beer in Mumbai and Pelican in Delhi and many others. These are practically single plant company and are likely to be there. The capacity of these local plants will also be utilized by large players in the game. We also have witnessed in the recent times that Haryana has become wet again and

Fig. 6.5: Many new beer brands have been introduced in the market.

Haryana Brewery which was closed for sometime has again started its operations. The foreign brands of beers are also in the market place. We have even the nonalcoholic beer in the market. In a recent visit to Bangalore city I have observed that there are number of foreign brands of nonalcoholic beer in Food World retail chain outlets and when made enquiries I was told that there is good demand for that. Non alcoholic beer are in fact two types. One is normal, produced from the fermentation of barley malt by traditional process and then alcohol is distilled out from the brew to make it comply with the specification of nonalcoholic beer. The other type is a formulated product and carbonated. The later variety is just like a soft drink. There are many foreign brands of beer available in India. Stroh is being produced and bottled in Rajasthan Brewery which has a large capacity and have both bottling and can filling lines. Foster, an Australian brand of beer is rapidly growing. South African Breweries has tied up with Narang Breweries and is fast making progress to enter into the Indian market. Others are lining up and therefore there are brisk activities in the Indian beer market.

There are lot of consolidation, market segmentation and strategic alignment activities on the anvil in brewing and distilling industry in India. United Breweries seems to be directing and making an all out efforts to be a significant and dominant player to protect their leadership in alcoholic beverages sector. The Chairman UB Group, sometime ago declared that he is looking for some strategic partner who can take around forty eight percent equity in the group's beer venture and search was on to find out a suitable partner. They seem to have identified a strategic partner in the leading European Brewer Scotish and NewCastle (S&N) who have taken twenty six percent of the equity in UB for price reported as INR 2.5 billion with option to acquire more in the later years.

This is a significant development. This will help UB to reduce its debt considerably, which is almost INR 3 billion currently. UB group after entering into an alliance with the European Beer S&N has finalised an acquisition plan to acquire GMR Vasavi's brewery in Vishakapatnam at a reported price of INR 400 million. This strategic acquisition will enable UB to make inroads into Andhra Pradesh, one of the largest beer markets in India. GMR Vasavi has an installed capacity of 125000 hectolitres with a licensed capacity of 245000 hectolitres. This acquisition will further strengthen the UB group's position in the Indian beer market and also possibly help them to gradually extend the market overseas to achieve their vision of becoming a global player.

In Mumbai one can get any brand of beer in can or in bottle. Danish beer Oranjolt in 330 ml sell in the local market at INR 90 a can. Miller beer is famous for light beer. It has been reported that Miller beer is planning to enter the Indian market. Some well known European brands are also likely to hit the market. Stroh has made canned beer a success with its tall pull ring easy open canned beer. With the introduction of Foster brand we have witnessed the smaller size bottle and also significant improvement in packaging quality. Earlier we had only white and amber coloured bottle and that too mostly recycled for strong and normal beer. We did not have real light beer. We also only have lager. The other varieties like porter, stout and ale are not known to the Indian consumers. The day is not that far when we will have all those varieties for the delight of the beer consumers here. The per capita beer consumption is one of the lowest in India but with the intense activities alongside the new varieties and brands the consumption level is likely to go significantly up. The local beer lobby is trying to bring beer consumption under the category of soft drinks and if that happens the distribution expansion will increase the consumption manifold.

New Investment in Breweries to Exploit High Growth Opportunities

Cobra Beer India, a subsidiary of UK based Cobra Beer – one of the fastest growing beer brands in UK – is investing about INR 500 million in a green field beer project in Hyderabad. At present the Cobra beer is being imported from UK and is marketed in India. The brand has seen good growth that influenced the company to decide to make significant investment of this magnitude. Additionally, company is also tying up with three more local breweries in north, west and south to produce their brand and to make the local plant conforming to international standards. The company is investing INR 100 million to upgrade these plants. The only other new brand of beer that has done well is Australian beer Foster. The focus of both Cobra and Foster are urban market. In fact Cobra and Foster have been doing much better in small size bottle of 330 ml and in canned beer category which goes well with the customers having light and casual drinking habits.

Only recently World's largest brewer SAB Miller has acquired 50% stake in the brewery business of Shaw Wallace. SAB Miller has announced that they will invest USD 132.8 million for acquiring 50% of the stake in the new joint venture where two leading brands of Shaw Wallace Haywards and Royal Challenge will be transferred. With this joint venture SAB Miller will have an access to 35% of the beer market in India which is estimated at 81 million cases and growing at a healthy rate of 12 per cent per annum.

United Breweries Group, the country's largest alcoholic beverage manufacturer and marketer have still control of about 41% of the total market. UB's Kingfisher itself is having about 30% of the total market. This brand has gone places and is doing well in many other countries as well. Having failed to rope in SAB Miller, UB group formed a strategic alliance with UK based beer major Scottish & New Castle (S&N) who picked up 26% equity in the new joint venture.

In coming months we will see the launch of many more beer brands coming both from the joint venture of SAB Miller with Shaw Wallace & Co Ltd known as Shaw Wallace Breweries Ltd and UB with its alliance partner S&N. The new brands that are on the card include 3 Lion and Carling Black Label from SAB Miller and Korenberg from UB-S&N.

UB group and Shaw Wallace will control with their partners in joint venture about 80% of the total all India market for beer.

The rural and country side market offers significant potential for the beer and the lead players as well as the new entrants including Cobra and Foster are now making new investment to increase production capacity to tap the opportunity. Currently the Indian beer market is estimated at 82 million cases of which 60 percent is sold in semi rural areas. Strong beer accounts for the 63 per cent of the total market or approximately 48 million cases of strong beer. Out of this 75 per cent goes to quench the thirst of the hinterland. As per the estimate available, over fifty percent of the total profit of the business in beer comes from rural and semi rural markets. And interestingly enough, this market is growing at the rate of 20 to 25 per cent per annum as against the over all industry growth rate of about 12%.

Rural market is thus big and growing even at a much faster rate. The big names in the strong beer segment such as Haywards 5000, Kingfisher Strong, Knock-out, Thunderbolt and Black–Night etc. have a distinctive advantage in the rural or semi urban segment. Among these five leading brands the strong beer sells around 37 million cases annually in the rural belt. The leading among those again is Haywards 5000 with 15 million cases of sales. Kingfisher Strong sells 8 million cases, Knock- Out 6 million cases, Thunderbolt 5 million cases and Black-Night 3 million cases. The other brands which are popular in rural segment are Bullet and Haywards 2000. It is thus no wonder that there is major thrust given by the big players in the rural market for selling beer. And to do that there are new initiatives both in terms of capacity expansion, new green field projects and significant marketing initiatives from the big players as well as from new entrants. Shaw Wallace is setting up four new greenfield breweries which will come under the joint venture fold for serving Kerala, Madhya Pradesh, West Bengal and Goa markets.

Fig 6.6: Brand leading the growth of the beer market.

After the capacity expansion Shaw Wallace Breweries Ltd will have a total beer manufacturing capacity of 31.7 million cases or almost 40 per cent of the total market as it exists now by the end of the current fiscal. At the same time, SAB Miller has bought four breweries including taking a controlling stake in Rochees Breweries located in Rajasthan and Mysore Breweries Ltd in Karnataka where SWC did not have any breweries at all.This gave the company through its leading southern brand Knock-Out an easy access to Karnataka, Andhra Pradesh and Maharastra. It also picked up Deccan

Breweries. They can therefore, now think to bring their international brands like Castle beer into India and at the same time continue to support the local well performing brands. SAB Miller has started its operation in India since October 2000 when it bought Narang Breweries located near Lucknow in Uttar Pradesh. SAB Miller and SWC together will have significant capacity and marketing and distribution muscle to take a major offensive to gain incremental market share.

The USD 9.1 billion company SAB Miller is seen to be obsessed with the acquisition. They have been acquiring breweries and beer brands in China, Europe as well in US. In India by now they have made their presence stronger and consolidated their position and with SWC joint venture which also will give them the management control, they are going to be a major force in beer industry. To that extent the leader in the category UB group will face now a formidable challenge. With this and also with the entry of other international brands of beer, this category is going to grow much faster. As the players are expecting and demanding for beer to be allowed to be sold in provision stores and supermarkets as it is done abroad, the market will literally explode. If distribution can cover wider networks including part of FMCG chain, beer will be consumed in public and consumption will increase manifold.

Wine Drinking Habit on the Rise in India

Indians prefer whisky in drinks. Sixty percent of our total of INR 280 billion hard liquor market is contributed by whisky sales. But the pattern is fast changing over the last five to six years. In that respect wine market in India is still in its infancy and is estimated to be about 0.5 million cases. Additionally, about 30000 cases of sparkling wine and champagne are sold annually in the country compared to 37 million cases of whisky, 11 million cases of brandy and 9 million cases of rum. While the liquor industry, in general, is said to be growing at a rate of about 15 percent, wine market is reportedly growing at a rate of 30 percent per annum.

This is a significant development particularly when compared with our experience of how difficult it was to promote wine sales in Indian market. In United Breweries we had one winery in Baramati in Maharastra and we used to produce white wine there but business never took off in spite of good effort. After considerable amount of effort and resources being spent to promote wine we realised that Indians don't drink for health nor do they like to be identified as sober social drinker with moderate drinking habits. This can be traced from the fact that although total liquor industry is about INR

280 billion, yet India Made Foreign Liquor (IMFL) accounts for only one third of the total liquor consumption in India. The rest is country liquor. Almost 90% of all forms of IMFL sold in the country are priced below INR 200 a bottle and whisky accounts for the sixty percent of the sales. Whisky therefore, serves the purpose of providing relatively cheap source of intoxication. Entire industry thus concentrated on promoting this whisky category. MNCs' share in whisky is around 10% but they have been successful only in the premium and super premium segments where MNC brands have about 30 % and 55-60% market share respectively.

During early seventies we did a lot of work on wine manufacturing. On experiental basis we used to produce large quantity of wine from wide variety of fruits and for considerable length of time did market development work but ultimately gave up seeing no opportunity. We thus thought that wine is not going to be a major business in India till we heard about a major wine project coming up a few years down the line. The first major wine project came up in Maharastra in the late seventies and if one has to go by the initial popularity of their sparkling white wine it was successful. Champagne India Ltd. was the first large public limited company to set up grape wine manufacturing project at a cost of INR 70 million with Australian collaboration.

Initially it was catering to institutional market and airlines but in the later years their brand of wine was retailed in all metro and other big towns. Their effort to promote the product through the retail outlets did not succeed and the company was able to keep going largely because of bulk order from some Australian Airlines. The company became sick. I always thought that the quality of this wine was good. Although their effort for retailing did not take them very far but the scenario is changing. Tilaknagar Distilleries in Maharastra is the other company who has a technical collaboration with Altier France for wine but they seem to be producing small quantity of sparkling wine for export market.

The youngsters are now increasingly seen to be more health conscious and they are consuming quality wine in parties or at home. Indians don't have the tradition to have wine with food at dinner or lunch but now I am hearing wine and cheese party being organised frequently. Imported wine and cheese bought locally are generally served in those parties. In coming years therefore we are going to see more international brands of wine in India and this trend is likely to increase; thanks to the growth of the younger population. According to the US Bureau of Census, by the year 2010 unlike most of the developed world, India is going to be a nation of young people - who will enter the productive age group and that at a time when rest of the world is greying.

The global trend of going grey is considered one of the most critical factors that will affect how business is done in the world a few years from now. There are three critical age bands - 0-14 years, 15-64 years and above 65 years. The first and the last are the dependent age groups whereas the middle one largely comprises the productive population and in India, 34.5 % would be in this group as against world average reported to be around 16 - 18 %. This younger and productive group will fuel the growth of health foods and drinks and my prediction is that the social stigma on drinking in India by then will disappear at least for wine and beer.

The other reasons cited for wine not becoming popular are its cost and one has to buy the full bottle like beer and consume it in one sitting and coupled with it the fear of unpronounceable French or Italian names and the aura of mystery attached to it which scared away potential wine drinkers. Thus the patrons at five star hotel stick to the brand "Chablis" which is easy to remember. Reading a wine label is no easy task and can be as intimidating as trying to decide which wine to have with what food. For the more traditional French, from where it comes from is top priority and hence French wines display this information most prominently.

But new world countries are not fastidious about the districts they come from - for them it is the grape variety. Hence wines from California, Australia and South Africa feature this on their label. The profile of the urban Indian drinker has changed dramatically in the last five years - from the brown sahib downing his pre-dinner peg of whisky to the young professional who works hard and plays hard, the Indian drinker has indeed come a long way. Sensible drinking now is the catch phrase of the times and the aim is to generally unwind and relax. The percentage of women drinking in India is also definitely increasing - thanks to the new status, freedom and social acceptance.

It is predicted that although it will take little time but wine market is definitely going to be big in India. No wonder that there is a frenzy of activity especially in the wine segment - with Australian, French, Italian, Californian and Chilean companies looking for distributors, opening offices here and undertaking aggressive promotion binges like wine and cheese evening and wine making dinners. Although the estimated size of the Indian wine market is currently reported to be around 4 to 5 million bottles but India is gradually emerging as one of the largest markets for wine.

The work ethics in cities dictates a modicum of sanity and sensibility during corporate lunches, functions, social get-together and high profile events, something that hard liquor cannot promise. The fraternity is increasing mainly because of the changing trends, health related attitudes, lifestyle statements and growing international influences. It can therefore be expected that wine will emerge as a major alcoholic beverage in coming years.

India Fast Emerging as a Major Market for Wine

Wine drinking habit is sharply increasing. Never before we have seen so much of development activities around wine. Earlier the volume was very low and growth was insignificant. Some pioneering work around Maharastra and Karnataka by taking initiative to grow seedless white variety of grapes and then linking the production both for export as fresh grapes as well as for conversion to grape wine has produced remarkable results. Not only that, one can conclude that grape growers have been successful in identifying market for the Indian grapes in overseas market. Also forward linkage with emphasis on production of quality wine is a very welcome scene. This is an unique example of creating success story utilizing our own capabilities for an upcoming identified market opportunity. In social circuit and parties serving wine is common now and it is a new culture. As heath foods is gaining more acceptance over the traditional synthetic and carbonated soft beverages , Indian who earlier preferred whiskey are seen to be turning towards wine which is no longer considered to be an expensive drink meant for elite class only. Instead, it is very much affordable for middle class population. Finding the right value proposition has done this trick.

There are many new brands that are introduced in the market and many new manufacturers have surfaced from no-where. In Maharastra itself there are about thirty wine manufacturers and the number is said to be still growing. Our Agriculture Minister Shri Sharad Pawar also reported to own a vinery located in his home constituency and he is very proud of being one of the oldest winery owners in the country. Some of the initiatives taken by Maharastra government in this regard have really yielded results. Maharastra has given 10 years excise duty holiday for those who are setting up wineries in the state using homegrown grapes from the state. This is a mandatory requirement and therefore bottlers have to put on the label this statement that the wine is made from grapes grown in Maharastra itself.

This step has dual advantage in the sense that not only the local tax authority can trace the product for excise exemption ensuring that grape farmers from the state is benefiting from the new found opportunity but in the long run wine from Maharastra grape will become synonymous with quality if the current momentum and growth in the export market is still persisting, as expected.

Fig. 6.7: Wine market is fast growing and is emerging as a global player.

We have some lessons to learn from this success. Although I don't believe that same model can be duplicated for all other horticultural category and there could be other models which will work for other fruits. But what is important to learn is that appropriate market linkage is absolutely essential and the total value proposition has to be right. Giving a excise holiday for ten years is a significant advantage in the sense that excise duty and sales tax in wine is still very high and vary widely from state to state. Thus depending on in which state the wine is manufactured a bottle of wine can be as costly as INR 450 to INR 650 a bottle. When Maharastra gave the tax holiday it becomes significantly cheaper for the consumer.

The wine drinking habits are growing will be indicative of the fact that manufacturers are focusing on export growth and exploiting alternative avenues for success. Also exploring possibilities for increasing demand in the domestic market. In absolute sense wine is still costlier in relation to other forms of alcoholic beverage but now it is within the reach of middle class. Grover Vineyards is trying to team up with the five star hotels to organize wine tasting sessions to give youngsters a chance to try out wine instead of other forms of beverages as promotional strategy. Industry is also expecting the govt. support for the growth of this trade by bringing it under the agro processing sector which will make it a central subject. If the license fees is reduced for wine selling through the bars and restaurants the product will get a wide distribution coverage.

The same company is projecting export growth targeting Australia and Russia as the potential market. Company is projecting a sales of 800,000 bottles this year a growth of about 20% over the last year. The country's largest wine manufacturer Chateau Indage Group has launched its first club at Athena bar and Mer!ot, a dining restaurant in Pune. The Marlot wine club will be focusing on the youngsters including the beginners to have different experience serving wines not only from India but also from best known wine variety from France , Italy and Spain as well as from South Africa , Australia, New Zealand, Chile and California. This club promises to provide unique experience to the wine lovers and fresher and beginners exposing them to go through the vineyards and wine manufacturing process and finally tasting the wine in the exclusive club of the company. This unique promotion definitely will give results delivering growth in consumption level.

If this experiment succeeds, soon we will have wine bars like beer bars and pubs. We definitely will see some of these wine bars to become a reality particularly in a few metro cities like Mumbai and Bangalore. Here again the Maharastra state which had mooted a policy on wine bar as early as 2002 and waited so long to become a reality to supplement the unique positioning of the grape growing centers of Nashik as the Napa Valley of India. The signal for opening wine bar seems to have now been given and Champagne Indage Ltd itself already applied for fifty such bar licenses in Maharastra. These licenses will be franchised in various districts and the company will provide Narcool chillers costing INR 100.000 to the franchisee running wine bars to hold the company's product. As far as wine is concerned Maharastra seems to be taking the lead with flexibility of policies that support growth of the industry. In order to support the local industry the govt. is increasing the import duty from INR 100 to INR 200 a liter for the imported wine which will make them costlier than local wine.

Seeing the opportunity and the kind of growth this wine market is experiencing the large players like Seagram , Foster and UB group have also announced their intention to become a player in the game. UB group has said that they are not even ruling out the possibility of acquisition or some joint venture with already established player in wine.

The wine experiment which is a holistic approach linking the farmers with the entire value chain will be an eye opener to other states to follow on their key category of major horticulture produce. Having succeeded in establishing Indian wine as global category is no mean achievement. In Mumbai models were called to crush grapes in a tub by dancing over it and celebrating wine festival. In deed, there is a cause for celebration.

7

Non-Alcoholic Beverages

Carbonated Soft Drink Industry

Soft beverages is a very large category covering natural and synthetic, carbonated and still, liquid and powder variety. Carbonated soft beverages are available in glass bottles, polyester bottles and in drawn aluminum cans. They are also sold in 1.5 litre PET bottles for home consumption. Besides, fountains dispense them in disposable containers. Cola, lemon and oranges are the major flavour segments that are being sold in Indian market. In lemon, we have both clear and cloudy lemon lime. Sprite is a clear lemon while Limca is a cloudy lemon lime holding dominant position in the market place.

As the market segment is dominated by cola, in the industry analysis, the market is often segmented on the basis of cola products and non-cola products. Cola products account for nearly 61-62% of the total soft drinks market. The brands that fall in this category are Pepsi, Coca-Cola, Thums-Up, Diet Coke, Diet Pepsi, etc. Non-cola segment which constitutes 36% can be divided into three major sub-categories based on the types of flavours available, namely: Orange, Cloudy Lime and Clear Lime.

Production of carbonated soft beverages has increased from 5,670 million bottles in 1998-99 to 6,230 million bottles in 1999-2000. This product group is a non-alcoholic flavoured/sweetened beverage, of which Cola, Orange & Lemon are some of the most accepted tastes in India. Manufacture of packaged drinks is governed by Food Products Order (FPO 1955) under Ministry of Food Processing Industry. The carbonated soft beverages earlier used to be produced in both post-mix and pre-mix plants. In course of time, post-mix plants were not encouraged and new projects were all under pre-mix process. Earlier, 240 bottles per minute (b.p.m.) plant was considered as good capacity. A few plants were of 320 b.p.m capacity. These days, most of the plants are of much larger capacity and also imported although local plants are available. Hilden is an old supplier of local plant for carbonated beverages.

The Phenomenal Growth

The kind of growth this market is witnessing now is phenomenal due to intense marketing activities of two players – Coke and Pepsi. All other players have disappeared from the scene and the industry is now revolving around only Coke and Pepsi.

The soft drinks market till early 1990s was in the hands of domestic players like Pure Drinks Pvt Ltd (initially a Coca-Cola Bottler and then after the exit of Coke introduced their own brand Campa), Parle Exports Pvt Ltd – manufacturer of well known brands like Thums-Up, Limca, Gold Spot etc which was subsequently sold to Coke, Dukes India Pvt Ltd – famous for their Mangola and soda brands which was acquired by Pepsi. Aditionally, there were many regional players. After the exit of Coke in 1977 with the initiative taken by the Govt of India, Modern Foods (a Govt of India Undertaking) introduced. Double Seven brand based on the concentrate formulation developed at Central Food Technological Research Institute (CFTRI), Mysore and the major bottler was Pure Drinks with its plants in all four major metro cities. Double Seven could never get market acceptance and Parle took the advantage of the gap and was successful in creating a major success story with its Thums-Up which has fought Pepsi, but when Coke re-entered the Indian market, Parle decided to sell its brands and business to Coke. The principal reason being franchise bottlers of parles gradually started shifting loyalty to Coke. Thus, with the opening up of economy and the entry of MNC players Pepsi and Coke, the market has come totally under their control. The only other MNC, Cadbury India Ltd tried to introduce their global brands like Canada Dry and Crush but subsequently withdrawn from the race. The carbonated soft beverages industry thus now got synonymous with Pepsi and Coke.

The phenomenal sales growth of carbonated soft drinks Pepsi (about 30 to 35 percent) and Coca-Cola (40 per cent and above) in the months of April and May 2003 has proved that there is a right price for everything - you just have to get to it.

In fact, since PepsiCo and Coca-Cola, the two US-based companies, set up operations in India, never have they achieved the kind of sales growth with their carbonated soft drink (CSD) brands as they have in the year 2003.

The success is mostly due to a cut-throat price war initiated by Coca-Cola India when it launched Coke in 200-ml packs priced at INR 5. Pepsi India was left with no choice but to follow suit. Not only this, Pepsi went one step further and slashed prices of its 300-ml packs to INR 6 because it didn't have 200-ml bottles. It can be pointed out here that during seventies and eighties carbonated soft drinks were sold only in 200 ml returnable glass bottles. In the later years Maha Cola (big Cola) concept came in and 300 ml bottles were introduced and price also started going up. The market has started taking a turn again and old price points and size have come back into play and interestingly enough it is triggering the growth of the market.

The two companies, which in the earlier years were unable to increase the sales of soft drinks and repeatedly requested the government to reduce the excise duty on them to help increase sales, have achieved an unprecedented sales growth now.

In fact, so great has been the sales growth of the soft drink brands that the companies now seem to be shelving its earlier plans to launch juices and other beverages in the domestic market. Sales of the two brands have outstripped the sales growth of juice drinks like Coke's Maaza and Pepsi's Slice. The two juice drinks were earlier said to be growing faster than Carbonated soft drinks (CSDs).

Led by a riveting advertisement campaign, Mountain Dew has already grabbed a 5-per cent share of the INR 70 billion carbonated soft drink industry since its launch.At the moment, PepsiCo India is putting its juice brand Slice under review. Originally launched in a mango flavour in returnable glass bottles, Slice was extended to cartons two years back. It has since then been introduced in litchi and guava flavours. Pepsi also launched coinciding with the World Cup – Blue Pepsi which was subsequently withdrawn from the market.

Coca-Cola India also says it has logged spectacular sales in the past few months. It claims it has registered a sales growth of over 40 per cent overall during the last summer months, while in a few urban pockets like New Delhi and Hyderabad the sales growth was as high as 70-80 per cent during the same period.

The company has also increased its village penetration from 9 per cent in year 2000 to 25 per cent in 2003 by adding 40,000 more villages. It has added 30 new lines since 2002 and has added 9 million cases of new glass bottles to its operations.

Compare this with the fact that it had about 20 million cases of glass bottles in the market during the last 10 years. The total number of Coca-Cola outlets has increased from 6,00,000 to 7,50,000 from 2000 and the company has given out additional 0.25 million refrigerators in the same year. Coca-Cola is also said to be putting its plans of launching juice and milk-based beverages on the back burner and grow CSD sales while the summer heat rages.

The market has high regional variations. While cola drinks have main markets in metro cities and northern states of UP, Punjab, Haryana, etc. orange flavored drinks are popular in southern states. Sodas too are sold largely in southern states besides sale through bars. Western markets have preference towards mango flavored drinks. Diet coke presently constitutes just 0.7% of the total carbonated beverage market.

The distribution network of Coca-Cola had 0.65 million outlets across the country in FY,00, which the company is planning to in-crease to 0.8 million by FY,01. On the other hand Pepsi Co's distribution network had 0.6 million outlets across the country during FY'00 which has increased to 0.75 million by FY'01.

Coca-Cola India claims a 58 per cent share of the soft drinks market; this includes a 42 per cent share of the cola market by Coke and Thums-Up put together. Other products account for 16 per cent market share, mainly led by Limca.

Fig. 7.1 In soft carbonated beverages it is the fight now between Coke and Pepsi.

Market Size

The entry of Pepsi and Coke has triggered the growth explosion in these categories. The following Table 7.1 gives the production figures of the carbonated beverages for the year 1997-98 to year 2001-02.

Table 7.1 : Production of Carbonated Beverages

Year	Bottles (in million)
1997-98	4,920
1998-99	5,670
1999-00	6,230
2000-01	6,450
2001-02	6,600

Source : Ministry of Food Processing Industry–Annual Report (2001–02)

The market was witnessing an average growth rate of 5-6% in the early '90s whereas in 1999-00 the category registered a growth rate of 7-8% per annum compared to around 20% growth rate a year earlier. In the year 2002-03 the carbonated beverages has demonstrated a significant growth of about 18% primarily triggered by the small 200 ml bottles at an invitation price of INR 5 per bottle. This strategy was primarily focusing on the rural market where unit price is always a key issue. Soft drinks industry can cover the rural market adequately with its large deeply penetrated distribution infrastructure covering the remotest areas. Even in places where drinking water is not available carbonated soft beverages are made available. Driven by health concerns and increased awareness of the importance of clean drinking water, bottled water sales are the fastest growing sector of the soft drinks market, with a compound annual growth rate in 1996-2001 of 9%. The expected size of the market under this category is estimated to be about INR 80 billion crores by the year, 2007 for both Pepsi and Coke to share.

This high expectation seems to have got a severe jolt from totally unexpected quarter. Both Pepsi and Coke have now got in-volved into a controversy that these popular brands of carbonated beverages contain pesticide residue in far excess of EU norms as determined by Center for Science & Environment (CSE), a Delhi based NGO. The impact of this revelation is so great that both Coke and Pepsi had to drop production upto 30 to 40% because of sudden and sharp decline in demand. It is interesting to note that our PFA (Prevention of Food Adulteration Act) under Ministry of Health, Govt. of India, does not have any standard for pesticide residues in beverages.

In spite of the existence of well entrenched distribution infrastructure, the aerated soft drinks industry in India is at a nascent stage with a per capita consumption of less than eight bottles, as given by the Federation of Indian Chambers of Commerce and Industry (FICCI). This stands lower than even that in the neighbouring countries such as Pakistan, Sri Lanka, Thailand, Indonesia and the Philippines.

The Rural Thrust

Both Pepsi and Coke are seeing the growth opportunity in rural India. Coke, for example, is expecting 30% of its revenue to come from rural sector where price and affordability is the major issue. Coca-Cola India's marketing plan for the coming summer peak sales season is vested with a rural thrust and rides on the back of its newly-launched 200-ml bottle, priced between INR 5 and INR 6 across the country. While the soft drinks sales showed flat growth in earlier years, sales are now significently up for the company as compared to the same period during the earlier years, largely on account of this aggressive pricing strategy.

The company had appointed 50,000 new outlets as part of its plans to cover one hundred thousand incremental outlets. The new outlets also covered 3,500 new villages. The company continues with its two-cola strategy, pushing Coke and Thums-Up in different cities or regions depending on the geographical preference. It can be noted here that Thums-Up brand equity is so strong that it sells still more than Coke. Putting both Thums-Up and Coke together Coca-Cola could fight Pepsi, otherwise Pepsi would have been way above Coke sales in terms of market share which was expected as Pepsi were the first entrant after the exit of Coke in 1977.

Coke Suffered for Late Re-entry

If Coke had continued and agreed to dilute the holding as stipulated by Govt of India in 1977, it would have gained. And this was publicly accepted by Coke. They have found therefore, the going is not as smooth which impacted their financial performance. Although Coke reentered India with a bang in 1993 following the country's economic liberalization program that started in 1990, with a promise – again along with few others, such as its rival cola giant Pepsi, and confectionery major Wrigley's, as well as Perfetti - that it would divest 49 percent of its stake in the company's Indian bottling operations to domestic shareholders in five years.

In 1996, when Coca-Cola made another investment of US $ 700 million in the country for acquiring bottling plants, the government extended the divestment clause. But Coke India has been seeking a complete waiver of the divestment clause, citing huge accumulated losses – estimated to be over US $ 400 million, sagging primary market conditions within the country; and the fact that the government had wavered this clause for several of its peers, such as Pepsi, Wrigley's, Perfetti and Dupont.

However, the Indian government insisted that Coca-Cola India divest its stake to satisfy the requirement of the divestment clause in the 1997 foreign collaboration agreement between the government and the beverage giant. The government's contention was that its foreign investment policies allow a divestment waiver only to companies that set up new or agricultural-based projects.And, since Coke-India had done neither - it has been expanding and making additional investments only through acquisitions, and not through the route of setting up of new projects (unlike its peers)– it could not allow a waiver to Coke.

But Coke's decision of divestment through private placements, too, has drawn criticism. Critics said that by opting to exclude the ordinary public from this process, Coke no doubt was observing the rule in letter but not in spirit. Clearly, the company is still not comfortable with public scrutiny of its accounts and business.

But to make divestment less painful for multinational companies, the Indian government announced a couple of carrots recently. First, the government clarified that the divestment clauses referred only to pruning of equity holdings and not allocation of voting rights – which means that divestments will not lead to loss of management control – and second, it offered a relaxation that divesting foreign companies need not go in for an initial public offering. Instead, they can offload to private investors, partners and employees.

Meanwhile, although the company is still floundering financially, Coke sources claim that the company had been quite a marketing success lately. In a release lately, Coca-Cola India said that its carbonated soft drinks business cornered an all-time high share of 60.5 percent of the all-India carbonated soft drinks market at the end of May 2002.

According to Coke, this is the first time since their re-entry in 1993 that they have picked up such a huge share of the Indian market. Quoting figures from the latest national retail audit report by ORG-MARG, a leading market research agency, Coke said that its market share in the carbonated soft drinks category had increased 1.8 percentage points. It is the fourth consecutive month that Coke India has recorded a market share increase over the previous month, as per the same release. The company broke even for the first time in Indian operations and made cash profit in year 2000-01.

However, its arch rival Pepsi, too, claims that it is leading the race against Coke, at least in the cola segment. Quoting IMRB figures, Pepsi said that its carbonated soft drinks category mopped up a 49 percent share of the overall beverages market, while its flagship cola brand, Pepsi-Cola, cor-nered a 50 percent market share during the same period.

In the recent past Pepsi's marketing strategies have been aggressively imitated by rival Coca-Cola, which has used promotions revolving around Hindi movies, cricket and music to promote its brands.

Coca-Cola India's strategy in India, in line with that in other markets, has been to have a large number of brands with a number of variants under each brand. At the same time, the company's mainstay remains carbonated soft drinks (CSDs). Hence, in the US market Coca-Cola has a number of variants under the Coke brand, including Cherry Coke and Coke Classic. Similarly, a number of variants exist under the Fanta brand. Coca-Cola India, some time back, had initiated the first cola price war by launching small 200 ml packs priced at INR 5. Now Pepsi India has fired the first salvo and lowered the price of its 300 ml pack from INR 8 to INR 6.

Industry sources say Coke India was able to reduce its prices from INR 7 to INR 5 because it acquired a big glass bottle manufacturing facility, which enabled it to offer smaller bottles at reduced prices.

Pepsi, on the other hand, valiantly though it is trying to keep pace with Coke's price initiative, lacks such a facility and is lagging behind in the 200 ml segment.

Pepsi's main concern at the moment is to try and slow down Coke's penetration of the market with its 200 ml packs and has chosen to focus on the 300 ml segment as it feels that, consumption of colas is bound to go up and 300 ml packs will be more popular. Factoring this in, Pepsi first brought down the price of the 300 ml pack to INR 8, and then to INR 6.

Pepsi is targeting its 300 ml packs at high-consumption markets like Delhi and Mumbai. Alongside the 300 ml packs, the company is also marketing 200 ml bottles priced at INR 5. The new price points are being communicated to the consumers through printed banners, truck-backs and point of sale merchandise.

Industry analysts say the strategy will work out if 300 ml at INR 6 looks more attractive than 200 ml for INR 5. Otherwise Pepsi may end up making huge losses as it has already spent huge amounts on advertisement including that on Cricket World Cup.

Soft drink sales have been rising and whatever be the outcome of the price war, the way cola prices are headed the soft drinks market is bound to get a boost.

Pepsi– HLL Joint Effort

In a path-breaking tie-up, two fast-moving consumer goods (FMCG) leaders, Hindustan Lever (HLL) and Pepsi Foods, have formed an alliance in India to jointly market, through a vending format, a full range of hot beverages and carbonated soft drinks from their portfolio of world-class brands.

HLL brings to the alliance a well-established presence and brand value in hot beverages, outstanding product development and backward integrated sourcing capability, expertise in vending and an extensive institutional channel base.

Pepsi has strong brands, rich expertise in on-premise retailing of cold beverages, extensive sales and distribution infrastructure, and a well-developed network of retail outlets and dealers who sell Pepsi through fountain machines.

The partnership leverages each other's strengths with an unbeatable business model that creates a powerful distribution base to market a unified portfolio of popular hot beverages and soft drinks through a combined fountain, vending and institutional initiative.

The area of collaboration for these two organisations will be in vending hot tea and coffee along with soft drinks across India. The alliance will make available leading brands of the two FMCG giants, Lipton, Taj Mahal, Bru, Pepsi Cola, 7Up, Mirinda and other popular carbonated soft drinks through vending machines and fountains.

With this alliance, HLL and Pepsi venture into offering hot beverages through the Pepsi distribution system for the first time in the country as part of their strategy to infuse new growth in the entire category of liquid refreshment beverages.

In this category, it is now a war like situation and the war is between the international rivals – Coke and Pepsi as it is there in other countries. All domestic and local regional players have either withdrawn or joined them as franchisee bottlers or sold the brand and business to them. It is unlikely that in future any other domestic corporation will venture into this category. Entry barrier is so high that it will be impossible for any other players, to venture into this fiercely competitive category. Of course, for the time being both Pepsi and Coke are fighting the greatest threat that they ever faced due to pesticide residue controversy. Bulk buyers and government stores and canteens have already boycotted Pepsi and Coke. What is worse – public opinion is against them.

Coffee Consumption is on the Rise

Tea and coffee form the largest beverage segment in Indian food industry and both fall under the hot beverage category. Tea is a common man's drink and also a source of energy and even a kind of relaxation and enjoyment for those who drink their morning and evening cup of tea whereas coffee is considered as a little up-market product because it is costlier. Because of its limited availability, price and consumption pattern and acceptance, coffee consumption remained stagnant at around 60000 MT for over a decade.

And there were only three major players Nestle, Tata Coffee and Brook Bond. However, according to the latest survey of the Coffee Board consumption has now increased and the current estimate has been put at around 70,300 MT with urban consumption stated as 70% or 49,600 MT and rest 30% or 20,700 MT as rural consumption. In the same study it was revealed that there was almost no increase in the consumption of coffee in urban India and therefore entire growth has been due to increased rural consumption and that too predominantly driven by south. The consumption is again skewed more towards filter coffee rather than the instant coffee. Almost 70% of this growth is contributed by the filter coffee and 30% by the instant coffee and the reason being stated as filter coffee is habit forming whereas instant coffee is not and as a result those who get hooked to filter coffee get addicted to the same and thus continue consuming this. In urban areas the consumption of filter and instant coffee is said to be almost same. Of the total consumption of coffee, 95% consumption takes place in south and the rest of the country consumes only the balance 5%. The penetration of tea is almost 93% but for coffee it is only 59%. The lot of untapped opportunities therefore, still exist. This new found growth has given some stimulus to this coffee growers. After years of hardship it seems to be looking up for them. The downturn in earlier years particularly in the year 2001-02 forced many players to go for amalgamation and mergers and acquisition of many coffee estates. And cost reduction was the only strategic course left for the players to survive in these hardships.

The growers were forced to sell the coffee beans to the middlemen traders who could export. Because of low margin and high cost structure of the business prevailing at that point of time some tried to diversify and others got stuck in the middle with no competitive advantage and therefore, suffered in the game. But now it seems that coffee growers are seeing some light at the end of the tunnel. Those companies who have integrated operations are likely to gain now. According to credit rating agency ICRA, companies like Tata Coffee Ltd are best suited to gain from such situation as they have the integrated operations in coffee business and diversified revenue streams from the sale of bulk coffee, instant coffee and also other plantation products.

Tata Coffee owned coffee estates, curing factories, roasting and grounding facilities and instant coffee production plant which no other company has. When instant coffee is the largest revenue spinner, they had the advantage to sell the coffee beans and other plantation products such as pepper, timber and tea which put them in an advantageous position which others did not have. The other brand of coffee which needs a mention include Café Gold of Hindustan Lever, Coorg 100% pure filter coffee and Coorg Double roast coffee of Tata Coffee. The Amalgamated Beans Coffee & Trading Co has its brand ABC Coffee Day. These brands, of course, are in addition of Nescafe of Nestle and Bru of Brook Bond, both being the instant coffee.

That the coffee consumption is growing can be understood from the figure given in Table 7.2, which will also give the regional dispersion in the consumption.

Table 7.2 : Consumption of coffee. (Quantity in MT)

Region	1998	1999	2000	2001
West	902	935	976	1021
South	7784	8143	8493	8901
North	486	508	534	564
East & North East	812	845	886	937

Source : CMIE data base.

The new coffee chains of Barista type have added to this growth. Incidentally, Tata has an equity (26%) in this venture as well. Seeing the success of the Barista many new coffee chains have surfaced. Notably among those are Café Coffee day, Qwiky, Movenpick in addition to Barista. Cafe Mocha is the new entrant in Mumbai. Within two years they have three outlets in the city. The Churchgate outlet is company owned but Juhu and Bandra outlets are franchisees. Café Mocha is opening an outlet in Goa and also in Delhi's Greater Kailash-I. The US giant and the world largest coffee retailing chain business Starbuck is planning their entry into the Indian market and as per the report, company has already started the ground work in this direction. Both Reheja group and Pantaloon are trying to tie up with Starbuck. Even company like Hindustan Lever is planning to enter the coffee retailing business and with Brook Bond in their fold this move makes ample sense for them. After long time with the series of acquisitions, food business has become a dominant and important strategic business for the Hindustan Levers like their parent Uni-Lever. The market share of the existing players in the coffee retailing chain as per the available report are said to be Barista 68%, Café Coffee

Day 27%, Qwiky 4% and Movenpick about 1%. The coffee chain phenomena has changed the market structure of the total coffee retailing market as such. According to the figure available in 1998, out of the total coffee retailing market coffee chain was contributing only up-to 3%. But by the year 2001 this has gone up to 9% and in the year 2003 this has further gone up to 12%.

The coffee is sold as we all know in many forms like fresh ground coffee, fresh coffee beans, instant coffee, instant standard coffee, instant decaffeinated coffee, filter coffee etc. And this coffee chain has added the type like cold coffee, Irish coffee, Cappuccino etc. The original hot beverage category as we used to call it and analyze it is no longer served only as hot cup of coffee. The Coca-Cola Company has launched their Georgia brand of coffee through the vending machine. The coffee business is now going to take new directions and there will be more players as it has happened in many other product categories.

Health Beverages are Being Relaunched

In the fruit juice market we have seen this fight earlier also for market share between powder beverages and natural fruit based beverages. And we are seeing it now again. In early seventies, the natural fruit beverages was available only in the form of Ready-To-Serve (RTS) bottled beverages and that too also only in glass bottles containing 10 to 15% natural fruit juices or pulp. We did not have aseptic-pack in those days. It came only in the eighties, even PET came much later. And mango was the 80% of the total bottled RTS beverage market, next to mango was the orange and the market for other flavours including the mixed fruit was very small. Our estimate was that RTS beverage was only about 10% of the total beverage market in those days and it is still approximately the same but the size of the market is much bigger now. Maaza was the only national brand and others were all regional. The leading amongst those was Mangola of Dukes in the western region, which was a market leader and Soma in south manufactured by the Enadu Group in Hyderabad. Besides, there were plethora of local brands surviving with small volume. Although market was small but there were many new brands of powder beverages launched around that time to get their own share of the health drink market. Maaza was also available in powder form in glass bottle and that too both in sweetened and unsweetened variety. It is curious to note that while RTS-mango is eighty percent of the market but in powder beverage segment orange flavour is the eighty percent of the market.

The reason could be that powder orange is a much better and acceptable product and mango in powder form was never that good. Today Frooty in aseptic-pack from Parle Agro is the largest RTS beverage brand in the country.

In the beginning of eighties, Cadbury had launched in Bombay and also in Delhi an apple drink in RTS segment under the brand name Appela. The product was bottled under contract arrangement at the Pure Drinks (the owner of Campa) plant. Cadbury also launched around that time a carbonated tea beverage by name 21. McDowell was the distributor for both these products. UB Group was holding about 15% stake of Cadbury.Cadbury in the earlier years made significant investment (reported to be INR 70 million) in an apple concentrate project in Kashmir and having failed in finding the profitable market for this concentrate abroad they thought of this carbonated apple beverage to be launched in the domestic market. Mr Prem Pandhi was the Managing Director of Cadbury at that time. Both 21 and Appela flopped and in fact both the brands did not take off at all and thus were short lived. Nestle's powder iced tea beverage Paloma was also launched around that time and it was withdrawn later from the market.

Nestle is going to relaunch the product. Although Appela was a failure but now we are going to see from Pepsi their Miranda - Apple. Nestle earlier had failed with their powder iced tea beverage and the reason, it was thought, that in India everybody drinks tea hot and therefore who will drink iced tea. But that did not deter them to relaunch their Paloma brand of iced tea again. Interestingly enough, even Lipton which is now under HLL fold is going to launch Lipton Iced Tea and will compete with other soft beverages and it has been reported that soon Tata Tea and even cola giant Coca-Cola may soon enter into this category. Expectation is that what has failed earlier might succeed now under changed market environment.

General Foods during early eighties was setting up their coffee plant near Mysore for manufacturing their international brand - Maxwell coffee in joint venture with Kothari to form Kothari General Foods (KGF). But Maxwell coffee was never launched. After setting up the project at a cost of INR 300 million KGF decided to withdraw and sold their plant to Nestle. Tang was launched in India around that time but did not succeed. At about that time Smith Kline Becheem (manufacturers of Horlicks) launched three variants of powder beverages in bottles and jars under the brand name Florida but that also flopped. In intervening decade there was no powder beverage in the market excepting Rasna, which we consider into a different class altogether. After all these years we are again seeing the old brands resurfacing in the market.

Tang has been relaunched and Dabur is distributing the product at a time when Dabur themselves are struggling to establish their Real Juice in cartons. In the meantime, we have seen many brands of fresh juice came and gone. Notably among those are Onjus of Enkay Texofoods and Jump-in from Godrej

Foods. In fact, I was curious to know why Godrej Foods after so much of marketing efforts for years finally decided to withdraw the brand and again launched a new fruit juice in aseptic-pack under the brand name X-s. So many brands came and gone in this category but only remaining thing is Aseptic-pack as packaging material which is still favoured by the manufacturers and marketers. I had the opportunity to visit Tetra Pak plant in Sweden during early eighties and even at that time I had seen that Robots were used to man some of their activities such as warehousing, etc. The only other global competitor of Tetra-Pak was Combiblock from USA but they did not survive while Tetra-Pak is still going strong. In India they formed joint venture with NDDV to form Hindustan Packaging Ltd. which got changed again to Tetra-Pak India Ltd.

PepsiCo acquired Tropicana, the largest selling fruit juice in the world from Seagram and also acquired the Gatorade brand when it took over Quaker Oats. Gatorade is very powerful brand of an isotonic drink (it replaces body salts after exercise) which occupies a niche but profitable segment in the US. No doubt, Gatorade will make its international debut shortly and have recntly been launched in Indian market as well. SmithKline Beecham Consumer Healthcare Ltd. also has a popular energy drink in their portfolio. Lucozade a very popular energy drink is available in three variants - energy, sports and solstice, besides orange and lemon flavors and this is also targeted against sports segment. Market information is that Lucozade will be launched in India soon and SmithKline is also going to relaunch their Rebena fruit drink in black currant flavor, which was earlier launched in Amla flavor and subsequently withdrawn from the market. Best Foods International also has launched a powder beverage by brand name Fresh Delite and there was aggressive school promotion carried out by the company in Delhi. When I was working for this company in late seventies we launched Trinka to fight Rasna in that segment but Trinka did not do well. Incidentally, Rasna has also a powder beverage to fight Tang. Recently, when I asked one of the senior executives of Pioma Industries that what would be their strategy and how would they like to react to the impending launch of Tang from Kraft General Foods. The reply was "We are fighting Tang in many countries abroad and we will fight them here as well - just wait and see".

What I am seeing is the same old game being replayed. Earlier we had RTS beverages in glass bottles, fruit juices in can and powder beverages (sweetened and unsweetened) in both glass bottles and also in sachet packs. And they were all fighting for the health beverages market category and over the years most of these brands disappeared. Today most of them have either already resurfaced or preparing plan to reappear in the market in their new Avatar by giving it a new look by changing the formulation, flavour, label and most importantly the packaging.

Food Business Designed Around one Fruit Variety – Seabuckthorn

The name sounds unfamiliar. No one has seen this fruit variety in Indian market. But this is a type of berry that grows in plenty in Ladakh as wild fruit. Locals consume it but rest is all waste. No one will also think of setting up processing plant based on an unknown variety of fruits and that too in Ladakh. The complexity of logistics management and cost will dissuade many from the basic thought of having any commercial venture based on this fruit. But those issues did not deter Mr. B.K.Mittal to go ahead to set up new food venture in Ladakh based on this fruit. Mr. Mittal is in the business of supplying prefabricated shelters to the army in Ladakh. It was a chance meeting for him with one officer in charge of Defence Research and Development Organisation (DRDO) in Ladakh who told him about the availability of this wonder fruit with very high nutritional values and also about the process developed by DRDO for its preservation and prospect of many product development opportunities. Mr Mittal got hooked to this idea and became the only official licensee for the technology in India. Ladakh Foods Ltd was thus born and its first product was a ready-to-serve juice. Seabuckthorn was subsequently introduced as Leh Berry juice in the market in aseptic pack. The product has now been rolled out all over the country.

Seabuckthorn is not a easy product to handle. The bushes grow wild in Ladakh over an area of 0.16 million hectres. The fruit has very short harvesting season which means that the product needs to be preserved as pulp for use through out the year. Although this fruit is unknown to us but it is not so to the rest of the world. The botanical name of the plant is hippophae rhamnoides which means that the tree that makes horses shining. The name comes from the observation made by the Greeks that horses that fed on these berries became noticeably more healthy. Seabuckthorn has thus had a reputation as a health giver since then. The Chinese are well aware of its value and there are as many as seventeen hundred companies in China involved in the business of selling this product as per the report. Ladakh Foods Ltd is thus the only counterpart in India. A business venture has become reality from nowhere.

DRDO's field research laboratory at Leh first became aware of the potential in the berries borne by the scrubby bushes and started working on it for developing the preservation and processing standards which was subsequently licensed to Ladakh Foods. Possibly for the reason that seabuckthorn, the name itself is unfamiliar the company has introduced the product as Leh Berry. Whether this decision is right or wrong is a different matter. But I thought that retaining the name of seabuckthorn in the product label design would have been a better idea as Leh Berry could be considered like as any other berry and hence the question – what is unique about it? This question would have been answered by the exotic name of the fruit. Big and funny sounding names also works well in the market place. Otherwise, how can Heineken beer will become so popular and like that there are many successful products.

Fig. 7.2 Food business designed around one fruit variety

Leh Berry seems to be claiming wonders to happen to those who will consume the product. It is bight yellow to orange in colour with slight spicy taste containing overdoses of vitamins, nutrients and anti oxidants. The product is said to have properties of reducing cholesterol and blood pressure, increasing resistance against coronary diseases and cancer and even helping HIV positive patients, delay the onset of the disease. Reports say that people in Delhi and Mumbai are mixing it with vodka to make a cocktail drink.

Ladakh Foods is currently working with the district forestry officials to begin the organized cultivation of the fruits in the region. This itself is an indication that the product is seen to have longer term prospects by the promoter. Although the visibility of the product is not that great but it appears to be picking up slowly. It seems that in Delhi and in part of Maharastra the product has found the acceptance. Initially I was wondering that how a small time fabricator could invest so much money to set up the aseptic filling line in a place like Leh based on a single fruit without any assurance of success and that too in a product category where there were many failures. But I came to know that Ladakh Foods only makes the pulp and the drink and the beverage is made by the Godrej Foods and who also distributes them. That makes ample sense as the product will be able to see its natural potential in Godrej's hand.

The company has now plans to launch a range of other seabuckthorn based products. They have now said to have launched a sauce and a jam made from seabuckthorn juice. The company also has plans to extract oil from seabuckthorn seeds to be used in cosmetic formulation. Incidentally, Godrej has the significant presence in cosmetic as well and therefore, will be the right partner for the Ladakh Foods in the game who can confine themselves making the pulp from fruit and oil from the seed for the Godrej to do the rest.

A new business is thus born from a single unknown fruit based on the technical initiatives of DRDO, entrepreneurial venture of Mr. B.K. Mittal and support of a big house like Godrej. That is how a good concept gets translated into potentially big business. Whether seabuckthorn will eventually become a big business or not only future will tell us but the basic direction of the venture is right. A new food business is thus born.

New Health Beverages Launched

In summer months food marketers try to launch new beverages, drinks and health foods to test the market acceptance of many product types and variants. Come summer and we have witnessed every year a few new launches. Most of them fail but a few succeed and that is the part of the game. There is this relentless effort from the brand marketers to create yet another success story. The failures do not dampen the spirit of the entrepreneurs. They know that one success will make good for ten failures. The development efforts on the part of the industry thus continues.

There were times when selling yoghurt was difficult. Jagatjit introduced fruit yoghurt during mid eighties and it failed. Today there are many brands of fruit yoghurt – both in set and stirred form – in the market. Mother Dairy, Amul, Nestle – all are in the fray. In addition, there are many local and regional brands. Corporations have even gone ahead with the launch of packaged flavoured butter milk and yoghurt drinks. Amul has launched recently their Masti Spiced Butter Milk which has been positioned as a health drink. The expected volume is about five million packets. The product has been introduced first in Vaishnu Devi in Jammu and in Silchar, a small town in Assam. Normally new launches take place in places which are likely to try out new products and in that consideration places like Chandigarh, Pune, Hyderabad, Bangalore are preferred options for the reason that these cities are cosmopolitan and modern in nature. Besides, focused media without much of wastage and spillage are available in these towns. These days marketers are trying different options. Only justification for launching in Vaishnu Devi could be that in there are constant stream of visitors from all over for darshan at the shrine which will give an opportunity to try out the product by people from all states at least marketing cost. The argument in favour of Silchar is that this is a milk deficient area and therefore any milk product is likely to succeed. Andhra Pradesh Cooperative Dairy launched flavoured milk.

This year Vijaya brand is extended to lassi and butter milk. Bangalore based Sun Valley now extended Masti Cool brand of flavoured milk to flavoured yoghurt. Yet another company in Bangalore, Balan Natural Foods launched yoghurt based flavoured drinks Miran Yo in many southern states. Masti Cool butter milk introduced by SunValley in Bangalore is extending the market beyond the southern and western states. In the north Amrit Banaspati is said to be launching yoghurt based fruit drinks under the same name Gagan under which they sell their flavoured milk in Delhi and in northern region. So many new launches on fermented milk food category are there to fight for a market which is estimated to be only about INR 300 million – an insignificant size in comparison to milk and milk products market which is pegged at INR 36 billion. The marketers therefore, are expecting significant growth of the market to justify the launch of these products.

The consumer behaviour is dramatically changing. Earlier these products were the domain of road side sweetmeat shops and dairies. The marketer have now upgraded these products by branding them and placing as more convenient, hygienic and reliable products for which consumers are willing to pay more. Tetra Pak first came into the Indian market in early eighties. The investment in the project (aseptic line) was so high that it was found to be difficult to market if the volume does not justify. These days every other product is packed in tetra pak including UHT milk as we find abroad which offers an additional advantage that products will not have any preservative and will

Fig. 7.3 New health beverages launched in the market

have a relatively longer shelf life. And therefore, food products in tetra pak can be positioned as natural health products.

Earlier the fruit juices market was growing very slowly. For decades the growth rate was about 10% or below. Now this market is growing at a rate of about 30% in volume terms and there are number of brands in the market including Real Juice of Dabur, Tropicana of Pepsi and Frooti of Parle Agro. No body thought that vegetable juice in tetra pak will be able to find a market. Few players including Godrej tried and now it has been said that this segment is also growing at 29% in volume terms. The health consciousness has increased significantly among the urban population offering new opportunities. The same group of customer segments is also the convenient seekers and therefore is willing a pay price for it.

We say that the products launched well ahead of their time do not succeed. Nestle tried their Paloma iced tea during eighties. It did not work. Now it is doing well. They sell iced tea through the dispensers as well. Lipton iced tea brand is going to be introduced in returnable glass bottles. Lipton is claiming that this is the first time in India. However, this is not the first time. We did it in 1983 to be exact. The returnable glass bottle requires different kind of distribution system which HLL do not have. HLL has worked out a strategic alliance with Pepsi to distribute this product. Lipton was present in iced tea market through tetra pak route for some time. In fact one liter iced tea in tetra pak in peach and lemon flavours was being retailed at INR 49. It did not get much volume and therefore HLL is now trying a different route. For this purpose HLL has to use the bottling and distribution facilities of Pepsi bottlers.

My own prediction is that it will fail again. The reason being that in the traditional soft drinks outlets we don't see the kind of customers who would have preferred this product. Recently the product has been launched in Bangalore city at INR 9 for 250 ml bottles. They now plan to extend it to 17 more cities across India. Why Pepsi has to rope in HLL to launch a product of this nature when they are capable of launching an iced tea themselves. The only reason could be that Lipton is already a lead player in tea, but that cannot be a great advantage for carbonated iced tea category. The greater advantage to Pepsi would be that at no extra cost they will be able to experiment with yet another product.

Because entire marketing expenditure will be on HLLs account. JWT has already been engaged to plan and work for this high profile new launch. In terms of Unilevers global strategy HLL is pursuing the food business very vigorously in order to become a dominant player in the category. HLL, as we know never succeeded in creating a new brand, particularly in food segment.

The entire food business has been built through acquisition route. Let us see what happens this time.

There are many other types of food and beverages invaded the market in the recent times. All are trying to find a place for themselves. There are many new players who have come up in the last three to four years time. There are oldies languishing not able to cope up with the new rules of the game. Innovation and competitiveness are the key success factors (KSFs) which requires new management style and skills. In highly competitive environment delivering KSFs better than competition will only ensure success.

MNCs Jumping into the Fray: Big Opportunity in the Bottled Water Business

Only a decade ago there was only one national brand in the mineral water industry and that was 'Bisleri'. We used to sell Bisleri in mid seventies and the volume was only about a 0.1 million cases, each case containing twelve PVC bottles of one litre each. There was hardly any retail selling and the volume used to come from only institutional segment such as hotels. No marketing executive wanted to be associated with Bisleri mineral water as that was a very small brand. There was only one small plant in Mumbai to take care of the national market requirement and that too used to run only once or twice a week. The scenario has drastically changed today.

After selling the mainline soft drink business including Thums-Up, Limca, Goldspot brand to Coke, Mr Ramesh Chauhan was left with only Bisleri mineral water and his brother Mr Prakash Chauhan with 'Frooti' beverages in aseptic pack. On one evening I got a call from Mr Ramesh Chauhan under whom I worked during my formative years in industry and whom I always consider a person who is extremely bright and knows almost everything of business that he does. Rameshbhai - as we normally call him - asked me to meet him in his home in South Delhi.

When I met him, he sought my help to improve the clarity and impact strength of PVC bottles by incorporating appropriate change in the master batch formulation used to make bottles through blow moulding process. PVC has two limitations in the sense that it is not biodegradable and hence not environment friendly and it has poor impact strength, besides being low in terms of bottle clarity. I did this job for him.Rameshbhai, at that point of time was having big ambition about mineral water business. He had drawn up plans to open up franchise bottling plants in major cities in India. He had also by then taken over direct control of major Bisleri water bottling plant in Mumbai, Delhi and Calcutta. He told me that his Bisleri will become a INR 2 billion brand in three years time. I thought Rameshbhai is dreaming. But no, today Bisleri mineral water is not only rightfully the No.1 mineral water brand in the country holding about 50 per cent market share in the organised bottle water market which has been estimated to be about INR 5 billion. This means Bisleri is already a INR 2.5 billion business. His brother, Prakashbhai also had introduced another brand of mineral water "Bailey" in competition with Bisleri. Bailey has notched up about 20 per cent market share which means between Bisleri and Bailey together they enjoy about 70 percent of the market in the organised sector. In the subsequent year of course, this scenario has changed.

The total mineral water market size now has been estimated to be about INR 11 billion and growing at a mind boggling rate of 60 percent per annum. There are about 200 brands in the market. In every railway station, we can find a local brand. And some of those brands are manufactured in garage or in the backyard using minimal or no facility. For obvious reasons, some of them will have doubtful quality. Besides, the empties of popular brand like Bisleri are refilled by unscrupulous people with ordinary tap water which may or may not be even potable and sold again in the market. This was possible for two reasons - one, of course, is our inadequate infrastructure to enforce food laws but in this case most strikingly the fact of the matter is that there is no standard laid down for mineral water.

Of late, of course, Health Ministry has issued guidelines for mineral water to be complied with effect from March 29, 2001. However, Bureau of Indian Standards (BIS) has specification for mineral water, but that is an optional standard. While I cannot comment on the new standards and regulatory guidelines being issued by the Ministry of Health, Govt. of India, on mineral water, but the requirement is not only for the mineral water, we need two separate standards for mineral water and natural spring water to distinguish between the two. The standards also need to be stringent enough similar in line as described by FDA covering chemical, bacteriological and bottling conditions including the labelling and licensing requirement. Only recently a standard for bottled drinking water has been prescribed.

Seeing that Bisleri is widely sold as spurious product, Bisleri changed the capping mechanism using ripped-open tear-off caps which cannot be easily copied by small timers and launched TV compaign to warn customers about duplicates in the market. Bisleri also introduced five litre economy pack in the market to be sold as family pack.

Although the market is dominated by two major brands, Bisleri and Bailey having combined market share of 70% in the organised sector but seeing the unprecedented growth rate in this market all leading multinationals are entering the fray. Coca-Cola and Pepsi have already introduced their brand Kinley and Aquafina respectively. Other leading Indian players include "Yes" brand of Kothari Beverages, "Ganga" from T-Series, "Aquapure" from Godrej, "Himalaya" from Mount Everest mineral water and so on.

Bottled water are of two types - the largest and popular segment where most of the brands belong including Bisleri is the treated water containing select minerals, sterilised usually by passing either through Silver Candles or by exposing under UV rays before bottling. The other type, which is in the premium segment is Natural Spring Water bottled after purification and sterilisation including ozonation. This is much costlier and the market is still very limited and will take some more time to evolve. The only Indian brand in this category is "Catch" - natural spring water from DS Group. They have set up a completely imported and modern plant at a cost of INR 120 million in Kullu and the product has been placed in the market at a price of INR 25 per litre as against the popular brands available at INR 10 to 12 per litre. Although Bisleri was originally in PVC bottle but now all the brands of bottled water are in PET bottles including Bisleri. In the premium water segment "Catch" has to compete with foreign brands. Nestle India recently launched its second premium mineral water brand "San Pellegrino" in India. This comes close on the heels of the launch of its premier brand "Perrier", in Delhi and Mumbai. The food major also plans to launch its bottled water brand "Nestle Pure Life"- targetted at mass market. Priced at INR 62 for a 500 ml bottle and INR 82 for a one litre bottle, San Pellegrino is being imported from Italy. Both Pellegrino and Perrier are sparkling water containing dissolved carbon dioxide. These brands are normally preferred as mixer with hard liquors. It has also been reported that Britannia will shortly introduce Danone's Evian brand of mineral water in the market.

Fig. 7.4 Pepsi brand Aquafina for bottled water.

Fig 7.5 Leading local brand Bisleri for bottled water.

To cash in on the opportunity, Bisleri is in talks with international bottled water majors - Nestle and Danone, to set up a joint venture for mineral water in the country. Danone is the second largest bottled water company in the world owns Evian and Volvic mineral water brands whereas Nestle has Perrier and Vitel brands. I was associated with the launch of McDowell's sparkling soda during late seventies and the product was doing well till early part of 80's. After that the company had withdrawn the support but the product was still available for many years in certain market by recycling the empties. Recently McDowell has launched its "Pure & Clear" brand of mineral water and is said to be re-launching McDowell's sparkling soda. With the liquor trade in their control they stand to gain from their launch of mineral water - Pure & Clear.

In the bottled water business with a MRP tag of INR 10 for one litre PET bottle, there is not enough margin for the manufacturers and marketers after providing for about 10 per cent for the distributor and between 30 to 40 percent for the retailers. It is in fact, the retailers who make the maximum in this trade. Bottled water also incurs high freight cost and hence cannot be distributed to a large area from one manufacturing location. The multiple manufacturing location through franchising route and very effective and wide distribution network are therefore the name of the game. In this game thus the premium segment players in natural spring water will have limitations because one cannot have the source of natural spring water in all locations.

The primary requirement of the consumer is safe drinking water. The price and distribution will therefore largely influence the buyers behaviour. In this game, soft drink majors will have an advantage in the sense that they have facilities to bottle product in multi locations spread all over the country and also have extensive distribution network. The fight therefore would be between Bisleri and Coke and Pepsi brand and we have to see who wins. Bisleri has definitely a first mover advantage. Nestle, Britannia and Catch have a long way to go in that direction and their distribution infrastructure are no match to the leading soft drink players. Besides, they will have to operate from one manufacturing location as long as they chose to remain in premium segment - the market that is still in its nascent stage.

One thing for sure is that bottled water market is going to witness an unprecedented level of intense marketing activity in coming years. It does not matter if we have many villages which don't have even drinking water or in villages in Rajasthan and Gujarat, women folk have to walk miles to fetch their daily drinking water - but bottled water will definitely be available - which all these large MNCs and domestic players will ensure.

8

Bakery, Biscuits and Breakfast Cereals

Bakery Industry in India - A Category Review

India is the second largest producer of wheat in the world. As per the figures of Agriculture Ministry, Govt of India, in 2003-04 India produced about 72 million tonnes of wheat which is 12 per cent of the world production. Most of the wheat produced in the country is suitable for production of bread and bakery products which is soft to medium hard with medium protein content. The major wheat producing states are Punjab, Haryana, Uttar Pradesh and Rajasthan. Durhum or hard wheat with high protein content and high gluten content is typically grown in central and western India. The quantity of Durhum wheat is small and is estimated to be about 2.5 million tones. Although acreage under wheat cultivation is steadily increasing , the productivity has been more or less stagnating at around 2.4 to 2.7 tonnes per hectre. In 2003-04, 72 million tonnes of wheat was produced from 26.62 million hectres of the farm land giving an yield of 2.7 tonnes per hectre. In India there are about 900 roller flour mills milling about 12.5 million tonnes of wheat utilizing less than 50 per cent of their installed capacity. As per the Ministry of food processing industry estimate there are about 400000 chakkis milling 42.5 million tones of wheat. The chakki milled wheat flour normally goes for direct household consumption and the atta (wheat flour) and maida produced in organized roller flour mills normally supply to the industry. Roller flour mill also produces other products including semolina (suji) and other bye products. With low capacity utilization the roller flour mills are not really doing well. Government through Public Distribution Scheme (PDS) distributes and sells wheat all over and Food Corporation of India (FCI) provides the major storage and infrastructure facilities for this purpose. FCI storage system is age old and inadequate and many studies indicated that there is a significant loss and pilferage takes place from FCI run storage godowns. The selling price of wheat by Govt. through PDS is quite low to cover Above Poverty Line (APL), Below Poverty Line (BPL) and Poorest –of- the-Poor(POP) consumers. These prices are now fixed at INR 6100 per tonnes for APL, INR 4150 for BPL and INR 2000 per tonne for the POP consumers. Needless to say that significant quantity of the wheat grains distributed through PDS comes back to chakkis and roller flour mills through parallel market linkages established traditionally by the middlemen. The reason being the market price is much higher. Even the cost of procurement of wheat including the holding cost reported to be around INR 9250 per tonne. It is clear therefore, that large part of the subsidy is wasted through this parallel channel as well as through the wastage and inefficiency of the system arising out of sub-optimal post harvest handling and storage.

Bakery Products

According to the industry estimates the market size of bread , biscuit and other wheat based products are as given in Table 8.1 below:

Table 8.1 : Market size for various sub-segment

	Value (INR billion)	Volume (million tonnes)
Bread	38.9	3.75
Biscuits	68.6	1.95
Grain Based Snacks	29.0	0.29
Branded Atta	13.5	0.90
Pasta Products	8.4	0.14
Total	158.4	7.03

According to the estimates, over 65 per cent of the total wheat produced in the country is utilized for atta production which in turn consumed for the preparation of chapatis.

Region-wise consumption of branded atta is said to be as given in Table 8.2 below:

Table 8.2 : Region-wise consumption of branded atta

Region	Percentage consumption
North	47
East	13
West	21
South	19

Bread

The total bread production in the country is estimated to be 3.75 million tones annually growing at a rate of about 6 per cent although the organized sector is said to be growing a little higher rate of 8 per cent. In 1977 government had reserved bread industry for the small scale. However, Britannia Industries Ltd (BIL) in private sector as well as Modern Food Industries Ltd, a Public Sector Undertaking were permitted to produce bread as per the installed capacity existed at that point of time. In addition to these two large players there were about 25 medium –scale and 1800 small scale manufacturers which together accounted for 45 per cent of the total production of bread in the country. In the unorganized sector it is said that there about 75000 bread manufacturers spread all over including some of those operating from even residential premises. South India consumes 32 percent of the total bread produced in the country followed by north which consumes about 27 per cent, west 23 per cent and east 18 per cent.

Increasingly, bread is finding popularity as item consumed in breakfast in place of traditional chapptis. Bread production has thus been on the rise. The manufacturers also introduced many bread variants. Health conscious people now also consume brown bread instead of white bread. Brown bread is all most 10 per cent of the total bread market. Milk bread is about 85 per cent, brown 10 per cent, fruit bread 3 per cent and balance 2 per cent is other specialty bread as per industry estimate. Earlier we had only whole bread but during last decade mostly sliced bread is being sold. One gets whole bread only in small towns produced in traditional ovens. The bakeries in India normally produce bread as well as cookies for the local market. The technology absorption in Indian bakeries therefore is still at various level. Some of the hotels in India produce excellent quality bread and other bakery products. The bread industry is increasingly dominated by the regional players . Many local and regional players have been able to create success stories and therefore dominance of big players like Britannia is gradually reducing. In fact Britannia wanted to get out of the bread segment because it is not very profitable. In Delhi we can see that Harvest Gold brand is quite popular and they are more visible than other brands.

Biscuit

The size of the biscuit industry is estimated to be about 1.95 million tones valued at INR 68.6 billion of which organized sector produces about 57 per cent of branded biscuits in volume terms and 64 per cent in value terms. In biscuit category we have two very large players Parle and Britannia. Besides, there are about 50 medium players and about 2500 small scale units. In the unorganized sectors we have over 30000 small, very small and tiny units spread all over the country. Our bakery industry thus quite big in that sense. Biscuit industry was also reserved for small scale earlier. It was de-reserved in 1997-98. Since then the industry is growing at a rate of over 10 per cent. Post de-reservation many local and regional players have started producing for Parles or Britannia as franchised units. These two large players also shifted the production to identified small biscuit units to reduce the cost. Britannia in due course of time closed down their Mumbai unit and has created a new unit in Uttaranchal to benefit from tax concession and low cost of labour. Britannia also acquired Kwality Biscuit couple of years ago.

Glucose and Marie are two varieties of biscuits represent the largest segments. As per the industry estimate, Table 8.3 below gives the contribution of various biscuit segments:

Table 8.3 : Various product segments in biscuits

Product segment	Percent
Glucose	44
Marie	13
Cream	10
Cracker	13
Milk	12
Others	8

Glucose biscuit which is the bulk of the biscuit production really delivers the volume and therefore takes care of large part of fixed overheads. Glucose biscuit is actually low margin biscuits. Businesses therefore constantly trying to create new brand of specialty biscuits which give them higher margin of profit. Some of the better known and successful brands in the market are thus Krack Jack, Good –day, Pure Magic, Little Hearts.

Per capita consumption of biscuit in India is only 1.9 kg , compared to about 10 kgs in USA and west European countries and 4.2 kgs in South East Asian countries.The reason of glucose biscuit sells the maximum is due to the fact that it is the low price mass consumption biscuit. This industry can grow at healthy rate if the price is brought down. It has been observed that whenever the excise duty is reduced the category was growing at much higher rate. But the reality is that the industry suffers from multiple tax levied on the category. The gross realization after taking care of the basic input cost and taxes and trade margins as prevailing will not be more than 25 %.The profitability of this category is thus low. The major marketing initiatives taken on the category has been by two lead players Parle and Britannia.

MNCs like Smith Kline Beechem (SKB) tried to create biscuit brand under Horlicks. Although this brand of biscuit still exists but the volume is low. They still produce the product through subcontract unit and promotion of the brand is a low key affair. Sara Lee entered this category and incurred huge loss for three years and exited from the category all together. Even Kellog introduced a few specialty biscuits in the market and made considerable efforts to market those brands unsuccessfully. Some of the local industries are really giving a strong fight to big players like Britannia and Parle taking advantage of low cost of production. There are therefore instances of regional success stories like Priya Biscuits, Bakeman etc.

Cake and Pastries

Although big players like Britannia produces cake but in this category most of the players are in small and medium segment. This category is small and numerous local producers have created success stories. The name that has created a name is Monginis. They have their own retail stores in all metro cities. In addition, there are many other local cake and pastry shops created good business proposition locally.

There are many bakery ingredients manufacturers are now selling even ready mixes to small bakers to help them producing good bread. These companies are also helping the small bakeries to improve the technology. In India we get bakery equipments and machineries supplying to small and medium size plants.

The industry is not very attractive and growth depend on price. Margin is low and large players finding it difficult to establish new brand. The only other large player entered this category is ITC. Their brand Sun Feast Marie Light is a success. But ITC has been spending a lot to create yet another brand which others cannot repeat.

Traditional Breakfast Habits Fast Changing

The breakfast eating habits are always traditional among Indians. In north it is roti (chapati), sabji (vegetables), achhar (pickles) and dahi (curd). In south it is idli (rice cake), dosa, uttapam and sambhar, chutni. In west and east also they have their own traditional styles and on the top of its sub-regional variations are in vogue. The breakfast food industry did not therefore change much to say the least. The younger generation in upper middle class and office going executives did favour toast with butter or jam and an egg preparation (either omelette, poach, fried egg or boiled egg) and a glass of milk which has fuelled the growth of bread industry pioneered by Modern Bread and Britannia on a national scale and a host of regional and local brands of breads.

This industry was reserved for small-scale sectors and in certain regions it is even price controlled. As a result, bread industry was never very profitable for large corporations. Some of the old and large players like Spencers have resorted to franchising. In some areas local brands were even preferred over large Pan India players. In Calcutta bread industry was very developed and many local brands became successful. Some of those brands are still existing - others disappeared. For example, once we had "FIRPOO" bread and Seth's (Sether roti) brand which were quite popular but I don't see those now. Some of the Calcutta hotels bake their bread, which are also popular. Great Eastern Hotel in Calcutta which is now owned by West Bengal government has their own bakery which supplies bread and other bakery products to local market. There was a time when bakery industry was quite developed in Calcutta. High quality cake, pastries, bread and speciality biscuits and cookies were available from couple of well known but not so large bakeries. Flurry's, for example, is still flourishing in Calcutta. But the industry has fast declined. In GK-I in Delhi one such shop is trying to do brisk business exploiting Calcutta's past glory on bakery technology.

For many years bread remained as one of the essentials in our daily breakfast menu. It started with a loaf baked in a traditional oven but later on bread from mechanised electrical oven, sliced bread, milk bread, masala bread etc. also were introduced.

Corn flakes appeared in Indian market in sixties. Hindustan Vegetable Products, a Govt. of India undertaking having their factory located at Najafgarh in Delhi and Mohan Meakins at their factory at Ghaziabad, first introduced cornflakes in Indian market. Hindustan Vegetables Products also used to sell Oats flakes and possibly still markets the same on a limited scale. While cornflakes were packed in polybags, oats were sold in printed tin container. Mohan's brand was "Champion" and was quite popular because that was the only nationally distributed brand of cornflakes. In late sixties one more brand from Calcutta was introduced. Calcutta flour mill-a unit of Shaw Wallace then and was managed by Shaw Wallace-Director Mr. Shantanu Chaudhuri, son of Mr Sachin Chaudhuri , former Finance Minister of India of Gold Control Act fame introduced his brand "Bingo" with a big bang. The technical support for the product development was provided for by Prof. Sunit Mukherjee of Jadavpur University. We were students then and were extremely delighted to see that Prof. Mukherjee was creating job opportunities. That hope was shortlived. "Bingo" failed in the market place although as a product and also in packaging it was a superior product than Mohan's "Champion" and therefore priced at a premium. Possibly distribution and pricing were major reasons of its failure.

In those days cornflakes was manufactured using traditional technology of gritting, cooking, flaking and drying. Of course, "Champion" is still manufactured using the same technology and still selling almost the same quantity as before of approximately 500 MT per annum purely on price front. By then, however, Cornflakes technology has changed and much superior quality flakes were produced by using extrusion technology. "Kellogg" in fact introduced cornflakes in Indian market using extrusion technology and that too in a lot of variants. Their products are priced much higher and with lot of marketing efforts the Cornflakes market, which was, stagnating at around 500-600 MT has grown in last few years to the tune of 4000 MT.

Fruit Juice drinking habits at breakfast in India is almost nonexistent. Some affluent families might be consuming freshly crushed fruit juice and that to mainly orange in season at breakfast. Last couple of years there are sustained efforts by couple of big houses including Dabur (manufacturer of "Real Juice") and "Tropicana" from Pepsi and to a certain extent by "Onjus" from Enkay Texofood to bring fresh juices at breakfast tables. Health and nutrition conscious households in upper income bracket now have added processed and preserved juices in their breakfast menu. This has fuelled the growth of the sterilised natural juices in paper cartoon and stand-up pouches.

Some years ago when cinestar Wahida Rehman returned from Canada with her young children to settle in Bangalore she realised that her children will be missing their favourite breakfast-Muesli. And then she decided to manufacture Muesli herself in Bangalore. Her product now sells in all premium food stores in metro cities.

Quacker Oats of USA have opration in India and introduced good quality oats meal for breakfast. With the exposure of media, children particularly in large and smaller cities are showing a distinct preference for western style breakfast and indulging parents, at least those who can afford are buying those for their children. Although at present very few households take meat preparations like sausage or frankfurters during breakfast in India alongwith eggs and toasts but that too will gradually be seen being encouraged.

Breakfast Cereal Industry Still Struggling to Make it Big

Indians like to have their traditional breakfast. And the taste varies along the regions. North Indians like puri bhaji, dahi, parota. While south Indians would like to have their favourite idli, dosa and sambhar and the like. East Indians don't have the established system of having breakfast. They have their morning cup of tea with biscuits or even with puffed rice and then take a full meal with rice before going to office. At least this is the trend amongst the middle class Bengalis. Marketers have tried to introduce many options but till date only bread has entered all kinds of households.Accordingly, bakery industry has flourished and most of those bakeries are small and cater to the local demand. The breakfast eating habits again has variations in each region where various religious groups have their own choices.

Fig. 8.1 A traditional south Indian breakfast : Idli, Vada, Sambhar.

For example, the breakfast in a marwari household will not be same as that preferred by Punjabi's. With such wide variations in breakfast habits the task before the marketer to make a big brand is always challenging. If someone likes it, all varieties of breakfast cereals are available in the market. Both local brands as well as imported international brands one can easily find in all reputed food stores. And these will include muesli, oats, porridge and of course corn flakes. In breakfast items other cereal products that are always there are bread and bakery items but they are all local and never a big national brand. Kellogg has been trying to make it big. But they realized that it is a long drawn battle for them. And the task is not easy. All these options for breakfast cereals were existing earlier as well but their quality was not as good. Mohan Meakin's Champion corn flakes is produced through the traditional technology of making corn grits, steaming it to make it soft and then pressing it and finally drying and packing. Extrusion technology helped improve the product quality tremendously and then it also opened up several new product innovation opportunities which has been captured by Kellogg. The volume of porridge, oats and muesli are so low that the big group has never attempted these products to manufacture and market. The only prospect that seems to be emerging is for corn flakes. Several local companies have attempted it and failed. But Kellogg seem to be determined to make it big and their struggle seems to be on going.

Kellogg is in India for about 10 years now and it is still not making profit. No Indian venture can pursue a business for such a long time with prospect of hope that some day it will become big anyway. It is only Kellogg that can take such a long term view of the business because it is their only business and it has to work for them come what may. Industry observers feel that it is too long and Kellogg might be fighting a losing battle. But Carlos Gutierrez, the global CEO of Kellogg does not feel so. When confronted with the question that Kellogg brand may not be relevant in India because of traditional breakfast eating habit of Indians, Mr Carlos pointed out that in Mexico the company operated for 20 long years before turning profit there and the company has the similar agenda for India as well. They have a commitment and focus and more importantly they have faith in what they are doing.

Carlos even said that he did not expect that Indian business will make any profit next two years but the next ten years this business will contribute to their earning per share in the global context. The fight is now to increase volume and achieve operational efficiency. The per capita consumption is so low that the task seems to be uphill for the local management. Kellogg also ventured into the chocolate biscuits. Although the product is still available, the biscuit venture seems to be very low key operation as they must have already realized that biscuit is still a difficult business. Of late, Kellogg has withdrawn from the biscuit segment now. Some observers believe that Kellogg has entered Indian market too early. But I don't think so. Even if they had entered now, ten years later the odds against them would have still remained same. By entering ten years earlier, at least they have taken early move and will therefore be able to keep other break fast global majors at bay. Other players will definitely get discouraged seeing the Kellogg's experience. If they succeed, which they will have to, they will reap harvest for the long time to come.

Kellog is present in 150 towns in India but they focus on 26 towns and of these 6 metros are their thrust areas. The product is distributed through 200 distributors. In ten years time breakfast cereals has achieved the highest penetration of up to 90 % in the processed food market in the organized retail environment which can be considered as their achievement so far. Realizing that the character of children is same world over, Kellogg is focusing on the children and it is said that they could directly reach about 300,000 children in the country and these children will drive the volume for the future. The break fast cereal as it looks like would be next generation product and Kellogg will be the major player in that segment.

In the breakfast cereal segment there are store label brands, particularly in the other variants of the category. But the growth rate is not that drastic and volume is not big for too many store label brands to find their own place in the market. Kellogg was, therefore, able to keep their dominance and perform better. In earlier years Kellogg reduced the advertisement expenditure but globally again they started spending to build the brand which is essential to justify the high price that they charge for their cereals. The high price of their products is also one of the reasons for the slow growth of the category. The metros and other major towns have to drive the volume. But Kellogg is not worried. They will eventually come out winner. At least that is what that they think and firmly believe in. Rest is history.

Indian Bakery Industry is Still a Mix of Traditional and Modern

Believe it or not, the reality is that there are an estimated 2 million bakeries across the country engaged in the production of bread, biscuits and other types of bakery products. In 1977-78 this category was brought under reserved for small scale and therefore for over two decades this industry has seen the proliferation of only small and unorganized players. The government implemented Abid Hussain Committee recommendation by de-reserving the category and by opening it up to large players in 1996-97. The major constraints this industry was facing was the availability of quality raw material at acceptable price – mainly wheat flour which was till recently canalized through State Trading Corporation (STC). Only recently the food grains sales and movement has been made open. One route open to the large players was to get the product manufactured through small scale and market it in their own name and that was exactly being followed by large players like Britannia. Spencer was earlier a large bread manufacturer. It was quite popular. In subsequent years Spencer adopted franchising route to keep their brand alive. Till today there are franchised bakeries of Spencer operating in the eastern and southern part of the country although their numbers are very few now. In subsequent years due to changes brought in excise duty regulation made these kind of operation unattractive. In case of bread even the price was fixed by the government in certain places like say Delhi making it unprofitable to operate.

During last two decades Britannia was consistently losing the market share on bread to their rival Modern Foods (then a Government of India Undertaking) as they had an unfair advantage of getting wheat at a subsidized rate from the government. That situation has now been corrected. Although it is a late realization on the part of the government that small scale has limitation to make the industry grow and therefore, they need the support of the large scale players for their survival. This industry is age old and thus awareness level is close to 100%. Penetration level is also very high, estimated to be close to 60%. Bread and cookies manufactured by unorganized sectors using traditional techniques are in fact popular snacks and food supplement for the lower and lower- middle income group people. The small scale players are therefore co-existing alongside the large players.

As per the estimate of the Food Processing Ministry (1998) the bread and biscuit market is said to be of 1.5 million tons (INR 21 billion) and 1.1 million tons (INR 60 billion) respectively whereas cake market has been estimated as 0.4 million ton. Over 80% of the bread is produced by small and unorganized sector and their contribution in the biscuit production is about 65%. While bread market is growing at a rate of 7% in volume terms, the biscuit market is growing at a rate of about 8 -10%. The growth rate of specialty biscuit is much higher at around 20% but the popular variety is growing only at 6-7% per annum. After Britannia introduced Tiger brand, glucose biscuit category is said to be growing at a relatively higher rate. Britannia since then is increasingly focusing on the premium segment to improve upon the margin of the business. The bulk of the volume of biscuit comes from glucose and Marie (Jacob Thin) kind of biscuits but they are high cost low margin products. You need them in your basket of portfolio for volume business which takes care of a large part of your plant capacity and also the fixed cost.

In bakery industry there is also a dominance of the regional players – they are big in their own right in the geographical areas they have chosen to cover. We therefore see many successful regional players – Ampro, Kwality in biscuit category and Harvest Gold and Wibs in bread category are some of those established brands to reckon with. Those who made it big in biscuits such as Britannia and Parle are not a significant player in cake. In cake category there are traditional manufacturers who, over the time made significant improvement in their product quality and presentations, leading among them is Mongini of Kolkata. In cake, one can see many local players doing good business. They have managed to establish themselves in their own locality on sheer strength of quality and service.

This old city of Kolkata was once hub for many well known bakeries and brands, most of those have now either disappeared or in the process of extinction. Great Eastern bread and loaf produced by Great Eastern Hotel was very famous once upon a time. This hotel is now run by Government of West Bengal and they still produce bread but on a very low key basis. In good old days in Kolkata we had Kolay Biscuit Company and Lily Biscuit Company and they were quite strong in the local market. Both of them have disappeared. Lily also used to produce bread. I worked in this company for a short period after my graduation but realizing that the company has bleak future, returned back to academics again. Kolay and Lily disappeared but two new biscuit company surfaced in the later years. One was started by a group of people who left Britannia and it seems that their company -Bharat Biscuit Company Ltd is doing reasonably well.

The other one, SAJ Industries was started by Aparna Agency who had a significant holding in Calcutta Chemicals which was in later years acquired by Shaw Wallace and finally by Henkel. Aparna Agency is a leading food distributor in Kolkata having Nestle and other reputed agency lines. Aparna Agency therefore, knows the market well. This company although struggling but showing signs of definite recovery. Their biscuit brand is known as "BiskFarm" and already a range of biscuits under this brand name were launched nationally. There is another biscuit venture started by the son of the former chief minister of West Bengal Mr Jyoti Basu. The plant was located in Burdwan and was doing contract production for Britannia. This plant is reportedly now lying closed.

Fig. 8.2 Local and regional players in biscuit giving tough time to large national players.

Bakery is one such category of food industry where survival rate is quite high and therefore we can see that most of the small players are thriving, although may not be doing very well. Last year I visited a small bakery located in Bamuni Maidan Industrial area in Guwahati who wanted to sell their factory to the DS Group and with sales proceeds, retire happily thereafter. The deal did not get through as the title of the property was not clear.This year when I met the gentleman again, I asked him about his business. He still makes and sells two thousand bread a day and as expected, not happy. This observation is however, valid only for small enterprises. Large players were seen to be highly susceptible. We have seen that highly diversified 35 billion US dollar food giant Sara Lee who started their bakery venture with a big bang but decided to close down after three years of operation incurring over INR 70 million of loss over a sales turnover of INR 530 million in the third year. We also have another major failure in Excelsia Foods - a company owned by Nestle which had ventured into biscuits and cookies in a big way and now lying closed looking for buyers for the plant and equipment and facilities. But Nestle again is venturing into biscuits through subcontracting route and so is ITC. Over the years only two big names continuing to grow and they are Britannia and Parle. But more names are likely to appear in the market in near future. Whether they will succeed or not is a different matter. Dalmia Biscuits, Bakeman etc are in the process of winding up. They will be fortunate if they get a buyer.

In the post liberalisation era we are seeing another class of bakery industry. These are bakery ingredients and ready mix marketer. Pilsbury has their bakery mix which is quite popular. Similarly, New Delhi based Calpro Foods Pvt. Ltd in association with Meiser Marken Ulmer Spatz of Germany has introduced a range of concentrate and premixes for production of specialty bread and cake and rolls for Indian bakeries. This company is targeting the small bakers to produce the quality products by holding on the key recipe so that they still remain their customer base for long time to come. We also have now a few European basic bakery ingredient manufacturers operating in the country. They only have trading activity here. Incidentally, all bakery ingredients manufacturers and for that matter food ingredients manufacturers are concentrating in south and that too in Chennai region.

One leading bakery ingredients manufacturer – Burn Philips, an Australian company who had acquired India's Yeast Company, erstwhile a company owned by Shaw Wallace – is quite active in this field. But there are others also in this business. And lastly, we have all kinds of biscuits, breads, cookies and speciality bakery products which are imported and available in all leading retail stores in India, particularly in metro cities, for sales through appointed distribution route. They come from all over. You name any brand and it is there. The global competition has significantly improved our local brands. Both Britannia and Parle have improved upon their recipes from whatever they had earlier and one can see now that the product quality is significantly better. If these large numbers of small and unorganized players have to survive they will have to imbibe better technology, sooner the better. Basic performing criteria for the bakery industry are now favourable. Also consumers are willing to try anything new and good. Bakers now therefore, have a job to do. And definitely they will have to be good at that.

In Biscuit the Fight is Between two Age Old Rivals : Parle Vs Britannia

In Indian biscuit industry Parle and Britannia are two leading names and they are age old rivals. Parle, a local player has displayed significant capability to contain their MNC rival Britannia's growth. It is worth reviewing their ball game for all these years for market dominance. The total biscuit industry in India is estimated to be about INR 38 billion putting organized and unorganized sectors together. And the branded biscuit market has been valued at INR 27 billion.

In volume terms this amounts to 0.8 million MT or 54% of the total volume. Out of the total branded biscuit market Britannia has about 30% market share and Parle controls about 38% of the market. The market is said to be growing at a rate of only 6 to 7%. The per capita consumption of biscuits in India is only 1.3 kg per annum as against about 15 kg per annum in developed countries. The biscuit market is segmented as premium, mid segment and glucose. The premium segment biscuits are priced at INR 70 a kg and above, mid segment is priced at INR 40 to INR 70 per kg and glucose is at INR 40 per kg. While premium segment is growing at the rate of 7%, glucose is growing at 10% per annum. Mid segment is growing at the rate of 12% per annum. Parle has the distinction of becoming the largest single brand biscuit producer in the world with 65% market share in the organized segment of the glucose market. With an annual sales volume of 180 million kg, Parle-G is the world's largest single biscuit brand followed by Italy's Mulino Blanco with 110.3 million kg. They have been able to create many new categories. Parle has launched first time in the Indian market a sweet and salted biscuit under the brand name Krackjack.

Britannia's 50:50 was launched much later. In glucose segment Britannia first tried with Glucose-D and then with Tiger. The first one did not succeed but Tiger brand has done well. The glucose is the largest segment accounting for 35% of the over all market, estimated as INR 15 billion. Britannia in fact, is an older company originally incorporated as Britannia Biscuit Company Ltd in Calcutta in 1918. Subsequently, they moved to Mumbai during early seventies and finally shifted their head quarters to Bangalore. Currently, Britannia's controlling stake is jointly held by Groupe Danone and Nusli Wadia of Bombay Dyeing. About 83% of the company's business is biscuits. Bread constitutes only about 5% of their business and cake and rusk is about 2%.

Over the years biscuit market has moved from core glucose segment and Marie offerings to the more value added variants. Parle's focus is the consolidation of its popular biscuit business and to add more variants whereas

Britannia has been busy stretching its portfolio of brands with more premium brands like Pure Magic etc. Parle is concentrating on its traditional brands Parle-G, Monacco and Krackjack. Britannia as all of us can recollect had a stated mission to make every third Indian a Britannia customer. But this mission seems to have not been pursued vigorously as planned earlier. After Sunil Alagh's unceremonious departure Nusli Wadia seems to be in no hurry to induct a new CEO. Only recently they inducted Ms Vinita Bali as CEO but with her induction the company seems to facing the resignations of scores of senior executives.

Fig. 8.3 In bakery industry it is the fight between two giants Parle and Britannia.

Britannia was spending lot of money earlier in advertisement. During Cricket World Cup, Britannia reportedly spent INR 120 million on their campaign "Britannia Khao, World Cup Jao". Their presence in the media now is not that dominant. Parle has been very steady in terms of their marketing efforts focusing on their key brand Parle-G. In May 2003 this biscuit brand has crossed the landmark of 30000 MT and that is 80% of their total biscuit volume. This single brand thus is keeping the entire company going as it is a huge volume. Over the years both Britannia and Parle started outsourcing their product from contract manufacturing units spread all over. Parle have 5 company owned manufacturing units and 32 contract manufacturing units. This itself is a long journey for a company which had only one plant in the suburban of Mumbai. Britannia has done an acquisition by taking over Kwality Biscuits in Bangalore. However, Parle delivered entire growth organically. Britannia has a very stronghold in the eastern and northern market whereas

Parle is stronger in western and southern market. It is also quite strong in UP. For Parle, Maharastra, Gujarat and UP contribute to 65% of their national sales. To cater to the northern market Parle has located one of their contract units at Bahadurgarh. While Britannia is predominant in the urban market, Parle have a very strong rural presence. They have extensive rural coverage to the level 1000+ population villages in the states of Maharastra, Gujarat, UP, MP, Rajasthan, Chhattisgarh, Northern Karnataka through 1800 strong stockists network.

Several MNCs have made attempt to enter biscuit category but none of them were very successful. Cadbury, Brook Bond, Nestle, Smith Kline Becheem (SKB), Sara Lee – all of them have entered this category. Cadbury and SKB are still there in the market with their Cadbury and Horlicks brand respectively. But the volume of these biscuits are small. They possibly wanted to exploit their popular main line brands but did not succeed. This market is highly competitive. In the popular, low priced segment local and regional players are quite strong. For example, Priya Gold in north which is making Britannia's life difficult in the north, particularly in UP. In the upper end of the market established players with strong brands with well entrenched distribution network make the task of the new players difficult. Even in this scenario the players still try to get a foot hold. ITC have made an entry into the biscuit category recently and they will also face either similar fate or will remain an insignificant player. Only time will tell us.

Biscuit is a daily consumable item. This is also consumed by all segments of the population. The rural market therefore, offers maximum opportunity for growth. Parle by virtue of their strength in rural areas have better chance of growth. The specialty biscuits and cookies are very profitable segment but the size of the market is still small. Britannia is trying to create and dominate that segment. Their Nutri-Choice etc brand has still to reach the volume to make it an attractive proposition for them. Britannia has presence in both cake and bread where Parle is totally absent.

Parle and Britannia are both admirable players in this category. Both are fighting to retain their dominance in their respective market and product segment. Together they are controlling the total biscuit industry. Others are local players or are regional players. While attempt is being made time and again to make big time entry into this category by various multinationals but those are abortive attempt. One does not see this scenario going to change in near future. Imported biscuits are of course hitting the market and many well known brands are seen to be selling in stores but their volume is not large. Biscuit industry in India has thus got synonymous with Parle-Britannia.

9

Meat, Poultry and Marine Products

Indian Meat Processing Industry- The Problems & Prospects

The fruits of liberalisation have not reached Indian meat processing industry, as yet and I don't see anything happening in a foreseeable future. The face of this industry has therefore not realistically changed and if at all it has, it is for the worse. Like many other processed food sectors meat and poultry processing also run and managed by family owned entities in traditional manner. Nobody has yet tried to look at the basic issues facing this industry. Even government has not taken any initiatives in formulating growth oriented policies to either upgrade this industry or to improve the quality and value of meat and meat products for international trade.

The major component of the meat industry in India is buffalo meat. India has a population of about 76 million buffaloes which is 50% of the world population of buffaloes and out of this 8.72 million buffaloes are slaughtered annually in organised slaughter houses - which is approximately 11% of the total population. And buffalo constitute approximately 80% of our total export. Sheep and goat is only 10-15% of our total export. Meat is normally exported either as fresh, frozen or processed. The price realisation in FOB terms for fresh and frozen is almost same and is around INR 30 per kg. whereas processed buffalo meat export fetched a price of INR 75 per kg. Fresh meat normally goes to nearby Middle East countries from Bombay airport. If one looks at the statistics of meat export from India one finds that it is declining. Although the global trade in meat has declined by about 2% during last two years, yet 1999 forecast is that it will show slightly upward trends. After experiencing a decline in export upto 1996-97 during 1997-98 India has registered a little growth (INR 7293 million) in buffalo meat export. But again in terms of total export of meat of all forms there was a decline.

The meat Industry in India is really concentrated in U.P. and Western regions. There are about 12 large meat processing houses in India whose turnover ranges from INR 100 million to INR 300 million and about 50-60 small meat processing industries located in these regions. Most of these processors depend upon the slaughtering of the cattle at the local municipal slaughter houses. At Deonar-Bombay we have the Asia's largest slaughter house. But many of these municipal slaughter houses are not organized on modern scientific lines to handle the large stock and to utilise all by-products profitably. As a results, we are not getting the competitive price to fight the global competition. Our meat only goes to a select middle east and South East Asian countries.

Amongst the large players in this field one can name Allanasons, Alkabeer and Hind Industries - all of them are major export houses. Meat industries in India thus belong to a handful of business houses in small and medium sectors particularly dominated by one religious group. Large corporate houses did not venture in this business at all. The only major venture from corporate sector in meat processing was from Brook Bond. In seventies, Brook Bond had set up large modern integrated slaughter house and meat processing plant for export at Aurangabad in Maharashtra. The plant has a capacity of handling 500 buffaloes per day and was equipped with the processing facilities to produce blood meal, bone meal etc and Dr. Sampat Kumar was the Director-incharge of the plant. Brook Bond's overseas experts were also working. The project failed mainly for three reasons - (i) non availability of so many buffaloes every day (ii) higher cost of production and therefore difficulty in marketing of by-products. The plant was finally sold to Allanasons - who are organised well in selling fresh and frozen meat in middle east market through their own retail outlets located there.

Allanasons therefore, are the importer of their own output to a large extent. They thus control the market. After Brook Bond's failure, no one in the corporate sectors has remotely thought about getting into this sector. Late Mr. H.P. Nanda, Chairman of Escort group of companies was keen in setting up an integrated meat processing plant in joint venture in U.P. We did lot of work in terms of collecting and collating information. The outcome of that was only a project report. The odds were found many, which were the major deterrent in getting into this sector. One reason, of course is the religious overtones in meat processing and animal slaughtering. The other reasons were availability of cattles. The organised cattle rearing is very labour intensive and there are too many pitfalls and uncertainties. Pollution control is also a major issue. The fodder is grown specifically to feed the cattles kept in a dairy farm and the projects are normally integrated in terms of milk processing, cattle breeding through artificial insemination programme, in-house veterinary services, fodder cultivations and animal feed plant and finally slaughter house and meat processing.

To organise this in India is a mammoth task and if one wants to do it. Govt. policies, infrastructural framework and political will are almost non-existent. Who then is going to bell the cat? I therefore tend to think that private sectors initiative in this sector cannot be forthcoming automatically. Besides, there are other issues such as in India only non-productive, non-milking buffaloes are allowed to slaughter and thus meat yield and quality of that meat from aged cattles are not very remunerative in global market where tender meat fetches a better price and are in demand. Also because the cattles in India grazes in natural grounds, Foot and Mouth Disease (FMD) is an issue. For this reason particularly in European and American market Indian meat is not accepted where meat from Australia/New Zealand are doing better business. America introduced trade barriers to stop Australia and New Zealand capturing global meat trade. On the top of it in India we trade buffalo meat as beef whereas all over the world beef meat is actually from cow which is not slaughtered here. This also has restricted the trade to a limited geographical area. As per regulatory practices, in the slaughter house in India goat and lamb is certified as healthy cattle whereas buffalo is certified as useless by veterinary surgeon before slaughtering.

One can, of course, argue that in developed countries like France and England where scientific feeding is done to improve the meat yield of the cattle has also gone through the catastrophy like "Mad-Cow" disease which has rocked the world trade in this field and as such we are much better leaving our poor cattle population to the grace of Almighty to grow on natural ground and also contribute to our national economy. Meat export itself gives us INR 1000 million a year plus the value of the by products. Are we not then supposed to improve the lot of this industry?

I generally believe that if an Industry has to do well in global market it has to first mature in domestic market. We can see that local meat industry is highly disorganised and quality control is almost non existent. A lot therefore, needs to be done to improve that. Value addition in terms of processing is another area where this industry is still in its infancy. Lazeez was a popular name in late eighties for meat and meat products in Delhi. I don't see that brand now in the market. Oberoi hotels run their own outlets (one such is in Vasant Vihar, New Delhi), for processed meat like sausages, meatballs, chicken drumstick, hotdogs etc. Others run that on selected outlets owned by them such a Nanz etc. for similar items. The processed meat industry did not grow because of limitation in frozen food outlets. Whoever has ventured in frozen industry have faced the failure including company like Hindustan Lever.

A silver lining is that in the subsequent union budget proposes to add a cold storage capacity of 1.2 million tonnes and modernise 0.8 million tonnes, and the Ministry of Food Processing Industries has announced an incentive scheme. Even grants and concessional bank loan are also given as part of the deal to encourage setting up cold storage. How much of that has happened we are still to know.

Fig. 9.1 Mutton Kabab a popular item of non-vegetarian food.

In poultry processing the scenario is worse. 1997-98 export of poultry meat was only INR 0.09 million dropped from INR 0.54 million of export on the previous year and is constantly declining over last four years. Here again the issues are poultry feed, modern veterinary service and scientific breeding. The successful models are Venkateshwara Hatcheries of Pune started by late Dr. B.R. Rao in private sector and Arambag Hatcheries in West Bengal in co-operative sector started in sixties by the initiative taken by the then Gandhian freedom fighter and Chief Minister of West Bengal late Mr. Prafulla Chandra Sen - popularly known as "Arambager Gandhi" (Gandhi of Arambagh) to the masses. But both these two successful poultry operations are in domestic business mostly sold through company owned retail outlets having freezer cabinet and covering the local market in Western and Eastern

India respectively. Venkateswara Hatcheries introduced their brand "Venkys" for the poultry products. Earlier the brand was heavily advertised but now media support is withdrawn. Of late, a poultry processing unit started with imported machineries having capacity of handling 30000 birds per shift at Noida, U.P. is on the verge of closing down and I was contacted to help them find out a prospective buyer.

The issue before us therefore, is a complex one and there is no easy solution. A holistic approach is required to make this industry grow and prosper.

Poultry Meat is the Fastest Growing Animal Protein

During 1990s buffalo meat was the largest animal protein segment in Indian diet. Almost 50 % of the total meat consumed was from buffalo meat and poultry meat was only to the extent of 16%. The scenario has changed now and buffalo meat constitutes about 37 % of the total meat consumption whereas poultry meat consumption has gone up to about 40% as can be seen from the following Table 9.1:

Table 9.1 : Animal meat consumption

Type of meat consumed	In 1991 (Per cent)	In 2003 (Per cent)
Buffalo meat	50	37
Goat & Mutton	30	20
Poultry	16	40
Others	04	03

Source *:* USDA report

The estimated production of poultry and poultry products is 1500 thousand tones in 2003 which was about 500 thousand tones in 1991 registering a growth rate of about 11 % whereas the growth rate of buffalo meat is only about 5%. As per the report of USDA the total production of buffalo meat is about 1.9 million tones. Over 20 % of this production is exported to countries like Philippines, Malaysia, Egypt and Middle east countries. As can be seen that mutton and lamb is relatively small segment and demand was always higher than the supply resulting in high price in domestic market. Per capita consumption of poultry meat has gone up from about 420 gms in 1991 to 1.5 kgs in 2003 and if we exclude the vegetarian population, the per capita consumption will work out to about 1.75 kgs per annum.

Although the poultry consumption is on the rise steadily the meat and mutton consumption is very slowly growing or almost stagnant. Whereas in export trade the performance of poultry is poor. India exports about 500000 MT of meat out of which almost 90 % is buffalo meat. The demand for Indian meat is also not growing as in international trade the demand is for lean hygienic meat. To grow in international trade we need to follow modern feeding and animal rearing programme. The total processing capacity in the country is about one million tones but the capacity utilization is hardly 50 % . These slaughter houses are in the control of the local municipal corporation. Deonar slaughter house in Mumbai is said to be modern and the largest in Asia. These slaughter houses are used by meat traders for selling meat in the local market as well as for export. Only a handful of players are large and fall in the organized sector in the meat trade. They are Hind Agro , Allana and Al Kabeer. Hind Agro is the only player in the country who have backward linkages with the modern male buffalo rearing facility. Their plant and facilities have been certified by the importing agencies and therefore are doing the business in an organized manner.

The poultry production is concentrated in west and south. Most of the poultry farms in west are located in and around Pune and in south those are located around Coimbatore. But in north and east there is no such concentration of processing zone. In West Bengal a large poultry processing facility exist in AramBag . This particular brand of poultry meat has in course of time become quite popular in the region.

The biggest single effort in the private sector for processing and farming of poultry meat has been initiated by Venkateshwara Hatcheries near Pune. They have modern plant and also have been successful in exporting in countries like Japan which is a very quality conscious difficult customer. As per the report, for catering to the Japan market for the processed poultry and poultry products a special process plant has been installed by Venkateshwara. Unlike buffalo meat, poultry processing plants have achieved fair degree of integration and therefore can hold the price line in the market and have been able to operate their own cold chain.

The meat and poultry processing industry has significant scope for development and there is a large potential for export. But the industry suffers from many constraints in terms of both socio-cultural , religious and political as well as technological nature. A holistic view therefore is necessary for ensuring the growth of this sector. As we don't slaughter cows we have a restricted market opportunity in the international market. For some identified market including middle east, buffalo meat is an acceptable meat normally sold as beef. The feed and the cattle rearing facility need to be improved in order to upgrade the hygiene and quality of meat. Besides, the feed quality restricts the productivity of the cattle meat. Disease surveillance is another important task. Food and Mouth Disease (FMD) is a critical issue for the meat export. Department of Animal Husbandry under Ministry of Agriculture , Govt. of India has identified three special zone which are declared as FMD free and the buffalo meat processing plants are located in those zones. First of all , these FMD free zones are required to be extended to cover a much wider area. Secondly , the importing countries should be invited to go through the inspection to officially accept these zones and process plants as meeting the standards of import as per the guidelines of Codex Alimentarius Commission.

The other factor that made Indian meat and poultry industry uncompetitive in the international trade is the cost. The inefficient supply chain management , poor infrastructure , lack of scale, absence of integrated process plant coupled with the socio cultural and political constraints have made this sector almost static in international trade. Only a few players who have established linkages in select countries are carrying on with the business. In the global trade cost is one of the most important factor to get entry and acceptance. The supply chain management therefore will be critical. The new entrants in the retail trade should be able to play a role in bringing about those desired improvements. The fruit and vegetable trade sector has already experiencing the signals of those improvements. Hopefully establishing cold chain and integrated meat processing plants with introduction of variety of products sold through refrigerated storage in the retail shelf will improve the scenario. Reliance and Wal Mart are expected to get into this trade as well. A holistic approach involving processors, Government departments, slaughterhouses and private organized retailing collectively can improve the performance of this potential sector.

Indian Seafood Industry Yet to Realise its Potential

During seventies there was a big expectation created in favour of marine food industry. In all seminars and symposia we used to hear food industry leaders and technologists talking about the big potential of fish export in the global market. "India is only scratching the surface as far as marine food processing is concerned", we were told. India with a long coastline of 8129 kms, two million sq. kms. of exclusive economic zone and 1.2 million hectors of brackish water bodies offer vast potential for development of fisheries. Against an estimated fishery potential of 3.9 million tons from marine sector, only 2.6 million tons are tapped. This leaves a substantial gap to be exploited.

Quick followed the investment from all bigwigs - Union Carbide, Voltas, ITC, Britannia - all of them had set up large process plants in different parts of the country following the coast line. Union Carbide had their plant in Vizag and Britannia in Thane. Union Carbide had even a fishing trawler with on board processing facility. But couple of years down the line, one by one, all these plants closed down. I had the opportunity to visit these plants to discuss the reasons of failure. In the later years, I was actively involved in the sea-food trade and visited many countries to tie-up the export of seafood. The orders can be obtained very easily. But while executing the orders, processors incur heavy losses.

The sea-food industry in south will tell you their fluctuating fortunes. Almost all of them will tell you that in this industry either you make huge money or incur huge losses - both being not within your control. This industry is thus strewn with number of pitfalls. Large corporate sectors thus found it almost impossible to manage. Those who have managed to remain in the business are actually small family owned enterprises and all family members are in the business. The suppliers, processors, buyers and in fact all stakeholders in the business are out to cheat you. It all starts from the landing station (Bunder) itself. The fisherman will show a grade of fish but finally give you a different grade if you are not very careful. You buy some quantity at bunder and weigh the same again in factory - it would be invariably less. Then there is process losses, shrinkage losses etc. And finally buyers and buying agents know the processors' problem. They know every day's rate, whether a particular processor is very keen to sell his product, otherwise he will incur more losses due to shrinkage of old stock etc. The price thus you get is never remunerative. Whereas the importer in Japan, Europe and USA will remove the packaging of the Indian exporter and put their own label and brand to sell in the local market at much higher price. The value addition was thus created overseas and not here.

Under the circumstances, the big players gradually switched over to contract processing. Britannia and Hindustan Lever still export seafish through the contract route. And you never make money in your contract export arrangement also. In contract processing at least processors get his 10 per cent contribution on his cost of production but exporter often had to sell at a loss just for registering some export turnover necessary to meet his import commitment. In the post liberalisation era business were not required to earn their foreign exchange for import as we have now large forex reserve. There are other problems arising out of non-availability of the grades required to execute an order. You may have produced various grades of shrimp, squid or cuttle fish but the order you got need some additional grades. Or after executing an order the processor is left with some grades for which no market is there. The only alternative left at that point of time is to sell at a loss by tieing up with the other exporters who might need these grades or offload it in the local market because storing it in cold storage will only increase the cost and also the shrinkage losses and associated discolouration with the resultant loss of value. While in Escorts, we had ventured into this game.

Fig. 9.2 In marine food industry the issue is value addition and branding.

Mr Anil Nanda, MD of Escorts gave the name of the brand "Blue Lagoon". We exported to Japan and Western Europe processing the material at the Thane plant of Hakeem Food Products Pvt. Ltd. and needless to say that we incurred loss largely because of pilferage after processing. The large players including MNCs like HLL, Pepsi etc who had export commitment, indulge in buying the marine export of processors by paying a premium which could be as high as 3 to 5% of the value of the export. Before the end of the financial year, large houses will invariably resort to this practice to meet their export obligation without really doing anything. Entire documentation will be done by processor -exporter in the name of the company wanting to book the export. Needless to say that premium increases as the year progresses. The management system and control mechanism from a distance just does not work in this industry. But in spite of all these problems, India is one of the largest marine product exporter in the global market. India's export of marine products stand at INR 6 billion.

I have been advocating my friends who are for longtime in this business that they should open their own offices abroad and try to market in the overseas market directly thereby make much larger profit. But they had many operational problems. Some of them of course did that and gained immensely from this approach. I remember the name of Firoz & Co. of Mumbai who had opened their office in London - all manned by the family members. In the later years, many more followed the similar approach and did report good profit from the operation. Otherwise, it is the same old story year after year. Cyclically they make either good profit or huge loss.

In post liberalisation era, things have changed for the marine food industry. We have now couple of players who have operations and marketing network overseas. Amongst those are Firoz & Co. of Mumbai and Transasia Corporation - Chennai. This industry is also subject to stringent quality control system. Most of the exporters now have implemented HACCP - to qualify as exporter to Europe and USA.

The Seafood Exporters Association of India (SEAI) in collaboration with Marine Products Export Development Authority (MPEDA) holds annual conference and exhibition every alternate year and this is a big show with lot of fanfare characterised by buyer-seller meet. If one participates in this conference one can see that every living things in the sea have a market. This show is therefore spectacular. The show is normally organized by, both SEAI and MPEDA alongwith Indian Fishery Industries and the Association of Shrimp Hatchery Owners and Shrimp Aquaculture Farmers.

This event is supposed to bring together leading players in the global seaford industry to a common platform where they can explore business opportunities and assess investment prospects, forge trade partnership and form technological alliances and transact business. Andhra Pradesh has emerged as the leader in aquaculture and deep sea fishing with its 40 per cent contribution of the total exports in the world. Vizag once a tiny fishing village, now became pioneer with its multiple activity in prawn aquaculture.Tsunami disaster had done significant damage to this industry. Vizag and Cochin thus earned its reputation to hold such a show.

Indian seafood industry recorded an all-time high export earning of nearly US$ 1.4 billion. The quantity exported last year was 343031 MT. Today India stands 3rd in global seafood production, having registered a growth rate of 300% over the last decade. Indian Seafood finds its way to as many as 75 countries around the world.

Although more than 200 units have implemented HACCP to qualify for export to EEC countries but lot need to be done in terms of infrastructural and technological upgradation. The significant growth in seafood export is due to aquaculture and Andhra Pradesh did significant contribution in this direction. Aquaculture Authority Bill is pending before the government to boost this sector further. But most important issue for this industry is still lying in its value addition. At current level it is only 15%.

Indian government is now in the process of finalising agreements with United States Food and Drug Administration (USFDA) and the Australian Quarantine and Inspection Service (AQIS) to ensure that marine product consignments from India cleared through the Export Inspection Council of India (EICI) are not subjected to routine and 100 per cent inspections by the concerned authorities in those countries. This means we are now looking for green channel for our seafood export.

Japan Marine Product Importers Association (JMPIA) who have visited and participated in the 13th Indian International Seafood Show 2001 have given clear indication that they are interested in setting up joint ventures with Indian processors. Japan being one of the largest importers of seafood particularly of shrimp from India, this would be a significant development. If things progress we can see definite improvement in value addition for this sector. And that is the most critical issue.

Processing and Value Addition are Major Challenges for Marine Products Industry

Indian marine food industry contributes approximately INR 270 billion in income or about 1.1 % of the GDP. Not only that fish is the main source of protein intake amongst population in coastal areas but it is also the major employment and livelihood provider in the coastal belt. Over 14.5 million people are engaged in fishing and fishing related activities. The current capacity of processing and cold storage are shown in the Table 9.2 below.

Table 9.2: Current built – up capacity of seafood industry

Built up Capacity of the Indian Seafood Industry					
Name of State	**No of Exporters**	**Freezing Capacity (Ton/d)**	**No. of Cold Storages**	**Storage Capacity (Ton/d)**	**No. of Fishing Vessels**
Kerala	287	1585.77	169	23086.50	2963
Tamil Nadu	286	524.55	67	5900.00	1562
Karnataka	43	186.40	26	3540.00	3226
Andhra Pradesh	95	779.50	53	7200.00	717
Goa	9	104.00	9	1275.00	420
Gujarat	64	2216.03	57	22925.00	426
Orissa	30	220.00	20	2460.00	414
Maharashtra	268	1327.11	39	19372.00	2932
West Bengal	99	340.00	30	3500.00	0
Delhi (UT)	92	0.00	1	15.00	0

Source: MPEDA

The sea food processing industry is quite well developed. There are about 1273 registered exporters in the country. The other infrastructure includes 215 ice plants, 481 shrimp peeling plants, 371 freezing plants, 471 cold storage units, 7 canning plants, 16 fish meal plants, 11 surimi plants. Around 95 per cent processing units are located and concentrated in 20 major clusters in 12 maritime states (Table 9.3). Most of the processing units are now HACCP certified.

Table 9.3: Coastal states where fishing and fish processing is a major industry

Maritime States of India	
Kerala	Maharashtra
Tamil Nadu	Gujarat
Pondichery	West Bengal
Karnataka	Orissa
Andhra Pradesh	Goa
Andaman & Nicobar Islands	Lakshadweep

Source: MPEDA

Over 80 per cent of the catch of the fish is utilized as fresh or chilled . About 6 per cent is said to be used for drying and curing, 4.7 per cent is utilized for production of fish meal and balance 5.3 per cent is utilized for freezing and export. Although there is an increasing trend now to produce value added fish products such as fish pickles, curried and extruded products. But that market is still not fully exploited. These products as well as canned fish has very big potential. However, main focus on international trade is still remained on frozen fish. The share of marine products export has steadily increased from INR 39.2 million in 1961-62 to about INR 63 billion in 2005-06 which is equivalent to 1.5 Per cent of the total export from India.

The main buyers are Japan, USA and West European countries and the major product is frozen shrimp and prawn including tiger prawn. While Japan was the single largest buyer of Indian sea food totalling about 31 per cent of the total exports from India but in year 2004-05 European Union collectively became the largest buyer from India.

Major marine products exported from India includes frozen shrimps, Individually Quick Frozen(IQF) shrimps, canned shrimps/prawns, lobsters, cuttle fish, squid tubes, fresh fishes, canned fish , dried fish, crab, clam, mussel, aquarium and ornamental fishes, dried shark fins and dried fish maws etc. Table 9.4 and Table 9.5 give the details of sea food exports from India by products and export figures by select countries and regions respectively.

Tabel 9.4 : Sea Foods export from India

Marine Products Export from India by Products							
ITC Code	**Category**	**2004-05**		**2005-06**		**Growth in Qunatity**	**Growth in Value**
		Quantity (MT)	**Value (Rs. Crores)**	**Quantity (MT)**	**Value (Rs. (Crores)**	**(%)**	**(%)**
0301	Live fish	60.8	6.32	43.3	5.54	–28.9	–12.3
0302	Fish fresh or chilled excluding fish fillets and other fish meat of code no. 0304	9931.0	91.65	10846.0	98.69	9.2	7.7
0303	Fish frozen excluding fish fillets and other fish meat of code no. 0304	144937.6	785.93	187869.7	1071.76	29.6	36.4
0304	Fish fillets & other fish meat (whether or not minced) fresh chilled or frozen	8959.2	78.13	13470.6	119.94	50.4	53.5
0305	Fish (dried and processed) and fish meat fit for consumption	6350.5	50.59	6608.3	44.04	4.1	–12.9
0306	Crustaceans (live, chilled, frozen, fresh and processed)	183604.0	4127.39	179843.1	3993.89	–2.0	–3.2
0307	Molluses (live, chilled, frozen, fresh and processed) and aquatic invertebrates	80332.5	764.06	95796.5	958.18	19.2	25.4
	Total	**434175.6**	**5897.75**	**494477.5**	**6292.04**		

Source: DGCIS

Table 9.5 : Export of sea foods from India to select countries

Exports of Marine Products from India–Select Countries/Regions						
Importing Country	**2004-05**		**2005-06**		**Growth in Ounatity (%)**	**Growth in Value (%)**
	Quantity (MT)	**Value (Rs. Crores)**	**Quantity (MT)**	**Value (Rs. Crores)**		
USA	96283.5	1644.2	107669.2	1704.0	11.8	3.6
Europe	102599.8	1580.5	112844.7	1783.4	10	12.8
Asia (excluding Middle East & Japan)	163258.9	1179.1	192431.0	1333.8	13.1	1.9
Middle East	13904.2	202.6	17877.8	248.52	28.6	22.7
Japan	46881.7	1101.2	45280.0	990.2	–3.4	–10.1
Total	**422928.1**	**5707.6**	**476102.7**	**6059.9**		

Source : MPEDA & FAO

The future prospect lies in deep sea fishing. Inland fisheries is growing at about 6 per cent per annum but holds a much bigger promise. For adequate development of this sector intensifying coastal aquaculture, sea farming, intensifying deep sea fishing and better management practices for sustainability are the key imperatives. Considering large processing facilities and availability of manpower importing raw material for processing into value added products and exporting back hold good promise for India.

10

New Food Products in the Market

Processed Food in the New Millennium

No one denies that the next millennium would be dominated by two sectors where knowledge revolution is taking place and that would be biotechnology and information technology (IT). Both IT and Biotech will shape the future of the industry in the next millennium. And processed food will be no exception.

In fifties and sixties India used to import primary food items - largely wheat and edible oil. Of course, oil we still import but otherwise India has become not only self sufficient in food but also a net surplus and exporter of food. The green revolution initiated by Dr. M.S. Swaminathan in agricultural front under the political initiatives taken by Late Prime Minister Mrs. Indira Gandhi had definitely delivered a great result. This is singularly the biggest contribution to the country by Mrs. Gandhi. During Jawaharlal Nehru's time we used to import wheat from USA under PL 480 scheme. A lot of stories used to float in the market about its quality which Indians used to consume three times daily. Surely, achieving the status of self sufficiency in food production will definitely influence the shape of things for processed food industry in India under WTO regime in the millennium.

The consumers will have wide choice to make and hence will expect greater value for money. They will be more convenience seeker and also more demanding. There will be higher level of awareness about safety, nutrition and effect on the environment. Marketers therefore have to be more careful and businesses will have to be knowledge driven and thus small and traditional operators will have difficult times. However, knowledge based small and medium food processors will continue to thrive and may even do better.

There will be two distinct kind of customers. One group, whose numbers will be very large who would like to buy convenient, safe, hi tech foods. Others, who belong to the affluent class will be very health conscious and will only ask for natural and organic foods. Processed food industries also therefore will divide along that line. It is expected that we will see many new processed food types. Also new preservation technologies will become popular. For example, Zeodration, freeze drying technology etc. Radiation technology will be more widely accepted.

During last three decades we have heard about application of radiation technology in the preservation of food where controversy still occasionally gains ground. But for certain category of food including grains, vegetable like potato, onion etc. (for sprout inhibition) and marine foods, there is a general acceptance of irradiated foods. In fact, grains are mostly irradiated now. In some countries they even have stipulation towards this end for agricultural products and insist on the certification by the competent authority under law before import.

Division of Food Technology under Bhabha Atomic Research Centre (BARC) in Mumbai has done great deal of work on gamma irradiation of foods. The work in this direction gained momentum when Prof. A. Srinivasan was heading that division. I recollect the collaborative work between BARC and Department of Food Technology and Biochemical Engineering of Jadavpur University headed by Prof. A.N. Bose. BARC used to irradiate fish at various radiation doses and Jadavpur University was assessing their physico-chemical and organoleptic quality. Prof. Dinesh Roy Chaudhuri was co-ordinator at Jadavpur and we have seen him regularly tasting irradiated fish and he is still hail and hearty - a living proof that irradiated foods can be made safe.

While it took long years for irradiated foods to be acceptable for certain category of foods and for certain markets, in the next millennium, consumers will get the details thereabout to decide which potato or onion variety to be purchased and from which food retail stores. Consumers will be seen picking up smoked irradiated processed salmon or say trout in a tray of 500 gms from deep freezer of a retail outlet in Delhi imported from say Norway. It is also expected that all global brands of processed and fresh food will be selling through Indian food retail stores.

The processed food products will have nutritional labelling. Consumers will carefully go through this label information before buying the product. Only known and well advertised brand will no longer be a guarantee of quality. Consumers will expect more disclosures on which their buying decision will depend. Nutrition labelling of food will thus become compulsory. Food marketer will have to put product informations on internet and as e-commerce will flourish consumers will buy goods from stores through net.

As there will be an increase in demand for natural and organic foods, those who are now venturing into this area are expected to derive rich harvest in the next millennium. ARC Harvest has just launched their high fibre whole wheat atta in Delhi market. Along the line there will be increased demand for health foods and speciality foods like diabetic foods, slimming foods, athletic foods etc.

The need for convenience will be increasingly felt. Food ingredients business will flourish. Processed ingredients or semi-processed foods will increasingly gain momentum. The likes of Daburs "Hommade" and Kissans "Curry Paste" will do much better. Quick cooking foods such as retortable pouch to take care of guests or hurriedly organised parties and gathering will sell more and thus more brands are likely to hit the market in the next millennium.

Genetically engineered food will be an acceptable primary foods for the masses. India will firm up its stand on imports of Genetically Modified (GM) food and seeds soon. GM foods and seeds introduction now being pioneered by transnational Life Science majors like Monsanto, Pioneer Hybrid, AgrEvo, Continental Grain and Ciba Geigy etc. - barring the last one all of them are US multinationals. There is lot of controversy particularly in Europe on safety aspects of GM-foods. Some of the very large food retail chain in Europe have even started hiring DNA finger printing laboratories to verify that the products they sell are free of foreign genes. India has already had its share of controversy over genetically modified seeds with the recent import of one million tonne of soyabean and Monsanto's BT cotton trials. As in India we don't have any food shortage now our dependence on GM-foods would be limited.

The controversy over safety and acceptance of GM-foods will continue as it has happened with irradiated foods over last three decades but that is expected to be resolved and if not for other reasons, at least for economic reasons many countries will accept GM-foods which might constitute a large part of raw material or basic material for processed food even in India.

If the trend really become as predicted we need to have new safety and food regulations. Governments' regulatory mechanism has to gear up for new criteria for licensing, certifications, control and monitoring and implementing global standards for food safety and health.

New Food Products are Hitting the Market

With the entries of new global players in Indian processed food industry we are now going to witness the launch of new items specially designed for specific markets and consumer segments. Some of these have already hit the market and there are others, which are in the pipeline. Marketers are experimenting with many new categories targeting particular consumer segments. This is definitely a phenomena of post liberalisation era and let us examine a few of them to understand what exactly is really happening.

The twenty-four billion dollar US -based foods major ConAgra has launched its best selling microwave popcorn brand Act II in the country. Act II is the first brand from ConAgra's global foods portfolio to be launched here. ConAgra is said to be the fastest growing food company in US. Two years ago they acquired ITC Agro-Tech and in line with the ITC's grocery line of business ConAgra has tried to consolidate the basic portfolio and now venturing into the branded FMCG market in select consumer segment. It is estimated that we have in India about 0.5 million microwave owning household. And the company is aiming at this small segment only. After having a successful test marketing in Pune in 1999 they extended it to other cities. There are innovation possible in this category such as butter corn which should have a sure fire appeal to Indian tastes and microwave owning consumers can definitely afford it. It has also been said that Act II brand will be used to promote a range of snack foods which will cater to a much larger market than the microwave popcorn. Act II is one of the largest selling microwave brand imported from Golden Valley Microwave Foods Inc. USA which has been launched in Indian market. ConAgra is drawing upon the expertise and capabilities of their US based facilities of their own and also of the Tiger Oats and is currently working on the development of products at its newly established research and development facilities at Secunderabad. As said earlier ConAgra in India is already in the branded dry grocery segment and also on the sourcing, distribution and export of agro commodities and the plans are to expand this range as well.

In western countries organic foods fetch a much higher price compared to the price of the traditional processed foods. UNDP has done a study on the global marketing prospect on organic foods and their report now is available for anyone interested. Food Industries in India now talking about the organic foods. A Pune based company has already launched grocery items which are being promoted as organic in nature and priced at a premium. Dabur is the largest player in branded honey in organised sector having a market share of about 70%. The company has now ventured into development of organic honey in Nepal with an intention to launch the product into the global market. To help them to become a global player in honey, Dabur hired an European consultant on a five-year contract. Honey has traditionally been used in India for special purpose and in religious activities by Hindus. Dabur has made honey, with their sustained campaign, a natural health sweetener and thus upgraded and brought it to the breakfast table. Agricultural Produce Export Development Authority (APEDA) under the ministry of commerce will soon introduce the certification for export of organic foods that the food products have been produced "organically". This has been announced in a seminar in Calcutta jointly organised by the Commerce Ministry, UNCTAD, Ministry of Environment and Forest, IIM- Calcutta and FICCI.

Similarly, the term "natural" has become fancy to many food marketer. Onjus of Enkay Texofood is said to be 100% natural. The company recently made a statement following a notice of enquiry issued by MRTPC. Dabur is also selling its "Real Juice" as 100% natural. So is "Tropicana" from the Pepsi's stable.

After successfully establishing itself in the ready-to-eat breakfast cereal segment, US foods giant Kellogg is gearing itself to introduce a range of grain-based products such as Rice Krispies, Treats and Nutri-Grain cereal bars. The company proposes to test market different grain based products with the Indian consumers for a period of 12 to 24 months for which the Indian company Kellogg India Ltd. plans to import various types of products from the parent company in USA. Soon therefore, we will see imported "Rice Krispies Treats" and "Nutri-Grain" cereal bars in Indian market and if test market is successful these will be subsequently produced in Kellogg's Taloja facility in India.

Nestle India Ltd. has recently launched two new milk products under "Junior Foods" category- "Nestle Growing Up Milk" and "Nestle Cereal Milk Drink" under the umbrella positioning of "Goodness of Milk plus more". Britannia also introduced Flavoured Milk in tetrapack upgrading the fluid milk from bottle and polypack to tetrapack which is actually a long life milk. Available indications are that they have difficulties in getting the market penetration. But I think on sustained effort this product will also find a profitable segment. In the confectionery category there are many new products we have seen now being marketed. Earlier we had only hardboiled confectionery, toffees and chocolates and chewing gums. We now have many new innovative products and also many international brands crowding the market and fighting for the market share.

Recently I chanced upon a Spanish company doing brisk business in slimming foods After talking to Mr. Santamaria, Managing Director of Sojivit India Pvt. Ltd. in Delhi I realised that the company is selling a range of slimming diet based on soya protein isolate. I thought that soya based foods excepting meat analogues from soya protein are already dead as far as Indian market is concerned but it seems that soya is reappearing in some other form for some other segment of the market. Mr. Santamaria himself wears a badge showing a message for the slimmers. The company markets food supplement for diet control. The complete plan for rejuvenating the metabolic system to ultimately control the body weight are sold under the brand name "Sojplan - Diet I Diet V" Mr. Santamaria gave it a unique name and calls it" Sojplan Cellular Nutrition Diet Programme". Another inter-national leader in food supplement and other related products including slimming products have entered the Indian market. Herbalife International of America Inc. have introduced their global products range in Indian market.

Some people still believes that soyabean has lot of prospects in terms of business potential. Arvind Chandra who runs a small industry of his own in Bombay by name "Vega Industries" dedicated himself in soyabean processing. In addition to soya paneer and tofu which he sells in the local market he has developed with his own initiative a range of pet-food based on soya-protein which sells under the brand name "Dogood". Whenever Arvind visits Delhi to meet his distributors he makes it a point to meet Mrs. Maneka Gandhi also to solicit her support for his campaign - "Make your pet a vegetarian" by feeding them on soya based diet.

Some of these new designers food will take time to become a significant category. Ironically, we had to wait for MNCs to come and introduce those new food items. Indian companies should learn lesson that in the competitive market unleashed by liberalization, innovation is the key to not only to success but also to survive.

New Launches in Tough Market Condition

In an apparently difficult market situation where most of the Fast Moving Consumer Goods (FMCG) companies have not faired well in terms of top line growth in business, processed food sectors, particularly the MNCs have reported relatively better results. Notably amongst them are Britannia, Nestle and Cadbury. It seems that their strategies have worked fairly well for them. For example, Nestle's strategy to hold on the price line to drive volume has paid off with healthy top line growth. Britannia also managed to report the real term volume growth by about eight percent. Similarly Cadbury's performance in chocolate and malted beverages can also be considered satisfactory. These are a few examples in a situation where most of the FMCG companies in household and personal care category did not report good results particularly in top line growth performance. Last couple or years businesses have resorted to cost cutting and belt tightening for most of them including bigwigs like Hindustan Lever for improving the bottom line objective.

The most striking feature of the processed food industry is their ability to create a few successful new brands under the same difficult market environment with recessionary trend already set in. And that is not a small achievement. Britannia introduced a new brand "Maska Chaska" and it did exceedingly well. In good old days we always thought that there were two sectors in the food processing industry which were relatively safer and the players were also reporting good operating results. These were dairy and sugar confectionery industries. Of late, Indian sugar confectionery market is not quite living up to its original promise. The growth rates have declined for the last few years and we expect that market will actually shrink by as much as two percent.

An increase in excise duty from eight to sixteen percent further complicates the matter. It can be pointed out here that marketer cannot just pass on the increased cost to customers. For example, the candy price cannot be pushed from say 50 paise to INR 1 because it would be quite substantial increase and a 75 paise price point is both consumer and trade unfriendly. Cadbury, which earlier was very bullish about sugar confectionery, has now put it on the back burner. It is believed that Cadbury wanted to get into this category through the acquisition route and that did not materialise. The reason being the asking price for the acquisition candidates were too high. In confectionery industry the leading players like Parle and Parry are just about breaking even and therefore the cost of acquisition is a serious issue for the Cadbury to get into this sector which is apparently not doing well. Parrys confectionery subsequently got sold. For the same reason, ITC has dropped its plan to get into sugar confectionery. Against that background why Perfetti is so excited? Obviously, in a market situation as explained above there are only two options - either grow the market by constantly introducing the new brands or capture volumes with the existing brands. For both the options one needs a lot of resources to support to succeed. But Perfetti has apparently chosen to take the first route.

In this difficult candy market the Perfetti's Alpenliebe is a big success. It sells about 15 million single pieces in a month. The brand pull is so good that it is available in small pan shops in remote areas. Total candy market in India is about INR 7500 million according to ORG-MARG estimate and Alpenliebe has already notched up a sales of about INR 100 million. The big opportunity in candy market is still the untapped rural segment. The small scale sector grabs a sizable portion of this market because they are exempt from 16 percent excise duty and 12 percent sales tax which large companies have to pay. The only way out for the large players is to get the product manufactured through third party in small scale following the lines that HLL does.

Against the same difficult market scenario the leading food companies are also launching new products. The latest from Pepsi's Tropicana range are two new fruit flavours namely mixed fruit juice and tomato juice both in one litre aseptic pack and priced at INR 68. Mixed fruit juice contains apple, pineapple, orange, mango and guava juices. The tomato juice also has been positioned as natural juice to be consumed directly and targeting SEC A and B class towns and consumers in the age group of 25 - 45 years. We have seen earlier tomato puree in aseptic pack but tomato juice is first time to be launched in carton pack. In earlier days we used to sell tomato juice in can and that too the market was only in hotel and restaurant segment. Tropicana, the largest in the world in the relevant segment has taken the lead in the juice segment, as expected, in the Indian market.

Fig. 10.1 New food in the market.

It has been reported that Coca-Cola has finalised a deal with Medimix, the Chennai based FMCG company to distribute its powder beverage Sunfill in Tamil Nadu to fight against the leader in the segment - Rasna which enjoys about 85% market share nationally. In a significant departure from earlier practices Sunfill will be manufactured through a contract source and will be distributed through Medimix which has strong distribution network in southern market particularly in grocery segment which Coca-Cola would like to encash upon. The total size of this market is estimated to be about 40 million unit cases. Coca-Cola attempts a penetrative pricing at INR 2 per pouch. The strategy is to approach the absolute low end of the market particularly the rural consumers as well as SEC C, D and E categories and the company is expecting a sales of INR 1 billion in next two years which later proved to be an unrealistic kind of expectation.

Medimix, is well known for their success in the herbal soap category and their distribution is quite strong particularly in south. With this association Coca-Cola will of course ensure the entry into the grocery segment and that too in remote areas which Rasna will have to take notice of. However, Rasna has survived such onslaught earlier and I don't see any reason why it will not display the same performance this time as well. I don't think that Tang of General Foods which was launched sometime ago and is distributed through Dabur has made much headway so far. And this is going to be yet another product from a formidable multinational like Coca-Cola. In these days of globalisation we will see the competition from all over. Recently, a Malaysian company has launched their entire range of fruit juices under the brand name "Natural Juice" in India through the trading route. In the end analysis, of course, all brands will not survive.

India has the Prospects to Become a Lead Player in Organic Foods

Of late we can see that there are lot of activities with respect to promoting organic foods both in the domestic market as well as in the international market. The results of course, are still to be seen. Till date the organic foods export is next to nothing. The estimate reveals that we have about INR 40 to 50 million worth of export from India under organic food category. There are about forty organic product producers located in various parts of the country and about fifteen odd exporters engaged in this trade doing and sharing this small but prospective business. Most of the export of the organic foods are in the commodity category dominated by rice and spice and also to some extent tea.

Whereas in Europe 24%, in US 7%, in Oceania 49% of the total agricultural area are under organic cultivation, in Asia it is only 0.33%. In terms of acreage India has 1711 hectares under organic cultivation as against US 900000 hectares and Germany and UK as 452270 hectares and 380000 hectares respectively. Therefore, in percentage terms in relation to total agricultural area our presence is miniscule and will not figure in any reckoning. As far as the domestic market is concerned Germany and United States are at the top. About 1.2% and 1.25% of the total food retail sales is organic amounting to USD 1800 million and 4200 million in Germany and USA respectively and growing at the rate of around 15 to 20% annually. The global forecast for the organic food stands at around USD 200 billion for the year 2000 in terms of retail sales value. As against that we will have to see our trade which is less than even one million in USD terms. That is next to nothing but our enthusiasm seems to be running high if one goes by the current events that are taking place in organic foods sector.

APEDA has been taking many new initiatives for the growth of this sector which includes conducting the awareness programme in north eastern states, Gujarat and Orissa. In these states pilot projects are being set up. Similar programmes are being organised in UP, Uttaranchal, Jharkhand and Karnataka with the involvement of the respective state governments. In the north eastern states APEDA has prepared product specific guidelines with respect to rice, sugarcane, pineapple and passion fruits with the involvement of NGOs and consultants. Techno economic feasibility reports have been prepared and the activities are being monitored. The government is also proposing a fifty percent subsidy on production costs up to INR 20,000 per hectare for spice growers in north eastern region. To promote organic farming in the country in view of its great export potential, the National Steering Committee under the chairmanship of Secretary, Ministry of Commerce approved the National Programme for Organic Production at its meeting on 2nd May 2001.

Under the National Programme for Organic Production (NPOP), documents like National standards, Accreditation criteria, inspecting and certifying agencies, accreditation procedure, inspection and certification procedure have all been prepared and approved by the National Steering Committee. These documents were prepared on the basis of the guidelines evolved by the representative international Organisation - International Federation for Organic Agricultural Movement (IFOAM), EU Regulations and Codex standards. To ensure the implementation of NPOP the steering committee formulated the National Accreditation Policy and Programme (NAPP). The National Steering Committee has designated APEDA, Coffee Board, Spices Board and Tea Board as accreditation agencies. In addition, the services of certain international certifying agencies such as SKAL and IMO are, however, available. In the month of July 2002 the government has also unveiled the country's first "India Organic" logo which will be used as an authentication mechanism for various organic products in the country as part of the ongoing efforts to boost their exports. India was the host of a global conference on organic foods held in the year 2004 where Indian products were displayed for the international traders from various countries, coming and participating in the event.

These initiatives will definitely go a long way to support the Indian exporters' effort to build this new trade. Organic trade has been growing at the rate of about 15% during last ten years and is expected to grow at 25 to 45% during the next ten years. We have therefore, a great opportunity.

The state government should take more initiatives in this direction to supplement the private efforts. My experience says that many initiatives really disappear if the market is not developed at the expected rate and therefore private exporters' effort should continue. In relation to organic food logo, I remember that in mid nineties, Ministry of Forest and Environment introduced the environment friendly food products logo and specification with lot of publicity. I was a member of that committee representing CII as the industry expert. But in the later years we found that there were no takers for that logo and the reason was very simple and that was market was not developed and there was no effort from the industry as well. Hence a concerted effort is very essential. I also strongly believe that for any product to do well in international trade, it is necessary to have a good domestic market as well. As for the organic products there is practically negligible small market at present. KVIC has recently introduced a range of organic foods under the brand name "Desi Aahaar" but they seem to be not doing well and they also have some operational difficulties. They appointed a consultant to help them in brand building whom they have selected by taking the lowest offer through sealed tenders. Obviously they will not get, the best talent at least cost. Seeing the visibility of the products, one can say that the products KVIC has launched have not taken off as yet. But we need to create a success story in domestic market.

Fig. 10.2 Organic foods hold great promise in India. Category is growing very fast.

The price differential between organic and other natural food products are so significant that getting mass market will be a problem for organic foods. Recently Punjab Agro Industries Corporation Ltd has drawn up plan for promoting organic foods in Punjab. Punjab Agro is proposing to involve farmers in a 250 acres of land which they have already identified for the purpose to help cultivating the product, in marketing the product in global market and finally some private investor should take over the entire business as a going enterprise. It is like build-run-own kind of proposition. KVIC is advertising these days for distributors for their organic products and telling them that distributors should be able to sell about INR 50 million worth organic foods in their chosen region and if they are ready they can go for discussion with the authorities. KVIC should know that distributors don't sell but they only help marketers to sell by organising the effective distribution. It is the marketer's responsibility to create demand for the products where KVIC is failing miserably.

India is gradually emerging as leading player in global trade in agro commodity. It is therefore very much possible for us also to become a lead player in organic food and organic agro business. But market development and supply chain management have to go in tandem. If farmers don't get the opportunity to sell the produce at right price then they will not continue to cultivate the organic foods for long. And for that purpose enterprising private exporters can play a lead role. The initiatives so far are still at the government level and as they are highly bureaucratic, I am afraid that they will not be able to create that kind of impact to make India organic exporters' competitive. We have learnt bureaucracy from British and that is reducing our potential. China was never under British and they therefore, are much faster and as observed by Tom Peter they have the advantage over us on that score what we call speed of action.

Pet Foods Might Emerge as a Large Category because of MNCs Sustained Marketing Effort

While in United States and Europe pet Foods is a very large multi billion dollar business and a very fast growing category, in India it is still almost non-existing. Pet foods that are available in the Indian market are produced by small time local players and we have the tradition of feeding pets with whatever we cook and eat at home. There is organized movement for feeding pets with vegetarian diets and some pet foods are in the market based on soybean protein. But the market is still unstructured, highly localized and very small. In late eighties Escort Group was seriously considering entering into this category with foreign collaboration and I was involved to carry out the feasibility of the project in India. This idea was from the late chairman of Escorts group, Mr. H. P. Nanda who used to tell me – "think about something new" whenever I tried to tell him that this is an untested and unknown category. But this is how he used to display his future vision. Of course, our findings were that the market has not yet evolved to warrant any significant volume.

Therefore, all the prospective collaborators that we talked to including Mars were not keen to make new investment in this new category. We then explored the possibility of manufacturing the pet foods here in India for the dedicated export to collaborator's market. That also did not work. My experience tells me that no one wants to invest in third country to buy back the products without having significant access to the market in that country. If there is any such joint venture formed those are short lived and they take advantage of the exit clause to get out of the collaboration. In the food industry there are many such instances. We, as a country tried that route to build export earnings but nothing happened and it was when the market has been opened up that we have significant foreign exchange surplus.

Many successive governments did not see the reasons till we reached a stage of bankruptcy and we had no other choice but to decide for an open market policy in 1991. We are seeing the opportunities, growth and new technologies only after that. And now we just cannot reverse. Pet foods is also going to be a new opportunity for the Indian food industry. Has anyone heard of any big project being even talked about on pet foods not to speak of any large facility being set up for the manufacture of quality and branded pet foods? But today the same is happening and global MNCs are trying to build a new category of food business for feeding pets in India.

Swiss fast moving consumer goods major Nestle has made its maiden foray into the pet foods business in India through its Nestle Purina Pet Care brand. They have appointed distributors for this new business and trying to build the category. American confectionery and pet foods giant Mars has already invested close to 5 million US dollar in a manufacturing unit in Hyderabad for this purpose and currently test marketing the products. Mars Inc operates in India through a wholly owned subsidiary christened Effem India Pvt Ltd. The company of course has basic permission to manufacture and market cocoa based confectionery products excluding those reserved for the small scale sectors. It has also permission to test market a range of pet foods under several brand names such as Cesar, Pedigree, Chappi, Pal, Chum, My dog, Whiskas, Kit e Kit, Thomas, Sheba etc. Their Hyderabad unit has an annual capacity of 5000 MT and the commercial production commenced in December 2002 and more than 100 MT of pet food products have been produced and sold from this factory. Of course, this volume is not sufficient for a full-scale launch and therefore Mars Inc. wants to carry out test marketing for an extended period and sought government permission before they undertake full-scale upgradation of the production facility which Government did not agree to.

As per the existing regulations test marketing time period allowed is up to two years and Mars is asking for further extension. Government is of the view that efforts so far have been made by Mars are not significant and their request for time extension is not justified and if Mars wants to continue the test marketing it can resort to Cash and Carry kind of trade without having involvement in direct retail trading. Possibly Mars will go for appeal and may even modify the application as they have the interest of getting into chocolate business as well. Mars business will be in direct competition with that of Nestle's and that is the reason why Nestle has pre- empted Mars by launching their pet foods range Purina. Pet foods range requires significant promotional support as the category is still small and unstructured. This will also call for a new distribution infrastructure which is not easy for a new MNC to organize. The current off take in a test market situation will not be attractive and therefore it is not surprising that Mars would like to continue the market development effort through the test marketing route. But the current regulatory frame work will not permit them to do so.

There is hardly any work done on pet foods in India. It is all with local small and unorganized sectors. Very few outlets retail pet foods, whereas veterinary medicines is already a big business. In developed market they have made many innovative products in pet foods category. There are numerous brands in this category that one can find in food stores in US. Even Mars has many successful brands and product lines in pet foods category. But in India Mars have to build this category from scratch and therefore cannot expect high volume in the beginning. If Mars is seeing the Indian opportunity on a long term basis it should utilize its installed capacity for supply to other markets and continue its effort for building the volume in the local market. Immediate volume prospect cannot utilize the capacity that they have set up. I know of two small soybean processing units in Mumbai who have introduced pet foods in Delhi through distributors route but their volume has not yet picked up. Vega Industries makes soya based pet foods . The reported sales of 100 MT of pet foods that Mars has produced since December 2002 is a significant achievement for a category of this kind.

It is not clear as yet how Mars will see this development but I can see that there is a big opportunity for them as a first mover in this category and although initial problems will be many but eventually they will be the beneficiary of their innovative approach. If the efforts of both Nestle and Mars continue in this direction we can look forward to seeing a new food business category. Animal lovers and of course, pets in Indian homes have good reasons to rejoice.

11

Constraints, New Initatives and Opportunities

New Initiatives From Food Industry in Select Category

When achieving the top line growth in the FMCG category (branded processed foods included) becomes difficult industries are forced to think of different strategies to fuel the growth of the business and profitability in a fiercely competitive market. All players are trying to create competitive advantage for their own categories exploiting all possibilities of generic strategies – namely cost advantage, differentiation and focus or in combination of those. Having the cost advantage over competition provides significant leverage to the industry as it can help them to deliver better value to the customers. And in a highly price sensitive market like India this gives opportunity for the significant growth of the market size.

Both Pepsi and Coke have demonstrated that the market growth can be much higher when the price of one bottle is brought down to INR 5 (Chota Cola in 200ml) or even INR 6 for 300 ml. But the cost advantage cannot be stretched to an unlimited extent and therefore other drivers of competitive advantage are now being increasingly seen to be exploited and leveraged. Extending the geographic boundary of the market and also increasing the penetration and depth of distribution are the other drivers to the growth and industries normally try to do that if the resources and product value proposition really support that kind of initiatives. These commonly known growth strategies are implemented on the top of and in addition to the normal marketing and promotional efforts.

Parle Products Ltd – the INR 14 billion biscuit and confectionery giant – is moving up the value chain to target the premium end of the biscuit industry.

The company has forty percent market share in the biscuit category and is planning to bring out variants of 'Parle-G', the largest selling biscuit brand in the world to secure a foothold at the top end of the biscuit market by introducing the two new variants of this popular brand. At present Parle has only Hide-n-Seek, a choco-chips biscuit in the premium segment. The other brands of biscuits in the company's portfolio include Monaco, Krack Jack, Marie, Cheeslings, Fun Centre, Jeffs and Sixer, the last three have now been consolidated under the brand Monaco. But, Parle-G, the flagship brand which is offered at INR 4 per 100gms against INR 14 per 100gms in case of Hide-n-Seek contributes more than fifty percent of the company's total turn over. Considering the importance and size of the brand in popular segment extending the variant in a different segments to make it a broad based brand is no easy task. But the company has ventured to do exactly that.

GP Goenka group flagship Duncan Industries has chalked out an extensive plan for its packet tea division. Duncan has four packet tea brands – Double Diamond, Runglee Rungliot, Sargam and Shakti. Their premium CTC leaf tea brand Double Diamond is now being slated to go national. Currently, the brand has the stronghold in Uttar Pradesh, Madhya Pradesh and Maharastra whereas their premium Darjeeling tea brand - Runglee Rungliot is being phased out as this brand is un-remunerative.

The only large consumer major in tobacco and hotels – ITC which is still continuing to operate from Kolkata is making significant investment in their new found food and agro business. ITC has now decided to extend its flagship foods brand, Aashirwad to spices and rice. ITC has already launched whole-wheat flour (atta) and iodised salt under Aashirwad brand and company believes that spices which is dominated by the unorganized sector offers significant potential. Interestingly, Hindustan Lever (HLL) has ventured into spices again even after the failure of Sona brand of spices from Brook Bond (now under HLL fold) which was subsequently withdrawn from the market. HLL has made a foray into the spice business under the brand name – Knorr Annapurna. HLL has also introduced rice under the Annarpurna brand. The market for spices in India is believed to be around INR 100 billion, of which the branded segment is only INR 6 billion and major players are MDH, Everest, Ashoka, Badshah etc. ITC's game plan apparently stems from their strategic synergies that they derive from agricultural products division for sourcing, ITC Welcome group hotels for specialist cuisine and the packaging division for backward integration advantage and finally strong brand equity and a very wide distribution network. The company therefore, strongly feels that growth will come by extending the product range which currently includes staple foods, confectionery, snacks and ready- to-eat food products.

Against that scenario the liquor major UB group is eyeing global market in addition to launching new products. The company is planning to take one of its brown rum brands to the international market. The group also plans to launch low-alcohol drink Shotz and regular- plus whiskey Derby Special in north India. Earlier we were only familiar with the terminology like RTS beverage in relation to soft and fruit based beverages. But in alcoholic beverages a new category is gradually emerging by name RTD (ready – to-drink). UB group is exploring the various models to aggressively grow the RTD category following the Australian – New Zealand franchise model for which company is contemplating creating a separate division to take care of manufacturing, bottling and distribution with an aim to convert about 5% of the beer drinkers into RTD category to see the kind of growth they are projecting.

When the competition is becoming intense and goings become tough organizations have to resort to different methods for growth, survival and consolidation of the business. And therefore we are seeing the response of the players in the form of various new initiatives. It is not essential that all new initiatives will deliver the expected results. But the businesses have to try all alternatives to finally discover a winning strategy that works. And thus the search goes on.

Outsourcing a Preferred Option for Large Food Processors

Because of competition from small and regional players who have lower cost structure the large players have distinctive disadvantage. As we all know in terms of generic strategies having cost advantage is a very important element of competitive advantage. All recent surveys tell us that the knowledgeable consumers are willing to buy the cheaper options in order to manage the household budget better which also give them additional fund to buy lifestyle items that their family needs. The established brands thus cannot get the same amount of premium that they were enjoying earlier. This phenomena is hitting the growth and profitability of large corporations. And they are therefore seen to be either reducing the price to hold on the market share or are no increasing the price even if the cost is going up. The price of the product i therefore an important determinant to ensure the growth and survival. Th discerning customers are not willing to pay for the organizational inefficiencies They have many options to select from. As a result, large organizations ar looking and exploring options for innovations to cut cost. The cost reduction i thus a prime agenda for corporations to pursue. One such options is to outsourc products from cheaper processing units who can meet the quality criteria bu will be able to supply at a lower cost than what it would cost the company to produce in their own manufacturing units.

Lowering price definitely helps increase the market size. Both Coke and Pepsi have demonstrated that the common principle of three A's (3A's), namely affordability, acceptability and availability really works well for the marketers. The soft drink giants have deliberately reduced the price and created a price option at INR 5 for 200 ml cola and the result was phenomenal growth. By lowering the price supported by aggressive advertisement the consumer base for Pepsi increased from 160 million in the year 2002 to 250 million consumers in 2004. But this remarkable growth has not given them incremental profit. Both Coke and Pepsi are now trying to strike a balance between the growth in sales and profit as ultimate purpose of any business is to make profit. The focus for the soft drinks major is on the upper segment which constitutes about 5 million customers but they consume larger quantity. As per estimate the average consumption of this top end customer is about 325 times a year. The industry has now felt that in order to fight the smaller players and also to fuel growth in lesser growing categories price reduction or creating lower affordable price option is not profitable. Sales growth cannot be at the cost of profit growth. The focus thus is on reducing the cost on one hand and looking for attractive segment on the other hand. And to reduce the cost one has to look for alternative options and innovations in supply chain management. Outsourcing is one such options to be explored and large industry is increasingly going for that.

Britannia Industries Ltd (BIL) has recently decided to shut down its Mumbai plant which is not cost competitive due to higher manpower cost. The biscuit industry is highly price sensitive and all manufacturers are under pressure to offer better value for money to consumers. Britannia is losing market to regional players like Priya Biscuit in north etc who are able to keep the cost structure lower. The regional players are now many having lower operating costs and overheads. In a category like biscuit the future growth potential is in the rural areas where cost will be a major factor for entry into those markets. Britannia was able to take many new cost cutting measures including organizational restructuring and de-layering and the effort is still on to reduce the cost further. As reducing the price without the consequential cost reduction will have many other problems arising out of lower profitability impacting the corporations ability to support the marketing initiatives required to keep the brand growing and healthy. BIL's current capacity to produce is said to be to the tune of 300,000 MT. They are in the process of closing down the Mumbai plant and adding a grass root plant in Uttaranchal having capacity of 45000 MT being set up at an estimated cost of INR 550 million. Uttaranchal will provide several tax incentives which will improve the margin on existing range. But at the same time company also decided to produce only 30000 MT of biscuits in company owned plant and will procure 210,000 MT of biscuits from contract packers across the country. This means about seventy percent of the total requirement will be sourced from contract vendors. Look at the advantage in terms of cost reduction. In Mumbai plant average manpower cost has been reported to be INR 19000 whereas the same would be INR 3000 in contract packing unit. The lower cost will help Britannia to reduce the price of certain brands to get higher market share. BIL currently enjoys about 38-39% market share and the brand is predominantly urban. Lower cost will enable the company to focus on rural segment to fuel growth.

The other food companies which are outsourcing in significant scale are HLL and ITC. In all these companies the percentage contribution of contract packers to the total volume are increasing every year. ITC has introduced in recent times many products in culinary category and also under grocery segments. All these products are outsourced. The outsourcing also give the large players an advantage of trying out many propositions in the market place and not all of them will really work. The downside risk is thus minimized. This is thus a win-win situation for both. Small companies who have idle capacity as they cannot market their products and therefore can utilize the capacity for large players. Earlier I have seen that contract packers were always happy as they were making easy money. But these days they are also under pressure as the big players are creating constant pressure on them to reduce the price further or not even lifting the stock as committed due to dynamic market environment. The pressure of large players are being passed on to the smaller players forcing them also to reduce cost continuously. In the process both have to become innovative and flexible to remain together in the competitive market.

Food Industry Now is More Customer Focussed than Before

The competition has forced the industry to be customer focused. Earlier the industry was designed around certain product categories, which were normally western style, and the attempt was made to make those products categories acceptable to customers. That task was enormous and thus many have failed. The categories did not grow and therefore only a few survived. Success rate of the food industry therefore was very low and it was not the investor's favourite. Financial institutions did not support the industry because their experience was very poor. The scenario is changing now. The success rate of new ventures has improved and even large corporations are again seriously considering the agro-based industry. I was surprised when I was told that an organization like Bharti Telecom has started a new agriculture based export business in collaboration with the UK based commodity traders and they are talking big business. Recently Bharti Group has formed a Joint Venture with Wal-Mart to enter into retail sector including food retailing in a big way.

The point that I am driving at is that new ventures are created by age-old traditional player by forward integration through customer insight. Organizations are looking at new initiatives by identifying new opportunities through a careful study and involving customers in the key decision making process. The increase in spending power of urban population and increased exposure to global trends are helping to open up new industry. The south India based V.G. Siddhartha's family has been owning coffee estate in south for the last 125 years. But in the year 2000 he got the bright idea of starting coffee retail chain in India. Today Café Coffee Day has 153 outlets in 37 cities in the country as against 120 outlets of Barista. This forward integration has definitely helped the group to go up in the value chain in the coffee beans business. They have more control on supply and quality assurance to satisfy the customers.

In the next phase in order to make the coffee cafes financially viable the other food products also have to be served through the same outlets which the group had identified through the organized customers contacts and carrying out the research. They found that offering light meal which is filling would be preferred by the customers than serving the traditional snacks. They thus decided to offer pasta and biriyani in those outlets. Here also they made the variations in the sense that in all places the menu is not the same. There are extensive variations and location specific menu were offered. Organising the supply line would be complex but to be in line with customer preferences will ensure the success. Haldiram's success story entirely revolves around customers preferred recipe. They have created their outlets in far away places. But customer travels those distance and those select outlets always run full.

Of course, they also sell their products through normal channel distribution and compete in certain categories with other big players in the field. The multinationals operating in India follow a model of country specific initiatives and thus one can find many products in their portfolio which are local taste preferences. Those who have violated this norm have not succeeded. We have instances where MNC is competing with local players in traditional food items. For example, Nestle has introduced a range of pickles under Maggie brand and competing with the local players. Also Pepsi has introduced bhujia and competing with Haldiram and Bikanerwala etc. In fact, Pepsi gets product made from Haldiram and Bikanerwala and also compete with them in the market place.

This is what we call cooperation and competition. These kind of ethnic products are not there in the portfolio of these MNCs anywhere. But local opportunity drives multinationals to introduce products which are designed to capture the local taste preferences. They are better marketer and hence go along with local taste preferences which makes the proposition more easily acceptable. Nestle in fact have globally over 7500 brands which includes local brands. They have about 45 brands which can be called regional brands and globally Nestle have only about 10 brands which can be called global brands. This dimension will explain how many products they introduce to exploit the local opportunity. One needs to think global and act local – the way multinational business model works.

Hindustan Lever is known for their innovativeness and systems approach to business. They took many initiatives to exploit the local opportunity. But unfortunately they did not succeed. Presumably, they were well ahead of the time, meaning that the products that they introduced by identifying the local needs were not timed right and they were well ahead of the time. Recently they introduced ready made roti (chapati). They test marketed it by placing the products in the railway station thinking that the travelers will pick them for use while traveling. Good idea, but the time may not be ideal for this concept. And idea may catch up later. Although a local player may be satisfied with low volume to start with but HLL has to make things big, otherwise it will not be profitable for them. Right timing to introduce products is very important. As per the survey, globally 28 per cent products in new launches fail because "it is too good nobody wanted it or better mousetrap nobody wanted". What I am trying to convey that only good product is no guarantee for success, it has to be timed right. This means that customer preferences at that point of time should signify the right volume of business opportunity. Otherwise the whole exercise can be futile.

There is no reason to think that local foods will have only country specific market. These days the market is globally integrated and that is why certain types of products have been globally acceptable. Thai foods and Chinese foods have become globally popular so also is Italian foods. If pasta and pizzas can be marketed globally why cannot we create global opportunity for our local products like idli and dosa? This is definitely possible. Some innovative players will be doing it? Pataka brand of pickles is very popular in UK market and also in other European market. This is an initiative of an Indian Gujarati entrepreneur setting up venture in UK. It has been reported that Chennai based Orion foods is now planning to introduce ready-to-eat Indian foods like Idli, Appams, masala Dosa, Vada, Bonda etc. in UK and US market. Such initiatives will increase in the near future.

The market opportunity for products exploiting local taste preferences will be increasing and we will see MNCs taking the move earlier to encash on those opportunities. Local players are expected to know the game better and therefore, any initiatives from their part is expected to create a success story if they can put up a value proposition for the customers preempting the MNCs. Few players are thinking in that direction. For example, MTR in south. But we don't see any such attempt in north or east. Otherwise Rosagolla, by now would have been a global brand. Possibly some MNC will make that happen some day. And we will watch that happening.

Rising Input Cost is Responsible for Declining Profitability of Processed Food Industry

Food Industry has registered relatively higher growth amongst the FMCG categories. The major players have registered a growth rate of about 14 per cent in the year 2004 over the previous year which is significantly higher than the growth rate which was averaging around 7 to 8% in the earlier three consecutive years. The Ministry of Food Processing Industry is expecting a growth rate of about 8% till the year 2007 which will further escalate to 10% by the year 2010. When there was sharp increase in the growth rate in the year 2004 everything looked brighter till I chanced upon a recent analyses of the industry. According the analyses done by the Industrial credit rating agency (ICRA) the yearly growth rate of this sector is highly variable.

It was 15% in the year 2001, 9% in the year 2002, 8% in 2003 increasing to 14% in fiscal 2004. But more important factor is the declining operating margin which was 6.7 per cent in the year 2000 to 5.8 per cent in 2004. This declining operating margin is arising out of the increase in the raw material cost. The raw material costs have increased from 68% of the operating income in 2000 to 71% in 2004. The operating profit would have further reduced but for lower employee costs and other overheads. Obviously industry tried to neutralize the rise in raw material price by reducing the overheads. At present about 1.5 million workers are employed directly by the industry which is projected by the ministry to go up to 37 million by the year 2025. It has been mentioned earlier that this industry is not the favorite of the financial institutions. If the projection of employment has to go up there has to be significant new investments. The ministry's projection for new investment in food processing is to the tune of INR 20 billion by the year 2010. But ICRA in their analyses has pointed out –"Projects originating from this industry need to be scrutinized in great detail for viability in each aspect of the value chain and in terms of appeal to consumers". Impacted by the reduced margin, food companies are also trying to manage the business with reduced working capital. The working capital to operating income improved from 78 days in 2000 to 70 days in the year 2004. This has helped corporations to report relatively stable return on capital employed (ROCE). The point that is being conveyed that competitiveness is getting reduced for higher input cost in terms of raw material in a situation where value addition is already lower for this category of industry. How can then Ministry of Food Processing Industry still keep hope for higher growth and higher investment ?

The industry is struggling to keep the price line competitive. As we all know that India is a very price sensitive market. The growth can only take place if the price can be lowered and brought under the affordability limit of the masses. Time and again this has been demonstrated. The carbonated soft drink market was registering a growth rate of about 10-12% for many years. Last year both cola majors, Coke and Pepsi, tried to break this barrier by introducing INR 6 a bottle and even INR 5 for 200 ml beverage. The growth was phenomenal. The category grew by 20% because of significant penetration of rural market. But industry found at the end of the day that their profitability has taken its toll because the lower price is not supported by the lowering of the cost. Both cola majors again decided to withdraw from this low price segment and focus again on the more profitable segment. They therefore, again gone ahead with the price increase to improve the bottom line performance. The market reacted sharply and the cola sales has come down by 20% again. The lowering of price to improve affordability had helped both cola majors to increase the sales of Cola from 160 million cases to 250 million cases. The initial strategy was to keep the lower price line for some more time till the cost is managed well could not be pursued because of rising cost of inputs such as sugar and freight etc. The total estimated cola consumers in the country is said to be about 250 million with consumption level lower than about 10 servings per year. But most profitable segment is only top five percent of this set whose average consumption is around 325 servings per year. For this hard core consumers price is not the major concern. One has to therefore decide on a trade off between volume sales against profitable sales. The obvious choice in the long run is thus to make profit for the business.

When the issue of affordability is the key to the growth of the Indian processed food industry coupled with the expectation of the policy makers to take Indian processed food to places around the globe the cost of production will play a significant role in terms of the keeping price line that will fuel growth and also make our products competitive. The raw material and packaging material constitute about 70 per cent of the cost of the goods. Therefore, keeping the price of agro commodities stable is essential. Otherwise, we cannot expect the growth rate to continue at the present level as we have experienced in case of cola beverages.

In a recent survey it has been found that the middle income group consumers are increasing in India. Even in terms of millionaires we have now about 70000 of them – a growth of about 14% over the year 2003. Unfortunately, the high income group offers a different kind of opportunity. This segment is there not to surge big volume business for the companies. Recently I was reading about the market potential of the costliest whisky brand and I was surprised that there are Indians who have ordered this brand. The most premium blended scotch whisky – 50 years old (matured) elite version of the brand 'Isle of the Skye' priced at INR 0.125 million per bottle is all set to enter Indian market. It seems that this brand has already hit the duty free shop here. This blend of whisky is matured for 50 years in wooden cask for special flavour and packed in typical style being followed for ages. Also no water is added or mixed with the beverages. The estimated market for this premium whisky in India is said to be 250 bottles per annum. In the year 2004 around 84 bottles have been imported into Mumbai. But this kind of market segment does not offer much avenues for the growth of the industry category as such.

There are two kinds of marketers one can find in industry. One – those who think that best product should be offered at least cost to be successful which may not be feasible. The other breed – thinks that anything can be sold at any price because they believe that there is a market for everything. In fact for sustainable development of a long term business proposition both these two types of marketers are wrong. In the product offering there has to be significant value perception for the consumers as well as a healthy margin for the manufacturers and for that matter all stakeholders in the entire chain. This is not happening and that is our main problem.

Industry has to work together to hold on the cost by going through all possible innovative measures. Government help will come as great relief to give the necessary support in terms of infrastructure and stability of the input raw and packing material cost. Failing which we will be only repeating the old level of performance and big time growth will remain a pipe dream.

Industry Constantly Relooking at their Product Portfolio and Investments

Heinz acquired Glaxo's food business comprising of Farex, Complan and Glucon-D along with the factory at Aligarh couple of years ago. Farex has now been put on the block for sale. Heinz is world leader in tomato ketchup but could not establish the product in India where Kissan and Maggi are the leading players. Farex has lost the market share over the years to Amul and Nestle in the baby food category and Heinz could not help it grow and therefore now looking for a buyer. Hindustan Lever divested their entire dairy food range covering Anik ghee and skim milk powder along with their Etah plant in UP to Nutricia – a Dutch food company.

Nutricia tried to revive that unit and also launched their own food supplements but could not make it a success story. Finally Nutricia exited from the business altogether by selling the business and brands that they acquired from HLL to the leading oil seed processors in MP, the Ruchi group owned by Agarwals. Kellogg introduced a range of biscuits and cookies and having failed to create a success story withdrawn from the category and now focusing on the core break fast cereal business where they are yet to make any profit. Britannia entered the dairy business with a big bang with its high profile launch of cheese (from cow milk) and later on the fluid milk in many metro cities. Recently, they have launched ghee as well. All are through the sub contract manufacturing route. Britannia has withdrawn from the fluid milk business altogether in a phased manner. And hived off other dairy product business in to a separate joint venture with a New Zealand based cooperative dairy. This has happened in spite of the fact that Britannia has the support of Danone – a French company and a leader in dairy business in Europe. Two years ago Sara Lee exited from specialty biscuits and cookies business after selling their plant in south to their distributors. ITC Agro sold their food portfolio to ConAgra who have also launched ACT II – a microwave based plain and butter corn.

They had a plan to launch a series of microwave based products. But microwave penetration is still not high to warrant a success story in that specialized category. Dabur had earlier set up a joint venture with Spanish group Agrilimen for confectionery products and subsequently withdrawn from the venture. Prior to that Dabur had joint venture with a specialty biscuit and cookies manufacturing company of Israel which ended up in loss and finally closed down. Dabur has been continuing with the joint venture having 50:50 participation in Dabon International between Dabur and French dairy major Bongrain SA which was set up in 1996. We thought that this is going fine but Dabur is now going to exit from this joint venture saying that cheese and dairy products is non strategic business for them.

Sometime ago Parrys have sold their confectionery business and the analyst thought that they might even exit from sugar business also in the long run but they introduced a new branded sugar as a value added product instead. Dhampure was the first sugar company to introduce branded value added sugar in the market. They have recently withdrawn from the category by saying that the category did not grow and consumers are not willing to pay 4-5 % extra for branded and value added sugars. ITC sold their food business earlier but came back again with renewed enthusiasm. HLL has created their entire food portfolio through acquisition when they could not create a single brand of their own. If ice cream is their core business, why they had to sell dairy factory , brand and business as log stock and barrel. HLL also acquired Dollop ice cream brand from Cadburys which they have abandoned. I can go on taking examples of businesses constantly relooking at their portfolio of brands and business and either retaining or divesting some of those to refurbish the portfolio which makes better business sense. We need to examine that.

The Chairman of HLL in his speech at the Annual General meeting (AGM) said that they saw a great growth potential in leading the evolution of consumers to branded and processed foods and thus HLL over the last few years made attempt to put in place the building blocks of a strong food business. As it exists Indian food industry is fragmented and lack scale and it was often commoditized with low margins. Businesses have recognized the fact that to change the food habits need huge investment which is not affordable even for a big giant like HLL. This has forced businesses including HLL to divest non value adding food business. Sometime ago HLL has divested their Vanaspati (Dalda, which is generic to the category) business to US based Bangi group but dairy business was not the similar and yet it was not adding any significant value to the HLL and therefore they even disposed off the same to Nutricia. As said by the chairman of HLL by reshuffling the portfolio the business was able to improve the margin by about 13 percent through product mix rationalization and also through cost reduction. They have cleared the supply chain of all old stock and geared up for fresh availability on shelf. According to them today the food business has a healthy margin and a supply chain driven by freshness and therefore food business will now invest for growth through relevant innovation.

Most players in processed food industry are not able to utilize their installed capacity and therefore there is extra fixed cost burden the processors carry. Too much competition and that too from small scale players does not allow marketer to realize optimal price and there is constant pressure on price. Too complex market structure and multiple trade layers eat up lot of available margins. Ever escalating media cost also eat into margins. For all these reasons marketers have constantly looked at their portfolio to make the whole category deliver at least expected profit. And that is the primary reason why we see constant reshuffling of the portfolio.

There were many new entrants to the category who got attracted by mere size of the market but consumption level is very low for the processed food. People still prefer the fresh. Changing this food habit needs enormous investment which business cannot afford in a category where success rate is very low. The processed food is still an urban phenomena and therefore growth has to be driven by the urban market potential which has its own limitation. If the price is reduced to get rural market penetration, it does not become a profitable proposition. The value addition in food trade is one of the lowest in India. In this scenario, players have to work hard to create more value and capture that value to deliver the incremental value to the customer in relation to the competition to survive in the game. And that is no easy task. Most of the new entrants realized this after they entered the market. A few of them still struggling thinking of very long term potential. Others have called it a day although they were very successful in many other countries around the globe.

Food Marketers Trying all Possibilities to Increase the Consumption Level

Processed food industry registered a modest growth despite the fact that FMCG sectors are going through a difficult phase and most of the companies are trying to deliver the bottom line growth by resorting to severe cost cutting, organisational restructuring and improving upon the operational efficiency to gain the confidence of the shareholders in an apparently recessionary market environment. The poor show of the food industry in India is due to the fact that promoters of food business have little or nil appreciation of the knowledge of the business. Most of the operators so far in this category, if we isolate large Indian and multi-national companies, are small traders venturing into the business with half-baked knowledge. The owners of the processed

Fig. 11.1 The key task at hand for marketers is to increase the consumption of processed food.

food industry in India have set up their enterprises by fishing disjointed information from scattered sources.

They are therefore not the natural owners of their businesses and that is why they are suffering. The other major reason of poor success rate of processed food industry is the market size here in India. It is small and growth rate is still smaller and as a result even the big players here have to struggle for the volume. This triggers a question - Are Indians eating less? That might sound incredible but if the latest data collated by the Central Statistical Organisation (CSO) is correct, that would certainly appear to be the case. According to the CSO data the expenditure on food actually declined by 1.4 per cent in 2000-01 in notional terms and by 2.7 per cent in inflation adjusted terms. This would mean on a per capita basis Indians ate less in 2000-01. It has been known for some time now that the consumption basket of the average Indian has changed in recent years in favour of healthcare, transport and communication services at the cost of the basic necessity of food and clothing. But the CSO data reveals that this pattern has accelerated significantly during year 2000-01, which means consumption expenditure on food products, has actually declined during the year. The per family consumption expenditure (PFCE) on food has declined from 50.6% in 1993-94 to 46% in 1999-2000 to 42.8% in 2000-01. This can also be due to inequalities in income distribution. The task of the food marketers therefore has become all the more difficult to maintain the healthy growth. And the players are thus exploring various means.

Battling the sluggish consumer spending scenario, Nestle India has decided to fight the slowdown by introducing 20 new products in the year 2002 across categories and imbibing the smaller packs and lower price points to extend the possibility of distribution coverage. This strategy helps them to increase penetration. The success of the INR 5 pack of Maggi 50 gms has been replicated in coffee products. In recessionary period, people prefer to buy small packs as one time expenditure is less. This method is effective to retain the brand loyal customers in recessionary market conditions.

Coke is focusing on 200 ml. segment this year. In seventies we had seen the soft carbonated beverage in returnable bottles in 200 ml. This gradually became 250 ml. and then to 300 ml. and the strategy was to deliver more quantity at the same price. The whole industry had to follow the changed rules triggered by multinationals and before that by Thums-Up. The history repeats itself, as we say. The new game is now smaller quantity in lesser prices. This requires huge investment in terms of bottles but the industry seems to be prepared for it. Pepsi has decided to uncork campaign for lemon cola. They seem to be concentrating on the lemon segment. The 200 ml. lemon launched in north is priced at INR 6 as against INR 9 for 300 ml. and the 500 ml. PET bottle at

INR15. The cloudy lemon lime pioneered by Limca has about 14% market share in the total aerated drink market where as clear lime constitute about 4%. Also cloudy lemon is favoured in north whereas clear lemon-lime is preferred in southern market. Pepsi is not a dominant player in lemon-lime segment but now they are becoming aggressive to take away a reasonable share of this market.

Britannia has definitely succeeded in some of their new launches in dairy segment. They therefore wanted to import dairy products through their joint venture with Fonteria Cooperative Group of New Zealand. Britannia will still focus on dairy segment for their growth. They will, of course, source the products through the third parties as they have done earlier. ITC is launching its new Atta brand. ITC has leased a 100 ton per day capacity plant near Delhi for northern India market for this purpose. It is not the first time that ITC is venturing into the food segment. ITC had their earlier stint in branded grocery business and they were quite big in edible oil segment, which was subsequently sold to Con Agra. But this time they entered again in this segment with wheat flour.

There are others who are trying to expand the market by extending to the new geographical locations. After a long wait, the United States has opened its gate for Indian spirits. In a major breakthrough for the domestic spirit industry, the Bureau of Alcohol, Tobacco and Firearms has given permission to Shaw Wallace & Company to sell Director's Special whiskey in the United States. They will be required to label the product as Indian Whiskey. But this is a major achievement for Shaw Wallace, in particular and the Indian liquor industry, in general.

The new initiatives are not limited to only large food processors. We can see actions in other areas as well. Agri export zones (AEZs), a concept introduced in the Exim policy 2001 to promote agricultural exports on the specific products from specific geographical areas are expected to reap optimum benefits from the concessions on transport subsidy and other benefits. There are several regions found for promoting the growth of specific category of agricultural products. For example, for leechi it is Uttaranchal, West Bengal and Bihar; for pineapple it is West Bengal and Tripura and for mangoes it is UP and Maharashtra etc. Globally growth of agro product export trails far behind the manufacturing sector export. The initiatives taken will help to realise the expected growth rate in this sector which has been pegged at INR 300 billion in next three year.

It has been seen that the average life span of an organisation is about thirty-five years. Those few global enterprises, which have survived much longer, have constantly undergone metamorphosis. Those who have refused to change died faster. When environment changes, it is therefore quite apparent that organisations are trying to do different things to remain floating. And it is needless to say that only those, which are trying to do different things, will survive.

Fads in Processed Food Industry

Fashion changes, so also has been seen for many processed food items which came and gone. Like fashion designers, marketers of food products translated the ideas and dreams of nutritionists, technologists and investors to create the demand of new types of food but many of these were shortlived. Investors rushed to make significant new investment in those processed food industries which disappeared like fads.

In late sixties protein food was one such fad. Prof. A.N. Bose - former Vice chancellor of Jadavpur University and a pioneer in food technology education and research in India - organised an international conference on "Protein Fortification of Food" in Kolkata. The conference was a grand success if one should judge by the global level of paticipation, involving industry representatives, nutritionists, technologists and policy makers, quality of presentations and deliberations. Prof. Bose is a towering personality, he could assemble who's who on the subject. In subsequent years many new protein foods hit the market. All leading multinational pharmaceutical companies introduced protein foods. And we have thus seen `Protinex' from Pfizer, "Protinules" from Alembic, "Spert" (derived from superior protein efficiency ratio) from Sandoz.

These products are actually protein supplement - to be mixed with milk and consumed and thus enriching the milk protein. The protein wave was so great that others introduced protein foods as variants. For example, Raptakos Brett introduced "Threptin" biscuit and Britannia "Probisk". Some of these products have disappeared and others still struggling to exist. This fad also drew the attention of the basic food marketers and thus we had protein fortified Atta etc. The first major investment in protein food industry was made by Tata Oil Mills by setting up an integrated groundnut processing plant in Mumbai - to produce peanut protein concentrate, protein isolate and also peanut protein based sterilised milk in bottles. Tata oil Mill is now under the fold of Hindustan Lever and this particular plant is closed down. Prof. Sulebele of University Department of Chemical Technology (UDCT), Mumbai had spent long years in popularising sterilised groundnut milk in bottle by associating himself in this project on a whole time basis and had to give up after seeing no light at the end of the tunnel.

Fig. 11.2 Many new products were introduced in protein food category.

The next fad in processed food industry was marine food. India has vast coastal line with three oceans and we were told that we were only scratching the surface. We have a gold mine of marine resource which we can catch, process and market globally - it was argued convincingly. And as expected, there was a beeline to set up fish processing plants. Some of them were

Fig. 11.3 Some foods did not survive long and disappeared like a fad.

ultramodern. Tatas, ITC, Britannia, Union Carbide had established modern freezing and processing plants. None of those are existing now. Union Carbide in fact had also processing facility on board in addition to having a plant in Vizag. After incurring huge losses they either closed their units or sold to smaller and traditional players in this line. Along the line Brook Bond had set up meat processing plant in Aurangabad and could not run it which subsequently Allanas took over and running profitably. Britannia's marine food plant at Thane was similarly sold to Bombay cold storage owned by B.R. Chopra of Bollywood fame. In subsequent years big business houses used to buy marine export to comply with the government requirement of balancing the import-export ratio. By then, big business houses realised that marine product processing is not a business where large corporate houses can make money. It is the domain of small business groups best run by family owned set up. While in Escort I tried to set up marine processing plant in New Bombay but after running it for two years it was again closed down incurring losses. This industry is strewn with several pitfalls and at every stage one can get cheated if not become extremely careful and if there is no personalised involvement.

The systems and procedures of large business houses really don't work here. The change in global market environment has forced this industry to upgrade the quality control measures by introducing Hazard Analysis and Critical Control Process (HACCP) and the industry is said to have invested over INR.1000 million in one year as per the report of the Indian Seafood Exporters Association. This step will help developing Indian Brand in international market particularly in EU. It can be pointed out here that unless we control the global market by introducing successfully our own brand directly in international market marine food industry will always remain very vulnerable and sooner we realise it is better. Shrimp is now put under Open General License (OGL) and imported shrimp has already hit Indian market. This is part of the deregulation as per WTO agreement.

During mid eighties soyabean- the golden bean and a wonder crop caught the eyes of the nutritionists and technologists. Soyamilk is nutritionally even better than cow milk and thus prospect of soyamilk and soyamilk based products were said to be very great. Examples were drawn from the international markets - "Vitasoy" in Hongkong is selling more than Coca-Cola in that country and hence why cannot we display the similar performance here in India - it was argued.

Only problems that encountered with soyamilk were presence of trypsin inhibitor, which gets destroyed on heating and beany odour due to lipoxygenase activity. Lot of work was done to take care of beany odour and Alfa Laval had developed plant to produce soyamilk having less or negligible beany odour. United Breweries Group was interested to set up this plant and we had worked in Alfa Laval's pilot plant in Lund, Sweden to perfect a product formulation to be introduced in India. The product when researched in India came closer to cow milk and was found to be acceptable by the target consumers. But unfortunately the project did not take off as by then UB's interest in food business faded and we in fact started looking around for buyers for Kissan and Dipy's which got subsequently acquired by Brook Bond.

UB did not go ahead with its soyamilk project even after doing great deal of work in that direction. But those who went ahead had burnt their fingers. Barring small timers, there were large business houses who had set up this project. For example, Great Eastern Shipping Group had set up their plant in Indore and had introduced flavoured soyamilk by name "Great Shake" in tetrapack. This plant was subsequently sold to Godrej who makes "Jump-in" fruit beverages there now. Amrit Vanaspati Group also had set up similar plant but their packaging plant was supplied by "Prepac" of France. They tried to popularise the flavoured soyamilk for two years and having failed now processing cow milk and selling pasteurised cow milk in Delhi market. By then smaller local brands also disappeared from the market. The biggest investment on soyabean processing was done by Britannia. At a cost of INR.250 million they had set up an integrated soyabean processing plant at Vidisha in M.P.- the heartland of soyabean. They also introduced edible oil (soyabean oil) by name "Vital". After one year this plant was sold to SM-Dye Chem - manufacturer of "Peppy" brand of extruded food. SM-Dye Chem now is said to be passing through the difficult time.

Then came the fad of snack food and extruded food. Potato Chips and expanded extruded ready-to-eat snacks projects started coming up in many places. TTK's "Fryum", Jagjit's "Binnys", Delhi flour mill's "Crax" and a half a dozen local and regional brands came and gone. "Crax" is still available in Delhi market but it is a very low-key affair. In potato chips Amrit Foods "Uncle Chips" brand can be considered successful which was subsequently acquired by Pepsi. Of course, Potato Chips now has again emerged as big category. In extrusion technology based project many suffered losses and closed down, examples are Rishabh Foods in Haryana, Oshi Foods in Bhopal etc. Rishabh is now trying to survive by subcontracting for Nestle, Cadbury and Dabur. Extrusion technology was used to produce low cost food by various State Government for school children feeding programme but those are heavily subsidised.

The lesson that we have learnt as far as processed food is concerned that a short-term euphoria cannot be considered as a long-term sustainable business. Of course, like multinationals, if a very long term perspective is taken such as Kellogg's who has declared that in India thev don't expect to make money at least in next twelve to fifteen years, then things could have been different.

But local industries cannot afford those kind of financial strains. Therefore, may be that where we failed earlier might become a profitable proposition now under MNC management where resources are committed for a longer term. Because, the fact of the matter is that although food habits do not change easily but on sustained effort it can happen slowly and surely.

Latest craze that I find when I visit food stores are different types of health foods such as "muesli" as breakfast cereals and muesli bars as snacks, also Kellogg selling variety of flakes on health connotation. Will they remain a long-term established products or will pass by again as fads as fashion changes? Only time will tell.

Perfect Timing for New Product Launch is one of the Key Factors for Success

We have seen that nine out of ten new products bomb in the market place. The failure rate is increasing further with ever increasing competition. These days failure rate is even higher. Marketers still try to create new business category with relentless efforts because ultimate dream of every marketer is to create and own a new category. Maggi and Rasna have just done that. But creating success stories is not an easy task these days. As a result, we don't see any big and remarkable success stories in food categories. Milkfood Ltd (a Jagatjit Industries group company) launched 100 % ice cream and have failed due to competition from Kwality ice cream. But the same company also kicked off flavoured and fruit yoghurt in the early 1990s and have failed. The company even introduced both fruit yoghurt and flavoured yoghurt and that too in wide range of flavours and fruits combination and both in the form of set and stirred variety to complete the range. And all of us were expecting a success story because they had taken the first move.During that time we were working on the development of the flavoured yoghurt in the food division of United Breweries Group (UB) .We did even product development trials and market research to project the demand estimate and the indications were favourable. UB group even started talking to Group Dannone for collaboration. Till date Dannone and Yoplait are the two successful global brands in this category. We initiated discussion with APV for the supply of the plant for the manufacturing of this product. But APV was setting up the similar plant also for Milkfoods and it was considered to be a very prestigious project for APV. They were telling us that we should speed up the process as the Milkfoods plant is fast coming up. As it always happens, everything do not fall in place in time and we had to reconcile with the fact that Milkfoods launched the product ahead of us in spite of the fact that we had conceptualized the product well ahead of them but they had an advantage in that they were already in dairy business and had a milk processing plant in Punjab.

Milkfood introduced the product initially in Delhi market and the availability was good in the sense that the product was available in all ice cream outlets including inside the cabinet of hand trolley vendors which contributes maximum sales. Product was priced at INR 6 per 250 gms cup. And we thought that the price was reasonable. But the product still failed. We then started analyzing the reasons of failure and our findings were that north was not the right place to launch the product. In north yoghurt is consumed everyday in the breakfast either as curd or lassi and the consumers will not replace their daily habit of consuming home made fresh curd or lassi. South could have been better place to launch any health foods as it was always been the case.

Ice cream consumption in north is high, because they cannot make it at home. Besides, at INR 6 for 250 gm yoghurt they could get one and half liter of fluid milk in Mother Dairy booth in those days. We thus could easily rationalize the failures. But we at UB could have also made the same mistake. Rest is the history – the product failed and subsequently withdrawn from the market. Today both Milkfoods Ltd and APV India Ltd disappeared from the Indian market. Dannone is said to be seriously considering introducing this product category in India. They will not set up the plant but will test the market through sub contract route. Time and again marketers including big players failed to create a new category. Hindusthan Lever did not succeed in dairy business and their Anik brand was practically a non starter. Finally, Hindusthan Lever could sell their plant at Etah in Uttar Pradesh to a new comer Nutricia who thought that they would make good use of this facility to market their nutritional supplement products. Now Nutricia has put the same plant on the block for sale. It is always an up- hill task to make a new product succeed.

Small quantity of set yoghurts were selling then in local isolated pockets but those were not a big success story to talk about. Even Amul and Mother dairy had set yoghurts in Delhi and Mumbai markets. Additionally, there were small local players. Those still exist today. But I would like to mention the case of Fun Foods Pvt. Ltd. – a Delhi based small company introducing the plain set yoghurt in the market. This company could enter the Indian Airlines and were exclusive supplier to them for many years. Fun Foods yoghurt was a permanent item in the Indian Airlines breakfast menu and they were selling everyday at least thirty thousand cups of set yoghurt to Indian Airlines alone producing this item from their small factory in Safdarjung Enclave in NewDelhi. Fun Foods had no experience in dairy industry before. For the last few years Fun Foods yoghurt is not there in Indian Airlines menu. The company still exists and markets a range of specialty foods like mayonnaise, salad dressing etc. in the local market but they are no longer in yoghurt. It is all over. If your product do not have consumer franchise only institutional patronage will not take you for long. Creating a success story for short term thus only is half the task–sustaining and growing it is another thing.

Timing and need gap identification are crucial for any marketer trying to create a new category. Take a look at companies that wanted to take on that challenge, but failed. Nestle probably felt that since India is largely a tea drinking country with a hot climate to boot, iced tea will be a winner. And it launched Paloma iced tea in the 1980s. Unfortunately, market was not ready and the product bombed. It has taken almost 20 years for Nestle to venture again in this segment. Both HLL and Nestle entered this segment recently. Timing therefore, is one of the most important rules of marketing to succeed.

ITC and Tata have Big Plans in Basic Foods for the Second Time

ITC Agro had earlier done significant investment in the areas of edible oil. They had gone for the backward linkages for this edible oil sector and launched the brand Sundrop sunflower oil. In Andhra Pradesh ITC had done significant agricultural extension work and contracted farmers for growing sunflower. But, couple of years ago they had sold their business to the US food MNC-Con Agra which is said to be the fastest growing food conglomerate in U.S. But after selling its earlier business in foods to Con Agra ITC Agro has renewed their interest in primary foods business again. One may wonder why? Tobacco business is always under public pressure and ITC had tried to find out avenues for diversification.

The recent one being in sports goods through organized retailing. Their Wills brand of cigarette has always been promoting the sports goods and therefore entry into this category is in expected line. Of late, ITC seem to have renewed their interest again in food business and therefore started talking about their aggressive plan into primary foods to be achieved through an integrated approach of agri business for which they have already worked out an inspiring agenda to be pursued. ITC with their well structured network of distribution penetrating the rural market, agri business should always been their priority and therefore we were surprised when they decided to sell their edible oil business to Con Agra after building it up from scratch. Although primary reason could be the fact that they were losing in that business but for the reason that their tobacco business is also agro based there were very valid reasons for them to continue which they did not. We were surprised earlier but not now when again they have renewed their interest in agri business.

Fig. 11.4 ITC launched a whole basket of processed food including primary food items.

ITC is primarily planning to leverage information technology for rural transformation to benefit from the marketing channel in a dynamic environment which ITC will provide. For that purpose they have taken e-choupal-an IT initiative to deliver real term information and customized knowledge to improve farmers decision making ability and thereby better align farm output to market demands and secure better quality, productivity and improved price recovery. India has all the basic ingredients for becoming a global player in the world trade of agro commodities. What we require is to deliver better quality at competitive price. This can be achieved by eliminating the colossal waste that takes place and for the involvement of multiple handling and intermediaries. Setting up direct marketing channel virtually linked to the mandi system for the purpose of price recovery and at the same time eliminating wasteful involvement of intermediaries and multiple handling, thus reducing the transaction costs and making the logistics more efficient. This model facilitates direct marketing channel in competition with the existing mandi system. Information technology initiatives are aimed at achieving all these. It can be pointed out here that IT initiatives can make all the difference. US food analyst had already predicted that due to drought conditions prevailing in India our basmati output will go down in the year 2003 by about ten million tons and therefore in global market there will be a short supply of basmati rice by about two million tons. US authorities therefore alerted their farmers that this two million tons will be an additional business opportunity for Taxas long grain rice farmers.

This example, will give an idea how the information is analyzed for business opportunity in a global environment these days. The government is taking many initiatives but private sectors can really make it faster. Towards that end ITC taking a lead role is appreciative. They have a significant advantage over other large players and MNCs in the sense that they have well penetrated rural and agricultural extension, service and distribution network as opposed to others like HLL who have only a well managed rural distribution net work. ITC had already launched Atta under the brand name "Ashirwad" in the markets covering Delhi, Haryana, Chandigarh, Meerut and Jaipur. This will be followed up by other staple foods with regional variants as per the plan. The food products that ITC launched is a cooked dal under the "Kitchen of India" brand. This also is said to be followed by other daily use products such as sugar and beverages. They are therefore getting into both staple foods and also value added processed foods. And both through contract manufacturing route.

Many may not recollect that in line with their usual business policies (to be there in all kinds of businesses) Tatas' were earlier in processed food business as well. Tata had OK brand of processed fruit and vegetable products and popular among those were Squash, Cordials and Jams in northern market. This was way back in seventies. Their manufacturing facility was located in Gaziabad and like many others in this trade they did not do well and finally this business was closed. Tatas were also having oil mills in Mumbai. Tata Oil Mills (TOMCO) was the pioneer in processing of groundnut oil. They were the first to set up peanut protein concentrate and isolate plant in the country. In seventies customers had to pay TOMCO in advance for peanut protein isolate. Subsequently, they also produced soya protein concentrate and isolate. Tomco also had soaps and detergents and were quite a leading player in that as well. HLL acquired that business couple of years ago. Tatas also had food flavour and fragrance business covering a wide range which still exists but operation is in low key. After quietly exiting from the food business they seem to be again interested in food business.

This time Tatas are venturing through Tata Chemicals which was earlier being looked after by Late Darbari Seth. Tata Chemicals is said to be entering into a broad category of foods including sugar, masalas and staple foods like rice, atta and dal. International consulting agency major Mckinsey & Co is helping Tatas to work out the detail game plan. Why Tata closed down their earlier business in foods is clearly understandable as they were required to focus on few key areas and foods definitely was not featuring amongst those. But why they have now again serious to get into the business? The answer lies in their success in Tata Salt brand which is still the number one branded table salt in India with well entrenched distribution network. They therefore, can piggy back on their salt success as they expect.

The reasons for the decision to enter into the basic food business by these two large groups could be different. But that does not matter. What matters to us is that these two big players with huge resources to their command will make difference to our long term game plan on agri business.

12

International Trade Opportunity in Select Food Category

Prospects of Fresh Fruits and Vegetable Export

India's fresh fruits and vegetables export has been very low all these years but it is increasing. Our main market for fresh fruits and vegetables is Middle East. In 1990 -91 India exported about 319 thousand MT of fresh fruits and vegetables worth in INR 1800 million which went up to 475 thousand MT having value of INR 3850 million which indicates that there is growth both in volume and also in the unit rate. Amongst fruits, mango and that too Alphonso mango has found a steady market abroad. Alphonso has significant demand in European market as well.

And if infrastructural support is there it can really become big. Besides , in addition to the infrastructural reasons we have a cyclical crop failure every alternate year which also is responsible for lacklustre performance of mango in export front. We are expecting that India has significant potential to become one of the key players in agricultural products in global trade. Although we are witnessing that there are significant improvement in export performance but that is nowhere near expectation and that too are achieved because Government is holding out a whole range of incentives to the exporters. Fruits and vegetables have been placed in the high priority areas for foreign technology and foreign direct investment. Automatic approval is also given to joint ventures in this area having up to 51 per cent foreign equity. The export thrust has been possible because of a very well developed market abroad. Although earlier focus was only on mangoes but during post liberalisation era we can see significant emphasis has also been given to other types of fruits including grapes, apples and oranges.

We can see some significant initiatives in that direction. The Agricultural and Processed Food Products Export Development Authority (APEDA) has signed separate memorandums of understanding with Maharastra government and the Rotterdam based Mother Dairy Fruit and Vegetables Ltd to boost export of mangoes (Alphonso) and grapes respectively to the European markets through the Agri Export Zones (AEZ). The Reserve Bank of India (RBI) has also recently cleared packing credit limit for these zones.

The packing credits cleared by RBI will be permitted for inputs such as seeds, pesticides , micro-nutrients and other materials imported by the exporters based at AEZ and supplied that to the farmers from whom they purchase the farm produce for export purposes. United Kingdom (UK) is a major target market and therefore APEDA's deal with Mother Dairy Fruits and Vegetables (MDFV) can provide significant support in UK market. As per understanding an MDFV representative will be relocated in the UK market to provide regular feedback to APEDA and also to the Pune based Grape Exporters' Federation about the prices, arrivals of mango and grapes from other competing countries, consumer feedback and the quality requirements of the specific markets. This representative will also explore possibilities of direct supplies to supermarkets in the UK and other European markets. As India's mango and grapes quality is good this would be a significant possibility. Fresh produce always have short season and on the top of that these are highly perishable and immediate action and decisions are therefore the key factors. These understandings thus can be expected to be beneficial.

Fig. 12.1 Big prospect for Indian fruits and vegerables in global trade.

The investment in this activity will be shared by various interested parties. The project entails a total investment of INR 350 million. Of this, INR 100 million will flow in from various central government agencies and INR 160 million will be from state government agencies and the balance from the private sectors. The agreement for mangoes will facilitate setting up of AEZs in the areas covering Sindhudurga, Ratnagiri, Thane and Raigad districts of Maharashtra. These initiatives of APEDA will therefore be largely going to benefit only one state and that is Maharashtra.

Not only mango and grapes, there is a distinct possibility that India can create market for apples and orange as well. Quite sometime ago Associated Cement Company Ltd (ACC) which was at that point of time a Tata Group company had taken initiatives to pack fresh oranges from Nagpur region for export. Dr Ganguly who was the managing director of ACC at that time took personal interest and a packing plant was set up for fresh orange export. ACC also had signed contract with the local orange growers. They exported some quantity but the project did not take off both for logistical reasons as well as for lack of market .The plant still exists and remained idle. Ideally the fresh fruits export business has to be located close to shipping port. It has to be either exported by air immediately on packing or it has to be transported through refrigerated containers and such facility should be preferentially available to this trade failing which it is not going to take off and on the contrary shippers are going to suffer tremendous losses. That has exactly happened to Tatas.

Government should set up storage and transportation facility and a centralised packing facility to be utilised by the farmers and then entire output to be exported through a nodal agency like MDFV. In that case we can expect to have competitive edge in the world market. MDFV can even take the product to the Europe and market directly and also through organised food retail chain and thereby add more value in the entire value chain. If a country like Brazil can become one of the largest exporter of orange from practically nowhere why cannot India? We definitely have a distinct possibility.

Indian Food and Agro Business Trade with the Middle East Countries

The geographical term Middle East was first coined in 1902 by the United States Naval Officer Alfred Thayer Mahan, originally referred to the Asian region south of Black Sea between the Mediterranean Sea to the west and India to the east. In today's context the term middle east collectively refers to the Asian countries of Bahrain, Cyprus, Iran, Iraq, Israel, Jordan, Kuwait,

Lebanon, Oman, Qatar, Saudi Arabia, Syria, Turkey, United Arab Emirates (UAE), Yemen and the African country of Egypt. It contains about 65% of the world's oil reserves. However, agriculture is still dominating the regional economy and in some countries like Iraq, Iran, Yemen, Egypt and Turkey agriculture contributes about 15 to 25% of their gross domestic products (GDP). The Indian business community frequently travel in these countries to establish contacts with all most all processed food and agricultural products importers in this region, more predominantly those who have regular trade with India.

The trading conditions in these countries are favourable for India for the simple reason that Indians are working there to facilitate the process of discussion and negotiation. The deal, of course, is invariably concluded by the locals directly. India having her geographical proximity to Arab world, our export business is significantly dependent on this regions' purchase. Many fruit and vegetable processing units and more importantly marine products and animal products including meat and poultry processing units who are dependent solely on the business from middle east and that too their business are in real terms customer specific in that region for years. Our export oriented processed food industry has therefore lot of dependence on middle east business.

With the middle east countries we have lot of fresh foods trade. Every day charter load of fresh fruits, vegetables, meat, fish and poultry including eggs are going from Delhi and Mumbai to these countries. But what we are doing now can go up significantly by improving the bilateral trade relations and business promotion. Our fresh food trade from India particularly fruits, vegetables, meat, fish, poultry and eggs will constitute a large part of this export. This has immense potential for further growth because we enjoy both cost and freight advantage. Very recently, in late August 2004 India and the six-nation Gulf Cooperation Council (GCC) put trade and economic ties on the fast track by signing a bilateral agreement in the Indian capital. India's Commerce and Industry Minister Mr. Kamal Nath and Kuwaiti Foreign Minister Mr. Sheikh Mohammed Al-Sabah signed a framework of agreement for economic cooperation that could eventually lead to a free trade pact.

Our bilateral trade had shown consistent increase with India's exports to GCC amounting to USD 7 billion and imports excluding oil from GCC amounting to USD 3.25 billion during 2003-2004. The significant part of this export is from food and agricultural products. Some of our leading processors and exporters have operations in the middle east and they have their offices, reprocessing centers, cold storages located in strategic locations in that country to enable them to add higher value in the entire chain till the products reach the ultimate customers. For example, Allanas in Mumbai who acquired the modern meat processing unit in Aurangabad in Maharastra from Brook Bond have even their own retail outlets in places like Dubai to sell their processed meat. Because of geographical proximity supported by the knowledge of the local laws, culture and practices such closely operated value chain is possible to manage to their great advantage. Similar practices are being followed by many other Indian processors like Lazziz as well. If one visits the local mandis and souks (bazaars) in Bahrain, Kuwait, Dubai etc. one can find that Indian vegetables are selling there which have been unloaded on the previous day in the local airport. If the infrastructure improves we can be more cost effective which will boost this trade further.

We don't have significant trade of processed and fresh food trade with other parts of the world. Excepting mango which goes to the EU countries as well, other fruits also to a limited quantity been exported to Australia, Japan and US has now almost come to nil as they have imposed very stringent phyto-sanitary conditions which our exporters and processors will find difficult to implement. India produces mango to the extent of about 6 to 700 thousand MT which accounts for the 60% (10 million mangoes) of the global production. Of course, the mango production goes through a cyclical trend. For example, in the year 2004 we had only 360 thousand MT as against 600 thousand MT produced in the previous year which is about 40% drop in production because of un-seasonal rains. We are seeing this trend for the last several years. In Maharastra, the 600 Km Konkan stretch is the major player in domestic and export markets followed by the Uttar Pradesh, Andhra Pradesh, Gujarat, Karnataka and West Bengal. The point that is being made here is that bulk of our mango both in the form of fresh as well as processed mango pulp – canned and frozen – are exported to the middle east buyers. Our dependence of the export trade to this region is therefore very significant.

If one looks at the figure of total processed food export from India it will be evident that about 50 % of the total comes from grains and marine products, another about 15 to 20% is contributed by vegetable and animal products. Processed fruit and vegetable contributes only 2 to 3 percent of our total export and almost entire part of this is directed towards middle east countries. As mentioned earlier entire fresh fruits, vegetables, meat and poultry and egg are also going to these countries, Indian industries should find it attractive to forge joint ventures with local partners to promote this business further. Also prospects of value added branded consumer products are very great. Opening up food retail chain with produce largely from India is a distinct possibility and the recent bilateral agreement is the step in that direction.

To achieve this we have to participate in all food trade fairs in that region and attempt to forge alliance. In the context of globalization, alliance and joint venture is an essential step for exploiting global market opportunity. And we have a great possibility in middle east. I am sure food companies cannot go and set up operations in Europe or US or in other developed countries excepting in the specific sectors like marine products. But doing so in the middle east countries is a distinct possibility, which our domestic producers should explore.

Global Trade of Indian Basmati Rice Facing Difficulties

India is a leading exporter of rice - particularly of Basmati rice in which only other country competing is Pakistan. Many made their fortunes in rice export and then ventured into other activities. In this connection, two names immediately come to our mind. They are Late Mr. Lalit Suri - owner of Hilton Hotels and Mr. Subhash Chandra Goel of Zee-TV both of them initially traded in rice and that too in a big way. In the later years as the name and the fame been achieved Subhas Chandra Goel quietly dropped his surname "Goel" to appear in his more media savvy new avatar "Subhas Chandra". Yes, we know him by this name now and many may not be knowing that he made his initial millions from rice export. So did Lalit Suri. In the later years Subhash Chandra ventured into his second project Essel Packaging. Lalit Suri's second project was a hospitality industry. He thus set up Holiday Inn hotel in Delhi, which is today Hotel Intercontinental.

This rice trade is increasingly becoming difficult and it is of late seen to be a political commodity. There was a time when Russia used to import from India huge quantity of rice through rupee trade and the deals used to be finalised in corridor of power. Person like Mr. Lalit Suri who has had inroads to the seat of power reaped big harvest in rice export.

Because of good monsoon, agricultural ministry has forecast a 5.75 percent increase in the kharif food grain output to a record of 108.4 million tonnes in 2004. The sharp increase in the output is mainly on account of the rise in Kharif rice output to 75 million tonnes as against 72.2 million tonnes produced in 2003.

Country's rice exports have shown a significant decline of about 60% to 1.7 million tonnes in the financial year 2000 compared to 4.5 million tonnes shipped during the same period previous year. Export of Basmati rice is estimated at 0.35 million tonnes, while non basmati rice is expected to be around 1.3 million tonnes in 1999-2000. The primary reason attributed to this fall in exports is the rise in domestic prices of rice.

While on the one hand we could witness an increase in rice production, on the other hand the export demand is not expected to be high. According to the officials of the All India Rice Exporter Association (AIREA), the world demand of rice for the year 2000 is expected to be low by 20 percent of 21.5 million tonnes as against 26 million tonnes recorded last year. Their expectation of Basmati and Non-Basmati export to touch 2 million tonnes in 1999-2000 because most of the rice consuming countries are expecting a good domestic crop all over the world and hence India will have to face a loss in demand.

Fig. 12.2 International trade is still in traditional commodities like rice and spices

India's rice exports are estimated to have jumped to around 4 million tonnes during 1998-99 against 2.3 million tonnes in 1997-98. But in 1999-2000 it was even be lower than that of 1997-98. 1998-99 performance was mainly due to unprecedented demand from certain Southeast Asian countries, where the crop was affected during earlier two years either due to EL-Nino or a dry spell. Accordingly, global demand for rice touched highest ever at 25-26 million tonnes in 1998-99 against 21 million tonnes in 1997-98. India exported large quantity to Srilanka and Bangladesh in 1998-99. Currently in India 5% broken rice is quoting a US$ 290-295 per tonne whereas Thailand is quoting US$ 270-285 and Vietnam is quoting US$ 230 per tonne.

With the introduction of genetically modified variety of rice in the world trade the rice trade have become increasingly difficult and it is surrounded by controversy. European buyers want now to do business with only those companies they trust. Since Basmati is a product they cannot differentiate into varieties themselves they prefer dealing with companies who can provide complete product traceability and an audit trail. So it is now trust combined with traceability. As food security is the biggest issue at the moment. European buyers are now beginning to insist that Indian exporters certify their rice as non-GMO and aflatoxin free as there is increasing awareness of the potential health problems.

Earlier we knew that aflatoxin is an issue with groundnut arising out of fungal infection but now we are told that this is also a problem with rice. As a consequence of this decision of European buyers merchant exporters could lose their European market. There are large merchant exporters like Pepsi, Hindustan Lever (HLL) who don't own rice mills will be the sufferer in addition to the host of other smaller and bigger players who are basically the merchant exporters as now buyer prefers to deal with exporters selling rice produced in their own mills. As merchant exporters like Pepsi and HLL have no mills of their own, buyers are increasingly diffident in dealing with them. Already HLL is losing its share in the French market because its biggest buyer there found discrepancies between one consignment and the next which was largely because HLL was to depend on many smaller units to source rice for export. Maintaining uniform quality was thus a problem. DNA tests have still not been accepted as conclusive tests to determine admixture.

Indian rice exporters wanted to split the Basmati into traditional and evolved which will have lower standard which Government had accepted in deference to the recommendation of Directorate of Rice Research, Hyderabad who argued that it would harm the growers interests. It is understandable that evolved varieties not necessarily can be assumed to be inferior to the traditional variety in grain length, elongation and fragrance and hence why should farmers suffer who need to introduce high yielding varieties to maximise profits on limited land.

There should be a differentiation between Basmati and Non-Basmati. Further differentiation between traditional and evolved varieties is unnecessary because European consumer does not care about what variety he actually eats as long as he enjoys the experience. In fact, the largest selling product in Germany is a mix between Basmati and Thai fragrant rice. "Uncle Ben" has introduced a Basmati, which is a mix of Indian and Pakistani, which is also very popular. Even European mills mix their Basmati according to the local taste. Govt. now proposes to introduce Voluntary Quality Control System (VCS) to be administered by APEDA. Currently inspection is done either by

Agmark, Export Inspection Agency (EIA) alongwith some international quality surveyors like SGS to check all export cargo. Although industry is not in favour of VCS but Govt. seems to be going ahead. According to new norms Basmati to be split into traditional and evolved and all exporters to compulsarily follow new classification.

System of VCS is for the first year after which it would be mandatory. All applications for commission payment or for settlement of quality complaints by exporters to RBI should be routed through APEDA. While registering contracts with APEDA exporters have to give complete statement of proceeds from all previous consignments and reasons for every shortfall. Exporters will also be required to inform buyers about the varietal admixture in every consignment. Exporters choosing not to join the scheme will necessarily have to be under the in - process quality control system of EIA to be eligible for exports at all and that too for one year only.

INR18 billion Basmati industries is now at the receiving end when it faces a sudden death of its US$ 200 million foreign market due to EU decision recently to end the customs duty derogation of ECU 250 per tonne. EU informed India that it needs to put curbs on free import of Basmati rice under pressure from the rice belts of Greece, Italy, France and Spain, which are burdened with huge intervention stocks although fact of the matter is that premium rice like Basmati constitute only small part of the total intervention stock. As the growth of Basmati rice in the European market was significant from 35000 tonnes in 1995 to 0.15 million tonnes in 1998-99, EU is geared about competition. Although Indian Govt. has taken it up strongly with Brussels but it is seen that Basmati is becoming increasingly a political commodity which goes against the basic traits of WTO advocating free market play.

In the stock market boom in 1994-95 more than a dozen rice exporters largely selling Basmati to the Middle East jumped on to the band wagon with initial public offer (IPO) at unheard of premia. Satnam Overseas, Chaman Lal Setia Exports, RT Exports and Khusi Ram Bihari Lal (KRBL) all those shares were oversubscribed and that too with a premium.

But the year 1999-2000 has turned out to be the industry's worst nightmare as all major players' face plummeting sales and a drop in profits. KRBL has reported a 52% drop in sales and 15% drop in profit in the quarter ended September 1999 from the corresponding period last year. Similarly Satnam Overseas, a significant player in the domestic market with Kohinoor and Trophy brands also reported 22% drop in sales during same year.

Indian Basmati has become the target of Pakistani ire because both exporters and Islamabad fear UK's Ministry of Agriculture, Food and Fisheries (MAFF) would declare Pakistani Super variety as inferior to traditional Indian Basmati as part of its move to define and differentiate between the Basmati variety exported from India and Pakistan through DNA fingerprinting. As rice is the second largest foreign exchange earner for Pakistan and basmati alone brings in US$ 250 million, this has led to an uproar within the community. Pakistan, therefore is shifting the line of control on Basmati to England by asking Asian Grocers and retailers in Britain to stop stocking Indian Basmati as a first step towards boycotting all Indian products. This should be viewed in the context that in UK there are about 1.5 million ethnic Asian population and fifty percent of that are Muslim. Besides, there are companies in USA who are duplicating basmati rice and even trying to pass long grain rice as basmati in the international market for which they have even taken patent rights. What is our Government doing about it?

13

Quality, Labelling and Regulatory

The Quality Issue Now Even Haunting Multinationals

There is a general perception that MNCs have better technology supported by the resources and the scale of operation and therefore, can produce superior quality products. And their Indian counterparts have, most often than not, smaller scale of operation and lesser access to resources and to the level of technology – therefore take short cuts to quality. The recent phenomena will change that perception. The quality issue for the processed food industry is so paramount that no processor can afford to undermine this and still think that they will remain in business. Unfortunately, however, reputed and well known brands are frequently coming under cloud of controversy on quality issue. And therefore this needs to be addressed, deliberated and action plan has to be evolved. In earlier days we used to face the complaints largely arising out of adulteration and non-conformance of quality specifications as given in the Prevention of Food Adulteration Act (PFA).

As per PFA, a foreign material found in the product would tantamount to adulteration and therefore punishable under law. And the food industry was constantly debating on the issue that there has to be a distinction between deliberate adulteration and for cases as it happens, which is unintentional. For example, an ant found in the bottle of food products, can never be intentional. But the law did not change and unscrupulous people used to take reputed manufacturers for a ride by engineering such incidence and then threatening to take the case to the health authority. Many such cases used to get settled outside. But a few such cases where big brands are involved, it used to get media attention. Long ago a Coca-Cola bottle was produced by a member of parliament on two occasions with dead lizard inside the bottle. But that did not tarnish the image of the company excepting some consequential embarrassment. And therefore, it was all business as usual thereafter. The issues related to quality failures and adulteration were mainly for the small unorganised players then. Today these issues are haunting the big players and even multinationals. And the effect on the business is thus very significant.

In the recent times we have seen three major quality controversies. The first one with the bottled drinking water. This had invloved all the well known brands including Bisleri. We have seen a row of debate across the country relating to BIS standards and its feasibility for implementation. Post this debacle all bottled drinking water manufacturers were advised to conform to the BIS standard. The next one that we have witnessed was with carbonated beverages and that too involving the brands like Pepsi and Coke. Delhi based well known NGO – Centre for Science and Environment (founded by Late Anil Agarwal) had broken the news in public that the pesticide residues in these products have exceeded EU norms. Whether we have in our food laws any such standard or not is another matter but such adverse publicity had greatly impacted the performance of the brands in subsequent months.

The public reaction to this issue was so great that government has to intervene and initiate action to put the public fury at rest. The whole controversy ended by forming a Joint Parliamentary Committee (JPC) headed by a prominent parliamentarian Sharad Pawar which has submitted its report but it was not conclusive. What is surprising that of late I find that a global company like Cadbury Schweepe's Indian arm Cadbury India Ltd got embroiled into yet another quality scam where number of instances have been cited about Cadbury Dairy milk chocolate containing worms. The couple of stores in Maharashtra and Goa have reported this in identical manner. Although the Food & Drug Administration (FDA) in Maharastra tried to give a clean chit to Cadbury after examining the stock in the factory but still the damage that has caused to the company is immense. Cadbury tried to react to the problem by saying that it is due to faulty storage conditions that prevailed in our trade. But if the company has to do business in India the corrective action needs to taken by the company itself.

We have come across yet another quality controversy involving Dabur Honey. But this complaint surfaced abroad and was reported in fine print in some leading newspapers in India and therefore escaped public attention. There was a health hazard alert in Canada that Dabur Honey might contain the antibiotic Chloramphenicol. The Canadian health authority had ordered immediate withdrawal of stock in 100gms, 250gms and 500gms sizes. Chloramphenicol in honey, as the report said, poses a risk of a serious blood disorder known as aplastic aneamia. This news spread in Europe like wild fire. Recently, we were told by a honey processors and exporters in Delhi that EU has introduced an embargo on the import of Indian honey into EU. Honey exporters are thus waiting for this ban to be lifted. This is a matter of great concern.

In a recent report appeared in the Economic Times it has been said APEDA has issued a warning that there is a danger of India being black-listed, unless the quality of its exports like meat and meat products, fruits and vegetables improves a great deal and they fully conform to the EU's standard. Of late, as stated in the report APEDA has been receiving complaints from EU countries about high residues of pesticides and chemicals in our products. This will greatly harm our prospect of global trade in agro and processed food products.

Pesticide controversy has greatly harmed both Pepsi and Coke. The Coke sales have been said to have fallen 11 per cent in the third quarter of 2003 because of the allegation that it contained high level of the pesticide residue. This would be the first time in the history of Coke that the company has to reconcile for the loss of sales on account of quality complaint. Same has happened to Pepsi as well.

When such things happen the competition also takes advantage of it. It has been reported that Cadbury also suffered in terms of sales in the last two months particularly in festival season. Amul has tried to take the advantage of this situtaion. Amul tied up with Campco for the increased supply to cover the gap in the market due to the decline in Cadbury's sales. It is like one party's loss is another party's gain. The chocolate production was reportedly stepped up from 4.5 tonnes per day to 7.4 tonnes per day during this period taking advantage of the sudden spurt in demand.

The industry also needs to know how to manage the crisis of this nature. Taking care of the quality is the prime task of the processors so that they meet the global standards. But if something of this nature happens how fast one can act to reduce the adverse impact holds the key in that scenario. I earlier thought organised sector and more so the MNCs have that well oiled machnery to handle such situation. But now we realised that big players are also equally vulnerable. We can only hope that we will learn from the experience. And that we will have to if we have to nurture our global ambition?

Coke and Pepsi are in Trouble on Account of Pesticide Residue Controversy in Soft Drinks

A lot of dust has been kicked off in the air with respect to pesticide residue in soft beverages, particularly in Cola. It all started with the earlier findings in the bottled water where all leading brands are reported to having pesticide residues much higher than the limits prescribed in Europe and other countries. The impact of this controversy was so great that the government was forced to form a Joint Parliamentary Committee (JPC) headed by Minister of Agriculture Mr Sharad Pawar. Since then Bureau of Indian Standard (BIS) has prescribed a standard for bottled drinking water. However, for soft carbonated beverages there is no such standards as yet adopted. It is still in the proposal stage. The Center for Science and Environment (CSE), a not-for-profit independent organization is picking up samples of only beverages for pesticide residues but not yet for other numerous food categories. The significance of this revelation is of that magnitude that the ripple effect of the same has greatly impacted the short term and long term performance of the two giant multinationals who are global leaders in the product category. Pepsi and Coke are world leaders in soft beverage business which they are managing across countries over centuries. It is therefore, expected that they know the business of water and soft drinks better than any body else. How come then again and again they are in-the midst of similar controversy. Knowingly no business will do anything to destroy their own image which they have so painstakingly built over the years. The question therefore, arises whether there is fundamentally anything wrong in our approach before we find and label someone as guilty.

There are other issues as well. That our cola drinks including Pepsi and Coke contain higher level of pesticide residues than their counterpart in Europe and America is one thing and labeling them as unfit for human consumption is a different matter. And in the absence of any prescribed standard which the businesses have to adhere to, it is not appropriate to raise so much negative publicity that some states like Kerala has decided to ban the Colas. There are instances even in America that such beverages have been banned to be sold in school premises. But that is on the consideration of nutrition and wholesomeness of the beverage. I have even heard that some of the school authorities in India as well have banned sales of soft drinks in their school canteen. These are understandable as there are other issues with respect to beverage ingredients which are not good for health if consumed too much which children normally indulge in. The reaction of our establishments based on one report on pesticide residue from CSE is thus anything but immature.

The matter has become now a political issue. And other organizations, Health Ministry, parliament all have added to that confusion. Coke to save their skin has approached UK based Central Science Laboratory (CSL) to challenge the findings of CSE in India. Our Health Minister Dr. Ramadoss made public statement that colas are safe. Possibly he has said that when CSL report contradicted the report of CSE. The minister even asked CSE to furnish more details about the test procedure and test protocol which is tantamount to saying that there is doubt about the report of the CSE laboratories. This he has said when confronted by a group of members of parliament accusing government for not taking cognizance or ignoring the report of CSE. The matter even went to such an extent that Bush administration also raised the issue with the government of India that if these two US multinationals are harassed there will be implications on the foreign direct investment (FDI) in India. This is an indirect threat. Back in India even pesticides company have also joined hands with Coke to discredit CSE. Agrochemical Promotions Group (APG) and Crop Care Federation of India (CCFI) who represent all pesticide manufacturers in India have joined Coke to dispute the CSE report. They said that use of pesticides in our country is highly regulated and there cannot be such situation that our ground water is contaminated to that extent. Our newspapers have carried all these reports in addition to articles and columns written both in favour and against CSE reports. The Health Ministry, in the mean time, announced that a comprehensive quality standard will be notified in January 2007 and for that an expert committee under chairmanship of Director General of ICMR is already examining the reports of CSE etc.

Anyone will accept that the quality of the end product will have a direct relationship with the quality of the basic ingredients. In beverages two major ingredients like water and sugar which will be the source of pesticides. Consumers therefore also would like to know what is the level of pesticides in our normal drinking water supply as well in sugar (both refined and unrefined) that we consume everyday. It is our common knowledge that many of our daily food items including tea and coffee contains several times higher level of pesticides than what has been reported for Coke and Pepsi. If the bottled water and beverage contains pesticide residues which is high it is likely that our drinking water supply from municipality as well as sugar we consume also contain the pesticide in higher amount. And no one was analyzing those and reporting. Why we will have to know these occasional and sensational news only from CSE. What is our public health laboratories doing? There are quality control laboratories set up in many institutions and universities. Even CFTRI at Mysore has quality control laboratory for testing trade samples. Why they have not reported anything so far. And every time we will start debate on a CSE report. And why CSE is only targeting the bottled water business, flavored or unflavored and not other businesses?

We all know that the in terms of use of pesticides in agriculture, India is much safer than even US and Japan where the quantum of pesticide used in agriculture is much more even if it is compared on the basis of per hectare of agricultural land. Why then we have so much of problems.

I have had association with this industry for many years. I must have set up at least twenty five of India's bottling plant. The process of refining of sugar, which goes through activated carbon treatment after making syrup to make it colorless and odorless should not have any pesticide residue left. Water is treated either though standard water softening processes or demineralized through ion exchangers to make it safe. And no bottling plant exists without these water treatment facilities. Why then Coke and Pepsi comes under fire every now and then? Both Coke and Pepsi are also being blamed for polluting environment as well for depleting the water level in the vicinity where they have set up the plant and when they draw water from underground through bore well.

Soft drink majors are not making profit. Additionally, they have to face many allegations, which threaten their existence. It is because they are large MNCs they are still there fighting out all odds. For any local company, for similar circumstances, they would have closed shops long ago. Food business in India is already in transition, these unhealthy development will slow down the growth potential. We need to be more responsible.

Nutrition Labelling of Foods

Consumers are exposed to a whole range of processed foods everyday. Those who do not want the inconvenience of preparing their own meals are willing to pay a premium for foods perceived to be of high quality and standard. One of their main bases of comparison is the information on the labels of these items. But our foods regulations in India are not elaborate and stringent enough to make it mandatory for the manufacturers to declare relevant information on the label to guide purchase decisions of the consumers.

In United States a regulation related to nutrition labelling was passed in 1973 but compliance was entirely voluntary unless nutritional claims were made or nutrients are added in the food products intended for sale. Although it was a voluntary declaration, manufacturers in United States and in other developed countries were complying with the requirement because of competitive pressure. In 1990 Nutrition Labelling and Education Act (NLEA) was passed and as a consequence it is now mandatory that all foods marketed in the US market must carry nutrition information in a standardised format. Also to encourage judicious purchase decision by the consumer, the information must indicate how the food contributes to a healthy diet. The regulations are result of the growing health and nutrition consciousness of the typical American consumer. A food and Drug Administration (FDA) survey showed that 55 percent of American consumers made their decisions based on what appeared on the panel. Similar survey in Australia showed that four out of five read food labels when make purchase of food items. Other consumer surveys have shown that well over half the shoppers worldwide are scanning the labels on food products.

The standard format called 'Nutrition Facts' must indicate according to the new Act, per serving size, total calories, calories from fat, saturated fat, cholesterol, sodium, total carbohydrates, dietary fibre, sugars, protein, vitamin A, vitamin C, calcium and iron. For easy understanding, the values are generally given in grams for each nutrient and as a percentage of recommended daily allowance to help the consumer not only compare food quality for various alternatives available but also to decide the daily food intake to meet the daily dietary nutrition requirement. This helps to maintain consumers' health and promote nutrition education.

Fig. 13.1 Nutritional labeling will help local brands gaining acceptance in global market.

As against that scenario in India we have a prevention of Food Adulteration Act (PFA) and to regulate processed fruit and vegetable product we have Fruit Products Order (FPO). While PFA comes under Ministry of Health,

FPO falls under the purview of Ministry of Food Processing Industry (earlier this was under Ministry of Agriculture, Dept., of Food). The entire scope of these two legislation is based on the minimum standard of Foods and related to prevention of food adulteration. Therefore, PFA and FPO only deal with permitted ingredients, limits thereof and safety standards. Our food labelling standards and requirement are not very stringent and are governed by both these regulatory authorities as well as by Packaged Commodities Regulations Order (PCRO) under Weights and Measures Act. Both PCRO and PFA have punitive power but FPO does not have. FPO can only cancel licences for any violations and default. Additionally, we have many product category specific legislation such Meat Products Order , Milk Products Order and Marine Products Order (MPO) as well as optional standards like BIS (Beaureau of Indian Standards).

Our food labelling standards are the minimum standards dealing with standards weights and measures of various categories of food, label size, size of the letters in the text of the declaration, nomenclature and other statutory declarations like maximum retail price etc. The product related information as required by law are minimal and limited to *contains permitted colour and preservative*, *contains no fruit juice* etc. The food laws in other countries even on these issues require that the manufacturers declare the name of food colour, preservative and other additives, if added. The food products which are not classified under PFA Act are called proprietary products and for proprietary, designed and fabricated foods the ingredient list in descending order need to be declared in addition to other statutory declarations. If the manufacturer claims any nutritional or therapeutic property of the food, rules said that the label should indicate the quantity present. Thus if manufacturer claims in the label that it contains vitamin and minerals the limit or quantity present should be declared. But if it claims "minerals and vitamins added" there is no such requirement for declaring the quantity present, which can obviously misled the consumers.

The way processed foods, ready-to-serve food and fast food consumption are growing there is definitely a concern whether consumers are getting the adequate nutrition from their daily rations. Towards this end, nutrition labelling, if made compulsory, will be of great help. Firstly, there will be a basis of comparison of quality from the wide choice that is available. Secondly, the manufacturers will have to be more careful about the processing methods and standards that are adopted in order to preserve the wholesomeness of food because it will be the responsibility of the manufacturers to ensure conformance to the declared standard till it is consumed.

We find in the market, lot of products including soft drinks, snacks, vegetable oil etc. with claim that the products are either low fat, fat free, low calorie, light (or lite) etc and these descriptions are used interchangeably. Consumers, in general, practically understand the same thing from all these claims and local food laws also don't differentiate them. Whereas US-FDA clearly defines such claims and manufacturers have to satisfy that. For example, as per US FDA low-fat means 3gm or less of fat per serving, fat free is 1/2 gm of fat per serving, and low calorie product should have 40 calories or less per serving. Light or lite is 50 percent less fat than standard product. US-FDA has also restricted the claims regarding relationships between a nutrient or food and the risk of a disease or health related condition. Only seven such relationships are allowed to be claimed. They are – relationship between calcium and osteoporosis; fat and cancer, saturated fat and cholesterol and coronary heart disease, fruit and vegetables and cancer, sodium and hypertension, grain products and cancer, folic acid and neural tube defects. The food exporters to United States will thus have to conform to these requirements.

In India food labelling standard is still in its infancy and only provide very limited information towards product quality, safety and wholesomeness. Sometime ago a very select category of foods like baby foods and fruit and vegetable products have been taken up for deciding about the Environment Friendly Labelling Standards at the initiative of the Ministry of Environment and Forest. But that is a voluntary standard and there were no taker for that in the Industry. Very recently an integrated food law bill has been submitted for legislation which should replace all existing and multiplicity of food laws that are in force. The integrated food law has subsequently been passed to be implemented by Food Standards and Regulatory Authority being formed. It would be a great service if the food labelling is made compulsory to incorporate nutritional and other quality details of the product so that consumers are not taken for a ride.

14

Indian Food Industry – Key Challenges

Managing Non-Tariff Barriers in Inernational Trade in Processed Food

Food Quality and Barriers to Trade

The world of business is all about competition and therefore, entry barriers whether it is tariff or non- tariff are anything but natural to trade. As tariff barriers are reducing across countries it is the non-tariff barriers which will make the life of food exporters more difficult. Under WTO guidelines , member countries are systematically reducing the tariff. In the recent union budget the peak rate of custom duty has been brought down to 12.5%. In course of time therefore, only NTB will act as a significant hurdle in the international trade and we should learn to live with it and manage business with these constraints.

Unlike tariff, NTBs are very difficult to define , monitor, police or even sometime quantify.

By quality we now mean conformance to certain standards and customer expectation. While manufacturers give more emphasis on conformance to requirement, design, specification including statutory and regulatory compliances but meeting customer expectations and buyers specification and standards could be different from regulatory requirement which are the minimum standard. The various dimensions that are specific to food quality are therefore performance, features, reliability, safety, conformance, durability, aesthetics and perceived quality. Reliability, safety and conformance are manufacturers led and are basic requirement. The other dimensions are actually customer specific. The most of the NTB issues thus arise from customer specific requirement which can be different from and in addition to legal or statutory requirement.

What are Non-Tariff Barriers

There are many types of non-tariff barriers such as :

Quotas: Established either on first come first serve basis or on a preferential basis to domestic and foreign residents. This quota regime also gradually disappearing.

Voluntary Export Restraint (VER): This is imposed as a quantitative restraints to reduce wasteful competition in principle. VERs are generally levied from the exporters to select countries so that exporters are not resorting to export by restricting supplies in the domestic market.

Domestic Production Subsidy: Governments bearing a portion of the cost of production to make local producers more competitive in the global trade. This issue is being discussed in various trade negotiations to bring in a parity but distortion exists.

Anti Dumping and Countervailing Duty: Dumping is actually selling products at prices lower than the costs of production. Antidumping measures are levied to counter unhealthy practices. Countervailing duties are imposed to counter enterprise and industry specific subsidies.

Product Standards: Although product standards are internationally accepted pertaining to quality, health and safety, etc but they can act as NTBs when applied absurdly to regulations regarding packaging, labeling, labour standards, environment protection etc.without due considerations to local conditions.

Sanitary and Phyto-sanitary Measures (SPS): This is imposed to improve human health, animal health and phyto- sanitary situation in all countries. But problem comes when it is practiced without due regards to the capability of compliance of many countries including India. This often deters market access for exports from India.

Domestic Content Requirement: Often government procurement policies hinder market access for foreign goods that do not possess the required domestic content.

Administrative Red Tape: Generally discouraged as wasteful economies, administrative red tape hinders trade facilitation by both delaying and discouraging trade.

Labour Standards and Practices: This covers issues related to engaging child labours, equal opportunity employers , not providing adequate and proper working conditions etc..

Fair Trade Practices: To ensure that all stakeholders in entire food value chain have got their legitimate share of the value creation.

Environmental Protection: To ensure that processors following environment friendly practices as well as green technology.

Traceability: Intends to trace origin of the problems in case of product failure to meet the standard. Not an easy task for compliance in our food value chain.

Implications in our Food Business

It can be seen that all NTBs are intended to improve the product safety, quality, environment, business processes. But problems come when it is difficult to adhere to based on the local conditions. Our food industry will have problems for compliance in NTBs related to employing child labour, equal opportunity employers (food industry in India employs child labour and women workers in production floor without due regard to legal requirements) and sanitary and phyto-sanitary measures. The other issues such as environment friendly technology, environment protection by taking care of the waste generated etc., fair trade practices and most importantly traceability could be serious issues which will act as big hindrance to our processed food trade.

For example, if a milk powder consignment gets rejected it will not be possible to trace the origin of the problems. This could mean that even individual cows and buffalos are to be traced. Our milk is not sourced from organized cow and buffalo rearing farm to ensure the safety and regulatory compliance at each such large farms. We source milk from all over through collection centers which are nothing but chilling plant and therefore we need to grow to a level from where we are now. Although we are number one milk producing country in the world but our contribution to global trade still less than 2 percent. These factors are partially responsible for poor performance in global trade. The industry therefore has to rise to the occasion to ensure the compliance.

There are many instances of rejection of Indian processed foods for issues arising out of NTBs. Mango pulp has been rejected by European Union (EU) for non-compliance to process standard. Coffee and tea also rejected by EU for not meeting technical standards. Frozen Fish and tea rejected by Japan for sanitary and phyto-sanitary measures (SPS). Similarly, meat, fish and dairy products, vegetables and fruits were rejected by USA on SPS measures.

The following Table will illustrate the consignments from the South Asia in the recent times facing NTBs of various nature. Table 14.2 provides details of shipments from India which are detained by USFDA

Table 14.1 : South Asian Countries facing NTBs (Export Facing NTBs at the major destinations for South Asia (percentage of total exports)

	Bangladesh	India	Pakistan	Srilanka
EU	91.01	55.45	71.30	83.41
USA	93.86	43.98	77.01	0.01
Japan	68.41	42.52	26.97	49.32

Table 14.2 : Countries facing detention of consignments for NTBs (Food Imports and Detention of Shipments by the US FDA):

Country Group/ Country	Export Value Million US$	No. of Detentions per Million US$ Import	No. of Detentions
May 1999-April 2000			
Total (52 Countries	—	9875	0.90
Mean	—	179	1.70
Range	—	11-860	0.1-11.0
India-all commodities	—	860	4.50
2001-2002			
India			
A. All commodities, Sept. 01-Feb. 02	138.82	364(997)	2.60
B. Shrimps, Dec. 01- June 02	69.84	49(88)	0.70
C. Mushroom, Dec. 01- June 02	0.19	6(30)	31.58

Table 14.3 and Table 14.4 will give the major reasons of detention of Indian shipments by USFDA

Table 14.3 : Major causes of Detention (Major Causes of Detention of Indian Shipments by US FDA)

A. All Commodities, Dec. 2001 - Nov. 2002

Causes of Detentions	No. of Shipments
Filthy	256
Salmonella	161
Not Listed	107
HACCP	88
List Ingredients	78
Nutrition Label	72
Pesticide	43

Unsafe Additives	37
Unsafe Colour	35
Direction, How to use (Not Given) etc.	28
Agricultural Residue	24
Color of Label Unsafe	17
Not Registered	16
Insanitary	15

Strategies to Manage NTBs

We should see the NTB as an opportunity to improve our quality , safety and processes as required for long term strategies for survival. We should not see these only as an obstacle. Businesses is all about competition and we can expect more of these even from individual buyers. For example large food retail chains are very powerful and they can ask for additional compliance. A recent case of honey export order received from a buyer in France who have stipulated a proof to be provided that beekeeper is getting their legitimate share of profit which will obviously come under fair trade practices. We had to invite the buyer to show him the proof of what is being paid to beekeeper as procurement price to prove that legitimate price is being given.

Some of our business have resolved these problems of NTB facing them which have been listed in Table 14.4 below.

Table 14.4 : Industry attempt to manage NTBs (How some of the NTBs were Managed)

Fishery Products	By Implementing HACCP Standards
Peanuts	By setting national standards for aflatoxin and promoting indigenous development of technology.
Rice	Standards for pesticide residues and exports to EU, USA and Japan
Spices	Experiences in dealing with aflatoxin standards and other SPS Measures.
Tea	Meeting standards on pesticide residues.
Organic Food Products	Experience in standard setting, certification, exports and institutional support to the organic sector.

NTBs have strategic implications and imperatives for all partners in the food value chain. Therefore, stakeholders at each interface has a role to play to meet the challenges of NTBs which would mean that strategic initiatives will have to be taken at farm level, industry level and country level. Firm level strategies would include product standards and SPS issues. Industry level initiatives will include labour standard and practices, fair trade practices , environment protection and traceability which can be collectively resolved as small players will find it difficult to comply with all these requirements . And the country level initiatives should cover all other types of NTBs as listed through bilateral, regional and multilateral negotiations

There are other strategic initiatives such as :

Rapprochement strategies:(as proposed by Jacob) which covers **harmonization** that involve standardization of regulation in identical form and **Mutual recognition** which means acceptance that alternative regulations, systems and standards can lead to the same level of food safety and quality. Hooker and Caswell equate this approach to **"Reciprocity"** in the Canadian -US free trade Agreement. **Coordination and Alignment** means global narrowing of difference between alternative technical regulations, systems and standards, perhaps based on voluntary international codes of practice.

These measures, however, can be taken at country level. At industry level some actions can be initiated such as training and facilitating formation of revised standards, interfacing with the entire value chain. And at firm level, we need to introduce the practices of quality systems management taking a holistic view of managing quality through internal processes and systems by voluntary compliance.

Conclusion

The food quality should be understood in its right perspective. Quality is not something better or superior but compliance to buyers requirement in addition to statutory and regulatory requirement and specifications. Entrepreneurs must learn to understand various dimensions of quality and its management that will give them a competitive edge over others. Food safety is a concern for everybody including consumers, producers and government alike and NTBs are intended to ensure safety to human , animal , environment and all stakeholders. Therefore, food safety is a basic proposition. Failure to adequately address food safety can result in fatal food borne diseases and consequent liability suits and economic losses. We need not have to be reactionary towards food safety challenges. Instead strategic initiatives to be taken at various levels.

Business, although selectively, have demonstrated ability to manage NTB related issues but this has to spread across industry. The goal of the respective agreements is to foster equivalent, though not successfully identical , SPS measures among members.

Quality raw Material at Acceptable Price –The Key to Success of Agri Business

Heinz, after a wait of five long years, had announced their impending launch of tomato ketchup for which they are the world leaders. Nobody knows tomato ketchup business better than Heinz. Bill Johnson - President and CEO of HJ Heinz made this declaration before launch of their ketchup and by that Heinz India is going to end the period of simply drifting with the Glaxo brands (Farex, Complan, Glucon-D and Nycil). Bill also elaborated saying that "making real ketchup is not easy. I would hardly call the products currently available (obvious reference to Kissans and Maggie) in the market ketchup. They have preservatives and flavourings while Heinz is completely natural. But that means using a special tomato which we have had to persuade farmers to grow and that has taken sometime". Bill Johnson also knows the ketchup serving technique better "Don't turn the bottle upside down and shake it because that clogs the bottle. With ketchup as viscous as Heinz's - a distinction the company is proud of since that shows how natural it is, it will flow in horizontal position of the bottle with little tapping by fingers on `57' mark engraved on the neck of the bottle of Heinz tomato ketchup". Kissan advertises the thickness of the ketchup and shows that it does not come out easily but Heinz will show it that it comes out naturally. The war on ketchup has thus hot up in the Indian market.

The ketchup manufacturing technology has undergone changes over the years. In good old days we used to make Dipy's and Kissan's brand of ketchup directly from the freshly crushed tomato juice and then concentrating it six folds in open steam jacketed boiling pan. We had the problem of the yield, wastage and thus batch to batch cost variation. Maggie came in the later years through subcontracted route and started making ketchup from the tomato paste as basic raw material which they were supplying to their contract manufacturers. Maggie helped the industry to grow many fold and introduced many variants which Kissans also followed with increased vigour.

To get consistent supply of the raw material we at Kissans and Dipys did lot of extension work to tie up with the farmers through backward linkages and we only succeeded to a limited extent. We used to buy tomato at a price varying from INR 3 to 4 per kg whereas to become internationally competitive the price should have been only fifty paise per kg and we were losing the global orders for the paste. At one point of time UB group were even considering setting up tomato paste plant in Kenya and did lot of studies on the project feasibility. One reason that we did not succeed was that the seed technology did not reach the stage to deliver the expected and required yield. We were only coordinating with the national seed corporation.

Heinz has to wait for five long years to get the right type of raw materials - a basic shortcoming of most corporate agri-business ventures is their inability to manage the raw material supply chain and this is the singularly most important reasons of failure of many process food industries. Whether it relates to dairying, solvent extraction for edible oil, fruit and vegetable processing, the story has been uniformly one of companies installing large plants and, then, struggling to ensure adequate raw material availability of consistent quality at acceptable prices to run these facilities at optimal capacities.

Agri business is a subject that no longer excites the corporations these days. The euphoria generated in the early years of reform peaked with the presentation of the much-hyped CII-Mckinsey report on food processing in late 1996 has died down. This is reflected in the languishing stocks of most agro-processing companies today.

Most of our agri businesses suffered from the nonavailability of quality raw material at acceptable price which factor corporate sectors consistently ignored and then succumbed. This is an age old issue we have been discussing with no avail. Rather than address this problem by forcing direct backward linkages with the farmers the processors most often sought to procure their raw material requirement from the open market riddled with middleman and commission agents who manipulate the prices.

Whether we like it or not the reality is that India's agriculture is characterised by the preponderance of small and medium sized land holdings which are not cost effective to serve the industries requirement. Corporations, therefore, have to provide the supports in terms of high yielding seeds and other inputs and extension work to make their cultivation remunerative and also provide them the comfort of assured buy back.

Those who have worked in those lines have benefitted. Pepsi sources its tomatoes from nearly 1000 farmers in Punjab at a price ranging from INR1.50 to INR1.90 per kg depending upon the distance to the processing plant. If the company were to buy this from the open market, it would have to shell out a minimum of INR 4 to 5 per kg and that too without having any guarantee of assured and acceptable quality of processing. While a price of INR1.50 per kg may seem to be ridiculously low from the farmers point of view but it is really not so - if we consider the average yield of 50 tonnes per hectre obtained from the improved saplings and package of practices provided for by Pepsi as against the average yield of 18 to 20 tonnes produced by the traditional farming techniques. At 50 tonnes per hectre yield farmer after taking care of all costs still nets an income of over INR 60000 per hectre.

And alongwith high returns are other advantages which include selling in bulk. It is much less cumbersome for the farmers to dispose of his tomatoes in truck load at the factory gate rather than hawk them in the nearby mandi in 20 kg baskets. The company guaranteeing buy back 50% of his produce as part of the contract arrangement also insulates the farmer from vagaries of price fluctuations often engineered by the middleman in the open market.

Our local agricultural universities did good work in close association with the farmers and private corporations like Pepsi also exploited the high yielding hybrid seeds for chilly (CH-1 and CH-2) developed by Punjab Agricultural University (PAU). Similarly, PAU has also developed high yielding chilly (M-522). Even for potatoes grown for the manufacture of chips need to have high dry matter and low sugar content. Central Potato Research Institute at Simla has developed Kufri Jyoti and Kufri Chipsona - two high yielding varieties for this purpose.

Contract farming - as it is generally known or in certain cases even captive farming by large corporate houses is the real solution to this problem. Alternative to that is the cooperative farming. And we have successful models already demonstrated by ITC in tobacco and sunflower, Pepsi in tomato and chillies, Nestle in milk for their Moga plant and Marico which has indeed pioneered safflower cultivation in the country. Barring Marico we have only multinationals showing us the way. Indian business houses only know to pass on the cost of their inefficiencies to consumers and thus would like and enjoy to work in a protected environment. Competition will teach them that there is no easier way to success.

Agricultural Commodities : Lifting of Restrictions Leads to Better Distribution

We as a country have come a long way from a stage when we were importing food grains to feed our countrymen to a situation today when we have not only surplus production but also we are now a net exporter of food grains. This journey towards the green revolution was quite a long one. In spite of this significant achievement we still have regional imbalances in distribution and have starvation deaths. It is not necessary to overemphasize that we are a country where in one state there were surplus production and in another state there were severe shortfalls causing even starvation deaths and still the movement of food grains were restricted. Only the recent budget has made this proposition for free and forward trading in basic agricultural commodities possible. Food industries can now buy the raw materials and inputs freely from the market instead of going through the agencies like State Trading

Corporations (STC). This kind of regulations that were prevailing were understandable when there was a shortage in agricultural productions but we have now even exportable surplus. Not only that, the food industry was suffering because the whole distribution network were not market driven. The Food Corporation of India (FCI) was not able to cope up with the demand for storage space required to stock the seasonal surplus and there were reports that grains were rotting in many FCI warehouses and also there were pilferage from those stock points on a large scale and the public distribution system (PDS) were not efficient enough to handle such situation creating regional imbalances in terms of availability and prices. Besides, the cost of maintaining that large inventory of food grains were also enormous. It is expected that the situation will now improve and the price and availability will be dictated by the prevailing market forces.

Government is now aiming to find long term export market for food grains to reduce the overflowing stock of FCI which will help not only to earn foreign exchange but also significantly reduce the stock level. As on February 1, 2002, the central stock stood at 56.335 million tonnes comprising of 26.134 million tonnes of rice and 30.201 million tonnes of wheat and the carrying cost of this alone will stand at a colossal INR 56.8 billion for the year 2001-02 which accounts for the 42% of the food subsidy. In 2000 this stood at INR 42.33 billion or 35.2% of the food subsidy. In the season starting in April 2002, 1.25 million tonnes of wheat was brought from Punjab alone. By March 1, 2002 India has exported 5.025 million tonnes of wheat alone which has made India the seventh largest wheat exporter with the foreign exchange earning of INR 400 billion and the export price has been pegged at INR 4250 per tonne. The government has also offered 3 million tonnes of rice for export during 2001-02 at a rate of INR 5650 per tonne of raw rice. The food grain stock situation is so comfortable that India has offered the surplus stock to certain country as grant or aid. The countries which have expressed interest to take advantage of this scheme are Bangladesh, Democratic Republic of Korea, Ethiopia, Eritrea, Madagascar, Yemen and Zambia. This is a significant change in our agricultural production scenario and therefore we are showing a clear sign of India emerging as a powerful agricultural economy.

If the enormous stock level of grains are managed well we would have been able to reduce the food and agricultural subsidy which takes its toll in budgetary deficit year on year. The slow action and responses on reforms on the part of the government are the major reasons for high cost of production of our processed food products. And those who are concerned are talking about it in all possible occasions but to no avail. Recently, in an Indo-Spanish trade show organised by PHD Chambers of Commerce in Delhi Mr Kisan Mehta, the former President of Coca-Cola Export Corporation in India and currently the Chairman of the Agri-Business Committee of PHD Chambers had mentioned that there is no change in this industry over the last thirty years and we are still discussing the same. This seminar was also attended by the Secretary to the Food Processing Industry and inaugurated by the Central Agriculture Minister. It was told to the delegates that in the food processing sector we only discuss about the opportunities and we can continue to discuss the same for next ten years to come. This is high time that we discuss some concrete action plans and key learning from some of those actions being taken in the recent past. Mr Chatterjee, the Chairman of SSP Industries - an old food processing plant and equipment manufacturer in India. Mr Chatterjee said in the same meeting "where is the opportunity, we are surviving only with some overseas projects that we get here, in India there is no project coming up and the Ministry only talks about the opportunity", he said. The need is to create healthy competitive environment for local industry to go global and form global alliances. This trade show was also organised to serve this purpose. What is the key role the Food Processing Ministry playing in this regard - every one wanted to know.

New Initiatives for Growth of Food and Agro Processing Industries

The competitiveness of India as a country is still in the lower order. In this year's ranking India's position is forty-third out of fifty four countries that were surveyed for global competitiveness ranking. Competitiveness is generally measured at three levels – country, industry and firm. Therefore, if India as a country is not competitive the question can be asked as how we can be competitive as an industry category. This question, of course, will be valid for all category of industries.

It has now become very clear to our policy makers and administrators that we need to do significantly different things to improve the growth of this industry. One of the major problems this industry is suffering is very low level of value addition. The high and fluctuating input cost, poor infrastructure and lack of developed market make the task of managing the growth process all the more difficult.

In the above context I can clearly see that govt. has taken two major initiatives. One is the creation of the Food Parks in all states and the other is the formation of Agri Export Zone (AEZ). Food Parks are apparently being created with an objective to provide all support services to the potential processors. Having set up these food parks govt. is now facing a new task of marketing those parks. Professional agencies are now being called to work as consultants to market those newly created facilities. Little they know that investors will only come after they are assured of the market of the food products that can be produced in those locations. In some of those food parks govt. is even willing to be a equity partner in addition to providing all other facilities and concessions that go with it depending on their locations. But still genuine promoters are not coming. In the context of our domestic industry growth is around 10% and capacity utilization is around 50%, the so called food parks are faced with an enormous task of finding investors to utilize the added capacity. If large players get growth or introduce new products small players can, however, set up manufacturing units in these parks as a support manufacturers or subcontractors. But that is also not happening.

The other initiative in terms of AEZ are centred around the main crop of the region. For example, north east and north Bengal have been identified as export zone for pineapple. Similarly, Himachal Pradesh and J&K for apple and Maharashtra for grapes. This according to me is a good initiative provided necessary support for processing and packing the exportable surplus and other related infrastructure for logistics are created around such identified Agri Export Zone.

Various task forces seem to be active for creating new policy frame work to faster growth of this sector. In the northern region, NRDC is meeting quite frequently to prepare agenda for action plan. We do not find that industry is well represented in those meetings. Most of the people involved are old familiar faces – obviously discussing old issues yet over and over again. It is expected that a new set of packages will be framed for approval of the govt.

In processed food industry a major cost is marketing. Financial institutions do not give loan for or to support marketing fund. For small processors marketing channel and support need to be identified. Tie-ups and joint ventures need to be materialized to exploit global opportunity. Only then these policy initiatives can deliver some useful purpose.

Food Industry Need to Learn From Past Mistakes and New Experience

It is needless to say that Indian Food Industry is now facing new realities. All of us are experiencing it but all don't learn similar lessons from the same experience as it all depends on one's own perception and background. When we had a relatively protected domain for us to operate we spent time endlessly discussing taxation, subsidy and drawback issues. We also of course, discussed and rightly so the issues related to availability of quality raw material and packaging material and poor infrastructure. But the main focus was missing in terms of building our own capabilities by constantly redesigning and upgrading the internal business processes on one hand and systematically developing the market taking the consumer insight and expectation into consideration on the other hand. Instead, we decided to continue to produce the same bottled and canned stuff thinking that customers will accept the same value proposition which did not happen. The market growth was low because of lack of any innovation and consumption expenditure on processed food in India was one of the lowest although as a percentage of total household expenditure is high. But those expenditure is not in processed food. As an industry we did not become competitive. India as a country is also not competitive and we are still declining and China is improving.

Country level competitiveness depends on the macro economic factors and other socio cultural factors including the speed, transparency and corruption of beauracracy where we have limited role to play. We can only be an opinion mobiliser and also may become an opinion leader. All these years we were only addressing the issues to improve the country level competitiveness when we were only a suboptimal local players. Now we are caught unaware as we need much higher level of competency to face forces of global challenges. If we had concentrated on market development focusing on our key customers to understand them better and deliver them the fruits of technological innovations in processing of primary foods to create the value added products we would have succeeded in increasing the consumption expenditure in processed food which is extremely low now. What we are seeing now is the result of aggressive marketing and development activities of select multinationals which we could have delivered. The result is in front of us – agriculture has improved so much so that not only we are self sufficient in food production but we are also exporting and that we are seeing a clear indication that India will and can become a global player in agri export business. Packaging industry has demonstrated significant growth in terms of quality and types of packaging material available. Even packaging machinery industry also has made significant improvement. Infrastructure has improved and further improving and even taxation also has reduced. Hence first reality is that everything else around us about which we were quarrelling about have improved but Indian processed food industry remained the same old. Whatever changes we see today is the result of marketing and development initiatives taken by the MNCs.

I would be failing if I don't narrate the success stories. Those who have taken the initiatives although their numbers are very few they are still a force to reckon with as they either took the first mover advantage or tried to be relevant with the changes in the market. For example, Parle Products - the biscuit and confectionery products manufacturer is still a force to reckon with whereas 35 billion dollar multinational giant – Sara Lee had to close down their biscuits and cookies venture after incurring losses consecutively for three years. Bisleri is still enjoying the number one slot taking advantage of the first mover in the category. So is the case of Pioma Industries - manufacturer of powder beverage and concentrate in Ahmedabad in a market where General Food's global brand "Tang" is struggling to establish their brand in India. And Thums-Up still sell more than the Coke and is rated number four brand in the ranking. The only other name that comes in my mind is Amul. These select few fall in the category of deliverers. The second reality is that barring a few players in select categories we could not create any formidable entry barrier to new entrants. Whatever barriers were there, were due to our market structure. Indian market is highly complex and our consumers who are different in different regions in their taste preferences and food habits and unpredictable compounded by low consumption expenditure. MNCs which counted on the population to project their sales number have severely burnt their fingers.

Competition existed earlier also, but the task was much simpler as it was a case of limited and that too healthy competition. We also had plethora of rules and regulations to protect us unduly. Today we not only have severe competition from the global players but we also need to face unethical and unhealthy competition. For example, age old and apparently loyal bottler of Bisleri in Kolkata overnight switched over to Coke creating a supply line collapse in that region for Bisleri. You name any brand, it is available through the trading route in Indian food stores and is competitive. Goods are being sold at or lower than the cost to capture the market. The third reality is that in the market it is now a war like situation and the differentiating line between ethical and unethical is gradually disappearing and diffusing.

We often hear that MNCs have deep pocket and that Indian companies have very limited resources which is grossly inadequate to fight the multinationals. This is true but we also should understand that in MNCs' there is colossal waste of resources as well. One has to know how the resources to be best utilized and how the every rupee spent can travel the maximum distance. There is therefore, also a game of wit, strategies, tactics and knowledge. And most importantly in the delivery of cost- value – benefit to customers better than the competition. If we cannot do that we don't have the right to be in the business. We should withdraw before customers force us to withdraw from the game. The fourth reality is that businesses are increasingly being fought from the strength of knowledge and efficiency and not simply on financial strength.

The retail trade is changing very fast throwing up new challenges to the marketers. Organised retailing is fast growing and there are many successful chain already showed the way as to how the shopping also can be pleasurable. The fifth reality is thus that there is proliferation of local brands and private store label brands giving opportunity to small and medium size players. Local player Fun Foods is en-cashing on that kind of opportunity.

Consumers are increasingly seen to be value conscious and brand conscious. The sixth reality therefore, is traditional grocery products are gradually upgrading to value added brands throwing up new opportunity. ITC, HLL, Cargil, Pilsburry etc are already in the game along side the local Shakti Bhog and Rose brand atta and Dhampure and Balarampur sugar and Tata salt.

Food service sector are emerging as a major opportunity for processed food industry. Restaurants, particularly the specialized food and restaurant chain including beverage chain such as Barista showed us the way. Industrial catering also has become big business now. Seventh reality therefore is opening up of the food service sector as an industry.

In the processed food sector there was always an issue of low value addition. In terms of value delivery it was always low. Major initiatives therefore, are necessary in terms of knowledge management, business process reengineering and technology management including taking IT initiatives and that is the eighth reality.

These eight new realities will lead us to the following four suggestions:

(i) Concentrate to improve upon firm level and industry level competitiveness. Market forces will take care of country level competitiveness.

(ii) We should learn to see ourselves as global player with global vision and mindset and organize all actions in that line. Only actions and actions alone will deliver the result.

(iii) Time and cost should be considered as very important elements of competitive advantage. Key imperative therefore, would be to reduce the technology development cycle. Simultaneous and parallel engineering and leapfrogging in terms of technical development rather than the traditional sequential development process that we follow. Innovations will be the key to deliver profit.

(iv) Direct R&D effort which has immediate impact on the business in terms of reducing cost, improving features and benefits of the product and services delivering incremental value derived from an in-depth understanding of what customers' needs are.

After citing eight ground realities and four quick suggestions I would like to conclude by sounding cautious optimism and venturing my own prediction about the industry. In spite of the fact that we missed the bus but everything is not still lost. Opportunity is enormous and we can put our act together to gain from that opportunity. If pharma companies and start up biotech companies can make it why cannot processed food industry. My own prediction is that in next 5 years or so there will be the emergence of new players and decline and death of the some of the old apparently known and established players. We say that change is the only constant. Those who will adjust and upgrade will survive. Others will have therefore to perish. Average life of an enterprise is estimated to be about 35 years and those few survived over century have constantly evolved over the years by redefining their businesses with the change of time. A study was conducted amongst Indian family owned businesses and it was revealed that Indian family owned business disintegrates and declines in third generation. Major initiatives therefore are necessary in the second generation when the residual value of the business is still there. As most of the Indian food businesses are family owned we should learn from these studies and put our act together for growth and prosperity. Have that clear vision and winning ideas and act fast.

Driving Growth in Consumer Spending on Processed Food Holds the Key for the Future of the Industry

The GDP growth rate in the year (2002-2003) is estimated to be around 4.4%, much lower than the expected, arising out of the poor performance in the agricultural sector. Agriculture accounts for about 20% of our GDP and 64% of the total employment whereas processed food accounts for only 2.5% of our GDP and only 1% of the employment. The value addition in the processed food sector is said to be INR 2000 billion in an industry whose size has been estimated to be INR 8000 billion. Scenario has of course changed since then and our GDP now growing at an average of 8% and contribution of agricultural sector is still declining. There is therefore, a need to boost the growth in the agricultural sector by bringing in drastic improvement in rural infrastructure covering roads, irrigation, cold storages and building network to connect the rural India with the rest of the world which will help reducing the wastage and middlemen intervention in the trading of the agricultural goods and produce for the processed food sector helping the industry to lower the cost and improvement in the productivity.

This calls for the significant investment in the rural India which is essential for the overall economic growth of the country. Industry is trying to introduce new products and add value to the basic foods by processing, packaging and branding but the market is still not responding to the efforts of the marketers and as a result most of the ventures are still not delivering the expected growth to make the proposition economically sustainable. We need the explosion in the consumption expenditure in the processed food which will be possible if the price of the processed foods category goes down significantly. We know that the consumption level of the processed foods in India is very low and even well below what we can see in the neighbouring countries. This is largely due to the fact that goods produced here are much more costlier for the reasons that inputs cost are higher, low level of productivity and high level and multiplicity of taxes. A holistic approach bringing changes in the entire value chain is therefore necessary. Of course, the improvement in productivity is the responsibility of the industry. But improving the rural infrastructure for the overall growth of the agricultural sector is the responsibility of the government. We need to generate rural employment through rural industrialization and that is possible only through establishing better linkages of the agricultural sector with food processing industry. If the infrastructure improves we can expect investment in the rural sector for processing of the prime foods for value addition and for marketing the processed food all over.

Indian market is highly price sensitive and therefore holding the price at the acceptable level determines whether product is going to be successful. We also know that the value addition in the processed food category is one of the lowest which is revealed by the low profit reported by the most of the players in the industry. The industry suffers from one hand of low consumption level and hence low growth and on the other hand from low level of value addition and hence low profit which further reduces the ability of the marketers to support the products for further growth. Industry is thus not able to come out of this vicious circle. It is trying to get buyers into the market by giving discounts and offering freebies for the consumers which we have witnessed during the last couple of years. The strategy is to post higher growth rate by offering more value to the consumers and that has worked for the majority of the players, of course at the cost of losing further in the bottom line. Low cost small scale family owned processors have therefore done better than the large organized corporations having higher cost structure. Big names and established players are losing grounds to the small players in the fight against the local players in their home ground.

A case in point is the significant performance of Priya Gold against Britannia in UP so much so that later has been forced to change strategy by cutting down the price to equal with the Priya brands and at the same time exploring all possibilities to reduce the cost further. In an apparently difficult market lowering the price helps to increase the consumption and the marketers are exactly trying to do the same. As processed food has direct linkage with the agricultural produce the increased consumption level of the processed food will help the rural life style in terms of up-gradation of both quality of life and increase in the rural income. It therefore makes good sense for the government to reduce the tax structure further for the processed food industry so that the products can be made further cheaper which will fuel the growth. Government gets increased revenue from the higher volume of the business and thus it will be a win-win situation for both government and the industry. It has also been seen that consumption level increase if the one time cost of the products is low which has encouraged industry to reduce the pack size of the products to make them affordable. For example, soft drinks majors Coke and Pepsi introduced 200 ml bottle at an attractive price of INR 5 per bottle. Within months there has been a huge spurt in the demand and the industry now is said to be growing at around 18 - 20 per cent. Because of lowering of prices the volume has shot up. And the trend reversed when price was increased. India has shown significant promise to emerge as a lead player in the global trade in agricultural export including export of organic foods. It is therefore important for us to do everything possible to help this sector to realize its potential faster. To make that happen we also need to help the processed food industry to realize its potential. And the only way we can help is by eliminating the wastage of agricultural produce by building infrastructure and networking the farmers with the industry and the market and by reducing the tax structure. Industry has to improve the productivity to enable industry to reduce the price of the food products to fuel the growth in demand. And that is the only way we can make it happen.

McKinsey Formula for the Growth of the Indian Food Industry

McKinsey had earlier prepared a much talked about report on Food and Agricultures Integrated Development Action (FAIDA). At the inaugural session of the FoodPro 2003 held at Chennai they made a fresh set of recommendation as part of the sequel to their earlier FAIDA report. Everyone knows that the prediction as given in the FAIDA report did not materialize and it remained only as potential opportunities for growth in the various sectors as identified by McKinsey. Initially there were lot of discussions on the report but as it happened always dust settled down and everyone forgot about it.

But it seems McKinsey has not forgotten about it and thus their Principal Mike Fernandes took this opportunity to air his views regarding the future direction for the Indian food industry. Although the suggestions given are not that no one knows about it but it makes sense to discuss those in its proper perspective.

There is a significant change in the domestic business environment impacting food business in particular. The most important is the growth of organized retailing in India, which is going to change the distribution system and margin of the trade. These organized retail chain demands more margin from the manufacturers because they buy in bulk. They take longer credit period and in the many product categories of food they have their store label brands which cuts into the market share of even many well known and established national brands. Many new stores are coming up in near future. It is expected that India will emerge as global outsourcing hub for food products.

With the opening up of the market there is flooding of the new brands and new food products. So the second change that is being evidenced is proliferation of food products in the market. At the same time consumption patterns also has been changing. There is lot of innovations in the category, many new food varieties have invaded the market. Many new players surfaced in the scene and at the same time some old players have appeared again with renewed enthusiasm. All these have collectively impacted the processed food industry on the positive side and we have witnessed growth in the category during last 7-8 years. But the scale of operation is still not very large. There are big players in the game like HLL, ITC etc. but they have not yet emerged big enough in the category.

For the purpose of integration between agriculture and the food processing the key core areas are dairy, wheat and horticulture. But all these three areas are still dominated by unorganized sectors. Big investment is not coming in these core areas because of low profitability. Major IT initiatives and infrastructure improvement will attract new investment. For example, Britannia did not find fluid milk market profitable and in the course of three to four months time they decided to withdraw their long life milk – Milkman from Kerala, Tamilnadu and later on from country's largest milk market Delhi, as well. In the infrastructure front we have made little improvement so far which has its own impact in terms of reducing the logistics cost, eliminating middlemen influence and eliminating the waste of basic inputs.

McKinsey, therefore, gave their own prescription to Indian food companies that Indian food companies should create market driven linkages rather than do it alone by building new infrastructure. As most of our units are suffering from low capacity utilization Mckinsey's second suggestion is that build low asset based manufacturing models and innovative distribution system. The third and most important prescription for food industry is to develop low cost business system to acquire pricing flexibility and competitive edge. The other day at the Annual convention of All India Food Processors Association (AIFPA) in Delhi this issue had come up and it was acknowledged the importance of reducing the cost in order to be globally competitive. But whenever those discussions arise members only look at Government and talk about reduction of taxes. Although there is a valid case of tax structure rationalization, industry should look inwards to improve firm level competitiveness.

The direction that Mckinsey has recommended for the Indian food companies are produce in large scale mass consumption products which appeal to the domestic consumers and ethnic international market at the same time. For westernized products focus on local and isolated market. Everybody cannot sell tomato ketchup in a market where even the world leader in tomato ketchup Heinz has failed. And thirdly customize the export orders. One cannot have a standard product for all markets in this category barring those who have build global brands over the years in certain food items.

There is clearly a merit in what has been suggested and Indian companies should direct their efforts to build enterprise incorporating these suggestions to emerge winner at the end of the game.

Efficient Logistics Management can Improve the Value Delivery

Lot of work is being done in supply chain management (SCM) to improve the value delivery of industrial products and other fast moving consumer products (FMCG). There are many consulting organizations who provide the specialized services in SCM areas to bring in improvement in total value chain. The processed food industry which falls in the FMCG category, however is not seen to be doing much in these areas to improve the value in spite of the fact that food products in India add very little incremental value and our industry is criticized for one of the lowest in terms value creation in comparison to the situation in many other countries. Even in comparison to the south east Asian countries our value addition is very low. In Philippines it is said to be 45% and in China it is 23% and as opposed to that we have an average value addition of less than 10%. The larger corporations such as Hindustan Lever (HLL) are very much concerned about that and they are trying to upgrade in terms of their value chain through improved SCM practices.

HLL Chairman made announcement to that effect and said that about 15%

improvement in value they could achieve. ITC is another company who are trying to use information technology (for example their e-choupal initiative) to improve the value in the supply chain management. The supply chain management covers end to end value chain including procurement, processing, in-bound and out-bound logistics, distribution till the product reaches the ultimate consumer and at each level of the interface there are innovation possibilities to upgrade in the value chain. And in this regard logistics offer considerable scope for improvement Our industry, as said earlier, suffers from low volume and there is no economy of scale and there is therefore no significant attempt to address these areas.

Fig. 14.1 Efficient logistics and supply chain management hold the key to improvement in reducing the cost of processed food.

The logistics issue is not drawing that much attention of our processors although it can be an eye opener to them if they are told about the possible value lost because of inefficient logistics management. The professional bodies and the ministry have got one issue very clear and that is the loss of primary produce because of non availability of adequate storage and processing facilities which is being highlighted in every forum for last thirty odd years or so and they have demanded installation of new cold storages along the line. The government also acceded to some of those demands of the industry and created a National Horticulture Board (NHB) who will be offering grant and banks will be giving loan at concessional rate of interest and expeditiously clear those applications for setting up new cold storages.

The issue that has escaped everybody's notice is that we have enough cold storage space and it is not fully utilized as yet. Most of our ice factories and cold storages have vacant space in the cold room and making losses and some of them even have closed down and still others are facing the threat of closure. This gives rise to the fact that there is mismatch between the quantity made available for storage and cold storage space available for utilization.

This has compounded the low return on the cold storages so far set up in the country. Another problem is with respect to their strategic locations. As most of the cold storages and ice factories are close to market centres and therefore in and around large cities which are used by the traders who keep their harvest for disposal to the nearest whole sale mandis. There are no cold storages close to growing centres compounded by uncertain power situations. The cold storage cost is very high due to high power tariff and there is lack of scale. There are few integrated logistics companies offering all India services. Our cold storages are small low investment and low technology type without any integration and scale. This concept has to change and only large players can make that happen.

All India Cold Storage Association (AICSA) which represents only Delhi based cold storages has about 44 members and their President said that 10 cold storages have recently closed down. Has any body asked when government is handing out loan and grant and Ministry of Food Processing is asking for setting up more cold storages why these existing cold storages are closing down? In one hand if we try to attract new investment and in other hand old investments become totally redundant and valueless where is the gain? We need cold storages but of different type, different scale, employing different technology located in strategic locations and integrated through total services such as fleet of efficient refrigerated container services across country or working and integrating it as a regional hub. Snowman, provides such integrated services across the country. This company is an initiative of the south based Amalgam group in Kochi whose primary business is seafood. But 85% of the investment has been made by Japanese company Mitsubishi Corporation and Mitsubishi Logistics, Hindustan Lever and another Japanese company Nichirei also have the equity stake in the company. Hindustan Lever will be a major user of this logistics services across country for their ice cream and frozen food business. And that is how businesses try to go up in value chain.

In logistics areas covering freight, insurance and transportation we have now couple of big parties including DHL, XPS and others. But they are engaged by very large groups in FMCG sectors and the whole economics work based on the improved logistics cost which is shared between manufacturer, marketer and logistic solution provider. The improved logistics also result in the drastic improvement in trade inventory and even total inventory in the systems as a result of efficient transportation and technology deployment. Of late, better communication & information technology and better infrastructure has reduced the travel time between two locations which improves the value. Most of our food processors are not able to harness these advantages still as they are either not having the volume or not having the knowledge of SCM practices.

In food processing industry logistics cost of primary produce plays an important role. Food Corporation of India (FCI) transports on an average 400000 bags of food grains every day from the producing centres to the various consumption centres by rail, road and inland water ways etc. The procurement centres, delivery centers as well as the quantum has been going up over the years. The logistics management therefore assumes significant role in reducing the cost of handling as well as waste due to lack of storage and handling facilities. We keep on reading various news about losses and pilferage in FCI godowns. Indirectly, any improvement in FCI system will have reflection in processed food industry as FCI handles two important inputs for food industry, namely wheat and sugar.

Recently, Association of Food Scientists & Technologist (AFST) has planned to address the value delivery issue on a pan India scale. They have organized one day conference in five major cities (Delhi, Kolkata, Hyderabad, Mumbai and Bangalore) but it seems that by design it is not addressing the entire value chain. The programme is focused on processing technology and packaging but not logistics.

Growth in Agricultural Sector Essential for Achieving Overall Growth Objective of Food Processing Sector

If India has to achieve its cherished growth rate of 10% in GDP, agricultural growth rate of around 4% is an imperative. In contrast, we have achieved last year (2004-05) a growth rate of only 1.1%. The Finance Minister has already mentioned this constraint saying that if farm sector growth is not touching 4%, the GDP growth rate can never be 8% and above.

The Agriculture Minister is quite optimistic about the higher growth prospect of farm sector. Till today, about 60% of our population is dependent upon agriculture for their livelihood. We have the largest cultivable land in the world but the farm productivity is also one of the lowest. Under WTO regime our farmers will be increasingly exposed to global competition and therefore we need to have comprehensive and holistic support plan and initiatives to make the farm sector more productive.

National Bank of Agriculture and Rural Development (NABARD) is entrusted with the responsibility for taking multi pronged initiatives such as building rural infrastructure, extending farm credit, providing the scientific and management support, crop diversification and multiple cropping, bringing in increased acreage under irrigated cultivation from the current level etc to raise the farm productivity. All these need to be offered in time for the farmers to benefit. The agriculture ministry is forecasting better farm output from the consideration of the crops to be harvested. This includes rice, sugarcane and oilseeds. Barring some regions, over all rain fall is also good but to say something conclusively one has to wait for the summer crops as well. On over all reckoning it is unlikely to go beyond 3% mark which is essential to get a GDP growth of about 7%. Government now has proposed a National Horticulture Board (NHB). Subsequently government also formed a National Commission on Farmers headed by Dr M.S. Swaminathan.

This commission is said to have proposed a huge budget for the Centre and States to spend on farm sector to significantly push the farm sector output. In 2003-04 our GDP grew by 8.5% when farm sector registered a 9.6% growth. As against that in 2004-05 farm sector growth was restricted to only 1.1% due to inadequate monsoon and correspondingly GDP growth rate was also low at 6.9 %.

The farm credit has gone up significantly in the current fiscal. It has been reported that the credit to the farm sector has gone to the extent of 25%. Lending by the private banks has gone up from INR 40 billion to INR 214.73 billion implemented through the priority sector lending directives. Incidentally, the rural credit recovery also has gone up. Percentage recovery in 2004-05 stood at 74.5% as compared to 72.6% in the year 2003-04. In real term, this would mean that the recovery has gone up to INR 250 billion in the year 2004-05 as compared to INR 210 billion in 2003-04. Although the overdue from the farm sector has also gone up from INR 79 billion in 2003-04 to INR 85 billion in 2004-05 and therefore real term recovery has to be read in conjunction with this increase in overdue as well. Rajasthan Electronics & Instruments Ltd has introduced small, handy and easy to carry electronic gadget loaded with simple accounting system software which can be connected to the main server to collect and settle the accounts of small farmers and societies in villages. The cash can be collected and an up to date account statement can be printed immediately for the farmer who has taken loan through micro credit extended to them. Their manufacturing facility is located near Jaipur. This can facilitate the rural credit recovery.

The growth of the food processing sector also incidentally hinges on the growth of the farm sector particularly for the reasons that the uninterrupted supply of standardized raw material at acceptable price is one of the most important criteria for the growth of the sector. Ministry of food processing has pegged the growth rate of processed food industry at 10% year on year basis. But the industry is not very confident about it. Industry as a whole is facing numerous problems in the sense that profit margins are declining. Some of the leading manufacturers and marketers including MNCs are squeezed in terms of margin very much and they are looking for ways and means to improve the productivity and profitability. Some of them are even trying to focus only on premium segment of the market for improved bottom line profit. But Ministry of Food Processing Industry (MFPI) seems to be ambitious in their growth projection and optimism.

The year 2015 vision document of MFPI is aimed at vast potential of the farm sector by trebling the size of the food processing sector and then also talking about generating more employment opportunity, enhancing the farm sector income and contributing to over all national growth. The objective of the document is also to increase the processing of perishables from its existing level of 6% to 20% and most importantly value addition from at around 7% now to an astronomical figure of 70% and finally increasing the India's share in global food trade from 1 % to 3%. Underlying assumption is that there will be an investment in infrastructure, capacity upliftment and marketing infrastructure for catering to increased level of consumption of processed food going up to 10 % from the current level which is a three fold growth. All these in next ten years.

Rabo India seems to have done a study on this and they assume that the fund will flow as incremental equity from the processing industries, loan from financial institutions, FDI as well as from government funding. We are not witnessing any new investment in capacity building so far. Lending agencies do not like to invest in the food industry. In the recent seminar on value addition through packaging in New Delhi organized by AFST a representative from Rabo India spoke about the opportunity and that too giving statistics how in many categories such as milk we are the largest producer etc. In the same seminar an old timer food processor was saying that he does not get the processing variety of tomatoes at acceptable price. The processing variety can go up with the total integration of farm sector with the global market requirement and therefore we need a holistic approach. If the value addition has to go up ten folds in ten years the cost of the products offering has to come down significantly to be competitive as there is serious limitation in raising the price of the product through offering of incremental benefits. And industry has to deal with this apparently very difficult task of delivering higher value than the competition.

A Holistic Approach is Needed for Growth of Agro Processing Sectors

Agro processing has been given the status of high priority sectors which will qualify for automatic approval of Foreign Investment Promotion Board (FIPB) for foreign equity upto fifty one percent. The Ministry of Food Processing Industry has drawn up a series of initiatives and action plans for the development of processed food sectors which include setting up of a national financial institution, priority bank lending, fiscal reliefs, assistance for upgrading standards to international levels, research and development activities, facilities for procurement through contract farming, assistance to encourage backward linkages etc. More such steps for the development of food processing sectors are still in the offing.

That the agro-processing sector is of high priority in the national agenda was there for more than a decade since Late Rajiv Gandhi's time and several governments have come and gone since then only repeating the same slogans. But our process food industries only have seen the entry of a few multinationals and closure of many domestic industries (some of them of course also grabbed by MNCs). The real term growth of the processed food sectors which can be measured by the growth in the consumption pattern have not yet taken place. As a result, we still don't see any significant change in the agro-processing sectors. It is still the same excepting a few new global brands have replaced old domestic brands. Earlier local companies were not doing well – today the new entrant MNCs are also not doing well and their all calculations have gone haywire.

We are expecting that export from agro sector also should increase but international market is highly competitive and to get an entry in the international trade lower price and superior quality are the key.

If the food processing sector has to flourish we will have to take a holistic view of everything and not simply anouncing some packages here and there. The primary focus has to be on the growth in the consumption pattern which will fuel the growth of the industry. The consumption has a direct relationship with price and the price can only be low if the basic inputs and tax structures are low. The primary inputs to the processing units are agricultural outputs and that can only be low if yield per hectre reaches the international level. Farmers should earn more from the incremental yield and not from a price protection mechanism of fixing the basic prices. This means government now has to set new policies, imbibe state-of-art technologies to maximise production from the existing areas under cultivation. By giving loans to the farmers alone will not help – he should be helped and taught how to generate money to repay the loan. Otherwise, what we are seeing today will further aggravate the situation. We hear that farmers are committing suicide for not been able to repay the loan.

In the name of providing level playing-field to domestic industries the government imposed an additional non-modvatable levy of 8% on imports.

Most of our basic packaging materials that are used in food industry will now be costing more. On the import of paper and paper board used for packaging material, custom duty had been increased from 20% to 30% which will increase the cost of composite packaging in food industry. Custom duty in citric acid, an essential food acid has been increased from 30% to 40%.

To add to the burden 8% excise duty has been imposed on packaged tea, branded butter, cheese and ghee, branded spices, meat and fish, skim milk powder and all other edible preparations when produced in factories. And finally on chocolates and food preparations maximum retail price (MRP) based excise duty has been extended. To top it all service tax has been proposed to be levied on slaughter houses using mechanical means.

In sum, these proposals are not going to help increasing the consumption because all budgetory proposals are indicative of inflation and consequent price increase in process food sectors. And if the consumption is not increased there will be no growth which will have its consequential effect on prices of basic agricultural commodities. Then what good it is only to declare agro processing a priority sector. Only fast track clearance of license is not enough. In fact that is only the starting point. Processed food must be within the reach of common people which alone can fuel the overall growth of the industry.

How do we Propose to Utilise the Production Capacity of New Food Parks

We have been raising the issue in various fora that India processes only about 5% of its total produce of fruits and vegetables and about 30% of its total produce goes as waste because of lack of adequate storage and processing facilities amounting to couple of thousands of milion of rupees loss to the nation. This we are hearing for the last thirty years. While it is no denying that it is absolutely necessary to stop wastage of all forms but no one has ever thought of investigating where these reported wastage takes place and was it possible to stop it. Without such valid information demands were made at all possible occasions that infrastructure for cold storage and processing facilities should be developed for the surplus produce.

Our experience tells us that what we produced in those days we could not sell and if at all we could sell those processed fruit and and vegetable products that was only a distress sales , most often than not at a price lower than the cost because entire stock would be useless if the processors could not sell the product before the expiry of the stock or before the start of the next harvesting season. Our process plant could not run in full capacity. So if we had processed the surplus we would have lost the higher value in terms the cost of input and the value that was added in processing the raw material. The key issue therefore was marketing and the fact of the matter was that we did not have a ready market for those processed fruit and vegetable products. Unfortunately, no one ever seem to have discussed this and related issues to find out a solution to the problem

There are over six hundred fruit and vegetable processing plants of various capacities in the country in the organised sector and eighty percent of those process plants are sick. They are not able to run the plant for want of orders. My question therefore is that do we need to have additional capacity? The story is similar in all most all the process food sectors. Hindustan Lever has acquired the public sector Modern Foods Industries couple of months ago and after their acquisition they have reported to have doubled the sales in volume terms. It was said that before acquisition the Modern Foods used to sell about 1.7 million loaves a week and now that figure has been reported as 3 million in a week which is more than double. Sales of modern bread was declining at the beginning of the year. This decline has been arrested and a 100 percent growth has been registered with various trade promotion schemes at major locations of Delhi and Mumbai where Modern Bread was not widely available and the brand name was on a downswing. And Hindustan Lever has achieved it by closing down two plants of Modern Foods and the third one is only partially operational and sourcing the additional requirement from the contract manufacturers. Only one plant of Modern Foods is fully operational. We should learn a lesson from that. And that is that production capacity is not really a constraint. What we really need is to build the marketing capability and the network and in that respect what government can do is the question. HLL is primarily focussing on three main issues including quality of the product, improvement in distribution and also leveraging on their strong procurement capabilities. If you cannot deliver the cost and quality leadership simply having production capacity has no advantage in today's competitive business environment.

Our requirement is to have an integrated approach. In that respect Karnataka Governments approach is more relevant. What they are doing is creating mobile processing facilities so that the farm produce can be processed immediately after harvesting and can be brought to the nearest storage facility to be despatched to the large process plants as semi-finished raw materials to be converted into the end product under a pre-agreed contract. This will safeguard both the processors and the farmers . Alternative to that approach is to create infrastructure to extend the life of the fresh fruits and vegetables so that they can be sold over a longer period as fresh products instead of converting them into the processed material and then finding it difficult to market as the fresh product will always have an assured market. And most importantly farmers themselves know how and where to market their produce. The only help that they want is to have facilities for extended shelf life of their surplus seasonal harvest at a reasonable cost.

But as against that what we are seeing that State Agro Industries Corporations are setting up multicrore food parks for processing. The latest in the list is Punjab Agro Industries Corporation (PAIC) who are all set to set up three food parks in the state involving an investment of INR 600 million. Besides this, PAIC would also set up four fruit and vegetable processing projects at a cost of INR 400 million which is expected to process 40,000 tonnes of fruits and vegetables annually. Maharastra Industrial Development Corporation (MIDC) has a pilot plant facility existing in Tarapur which is normally given on rent to the parties who would like to do any scale up work or want to take a commercial run to see that the process is working fine before going for investing in large scale project.

This facility was useful particularly for those who are developing the new processes. The same MIDC recently has announced that they want private parties to invest in their proposed aspetic pack plant which will be used as contract plant for others to produce products and market. At least MIDC is clever enough to involve the private parties to finance such ventures and private parties if interested to invest will ensure that the plant is booked for the potential buyers who have either established a brand or have the marketing skill and resources to create a new brand failing which these investments will be futile and we will in the long run be creating more sick and unviable units. The creation of units in Public-Private-Partnership (PPP) model is a good idea. Why our ministry is not taking into the account of the experience of our already existing installations and capacities is not understandable. Also why we are not thinking of making use of already made investment before deciding on the creation of new capacity. Under the state agriculture department there are numerous small fruit and vegetable processing facilities existing which are located in multiple locations in close proximity to growing areas. None of those are having any job. In Escorts we got a very big order of canned pineapple from Germany. This order was offloaded to three parties one in private sector (Changia Food Products Ltd in Siliguri) and two in those government owned process plant one under West Bengal Government in north Bengal and the other under Manipur Government near Imphal. We gave advance and also supplied the can to produce the goods in time to execute the order. Needless to say that none could execute the order and we could not even recover advance money from Changia who went into liquidation after trying for BIFR to take over. These small processing plants under state government were having one in-charge who can be described as partly technically trained with two or three helpers. In district headquarters these small process plants occasionally train housewives to make squash, cordials, jams and ketchup at home and beyond that these small processing units have no other utility.

When UB Group sold their Kissan and Dipys business to Brook Bond we had at that point of time nine production units spread all over in locations like Mumbai, Nasik, Bangalore, Bagalur, Bareilly and Nepal and all these plants were producing all products. Post acquisition, HLL has closed down all units except Bangalore and also withdrawn Dipys brand from the market and resorted to outsourcing in the later years. Such is the condition of the production facility that we already have. Some efforts are necessary to upgrade them and make them useful to be productive. What are the actions in that direction? If the existing capacity is not utilised fully for valid reasons is there any valid reason of creating new capacity? Who is going to utilise these production facilities being created in Food Parks in all state and for whom? Has the State Agro Industries Corporation tried to seek a justifiable and convincing answers for these questions?

What Government can do to Promote Food and Agri Business

What government can do to help this sector grow faster in the domestic market and also to be able to integrate faster with the international market?. We all know that food and agricultural sector holds a great promise to emerge as the lead player in the global market. Many international procurement agencies and commodity traders have realized this and therefore forged local alliances to source agro commodities including fruits and vegetables to be sourced from India to be marketed in the European and other developed countries. Recently, Bharti Telecom Group – the largest in the telecom sector – has set up a venture for export of agricultural produce in joint venture with the largest commodity trader of UK. A telecommunication group recognizing the power of the agricultural sector is worth taken note of. The Middle East countries have signed agreement for increasing the agricultural products trade with India.

The earlier governments have made attempts to support this sector but nothing significant really happened for which I don't really blame the government. Because our industry associations really lost focus on what are the critical issues for them which will have long term implication and more particularly which will improve their competitiveness. None of them are realizing that if they are not going to become global player in course of time they will not exist. The food industry associations' demands therefore were limited to reduction of taxes, levies and controls. What they should be more concerned about are those issues which will help them to go up in the value chain and become more competitive. The earlier budgets have thus granted only such concessions in periodic dose to keep the industry lobbyists in great humour. The recent union budget have really provided many incentives including much desired tax holidays and investment allowances. But industries have failed to exploit this advantage for creating new capacities and new investments. While government has directed the financial institutions to support this sector generously but the fact of the matter is that this sector is not the favourite of the financial institutions. The reason is very simple and that is the earlier loans given to the food sector have not been repaid. The food sector still is not investors' friendly and credit rating is low. The failure rate is also quite high in processed food sector.

The government, therefore, should look at the issues which will improve the competitiveness of this sector. The finance minister has already sounded that the focus of the next budget would be agricultural sector and rural India. If the necessary impetus is given there it should serve a long way to help this sector to grow faster. This industry needs the integration with rural India where basic agricultural production is there. We will thus require an excellent road and communication infrastructure for faster movement of goods and services across states and countries at a much lower cost from rural India. Investment in this areas should, therefore, be preferentially mobilized through private and public investments in infrastructure. Secondly, we need to create food processing units in small and medium sectors in rural India for generating local employment to improve the purchasing power of the rural population to help them integrate with the mainstream. We cannot have an isolated development approach without involvement and support of everyone who are the stakeholders in the development process. This is a mammoth task but we need to accomplish that very fast. This task will involve upgrading the health service and education and up-skilling the rural population in terms of improving their capability to work in the rural sectors.

The government extends grants to many NGOs including self seeking NGOs for that kind of purpose. While NGOs help is definitely required but there are NGOs which promote their own interest at the cost of exchequer. Those should be identified and denied any grant in the name of rural upliftment. This will also help the small and marginal farmers to find direct market for their produce in the local areas where processing units are located. The government has taken initiatives to create agri export zones and food parks in various states etc. But these attempts did not produce any results particularly for the reasons that the appropriate linkages have not been established. In this task large industries which have a marketing network need to be integrated and supported by small enterprises in rural sectors and in the long run this small and medium rural industry will develop themselves to become capable to market their produce directly to end customers. The large existing industries should be allowed to shift their factories to the rural sectors to become cost competitive. The large industries should be allowed the investment allowance if they plough back their profit to set up new units in rural sectors in all states irrespective of the location.

If the industrial infrastructure is not in place, setting up industry with tax concessions will not make the units viable. The new investments in the state sectors particularly in the difficult states should be channelised through the central investment council which will have the responsibility to assist the investors to set up their units in time without being subjected to the requirements to satisfy multiple agencies. Towards this end expeditious implementation of unified food laws will come as a great help. After so many months this draft of unified food laws have now been cleared by the parliament and awaithing to become an Act. The government should set up a Central Food and Agricultural Sector Entrepreneurship Development Center headed by a competent person and governed by a body consisting of successful and knowledgeable people in this sector who were party to creation of successful enterprises. The role and the mandate of this institution will be creating successful food ventures through entrepreneurial development activities. This should be an autonomous institution started with public fund but within reasonable time frame should become self sufficient. This institution will carry out market research, pilot study for test marketing of products, technology transfer, assess the techno-economic viability of the proposal and will work in close cooperation between the prospective entrepreneurs and funding agencies and the similar such roles.

The government earlier had granted the income tax holidays for the new investments in food processing units expecting that a lot of new companies will come up. Businesses generally are set up when a market is identified which can be exploited. Seeing the performance of the existing units where even established global players with enormous resources are finding it difficult to create viable business, new players are hesitant in putting their limited resource in new food business. One should appreciate that if businesses make profits paying income tax is not an issue but if business does not make profit at all what good it is to have the facility of income tax holiday? Therefore, it is better to help the industry to make profit and then ask them to pay tax. And the profit can increase either by reducing the cost or increasing the sales. Subsequent government budgets should come as help to improve the both.

Emergence of Electronic Commerce in Processed Food Sector

The Organization for Economic Cooperation and Development (OECD) defines electronic commerce as a new way of conducting business on line, qualifying it as business occurring over networks, which use nonproprietary protocols that are established through an open standard setting process such as the internet. The ability of the internet to bring together distant parts of the world in global electronic market place and information exchange has a far reaching and potentially beneficial impact on both the developing and industrialized economies alike. Therefore, India also has a huge potential for internet and electronic commerce. Internet penetration in India is expected to be over 10 million by 2006 with e-commerce growing at a CAGR of over 200 per cent. E-commerce covers three types of transactions, namely, business-to-customers (B2C), business-to-business (B2B) and business-to-government (B2G).

Most of the business in India have recognized e-commerce and the internet as being the integral to their future business growth strategic framework. On the supply chain front B2B transactions are part of the regular business process with much higher efficiency and lower cost for most of the corporations in the FMCG sector, small and medium enterprise included. However, only very large corporations have either implemented or in the process of implementation of costly customer relationship management (CRM) interfaces to build bridge with their ever evasive and difficult to retain customer base by providing significant value to their customers in terms of service quality delivery. Those organizations who have taken initiatives to provide customers an opportunity to shop on line by accessing their portal which provides all the relevant information for customers to take decision are experiencing the growth in the e-commerce transactions. Let us capture such initiatives in the processed food ventures.

While organizations are seeing it an additional and powerful source of conducting business today but at the same time old traditional ways are to still continuing parallely in a complex and very large market that India is. Therefore, no one possibly will consider it as the only way to do business. Reliance Infocom is planning to launch its nationwide chain of web stores. The group has made a foray into coffee retailing business by launching a coffee brand called Java Green which will be sold in its over 700 web stores across the country. The first coffee retail outlets will come up at Spencer Plaza, the largest shopping mall in Chennai. It has been said that Qwiky, the Chennai based coffee bars housing Reliance Infocom's web stores who have experience in this line of business will be helping Reliance in their new venture.

If the experience is successful other beverage brands such as Java Roll and Java Wrap will also be sold through these coffee outlets.

ITC's E- choupal initiatives is a mega venture in the direction of harnessing the power of information technology to penetrate the huge rural market for mutual gain by eliminating the hurdles and non value adding activities of the intermediaries in the business of selling the agricultural outputs to the global market. Building up an infrastructure of that magnitude across the country is an uphill task which a company of the size of ITC can undertake. ITC is said to have covered soyabean producing areas of Madhya Pradesh already and is now pushing into the wheat heartland of UP. In MP it is catering to more than 6000 villages. Last year the company traded the soyabean worth INR 1.6 billion and this year in one season alone they have exceeded that volume. Even competitors of ITC in agricultural commodity trade accepts that ITC has done a remarkable job.

Look at the way how the agricultural output used to reach its ultimate buyer. Conventionally, a typical farmer sold his produce to a small trader called the Kaccha Adat. This man, in turn, sold it to larger trader called the Pakka Adat. From here the produce found its way to the local mandi or the market where large traders came into the picture. Brokers surfaced at this stage and got the soyabean sold to processors like ITC. Traditionally, these brokers were the people who controlled the information on prices and supplies and hence were quite powerful. The e-choupal model has made those powerful brokers quite upset. A new role therefore has to be found out for them and in this new initiative they have been made to work as co-ordinators (samyojaks) who nominates village level sanchalaks and get 1 per cent commission on their service for documentation etc. After the initial reservation and resistance they offered, these middleman finally accepted the reality seeing that although margins have come down in the process and became transparent, their earnings will still be the same as they will trade higher volume. At the end of all these excercises ITC reduced the cost of procurement to INR 200 a tonne from INR 700 a tonne as it was costing earlier. That translates into immediate savings of INR 500 per tonne for both the farmer and ITC to share.

The new e-commerce and e- business opportunity will open up fresh chapters which will make the business transactions not only transparent but will benefit all involved in the process. In the knowledge economy the farmers will also eventually emerge as knowledge workers. The major policy initiatives will therefore be necessary to harness the significant possibilities that internet revolution will offer to all businesses. And processed food industry should make a note of it and take the necessary actions.

Financing Food Processing Units

Most of the players in the industry are in small and medium scale who have not performed well so far. In this sector financial institutions do not like to extend loan because of the past experience. This industry therefore has been considered as high risk industry. Further there are several regulations which limit availability of finance in this sector, including the definition of priority sector lending, the cooperative Act and the Warehousing Corporaton Act. Besides, crop insurance issues schemes in India have faced several issues including assessment of farm yield, lack of valid past statistical data to calculate premia, high premium for certain crops, administrative hurdles in managing claims-rendering very limited benefit to farmers.

FDI in Food Processing

FDI in food processing sector is low constituting only 4 per cent of the total FDI during the period 1991-2004 and actual inflow is again still lower to about 28 per cent of the FDI approved (INR 4.2 billion out of INR 11.6 billion approved so far during this period).This performance is despite the fact that 100 per cent FDI is permitted in all sector except retail, plantation and alcoholic beverages.

Government Support

Although Government has announced several incentives to promote new investment in food processing the reality is that nothing much happened. The reason being government support is inadequate and procedural hurdles are far too many. Those who received the grants and concessions could not benefit from it. This has to address the sector specific issues and government has to work in close association with the industry to ensure that the supports and incentives given are fully utilised for the purpose. A strong monitoring mechanism thus also has to be in place.

The industry which is predominantly constituted by small and unorganised sector requires the skill and experienced managerial input if those small enterprises are to deliver result. The development of skilled human resource in all functions of enterprise management is therefore a key issue. Institutions should be encouraged to offer short term management development programme specifically directed to meet the need of small entrepreneurs running the process food industry. The other important issues include the research and development effort as well as rationalisation of tax structure and safety and regulatory issues.The regulatory authorities has to demonstrate the ability to implement safety and quality and hygiene to provide the credibility of the

Organised food distribution in India did not grow for the simple reasons of poor infrastructure, technology and capital. Foreign Direct Investment (FDI) in retailing is still restricted excepting in cash & carry format. The restriction on FDI in food retailing comes from the apprehension that this might create employment amongst small family owned retailers and shopkeepers and also at the same time reduce the bargaining power of the farmers. However, in reality the experience in other countries will teach us that it has helped in employment creation, elimination of middlemen to reduce complexity and improve efficiency, increased access to information for farmers and finally cost savings for the consumers

Export of Food Products

India has about 1.5 per cent amounting to INR 360 billion in 2003-04 share of global agricultural export (approx USD 522 billion) despite enjoying the leadership in production of some of major crop and agricultural products. This again is constituted largely by primary processed items and commodities where price realisation is very low. The reason for this lacklustre performance is arising out of our low competitiveness in global trade, poor perception of products in global trade , non-tariff barriers coupled with short life cycle of the products.

Most exporters in India lack in scale.For example, the largest fresh food exporter has registered a turnover of INR 500 million only. The economy of scale has thus rendered these exporters uncompetitive. Our food traders are only playing an opportunistic role and are not establishing themselves as long term players of significance in the global trade. Our food trade in global market could not so far establish any name or brand to reckon with due to lack of technical and managerial expertise compounded by the low investment and capital inflow.

Financing of Processed Food Sector

Financing of Farmers

Farming community often rely on credit from unorganised source including moneylenders who often exploit them. This is the result of limited access , timeliness, availability and adequacy of credit from organised sources. Problems of the banks extending finance is the fear of default in case of crop failure or in the absence of an assured market for their produce and in addition, farmers do not have the ability to provide collateral as security.

15

Future of Indian Processed Food Industry

Future Depends on Ability to Exploit Opportunity

The future of processed food industry in India lies in our ability to exploit the opportunities ahead of us. The role of the food industry becomes very critical for two reasons namely, the food production is expected to grow significantly. In next ten years the production level is estimated to be almost double. With low farm level price and huge wastage, processing can offer some solution even now. The other reason which will impact the processed food industry is the new retail revolution that the country is witnessing with the entry of global leader like Wal Mart and with the entry of organisation like Reliance. These large food retailers will bring in efficiency in the supply chain integrating the back end and will help domestic market to grow giving opportunities for the food processors to get avenues to market their products. These large format retailers are also expected to source merchandise from India for their stores abroad.India therefore , can have an opportunity to become global food supplier particularly because we have the distinction of becoming the largest producer of many agricultural commodities in the world. We could not add much value to the processed food items and we could not emerge a cost effective producer to make any impact in the global trade opportunity. In the global trade of food and food products India remained an insignificant player. The processed food is still considered an item of luxury in India and the prices are quite high for general consumers to try. Moreover, fresh is always available and is cheaper than processed items, the domestic industry therefore, did not grow. Food processors did not perform well and many initiatives and new ventures failed. Although market has grown over the years and many new products have

Exhibit 7: Investment required to achieve the vision

		(INR bn)	
	2003-04	**2009-10**	**2014-15**
A. PROCESSING			
Fruits and Vegetables	70	40	110
Dairy	217	101	318
Meat and Poultry			
Buffalo Meat	8	9	17
Poultry	1	2	3
Marine	16	64	80
Edible Oil			
Refineries	3	3	6
Non-Alcoholic Beverages			
Tea	53	15	68
Grain based products			
Rice milling	24	19	43
Flour milling	15	18	33
Breads	5	5	10
Biscuits	13	12	25
Snack & Ready-to-Eat foods	5	6	11
Pasta based foods	1	2	3
Sugar and Sugar based products			
Sugar	75	75	150
Confectionery	1	2	3
Chocolates	8	11	19
Alcoholic Beverage			
Wine	5	4	9
Sub-total	520	390	910
B. OTHER INVESTMENT – MARKET DEVELOPMENT AND INFRASTRUCTURE			
Market Development fund	5	2	7
Institution (s) for food technology/ management	2	1	3
Food testing laboratories	3	1	4
Food Parks	20	30	50
Cold chains, abattoirs, packaging centre etc.	10	13	23
Total	**560**	**437**	**997**

Source: Rabobank analysis, pertains to organizd sector.

Appendix-II

Global Food Market Outlook- 2007

World Wheat Market at a Glance

	2004-05	2005-06 estimate	2006-07 forecast	Change 2006-07 over 2005-06
	Million tonnes			%
World Balance (milled basis)				
Production	632.0	624.5	591.8	–5.2
Trade	110.8	110.1	110.0	–0.1
Total Utilization	618.8	623.2	621.7	–0.2
Food	437.7	442.4	445.6	0.7
Feed	111.1	113.2	112.2	–0.8
Other Uses	70.1	67.6	63.9	–5.6
Ending Stocks	175.5	174.7	147.0	–15.8

Source : FAO

World Wheat Imports

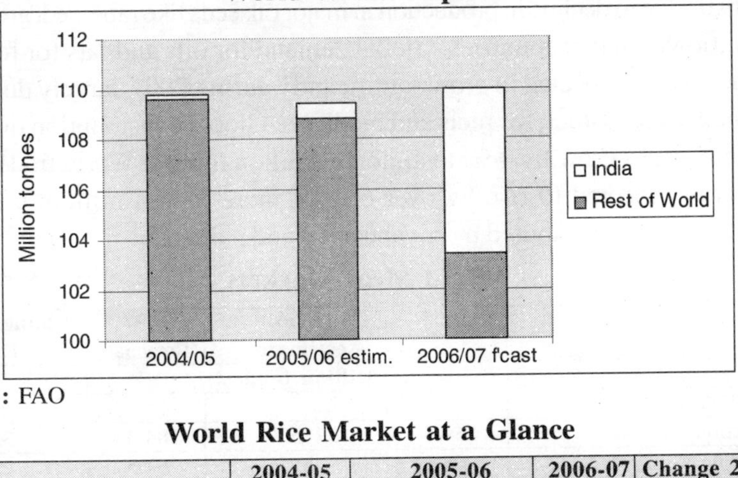

Source : FAO

World Rice Market at a Glance

	2004-05	2005-06 estimate	2006-07 forecast	Change 2006-07 over 2005-06
	Million tonnes			%
World Balance (milled basis)				
Production	406.9	421.9	420.9	–0.2
Trade	29.8	28.6	28.9	1.1
Total Utilization	413.8	416.4	420.6	1.0
Food	361.6	367.2	372.2	1.4
Ending Stocks	99.2	105.3	104.7	–0.6

Source : FAO

Rice Exports by the Major Exporters

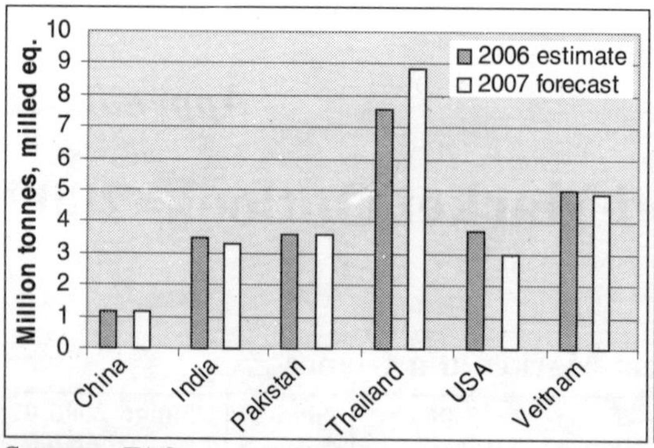

Source : FAO

Share of Global Dairy Exports (Avarage 2004-06)

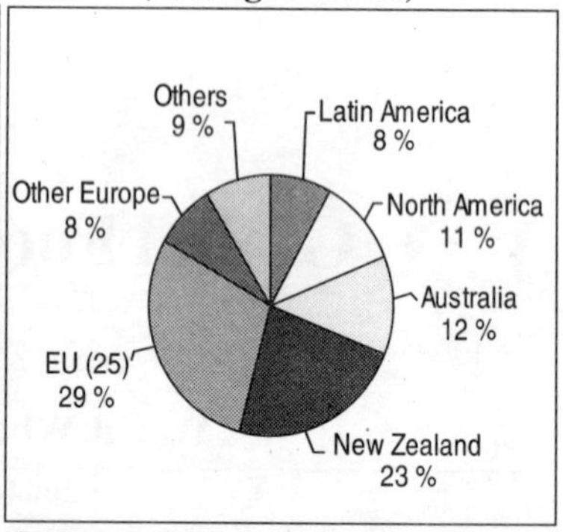

Source : FAO

Sugar: Global sugar production for 2006-07 is forecast to increase to 155.5 million tonnes largely due to higher output in Brazil, India, China, Indonesia and Thailand where as Sugar production in developed countries is expected to drop by about 9 percent in 2006-07 to 39.1 million tonnes. Output in EU for 2006-07 is estimated to have decreased by 23 % from 21.4 million tonnes in 2005-06 to 16.5 million tonnes in 2006-07. World sugar consumption is estimated at 152.1 million tonnes , a 1.5% growth from 149.9 million tonnes in 2005-06.

Oilseed : Global oilseed production is forecast to register only marginal growth in 2006- 07 due to decline in production in major oilseeds like rapeseed, groundnut and sunflower in key countries. Global demand for oils and fats for food and non-food use is expected to grow significantly during 2007 largely due to use of oilseeds as feedstock for fuels and biodiesel. Global consumption of oil and fat is forecast to grow by 4 % to almost 6 million tonnes. World trade in fats and oils is expected to rise by over 6 % or more than 4 million tonnes in 2006-07 largely contributed by soyabean oil and palm oil.

World Meat Markets

	2005	2006 estimate	2007 forecast	Change 2007 over 2006
	Million tonnes			%
World Balance				
Production	269.1	275.7	284.3	3.1
Bovine meat	64.5	65.7	67.5	2.8
Poultry	82.2	83.1	85.5	3.0
Pigmeat	104.0	108.0	112.0	3.7
Ovinemeat	13.1	13.5	13.8	2.7
Trade	20.9	20.7	22.0	6.7
Bovine meat	6.6	6.6	7.2	9.2
Poultry	8.4	8.2	8.7	6.4
Pigmeat	4.8	4.8	5.0	4.2
Ovinemeat	0.8	0.8	0.9	4.6

Source : FAO

Appendix-III

Market Indicators in Food Retail & Catering Industry

Table 1 Consumer Expenditure on Food in Retail 2000-2005

INR bn	2000	2001	2002	2003	2004	2005
Total	5,653.9	6,229.7	6,124.9	6,404.7	6,841.0	7,310.9

Source: Official statistics, trade associations, trade press, trade interviews, Euromonitor International estimates

Market Data

Table 2 Units, Transactions and Value Sales in Consumer Foodservice: 2000-2005

	2000	2001	2002	2003	2004	2005
Units	740,120.0	818,022.0	909,999.0	1,019,044.0	1,137,196.0	1,268,834.0
Transactions (mn)	28,170.0	32,030.4	36,664.3	42,213.2	48,799.6	56,305.8
INR million current prices	1,044,133.3	1,252,006.0	1,427,207.7	1,622,997.6	1,841,950.6	2,117,550.4
INR million constant prices	1,044,133.3	1,207,511.5	1,318,572.6	1,444,484.2	1,579,838.3	1,746,235.7

Source : Official statistics, trade associations, trade press, company research, store checks, trade interviews, Euromonitor International estimates

Table 3 Units, Transactions and Value Sales in Consumer Foodservice: % Growth 2000-2005

% growth	2004-05	2000-05 Cagr	2000-05 Total
Units	11.6	11.4	71.4
Transactions	15.4	14.9	99.9
Value current prices	15.0	15.2	102.8
Value constant prices	10.5	10.8	67.2

Source : Official statistics, trade associations, trade press, company research, store checks, trade interviews, Euromonitor International estimates

Table 4 Consumer Foodservice by Independent vs Chained Outlets: Units/Outlets 2005

Outlets	Independent	Chained	Total
Cafés/bars	59,204.0	1,169.0	60,373.0
Full-service restaurants	468,380.0	947.0	469,327.0
Fast food	47,171.0	573.0	47,744.0
100% home delivery/takeaway	92.0	78.0	170.0
Self-service cafeterias	–	–	–
Street stalls/kiosks	689,900.0	1,320.0	691,220.0
Consumer foodservice	1,264,747.0	4,087.0	1,268,834.0

Source: Official statistics, trade associations, trade press, company research, trade interviews, Euromonitor International estimates.

Table 5 Food vs Drinks Split 2005

% value analysis	Food	Drink	Total
Cafés/bars	35.0	65.0	100.0
Full-service restaurants	79.0	21.0	100.0
Fast food	66.0	34.0	100.0
100% home delivery/takeaway	90.0	10.0	100.0
Self-service cafeterias	–	–	–
Street stalls/kiosks	83.0	17.0	100.0
Consumer foodservice by type and chained/independent	71.1	28.9	100.0

Source: Official statistics, trade associations, trade press, company research, trade interviews, Euromonitor International estimates.

Table 6 Sales in Consumer Foodservice by Location 2000-2005

% value	2000	2005
Stand-alone	84.3	80.9
Retail	2.9	4.7
Travel	2.7	4.2
Leisure	0.9	1.3
Hotels	9.3	8.8
Total	100.0	100.0

Source: Official statistics, trade associations, trade press, company research, trade interviews, Euromonitor International estimates

Table 7 Forecast Units, Transactions and Value Sales in Consumer Foodservice: 2005-2010

	2005	2006	2007	2008	2009	2010
Units	1,268,834.0	1,417,661.0	1,568,487.0	1,715,912.0	1,869,094.0	2,018,359.0
Transactions (mn)	56,305.8	64,435.9	73,130.1	82,285.1	91,542.4	100,471.6
INR million	2,117,550.4	2,353,668.9	2,612,311.4	2,899,351.5	3,180,006.8	3,459,735.9

Source: Official statistics, trade associations, trade press, company research, trade interviews, Euromonitor International estimates.

Table 8 Forecast Units, Transactions and Value Sales in Consumer Foodservice: % Growth 2005-2010

% growth	2005-10 Cagr	2005-10 Total
Units	9.7	59.1
Transactions	12.3	78.4
Constant value	10.3	63.4

Source: Official statistics, trade associations, trade press, company research, trade interviews, Euromonitor International estimates.

Table 9 Leading Chained Consumer Foodservice Brands by Number of Units 2005

	Global Brand Owner	Outlets
Coffee Day Xpress	Amalgamated Bean Coffee Trading Co Ltd	330.0
Café Coffee Day	Amalgamated Bean Coffee Trading Co Ltd	266.0
Indian Hotels Co Restaurants	Indian Hotels Co Ltd	168.0
Baskin-Robbins	Pernod Ricard Groupe	135.0
Barista Coffee Co	Barista Coffee Co Ltd	130.0
Java Green	Java Green Pvt Ltd	130.0
Pizza Hut	Yum! Brands Inc	118.0
Domino's Pizza	Domino's Pizza Inc	100.0
McDonald's	McDonald's Corp	84.0
Subway	Doctor's Associates Inc	56.0
Smokin' Joe's	Smokin' Joe's Pizza Pvt Ltd	47.0
Pizza Corner	Global Franchise Architects Co Ltd	45.0
Hot Breads	Oriental Cuisines Pvt Ltd	40.0
Kamat	Rangappa Kamat Group of Hotels Ltd	35.0
Wimpy	Wimpy Int Ltd	30.0

Nirula's	Nirulas Corner House Ltd	1.8	1.6	1.5	1.5
Hot Breads	Oriental Cuisines Pvt Ltd	2.3	1.9	1.7	1.5
Smokin' Joe's	Smokin' Joe's Pizza Pvt Ltd	1.6	1.5	1.5	1.5
KFC	Yum! Brands Inc	0.5	0.5	0.7	1.5
Pizza Corner	Global Franchise Architects Co Ltd	1.2	1.2	1.1	1.2
Sarvana Bhavan	Hotel Saravana Bhavan	1.8	1.6	1.3	1.2
Ashok Comfort	India Tourism Development Corp	2.1	1.7	1.4	1.2
Ashok Classic	India Tourism Development Corp	1.9	1.6	1.3	1.1
Java Green	Java Green Pvt Ltd	–	0.0	0.9	1.0
Baskin-Robbins	Pernod Ricard Groupe	–	–	–	1.0
Coffee Day Xpress	Amalgamated Bean Coffee Trading Co Ltd	–	0.1	0.6	1.0
Dum Pukht	ITC Ltd	0.6	0.9	0.8	0.9
Peshawri	ITC Ltd	0.8	0.8	0.8	0.8
Subway	Doctor's Associates Inc	0.3	0.6	0.6	0.7
Sagar Ratna	Sagar Ratna Hotels Pvt Ltd	0.8	0.7	0.6	0.6
Trident	Oberoi Group	0.9	0.9	0.6	0.6
Dakshin	ITC Ltd	0.5	0.5	0.5	0.5
Ashok Elite	India Tourism Development Corp	0.8	0.7	0.6	0.5
Ruby Tuesday	Ruby Tuesday Inc	0.1	0.2	0.4	0.4
Mocha	Impresario Entertainment & Hospitality Pvt Ltd	0.1	0.2	0.2	0.3
Amorettos	Amoretto Retail Pvt Ltd	–	0.2	0.3	0.3
US Pizza	US Pizza	0.3	0.3	0.3	0.3
ChicKing	Al Bayan Group	0.2	0.2	0.2	0.3
Qwiky's	Qwiky's Corp	0.2	0.2	0.2	0.2
Swirl's	Unilever Group	–	–	0.0	0.2
TGI Friday's	Carlson Cos Inc	0.1	0.2	0.2	0.2
Costa Coffee	Whitbread Plc	–	–	–	0.2
Kamat	Rangappa Kamat Group of Hotels Ltd	0.2	0.2	0.1	0.1
Baskin-Robbins	Allied Domecq Plc	1.1	1.0	1.0	–
KFC	Tricon Global Restaurants Inc	–	–	–	–
Pizza Hut	Tricon Global Restaurants Inc	–	–	–	–
Others		39.5	37.0	35.4	34.3
Total		100.0	100.0	100.0	100.0

Source: Trade associations, trade press, company research, trade interviews, Euromonitor International estimates.

Calorie Consumption

Table 12 All India average , per capita food intake in Kilocalories/ day

All India	1972-73	1993-94	1999-2000	2004-05
Rural	2,226	2,153	2,149	2,047
Urban	2,107	2,071	2,156	2,020
Bottom 30%	1,505	1,678	1,626	n.a
Middle 40%	2,170	2,119	2,009	n.a
Top 30%	3,161	2,672	2,463	n.a

Source : NSSO 61st round; and Mahemdra Dev and Evenson 2003

Table 13 Statewise averages, per capita food intake in Kilocalories / day

	Rural 1972-73	Rural 2004-05	Urban 1972-73	Urban 2003-04
Andhra Pradesh	2,103	1,995	2,143	2,000
Assam	2,074	2,067	2,135	2,143
Bihar	2,225	2,049	2,167	2,190
Gujarat	2,142	1,923	2,172	1,991
Haryana	3,215	2,226	2,404	2,033
Karnataka	2,202	1,845	1,925	1,944
Kerala	1,559	2,014	1,723	1,996
Madhya Pradesh	1,895	1,933	2,229	1,954
Maharastra	1,895	1,933	1,971	1,847
Orissa	1,995	2,023	2,276	2,139
Punjab	3,493	2,240	2,783	2,150
Rajasthan	2,730	2,180	2,357	2,116
Tamil Nadu	1,955	1,842	1,841	1,935
Uttar Pradesh	2,575	2,200	2,161	2,124
West Bengal	1,921	2,070	2,080	2,011

Source : NSSO 61st round , 2007

Bibliography

1. Baisya, R.K.,Effect of liberalization of Food and Dairy Industry. Processed Food Industry, Volume 1, December 1997, pp 8-10.
2. Baisya,R.K., Nutrition Labelling of foods. Processed Food Industry, Vol.1 Issue 1, January 1998 pp 9-11.
3. Baisya, R.K., Multinational Food Companies can upgrade the Industry. Processed Food Industry, Vol. 1 Issue 1, March 1998 pp 8-10.
4. Baisya, R.K., Swadeshi Policy and Food Processing Indsutry. Processed Food Industry, Vol. 1 Issue 1, April 1998 pp 8-10.
5. Baisya, R.K., A Holistic Approach is Needed for Growth of Agro Processing Sectors. Processed Food Industry, Vol.1 Issue 1, July 1998, pp 8-10.
6. Baisya, R.K., Can Processed Food Industry be Cheaper than Fresh Food in India. Processed Food Industry, Vol. 1 Issue 1, August 1998.
7. Baisya,R.K., Implementation of Food Laws is the Basic issue. Processed Food Industry, Vol.1 Issue 1, September 1998
8. Baisya, R.K, Acquisition of Domestic Food Business by MNCs. Processed Food Industry, Vol. 2 Issue 1, November 1998 pp 7-8.
9. Baisya, R.K., MNCs Influencing Growth of Processed Food Industry, Processed Food Industry,Vol.1 Issue 1, December 1998.
10. Baisya, R.K.,Global Competition in Processed Food, Processed Food Industry, Vol. 2 Issue 2, December 1998 pp pp 7-8.
11. Baisya, R.K.,Technological Upgradation Leading to Superior Quality. Processed Food Industry, Vol. 2 Issue 3, January 1999 pp 7-8.
12. Baisya, R.K.,Proliferation and Extension of Food Brands. Processed Food Industry, Vol. 2 Issue 4, February 1999 pp 7-8.
13. Baisya, R.K., MNCs' Entering Traditional Foods Sectors. Processed Food Industry, Vol. 2 Issue 5, March 1999 pp 9-11.
14. Baisya, R.K.,Food Retailing Has Now Become Industry. Processed Food Industry, Vol. 2 Issue 6, April 1999 pp 7-8.

15. Baisya, R.K.,Imported Foods in Indian Market. Processed Food Industry, Vol. 2 Issue 7 & 8 May and June 1999 pp 9-10.

16. Baisya, R.K.,Fads in Processed Food Industry. Processed Food Industry, Vol. 2 Issue 9, July 1999 pp 9-11.

17. Baisya, R.K.,Food Industry in India. Processed Food Industry, Vol. 2 Issue 10, August 1999 pp 9-10.

18. Baisya, R.K.,Food Service industry has now come to stay. Processed Food Industry, Vol. 2 Issue 11, September 1999 pp 9-10.

19. Baisya, R.K.,Indian Meat Processing Industry – The Problems and Prospects. Processed Food Industry, Vol. 2 Issue 12, October 1999 pp 7-9.

20. Baisya, R.K., MNCs Rewriting the New Rules of the Game. Processed Food Industry, Vol. 3 Issue 1, November 1999 pp 7-8.

21. Baisya, R.K.,Fast Food Restaurants in India is the Latest Craze. Processed Food Industry, Vol. 3 Issue 2, December 1999 pp 11-13.

22. Baisya, R.K.,New Food Products are Hitting the Market. Processed Food Industry, Vol. 3 Issue 3, January 2000 pp 7-8.

23. Baisya, R.K.,Processed Food in the New Millennium. Processed Food Industry, Vol. 3 Issue 4, February 2000 pp 7-8.

24. Baisya, R.K.,Breakfast Habits Fast Changing from Traditional to American and Continental. Processed Food Industry, Vol. 3 Issue 5, March 2000 pp 6-7.

25. Baisya, R.K., Why MNC go through Acquisition Route for Growth Strategy. Processed Food Industry, Vol. 3 Issue 6, April 2000 pp 6-7.

26. Baisya, R.K.,Food Research Institutions in India Produce Little Value. Processed Food Industry, Vol. 3 Issue 7, May 2000 pp 7-9.

27. Baisya, R.K.,Global Trade of Indian Basmati Rice Facing Difficulties. Processed Food Industry, Vol. 3 Issue 8, June 2000 pp 7-9.

28. Baisya, R.K.,Quality Raw Material at Acceptable Price – the Key to Success of Agri-Business. Processed Food Industry, Vol. 3 Issue 9 & 10, July and August 2000 pp 8-9 & 12.

29. Baisya, R.K.,Sweetmeat Industry Talking about Going Global Fearing MNCs. Processed Food Industry, Vol. 3 Issue 11, September 2000 pp 6-7.

30. Baisya, R.K.,MNCs Fail to Make Dent in Domestic Alcoholic Beverage Industry. Processed Food Industry, Vol. 3 Issue 12, October 2000 pp 11-13 & 35.

31. Baisya, R.K.,Milk has graduated from the status of a commodity to brand. Processed Food Industry, Vol. 4 Issue 1, November 2000 pp 11-12.

32. Baisya, R.K.,MNCs Jumping into the Fray: Big Opportunity in the Bottled Water Business. Processed Food Industry, Vol. 4 Issue 2, December 2000 pp 10-12.

33. Baisya, R.K.,High Brand Loyalty: MNCs Facing Difficulty in Establishing New Foreign Brands. Processed Food Industry, Vol. 4 Issue 3, January 2001 pp 6-8.

34. Baisya, R.K., Food Industry in India in the New Millennium, Indian Food Industry, Vol.20 No.1, Jan./Feb. 2001

35. Baisya, R.K.,How Do We Propose to Utilise the Production Capacity of New Food Parks?. Processed Food Industry, Vol. 4 Issue 4, February 2001 pp 7-9.

36. Baisya, R.K.,New Set of Food Traders Launching Global Brands Through Free Imports. Processed Food Industry, Vol. 4 Issue 5, March 2001 pp 7-9.

37. Baisya, R.K.,Indian Sea Food Industry yet to Realise its Potential. Processed Food Industry, Vol. 4 Issue 6, April 2001 pp 7-10.

38. Baisya, R.K., Consumers Goods Industry in India in the New Millennium – The Shape of Things to Come, Chaos, Dms IIT Delhi – Delhi, Issue 3, April 2001.

39. Baisya, R.K.,Wine Drinking Habit on the Rise in India. Processed Food Industry, Vol. 4 Issue 7 & 8, May and June 2001 pp 7-9.

40. Baisya, R.K.,Once Again Health Beverages are Being Relaunched. Processed Food Industry, Vol. 4 Issue 9, July 2001 pp 6-8.

41. Baisya, R.K.,Indian Dairy Industry: Total Change of Complexion. Processed Food Industry, Vol. 4 Issue 10, August 2001 pp 6-9.

42. Baisya, R.K.,Some traditional Indian food brands survived the test of time. Processed Food Industry, Vol. 4 Issue 11, September 2001 pp 6-8.

43. Baisya, R.K.,Amul Emerging as a Giant in Processed Food Industry. Processed Food Industry, Vol. 4 Issue 12, October 2001 pp 10-12.

44. Baisya, R.K.,Yet Another Major Food Joint Venture Breaking Up. Processed Food Industry, Vol. 5 Issue 1, November 2001 pp 6-8.

45. Baisya, R.K.,New Launches in a Difficult Market Situation. Processed Food Industry, Vol. 5 Issue 2, December 2001 pp 8-9.

46. Baisya, R.K., In Key Categories it is now the Fight Amongst Only Multinationals. Processed Food Industry, Vol. 5 Issue 3, January 2002 pp 9-10.

47. Baisya, R.K.,Beer Industry is going to Witness Many New Brands. Processed Food Industry, Vol. 5 Issue 4, February 2002 pp 8-9.

48. Baisya, R.K.,Prospects of Fresh Fruits and Vegetables Export. Processed Food Industry, Vol. 5 Issue 5, March 2002 pp 8-10

49. Baisya, R.K.,Agricultural Commodities: Lifting of Restrictions Leads to Better Distribution. Processed Food Industry, Vol. 5 Issue 6, April 2002 pp 6-7.

50. Baisya, R.K., New Generation Ice Cream Parlours To Be Designed Like Coffee Parlours. Processed Food Industry, Vol. 5 Issue 7, May 2002 pp 6-8

51. Baisya, R.K.,Food Marketers Trying All Possibilities to Increase the Consumption Level. Processed Food Industry, Vol. 5 Issue 8, June 2002 pp 5-6.

52. Baisya, R.K.,Indian Bakery Industry is Still a Mix of Old Traditional and New Modern. Processed Food Industry, Vol. 5 Issue 9, July 2002 pp 7-9

53. Baisya, R.K.,New Initiatives for Growth of Food and Agro Processing Industries. Processed Food Industry, Vol. 5 Issue 10, August 2002 pp 34.

54. Baisya, R.K.,.ITC and Tata have Big Plans in Basic Foods for the Second Time following HLL Line. Processed Food Industry, Vol. 5 Issue 11, September 2002 pp 9-10

55. Baisya,R.K.,India has the Prospects to Become a Lead Player in Organic Foods. Processed Food Industry, Vol. 5 Issue 12, October 2002 pp 9-10

56. Baisya, R.K., After Salt it is now Sugar Graduating to Value Added Brands. Processed Food Industry, Vol. 6 Issue 1, November 2002 pp 8-9

57. Baisya, R.K.,Agricultural Output and Consumption Expenditure on Decline: Punjab Requires New Direction in Food Processing. Processed Food Industry, Vol. 6 Issue 2, December 2002 pp 9-11.

58. Baisya,R.K.,Food Industry Need to Learn from Past Mistakes and New Experience. Processed Food Industry, Vol. 6 Issue 3, January 2003 pp 7-9

59. Baisya, R.K., Emergence of Electronic Commerce in Processed Food Sector. Processed Food Industry, Vol.6 No.4, February 2003. Processed Food Industry, Vol. 6 Issue 4, February 2003 pp 9-10

60. Baisya, R.K.,Driving Growth in Consumer Spending on Processed Food Holds the Key for the Future of the Industry. Processed Food Industry, Vol. 6 Issue 5, March 2003 pp 10-12

61. Baisya,R.K., New Chapter to Begin with the Proposed Joint Ventures Between Dairy Co-operatives and MNCs. Processed Food Industry, Vol. 6 Issue 6, April 2003 pp 8-10

62. Baisya,R.K.,New Initiatives from Food Industry in Select Category. Processed Food Industry, Vol. 6 Issue 7, May 2003 pp 10-12

63. Baisya, R.K., Alcoholic Beverages-Indian made foreign Liquor- A category Review, Indian Food Industry, vol22, no3 May-June 2003, pp 18-24.

64. Baisya,R.K.,Pet Foods Might Emerge as a Large Category Because of MNCs Sustained Marketing Effort. Processed Food Industry, Vol. 6 Issue 8, June 2003 pp 7-8.

65. Baisya,R.K.,Foreign Fruits & Vegetables Flooding the Indian Market. Processed Food Industry, Vol. 6 Issue 9, July 2003 pp 11-13

66. Baisya,R.K.,Perfect Timing for New Product Launch is One of the Key Factors for Success. Processed Food Industry, Vol. 6 Issue 10, August 2003 pp 8-10

67. Baisya,R.K., Organic Food Production in India : The Road to the Future, Middle East Food, Vol. XVIII, Issue 4, July- August 2003, pp 43-44

68. Baisya,R.K.,New Investment in Breweries to Exploit High Growth Opportunities. Processed Food Industry, Vol. 6 Issue 11, September 2003 pp 9-11.

69. Baisya R.K., Carbonated Soft Drink Industry, A category Review, Indian Food Industry, Vol 22, No 5, Sept- Oct 2003,pp 24- 27.

70. Baisya,R.K., Why milk food beverages category is stagnating. Processed Food Industry, Vol. 6 Issue 12, October 2003 pp 10-12

71. Baisya,R.K.,The Quality issue now even haunting multinationals. Processed Food Industry, Vol. 7 Issue 1, November 2003 pp 11-12

72. Baisya,R.K.,Dairy Industry –A category Review, Indian Food Industry,, Vol 22, No 6, November- December 2003, pp 20-23.

73. Baisya,R.K.,Sugar confectionery Industry has seen many new products from the recent entrants. Processed Food Industry, Vol. 7 Issue 2, December 2003 pp 9-11.

74. Baisya,R.K.,Mckinsey Formula for the Growth of the Indian Food Industry. Processed Food Industry, Vol. 7 Issue 3, January 2004 pp 9-10

75. Baisya,R.K.,Recent Acquisitions in Indian Food Industry. Processed Food Industry, Vol. 7 Issue 4, February 2004 pp 7-9

76. Baisya,R.K.,Interim Budget and Food Processing Industry. Processed Food Industry, Vol. 7 Issue 5, March 2004 pp 13-14

77. Baisya, R.K., Indian Dairy Industry- A category Review, Indian Food Industry, Vol 23, No 3, 2004, pp 23-29

78. Baisya,R.K.,Food Business designed around one Fruit Variety – Seabuckthorn. Processed Food Industry, Vol. 7 Issue 6, April 2004 pp 6-7.

79. Baisya,R.K.,The Game of Two Age Old Rivals: Parle Vs. Britannia. Processed Food Industry, Vol. 7 Issue 7, May 2004 pp 8-11.
80. Baisya,R.K.,Coffee Consumption is on the Rise. Processed Food Industry, Vol. 7 Issue 8, June 2004 pp 6-8.
81. Baisya,R.K.,Oppourtunities for MNCs in Indian Processed Food Sector. Processed Food Industry, Vol. 7 Issue 9, July 2004 pp 6-7
82. Baisya,R.K.,Breakfast Cereal Industry still struggling to Make it Big. Processed Food Industry, Vol. 7 Issue 10, August 2004 pp 10-12
83. Baisya,R.K., Outsourcing a Preferred Option for Large Food Processors. Processed Food Industry, Vol. 7 Issue 11, September 2004 pp 12-14.
84. Baisya,R.K.,Indian Food and Agro Business Trade with the Middle East Countries. Processed Food Industry, Vol. 7 Issue 12, October 2004 pp 12-14.
85. Baisya,R.K., Confectionery Industry is Seeing Major Activities for Growth. Processed Food Industry, Vol. 8 Issue 1, November 2004 pp 8-10
86. Baisya,R.K.,Food Industry Now is More Customer Focused than Before. Processed Food Industry, Vol. 8 Issue 2, December 2004 pp12-15
87. Baisya,R.K., How Acquisitions have changed market Dynamics in Indian Food Industry. Processed Food Industry, Vol. 8 Issue 3, January 2005 pp 11-13.
88. Baisya,R.K., Product Labeling- Reading Between the Lines , Times Food Processing Journal , Dec-Jan 2005, pp 40-42
89. Baisya,R.K.,What Government can do to Promote Food and Agri-Business. Processed Food Industry, Vol. 8 Issue 4, February 2005 pp 9-12
90. Baisya, R.K., Lure of the East :Prospect of Food Export to Middle East Countries, Times Food Processing Journal, Feb-March 2005, pp 12-15
91. Baisya, R.K., Status of Food Machinery Manufacturing Industry in India, Times Food Processing Journal , April-May 2005, pp 4-8
92. Baisya,R.K.,Impact of Tsunami Devastation on Indian Seafood Industry Processed Food Industry, Vol. 8 Issue 5, March 2005 pp 13-15.
93. Baisya,R.K., Implications of Union Budget on Processed Food Industry. Processed Food Industry, Vol. 8 Issue 6, April 2005 pp 8-11.
94. Baisya,R.K.,New Health Beverages Launch in Summer Months. Processed Food Industry, Vol. 8 Issue 7, May 2005 pp 10-13.

95. Baisya,R.K.,Food Retailing will Soon Become a Major Force for Growth of Indian Food Industry. Processed Food Industry, Vol. 8 Issue 8, June 2005, pp 8-10.

96. Baisya,R.K.,Rising input cost is responsible for Declining Profitability of Processed Food Industry. Processed Food Industry, Vol. 8 Issue 9, July 2005, pp 8-10.

97. Baisya,R.K.,Industry Constantly Relooking at Product Portfolio and Investments. Processed Food Industry, Vol. 8 Issue 10, August 2005, pp 12-14

98. Baisya,R.K.,Efficient Logistics Management can Improve the Value Delivery. Processed Food Industry, Vol. 8 Issue 11, September 2005 pp 8-10

99. Baisya,R.K., Growth in Agricultural Sector Essential for Achieving Overall Growth Objective of Food Processing Sector. Processed Food Industry, Vol. 8 Issue 12, October 2005 pp 12-14.

100. Baisya,R.K., Drink to your health, Times Food Processing Journal, Oct-Nov 2005, pp 21-26.

101. Baisya,R.K., Confectionery Industry is Seeing Major Activities for Growth. Processed Food Industry, Vol.9 No.1, November, 2005, pp 8-10.

102. Baisya,R.K., Proposed Integrated Food Law Needs Careful Review and Much Wider Discussion. Processed Food Industry, Vol. 9 Issue 1, November 2005, pp 10-14.

103. Baisya,R.K.,Organized Retailing Can Help Food Processing Industry to Grow. Processed Food Industry, Vol. 9 Issue 2, December 2005, pp 10-12.

104. Baisya,R.K.,India Fast Emerging as a Major Market for Wine. Processed Food Industry, Vol. 9 Issue 3, January 2006, pp 10-12.

105. Baisya,R.K., Problems of Processed Food Industry, Indian Food Packer, Jan-Feb 2006, pp 11-12.

106. Baisya, R.K.,Industry Exploring Entry into Global Market. Processed Food Industry, Vol. 9 Issue 4, February 2006, pp 10-12

107. Baisya,R.K.,Union Budget and Processed Food Industry. Processed Food Industry, Vol. 9 Issue 5, March 2006, pp 14-16

108. Baisya,R.K.,Food Professionals not Playing Participative Role in Policy Making. Processed Food Industry, Vol. 9 Issue 6, April 2006, pp 8-10.

109. Baisya,R.K., The retail Recipe, Retail Biz (a publication of Economic Times) Vol. 3 Issue 9, April 2006, pp24-25.

110. Baisya,R.K.,Relevance of Traditional Technology in Modern Food Industry. Processed Food Industry, Vol. 9 Issue 7, May 2006, pp 14-16.

111. Baisya,R.K.,Contract Farming will Ensure Farmers A Direct Outlet. Processed Food Industry, Vol. 9 Issue 8, June 2006, pp 8-10.

112. Baisya,R.K.,Implications of Non-Tariff Bariers in Global Trade of Processed Food. Processed Food Industry, Vol. 9 Issue 9, July 2006, pp 10-12.

113. Baisya,R.K.,Linking Farmers to Consumers through an Integrated Food Value Chain. Processed Food Industry, Vol. 9 Issue 10, August 2006, pp 10-12.

114. Baisya, R.K., Why we are not able to export dairy products despite being the largest milk producers in the World. Process Food Industry, Vol. 9 No. 10, September 2006, pp 11-13.

115. Baisya,R.K., Strategies to Manage the Non-Tariff Barriers in Global Trade of Indian Processed Food, Indian Food Industry, Sept-Oct, 2006, pp 11-14.

116. Baisya,R.K.,Coke and Pepsi are in Trouble on Account of Pesticide Residue Controversy in Soft Drinks. Processed Food Industry, Vol. 9 Issue 12, October 2007, pp 11-12

117. Baisya,R.K.,Local Producers should know to Deliver Higher Value to Customers to fight MNC competition. Processed Food Industry, Vol. 10 Issue 1, November 2006, pp 15-16

118. Baisya,R.K.,Retail Revolution is Finally Arrived Impacting Our Food Industry. Processed Food Industry, Vol. 10 Issue 2, December 2006, pp 14-16

119. Baisya,R.K.,Bakery Industry in India – A Category Review. Processed Food Industry, Vol. 10 Issue 3, January 2007, pp 10-14.

120. Baisya R.K., Poultry meat is the fastest growing Animal protein, Processed Food Industry, Vol. 10, Issue 4, February 2007, pp 10-12.

121. Baisya R.K., Growth Oriented Budget but Nothing Significant for Industry, Processed Food Industry, Vol. 10, Issue 5, March 2007, pp 14-16.

122. Baisya R.K., Processing and Value Addition are Major Challenges for Marine Products Industry, Processed Food Industry, Vol. 10 Issue 6, April 2007, pp 14-16.

123. Baisya R.K., Meat Industry is Stagnating while Poultry Market is fast growing, Processed Food Industry, Vol. 10, Issue 7, May 2007, pp 14-16.

124. Baisya R.K., Food & Grocery Retail Market in India, Processed Food Industry, Vol. 10, Issue 8, June 2007, pp 10-15.

Index

ABPP